The German Prosecution Service

Shawn Marie Boyne

The German Prosecution Service

Guardians of the Law?

Springer

Shawn Marie Boyne
School of Law
Indiana University
Indianapolis
Indiana
USA

ISBN 978-3-642-40927-1 ISBN 978-3-642-40928-8 (eBook)
DOI 10.1007/978-3-642-40928-8
Springer Heidelberg New York Dordrecht London

Library of Congress Control Number: 2013954378

Printed on acid-free paper

Springer is part of Springer Science+Business Media (www.springer.com)

To my parents,
John and Mary Jo Boyne

Acknowledgments

When I left the practice of law after 9 years to begin my Ph.D. studies, I believed that I could make it through the process as the result of my own drive and determination. I was wrong. Without my indefatigable dissertation advisor, Kathryn Hendley, at the University of Wisconsin, I am confident that I would never have persevered to complete this project. The other members of my dissertation committee, Don Downs, Tamir Moustafa, Michael Smith, and Walter Dickey, read through early drafts of my original manuscript and provided crucial insights along the way. Howie Erlanger provided me an early home as a graduate fellow in the Institute for Legal Studies at the University of Wisconsin Law School. Pam Hollenhurst, the ILS Institute's Associate Director, often made me feel at home in the law school—though my primary home was across the quad in the political science department.

One cannot go to a foreign country and gain instant access to a wide network of prosecutors, judges, and defense attorneys without a network of individuals who believe in your work. During my first trip to Germany, Liane Wörner at the Justus-Liebig-Universität adopted me as a sister and scheduled a whirlwind initial research trip around Germany that only heightened my interest in the country's legal system. Also, I cannot forget the early stewardship provided by Professor Dr. Walter Gropp, who also helped to guide my transition from graduate student to law professor. Matthias Wörner and Martin Dege often helped me, not only with my German, but also with basic advice on the country not found in guidebooks. In Gießen, I also thank Professors Richard Giesen, Bernd Hecker, Arthur Kreuzer, Thilo Marauhn, and Gabriele Wolflast, all of whom graciously shared their network of professional contacts with me. I am also grateful for the assistance provided by Professor Udo Ebert and Eberhard Siegismund of the German Federal Ministry of Justice. Many individuals opened their homes and offices to me as I travelled throughout Germany. Among those, I wish to thank Susanna Erb, Bernhardt Becker-Flugel, Kathi Fröhlich, Ursus Koerner, Michael Nagel, and Sabine Wolski.

I often became lost in my extensive travels throughout Germany. I would not have found many of the locations that I was travelling to without the help of numerous ordinary German citizens. I am particularly grateful to the couple who found me wandering looking at a map in a residential neighborhood looking for my hotel. Not only did they walk me to my intended destination but they also gave me a bus ticket and directions to the prosecution office. It turned out that the gentleman was a retired judicial employee. He was fascinated with my project.

The opportunity to participate in the Berlin Program for Advanced German and European Studies at Freie Universität during the 2005–2006 academic year was an unbelievably rich research experience. The program director, Karin Goihl, not only takes each fellow under her wing, but she also provided me with helpful assistance when I needed help navigating my way around Germany. During that year of fieldwork, I was also privileged to bounce my initial research ideas off of the members of the Young Researchers' Group on Comparative Micro-Sociology of Criminal Procedure, led by Dr. Thomas Scheffer, also housed at Freie Universität-Berlin, Germany.

After finishing my dissertation, I returned to Germany to continue my research as a DAAD postdoctoral fellow at the Max Planck Institute for Foreign and International Criminal Law. The Institute's library and staff are an incredible resource. During these periods, Prof. Dr. Ulrich Sieber graciously lent his support to my project enabling me to expand my interviews and observation activities across a wider cross section of Germany. In the interim period, I have rewritten and updated most of my original dissertation. I gathered the confidence to do so after participating in the *Annual Comparative Law Works-in-Process Workshop* held at Yale Law School in February 2011. At that workshop, I received helpful feedback from Jacqueline Ross, Mortimer Sellers, Kim Sheppele, Jim Whitman, and the workshop participants. I also presented portions of my work at the McKinney School of Law's Junior Faculty Workshop where Marcus Dubber and Cynthia Adams critiqued my work. Like many developing scholars in the Midwest, I owe a debt of gratitude to the Washington University School of Law's junior faculty workshop where I presented several chapters of my work.

The Robert H. McKinney School of Law provided me with a semester of junior faculty research leave as well as funding from the John S. Grimes Fellowship in order to complete this book. Without the funding that I received from the DRIVE fellowship at Indiana University–Purdue University, I would not have had the funds to support the transcription and translation of my numerous interviews. With respect to the translation and transcription work, I cannot heap enough praise on Anna Baxter who worked on the project tapes for 3 years. At the law school, research librarian Richard Humphrey is an incredible person to have on your team. My faculty assistant, Faith Long, somehow survived the final 2 months of editing intact—demonstrating a degree of dedication that often matched my own. I would also like to thank my colleagues and students at the Robert H. McKinney School of Law, whose ongoing support and encouragement of my teaching and research have made my job the "best job on earth."

Finally, I cannot say enough about the prosecutors, judges, and defense attorneys whom I interviewed. Their hospitality and patience with my German language skills was extraordinary. I always looked forward to being invited to their morning "coffee meetings" where institutional knowledge and norms were informally shared. Sometimes my language skills helped me to break the ice with younger prosecutors who loosened up after observing me make mistakes. I remember in particular during one interview that I tried to ask a young prosecutor to describe a case that he had handled in which he was proud of the result. I mispronounced the German word for case (Fälle) and the question morphed into—What mistake (Fehler) are you most proud of? After the prosecutor realized what I was trying to say, we both broke into laughter. Gratefully many prosecutors spoke fluent English. Those who didn't were extremely patient with my language skills. Had so many individuals not found the time to spend with me, this book would never have made it off the ground. In deference to maintaining the anonymity of my interview subjects, I cannot cite them by name.

Writing this book was an iterative process that required the help of so many people that I am sure that some individuals will go unnamed. So many individuals guided me through the German legal system to whom I owe an enormous debt. In addition to my interviews with prosecutors and judges, I spoke with members of law enforcement, defense attorneys, officials employed in crime labs and prisons, social workers, as well as some defendants. All of them contributed to my understanding the complexities of the German criminal justice system.

My only regret in this whole process is that my mom, Mary Jo Boyne, who traced her roots back to Germany, did not live to see the book completed.

Indianapolis, IN Shawn Boyne
2013

Abbreviations

§	Section
§§	Sections
BGH	Federal Court of Justice
BGHSt	Federal Court of Justice Criminal Law Panel
BVerfGG	Federal Constitutional Court Decision
BvR	Federal Constitutional Court Decision
DVJJ	German Association for Juvenile Court and Juvenile Offenders
GG	Basic Law of the Federal Republic of Germany
GStA	General Public Prosecutor
GVG	German Code on Court Constitution
JGG	German Act on Juvenile Courts
LOSTA	Leading Public Prosecutor or Chief Office Prosecutor
NBG	*Niedersachsen* Civil Service Law
OStA	Senior Public Prosecutor or Department Manager
RiStBV	Guidelines for Criminal and Fine Proceedings
StA	Public Prosecutor
StBG	Code of Criminal Law
StPO	Code of Criminal Procedure

Contents

Chapter 1
Introduction

> There are few bases for being able to radically change whatever society one is living in. There are many bases for making better use of its possibilities (Luhmann 1992, p. 182).

1.1 The Rechtsstaat and the Twenty-First Century

As the twenty-first century enters its second decade, Germany stands clearly on Europe's center stage. Propelled by an economy that has served as an engine of Europe's economic growth as well as a safety net for Europe's more troubled economies, German influence has been a driving force behind the continuing growth and form of the European Union (EU). Within the EU itself, German policy has decidedly influenced the contours of European policies regarding trade, environmental policies, security and justice, and human rights. In the legal arena, Germany's Basic Law has arguably supplanted the U.S. Constitution as a model for new democratic constitutions (Bahners 2009).

Despite Germany's influence on the European stage, Germany and its European partners face critical social, economic, and political problems that threaten the societal foundations of the democratic welfare state. While the aging of the European workforce calls for a narrowing of the each state's extensive social-welfare net, reforms designed to redefine that net stoke civil unrest. Just as challenging, ongoing tension over the integration of immigrant communities in both Germany, as well as into the larger European society, erupt on a regular basis and stoke anti-immigrant rhetoric and distrust. While centrist political elites frequently condemn such rhetoric, laws and norms of discourse that attempt to prevent and punish racist speech have at times ironically hamstrung public debate. Political reforms aimed at tackling integration challenges are often stymied.

Yet, as the tides of socioeconomic change have ebbed and flowed, post-war Germany's commitment to legal foundations of the state, the German *Rechtsstaat*, has continued to deepen. Since the creation of the post-war German *Rechtsstaat*, German policymakers have demonstrated increasing fidelity and trust in the law's

S.M. Boyne, *The German Prosecution Service*, DOI 10.1007/978-3-642-40928-8_1,

ability to regulate and structure society. Indeed, the German Constitutional Court's decisions today constrain political action to an extent that is scarcely imaginable in common law states such as Great Britain and the United States. While the law and legal regulation play an integral rule in preserving societal order in many countries throughout world, it is difficult for outsiders to comprehend the degree to which law shapes daily societal interactions in Germany. Indeed, law is truly the glue that regulates German societal interactions.

What is a *Rechtsstaat*? To begin, there is no precisely equivalent concept in Anglo-American law. While it is tempting equate the concept with the common law rule of law state, seen through the lens of nineteenth century European liberalism, the starting point might be more accurately stated as a state governed by the law of reason. A common denominator shared by rule of law states and the *Rechtsstaat* is the fundamental imperative that it is "the state's duty to wield its power through laws in accordance with fundamental principles of legality" (Rosenfeld 2001, p. 1319). Scholars have drawn the key distinction that in a rule of law state, a tension exists between the law and state power. It is an individual's societal or civil rights that protect the individual from the power of the state (Loughlin 2010). Conversely in a *Rechtsstaat*, the relationship between law and the state is more symbiotic (Rosenfeld 2001). Rather than existing in tension with the state, rights are an integral part of the state's legal foundation. Indeed, according to German philosopher, Jürgen Habermas, in the German state, certain fundamental rights are the precondition for the establishment of democracy (Loughlin 2010).

The gap between these foundational conceptions of state power has widened during the last century. The original nineteenth century concept of a *Rechtsstaat* has expanded to embrace the "freedom, equality and autonomy of the individual within the framework of a unified legal order" that is defined by legislation and implemented by independent courts of law (Kommers and Miller 2012, p. 48). According to noted German constitutional scholar Donald Kommers, as the nineteenth century progressed, the concept of a *Rechtsstaat* evolved to "integrate state and society and to proclaim the unity of law and state" (Kommers and Miller 2012, p. 48). While this unified conception of law and state was a product of the emergence of European political liberalism, the modern conception of basic rights, in particular, the inviolable right to human dignity came to prominence only in the post-war period. Most importantly, the West German Basic Law, which today represents the Constitution of reunified Germany, "not only subjects law to the concept of justice; it also creates a fundamental system of values in terms of which all legislation or other official acts must be assessed" (Kommers and Miller 2012, p. 49). Prior to the adoption of the Basic Law, the continuity of rights in the positivist *Rechtsstaat* was subject to the legislature's continuing will. Rosenfeld (2001, p. 1328) has traced the evolution of the *Rechtsstaat* concept, noting:

> Although today's *Rechtsstaat* in some sense incorporates elements of both its Kantian and positivistic counterparts, it is in key respects different from its predecessors and thus raises novel questions regarding law's legitimacy. Like its Kantian counterpart, today's *Rechtsstaat* enshrines fundamental rights above the realm of ordinary laws, although these rights are substantive rather than formal and differ significantly in content from

their Kantian predecessors. On the other hand, like its positivistic predecessor, today's *Rechtsstaat* institutionalizes legality, but it is a legality that is not merely dependent on consistency and predictability, but also contingent on constitutional conformity and on the realization of constitutionally recognized substantive goals.

At the risk of oversimplifying the differences between the two concepts, one might predict that, in a rule of law state, state power will trump individual rights more frequently, than in the Rechtsstaat as courts weigh the relative importance of state interests and individual rights across various contexts. A prime example is the American war on terror where courts have often privileged the state's interest in security over an individual's right to privacy (Huysmans 2004). In contrast, although some rights in the *Rechtstaat* may be subjected to a proportionality review, the right to human dignity is an absolute right not subject to judicial balancing (Lepsius 2007).

Indeed, as Germany has navigated its way through reunification, EU expansion, and the rise of radical Islamic terrorism, the judiciary's commitment to the *Rechtsstaat* has altered state policy and underscored the state's ongoing commitment to fundamental human rights. Political leaders who have attempted to implement policies that threaten individual liberties have had to contend with an increasingly activist Federal Constitutional Court (*Bundesvefassungsgericht*). Emboldened by a Constitution that balances international human rights with the state's interest in preserving a democratic state, the broadening scope of the FCC's decision-making underscores the German judiciary's deep commitment to the *Rechtsstaat* ideal.

Perhaps nowhere is evidence of the law's pervasive constraining impact as clear as in Germany's response to terrorism. While the United States declared "war" on terrorism and sought to defend its response by reframing international law, German policymakers crafted, and the German public supported, a more measured response more carefully bounded by international legal norms. While the German government has at times attempted to privilege state power at the expense of basic rights, Germany's top court has not hesitated to intervene-ruling, for example, in 2004 that the state could not lawfully monitor individual computers absent a judicial order.[1] Furthermore, 2 years later, the FCC held that the military could not shoot down a plane commandeered by terrorists.[2]

1.2 American Power and the American Prosecutor

In contrast to the restraint exercised by the German government in the post 9/11 era, the United States has declared a "war on terror." The scope of state power has expanded and the intrusiveness of federal government's investigative powers has increased. While legislation like the PATRIOT Act has drawn the attention of

[1] BVerfG, 1 BvR 2378/98 of March 3, 2004.

[2] BVerfG, 1 BvR 357/05 of February 5, 2006.

organizations and individuals who are concerned about human rights and civil liberties, these developments have overshadowed long standing systemic problems in the nation's criminal justice system. In particular, the gross underfunding of indigent defense services, coupled with a rapid growth in prosecutorial power and discretion, have transformed a system premised on a battle between equal parties into one in which a powerful prosecutor dictates the course of justice. As the government's relative power in the courtroom has grown, many prosecutors have abandoned their duty to seek justice in favor of a single-minded pursuit of convictions. While a large number of prosecutors stay within ethical boundaries, there is also mounting evidence that suggests that prosecutors ignore their constitutional obligation to reveal exculpatory evidence (Cohen 2013), mislead jurors (West 2012, pp. 6–7), and privilege political considerations over the dictates of justice (Gordon and Huber 2009, p. 1434). In key respects, the rise of American prosecutors' unbounded power and the dominant role that prosecutors play in shaping the face of justice in America today is but one symptom of the law's inefficacy in halting the growth in the government's punitive power. In both the courtroom and in the public sphere, the arc of justice is bending in the favor of the state's increasing power. The law has proved to be an imperfect tool in halting this advance. Since prosecutors operate within the framework of a rule of law state, this portrait of prosecution practice calls into question whether or not prosecutorial decision-making conforms to the requirements of a rule of law state (Raz 1979).

1.3 The Adversarial System and the Quest for Truth

The Anglo-American system of justice is premised on the assumption that the truth will emerge from a battle between the parties. In structuring the criminal process as a binary process, our founders assumed that members of the jury would possess the insight necessary to sort the true from the false. However, for decades dozens of scholars have called into question the accuracy of the system's underlying assumptions (Luban 1989). As the advent of DNA testing has drawn attention to the problem of wrongful convictions, those concerns have intensified. Research conducted by the Veritas Institute found over 800 cases of prosecutorial misconduct in California between 1997 and 2010.[3] Studies like these have led a growing number of scholars to question whether prosecutors are working harder to secure convictions than to achieve justice.

Extensive scholarship on the American system criticizes prosecutors for abandoning their truth-seeking duties. Scholars such as Culp Davis (1976), Pizzi (1999), and Kagan (2001) argue that the adversarial nature of the American criminal justice system influences behavioral norms. Proponents of this argument maintain that, the system's underlying normative assumption that the truth will

[3] Veritas Initiative, First Annual Report (2011) 11.

emerge from a battle between parties emboldens prosecutors and defense attorneys to treat trials as contests. Pizzi (1999), who has derisively criticized the American system for producing "trials without truth," has alleged that a "conviction mentality" motivates prosecutors to privilege securing convictions over achieving justice. Although the system attempts to screen out evidence that may bias jurors, some commentators have charged that those complex procedural rules allow lawyer to dominate trials. Despite the fact that disciplinary rules govern the behavior of attorneys and prosecutors, neither ethical guidelines nor legal sanctions have proven robust enough to deter prosecutors' unethical behavior (Rudin 2011). Comparative law scholars have joined the chorus of critical voices. For example, the eminent legal historian, John Langbein, considers American trials to be a "truth defeating enterprise" (Langbein 1985).

The most serious allegation against the system is that the parties no longer view the criminal process as a search for the truth, but rather as a quest for victory. According to proponents of this argument, the adversarial nature of the process has affected how lawyers view the system's end results. Although prosecutors possess an ethical obligation to pursue justice, some prosecutors seem driven by a "win at all costs" conviction-oriented mentality (Ma 2002). In this context, winning trials, securing stiff sentences, and boosting the district attorney's reelection chances can overshadow due process considerations. As a result, prosecutors may be disinclined to pursue certain leads or to disclose exculpatory information despite the fact that the law and professional rules of conduct mandate disclosure. Influenced by the institutional orientation of the prosecution function, even conscientious prosecutors may develop the attitude that all defendants are guilty and convey their conviction-oriented mentality to new hires (Miller and Remington 1969).

Given that over 95 % of cases in the American system are resolved through the use of plea bargains rather than trials, the vision of justice being settled by a jury of one's peers occurs with greater frequency on television screens than in real life. Given that only a small percentage of cases are resolved at trial, one might wonder the extent to which courtroom battles sidetrack the search for truth. In response to that criticism, Pizzi (1999) has argued that the adversarial process's conflictual nature colors case investigation processes as well leads prosecutors to suppress exculpatory evidence.

High case loads affect the ability of both prosecutors and public defenders to discover the truth. The drive for efficiency, motivated by the need to process a large number of cases with limited resources, is a dominant force shaping prosecutorial practice in the United States today. On the defense side of practice, most Americans cannot afford to fund an effective defense effort in a felony case. As a result many suspects are represented by public defenders who lack the time and resources to mount a defense that might dislodge the coercive leverage that the state possesses in the plea negotiation process (Alschuler 1968). In a number of cases, less than effective defense efforts have culminated in the state's execution of an innocent defendant.

1.4 The Most Objective Civil Servants in the World

Against this backdrop of criticism, in the 1980s comparative law scholars began to suggest that the model of German prosecution practice, with German prosecutors' commitment to objectivity, offered instructive lessons for an American system besotted by claims of prosecutorial overreaching. While scholars have condemned American prosecutors for their "conviction mentality," for decades, comparative legal scholars held up German prosecutors for their dedication to objectivity. As the supervisor of an objective investigation process that is not driven by the desire to secure a conviction, German prosecutors spearhead a truth finding process that commences with an objective investigation and continues through to main proceeding where the chief judge overseas the presentation of the evidence (Langbein 1979). Described by one scholar as the "most objective civil servants in the world," German prosecutors are inculcated through their training and socialization processes with the mandate to serve, not as zealous adversaries, but as "guardians of the law." This optimistic assessment of German prosecution practice also reflects the conviction of many German legal scholars that prosecutors in Germany's inquisitorial system function as second judges dedicated to finding the objective "truth." Instilled with the vision to serve as "guardians of the law,"[4] German prosecutors lack the thirst for winning that their American colleagues display in the courtroom (Langbein 1979). Protected by the guarantee of life time employment, German prosecutors appear to be insulated from political influence and free to enforce the law as it is written. On paper, the German model of prosecutorial decision-making appears to more effectively balance a state's desire for retribution with the need for justice than America's conviction oriented system.

Indeed, German scholars have enthusiastically promoted the key ideals and orientation of the German system (Dubber 2005). This publicity has led reformers in Italy, Spain, South Korea, Latin America, and Japan to look to the German model for inspiration (Dubber 2005, p. 1054; Ma 2002). The reputation of the German system has even attracted the attention of American scholars (Foster 1996). For several decades, American scholars, seeking an antidote to the problems created by widening prosecutorial discretion in the United States, praised the German model because the system's commitment to the bedrock principal of mandatory prosecution appeared to constrain prosecutorial discretion (Langbein 1979, pp. 201–212; Kagan 2001 p. 232). That principle, which requires prosecutors to file charges in all cases in which sufficient evidence exists to believe that a crime has been committed, aims to ensure that prosecutors enforce the law in a uniform and non-arbitrary

[4] *See* "Waldenburg" Training Materials (on file with author) (stating that German prosecutors do not function as parties but they possess a duty to be objective and to ensure that justice is administered according to the law). From 2004 through 2010, the author conducted field research in 16 different prosecution offices in Germany. To protect the anonymity of the interviewees, fictitious place names and a numerical coding system have been used to identify documents and interviewees.

manner.[5] At first glance, then, German prosecution practice seemed to offer a striking exception to the mantra of American law and society theorists that the law is not enforced as it is written.

A key factor that drove German scholars to promote the advantages of the German prosecution service was the fact that many of these scholars possessed the civil legal tradition's positivistic faith that legal practice accurately mirrored the law on the books. The scholars' faith in the prosecution service's objectivity reflected their conviction in the law's ability to shape prosecutorial practice. As a prime example, part of this optimism rested on the assumption that prosecutorial practice mirrored prosecutors' obligations as they were stated in the statutory code. Thus, because the Code of Criminal Procedure obligates prosecutors to investigate the facts that weigh for and against a suspect's guilt, scholars presumed that all prosecutors faithfully followed that mandate.[6] Indeed, time and time again, scholars have cited particular code provisions as conclusive evidence of prosecutorial practice. To American scholars, familiar with the rich tradition of law and society scholarship in this country, the comparative paucity of research in Germany that explores the gap between the law on the books and the law in practice has been puzzling (Goldstein and Marcus 1977; Langbein and Weinreb 1978; Goldstein and Marcus 1978). Writing in the 1970s, Goldstein and Marcus (1978, p. 1575) offered one explanation for German scholars' hesitancy to explore this gap:

> It should be noted that American scholars frequently assume that the American system deviates from its formal requirements. The writing on European systems, however, reflects the contrary assumption that differences between practices and formal requirements are bad and to be avoided. This attitude may explain the reluctance to develop an empirical literature that searches for such differences.

1.5 Cracks in the Edifice

For decades, scholarship that described prosecutorial practice in Germany contended that the normative ideal of objective decision-making shaped prosecutorial practice. As one example, in 1979, German legal scholar Klaus Sessar asserted that prosecutors' attention to the law, rather than pragmatic concerns about costs and efficiency, guided decisions to prosecute (Sessar 1979). In that same year, John Langbein boldly declared that Germany was a "land without plea bargaining" (Langbein 1979, pp. 204–205). Typical of the faith that German scholars vested in the theory of limited discretion are Dr. Jescheck's comments (1970, p. 511):

> Certainly even the "legality principle" contains an unavoidable degree of discretion-namely, that the obligation to press charges arises only if 'sufficient factual clues' are available. If on the results of the investigation, however, it is merely a question of whether

[5] See §152(2) StPO and §172.

[6] *See* §§160(2) and §296 (2) StPO.

> there exists proof sufficient for conviction of the suspect, the prosecutor is still obliged to file the charge. He may not take the question upon himself whether it might not be in the interest of the state or more expedient for the parties to drop the proceedings completely. The legality principle does not arise-as one might suppose-from any absolute requirement that the state revenge every criminal act, for modern German penal law recognizes many sanctions which are entirely free of any retaliatory objective. The decisive idea is rather that it is one of the primary tasks of the state to guarantee fairness and justice without consideration of the individual involved, and without considerations of expediency, matters which have very little to do with retribution.

Despite scholars' bold claims about the law's efficacy, in the late 1970s, shifts in practice began to emerge. Significantly, tightening resource constraints began to impinge on prosecutors' ability to conduct the resource-intensive truth-finding process originally envisioned by Germany's post-war Code of Criminal Procedure.[7] As the resource constraints became more severe, rising caseloads forced legislators to carve out ever larger exceptions to the principle of mandatory prosecution specifically granting prosecutors greater discretion in handling minor crimes cases (Sessar 1979, p. 256).[8] Despite these changes, many scholars continued to maintain that German prosecutors' duty to function as "objective" fact-finders had not changed and that prosecutorial discretion in Germany was limited. For example, Sessar (1979, p. 257) argued that "dismissals of felony cases was (and is) not permitted by law." In the late 1970s, both Sessar and Weigend claimed that the government increased prosecutorial staff to respond to rising case loads (Sessar 1979, p. 261; Langbein and Weinreb 1978, pp. 45–46). Even the eminent Roxin (1991) argued that, although practical developments have lead to a growth in the number of exceptions to the principle of legality, those exceptions had not overtaken the principle's theoretical validity.

For quite some time, the number of dissenting voices who questioned whether or not the principle of legality was still honored in practice was limited. When criticism did exist, it tended to attack a narrow range of practices. Some scholars conceded a bit of ground by admitting that, although prosecutors possessed the discretion to dispose of minor crimes, they were bound to apply the principle of mandatory prosecution to serious crimes (Jescheck 1970; Culp Davis 1976; Hermann 1974; Felstiner 1979; Langbein and Weinreb 1978; Weigend 2004).

Yet, fiscal constraints, combined with the emergence of new types of economic crimes, continued to put pressure on the ability of the prosecution service to fulfill the ambitious fact-finding function mandated by the German Code of Criminal Procedure (StPO). Moreover, the forces of globalization have nurtured new forms of criminality that have outpaced both developments in the law as well as the capacity of judicial institutions. One source of constraint is the fact that in some cases, the "technology" of prosecutorial practice has not kept pace with the sophistication of criminal activity. For example, while organized criminal actors have exploited global communication networks to commit crime, some police and

---

[7] *See* §§244, 249, 252–60 StPO.

[8] §153(1).

prosecution offices continue to rely on internal bureaucratic practices that use handwritten instructions to direct investigative activity. As corporations and individuals utilize technology to circumvent the law, thick case files may languish unread in courtroom offices for months. Although sophisticated criminals can launder money with the push of a computer button, judges on the front lines are buried in paperwork. Both judges and prosecutors often lack the capability and resources to diligently review complicated cases on a timely basis.

As workload pressures in both prosecution offices and the courtroom chambers continued to intensify, both prosecutors and judges were caught in a vise between trying to fulfill their legal duty to investigate the material truth and rising organizational pressures to close cases quickly. To balance these competing concerns, prosecutors began to use a variety of procedural mechanisms to dismiss cases or defer prosecution in the majority of cases that crossed their desk. As a result, today many cases no longer enjoy a full investigation of the facts. Consequently, in some cases, the resulting punishment is proportionate only to a vague outline of criminal activity contained in an incomplete file. In cases resolved through confession agreements,[9] the court may settle for a version of the "truth" which may be largely painted by the suspect themselves, rather than expend the time and resources required for a full investigation of the facts surrounding the crime.[10] Although German prosecutors possess broad investigative powers, they no longer possess the resources to initiate the extensive search for the material truth envisioned by civil law tradition legal theorists.

The development that has caused the greatest consternation among German legal scholars has been the growth of case settlement practices that initially developed outside the boundaries of the formal law (Thaman 2007, pp. 43–44). While the Federal Constitutional Court acknowledged that the practice of negotiated settlements was not per se unconstitutional in 1987 (Esposito and Safferling 2008), it was not until 2009 that the legislature finally sanctioned the use of negotiated settlements.[11] The course of this practice-driven change in the Code of Criminal Procedure, sanctioned first by the judiciary rather than by the legislature, ran sharply counter to the civil law tradition's circumscribed vision of the judicial role as well as the positivist vision of the nature of law itself (Weigend 2008). Yet, since the disposition of major crimes continues to require that a judge conduct a main proceeding, this practice appears to remain consistent with the principle of mandatory prosecution.

While the principle still exists on the books, a growing number of scholars have concluded that the widening range of discretionary decision-making authority that German prosecutors now possess has substantially undercut the force the principle

---

[9] An abbreviated criminal procedure involving an agreement between the defendant and court that is roughly similar to an American plea bargain.

[10] In the absence of a confession agreement, it is the duty of the court to establish the truth through the taking of evidence. See §244(2) StPO.

[11] *See* §257c StPO.

in practice (Eisenberg and Conen 1998; Weigend 2004; Elsner and Peters 2006). As Elsner and Peters (2006, p. 234) state "[t]here is a clear trend moving away from the principle of legality towards more powerful and independent prosecuting institutions." Scholars such as Geisler (1999, p. 11) argue that the judicial community is no longer adhering to the law with respect to the prosecution and disposition of minor- and middle-level criminality and that prosecutors are ignoring the principle of legality. In 2004, the respected scholar, Weigend (2004, p. 215) wrote that "[t]oday prosecution is in effect mandatory only with respect to most felonies."

Although the German Code of Criminal Procedure has, in some ways, evolved to more closely represent the discretionary decision-making opportunities available on the ground, it is worthwhile examine the extent to which prosecutors still serve as "guardians of the law." Although the law no longer requires prosecutors to investigate and prosecute every case, the code provisions on the books that attempt to mandate objectivity still exist. With a wide range of decision choices before them, the role of German prosecutors has shifted from serving as chief of the investigation process to more of a gate-keeping function. Under the stress of rising caseloads, through their daily decision-making, prosecutors determine what actions should be sanctioned as well as those that do not merit punishment.

The widespread scope of the changes in prosecution practice have called into question prosecutors' degree of fidelity to the remaining parts of the statutory code that mandate that prosecutors function as objective decision-makers. Given that prosecutors, with the judiciary's indulgence, bent the law to accommodate the demands of daily practice, some scholars have declared that the inquisitorial ideal of sharply constricted prosecutorial discretion is dead (Weigend 2008).

Indeed these developments have prompted scholars to criticize the growing gap between the inquisitorial ideal of a thorough fact finding and adjudication process and current prosecution practices-some of which have short-circuited the truth-finding process (Erb 2004). In particular, scholars such as Weigend (2008) have sharply criticized the growing ambit of prosecutorial discretion and the rise of negotiated settlements in so-called "minor" crime cases. While there has always been some wiggle room in the charging process, the increasing use of settlement agreements has critically weakened the prescriptive force of the principle of mandatory prosecution. Scholars are not alone in criticizing the expansion of these new procedural mechanisms. During my interviews with judicial officials, several judges at the appellate level, who do not face the same day-to-day workload pressures as prosecutors and trial court judges, joined in this criticism of prosecutorial practice.[12] One outspoken appellate judge accused prosecutors of having adopted an "in and out box" mentality that privileges efficient case closing strategies at the expense of conducting an extensive investigation designed to discover

[12] Appellate Judge Interview [22FE], 22 July 2004.

the truth.[13] Another appellate judge related to me that "in the majority of low-level crime cases, prosecutors do the work of administration and not of justice – they get their papers signed and that is that."[14]

1.6 The Silver Lining: Embedded Normative Values

While scholars might be quick to mourn the demise of optimistic claims from the "land without plea bargaining," the mandates established by German law have always set a standard that was primarily normative, if not mythological, in character (Weigend 2010). Even if the prescriptive force of those norms has weakened, it is important to remember that the current performance of adversarial systems falls far short of their own truth-finding aspirations. The emergence on German soil of a practice akin to plea bargaining has not turned members of the German prosecution service into conviction-driven prosecutors. Indeed many of the core features and underlying normative assumptions of Germany's inquisitorial criminal justice system remain in place. While it is true that the pressure of high caseloads and limited resources have encouraged prosecutors and courts to pursue negotiated settlements in many minor crime cases, statutory restrictions ban the use of "confession agreements" in major crime cases.[15] However, as I will detail in Chap. 6, the list of crimes included in the German category of "minor crimes" is an expansive one that includes some crimes that are considered to be felonies in the United States. Nevertheless, charges in cases involving premeditated murder, for example, may not be negotiated downwards as they may be in the United States.[16]

Given these restrictions, it is worth examining how German prosecutors today interpret their duty to function objectively and translate that duty into trial practice.[17] While recent critics have derided the use of confession agreements to short-circuit the truth finding process, it may be short-sighted to conclude that the use of those agreements has completely undermined prosecutors' commitment to objectivity. The simple rise in the numbers of confession agreements tells us little about the stance that prosecutors take in the courtroom and whether and how their daily decision-making reflects a commitment to viewing the evidence objectively.

---

[13] *Id.* ("If this would be my room, you would find furniture over there . . . On one side you would find the remark 'entrance' and on the other side 'exit.' And this is the perspective of a good public prosecutor. That what is coming in now today has to be finished.").

[14] Appellate Judge Interview [13MU], 10 April 2004.

[15] *See* §153 StPO.

[16] Appellate Judge Interview [22FE], 22 July 2004.

[17] Given the differences in the procedural posture of adjudicatory hearings in Germany, I refer to these hearings as "main proceedings," which is a rough translation of the German term for those hearings, throughout the rest of this book.

Despite the fact that the scope prosecutorial discretion in Germany has increased, it is worthwhile to scrutinize what it means for prosecutors to function "objectively" in a system where success is not measured in terms of convictions and the length of the defendant's sentence. Once we push to the side our fascination with German plea bargaining, a rich menu of research questions remains. Most critically, when handling allegations of serious criminal activity, do German prosecutors honor their normative mandate to investigate and prosecute those cases through an objective lens? How do prosecutors define objectivity? To what extent are members of this unelected bureaucracy influenced by political considerations?

Given that disciplinary rules have proven to be largely ineffective in constraining those prosecutors in America who are willing to pursue convictions at the expense of justice, it is worthwhile to examine the extent to which the bureaucratic structure and organizational ethos of the German prosecution service constrains decision-making. Similarly, although elected district attorneys in the United States ignore the popular will at their own peril, it is an open question whether the protection of lifetime employment that German prosecutors enjoy fully insulates their decision-making from political influence. To the extent that prosecutors are not driven by political considerations or the desire to win, it is important to understand what factors do influence the evidence-gathering and prosecution processes, as well as how those factors shape criminal justice outcomes.

1.7 Why German Prosecutors?

Although they are charged with viewing case facts with a judicial lens, prosecutors' ability to craft and develop practices, such as confession bargaining, in the shadow of the law demonstrates that even in countries with a civil law tradition, it is not the law alone that guides decision-making. As the boundaries of prosecutors' discretionary decision-making have enlarged, it has become more important to understand how German prosecutors exercise that discretion and thereby define the face of "justice" in Germany today. If we needed to be convinced of that fact, the evolution of the practice of "confession bargaining" over the past 30 years outside the statutory framework, conclusively demonstrates that the face of justice is no longer being painted by the law in the code books. To understand how prosecutors make decisions in the course of their daily practice, it is necessary to observe, question, and "participate" in those practices.

I devoted over 3 years to studying and observing German prosecution practice in 15 different prosecution offices scattered throughout Germany between 2005 and 2010. I sat in prosecutors' offices and listened to them lead me through their case screening decisions. I read scores of heavily documented case files. I interviewed over 100 prosecutors, judges, and defense counsel in both large and small cities throughout Germany and gained close access to their work practices. As a former prosecutor in the United States, I was able to compare my observations of German practice with my own experiences as a prosecutor. Proud of their system, most of my German hosts were happy to open their office doors to an American visitor. In the course of my research, I gathered a more nuanced understanding of prosecution practice than is painted by many comparative legal scholars today.

Although research into prosecutorial discretion in the United States is extensive, scholars' long denial of prosecutorial discretion in Germany has created a large gap that hampers comparative studies of prosecutorial practice as well as reform efforts. Thus, the extent to which German prosecution practice actually reflects the normative vision of objective fact-finding is an intriguing question that this book aims to explore. To date, no comprehensive study of German prosecution practice has been published in English. Even though prosecutorial discretion in Germany has increased and the principle of mandatory prosecution has lost some of its regulatory force, it is worthwhile to determine what factors drive prosecutorial decision-making in a system where success is not measured in terms of trial victories. Despite legal scholars' recent criticism of prosecutorial practice, many of the core features and underlying normative assumptions of Germany's inquisitorial criminal justice system remain in place.

Sociological studies of the prosecution service exist. To date however, the bulk of that research explores how the bureaucratic organization of work practices affects case dispositions. For example, Asmus (1998) argues that bureaucratic practices undermine prosecutors' application the principle of legality as prosecutors, besieged with a crushing case load, must adopt efficient strategies to close cases. While this research has broken important ground, it casts little light on prosecutorial decision-making in the courtroom and ignores prosecutorial practice in major crime cases.

Absent a detailed understanding of how prosecutors themselves interpret their duty to prosecute cases objectively as well as the role that collegial norms play in binding decision-making, scholars cannot ascertain whether organizational factors reinforce or undermine the system's normative goals. To the extent that German prosecutors seek to honor their normative mandate to investigate and prosecute cases through an objective lens, understanding how German prosecutors interpret and honor that duty will further our understanding of how normative values are embedded in the day to day practice of bureaucratic organizations.

It is also evident that, if no trace of the goal of objective decision-making remains in prosecutorial practice today, the gap between the normative goals of the law and practice undermines the German *Rechtsstaat*. As long as stakeholders in the legal system either continue to invoke the myth of mandatory prosecution or lambast the demise of the system, they risk failing to confront the challenges that the judicial system currently faces. The continued over-reliance on the principle of mandatory prosecution as the guarantee of prosecutorial neutrality threatens to undermine the achievement of the normative goals that the German legal system purports to advance.

Finally, to the extent that prosecutors are not driven by political considerations or the desire to win, it is important to understand what factors shape the evidence gathering and prosecution processes. Ultimately, to determine whether or not the organization of German prosecution function requires reform, we must understand how the factors that influence decision-making affect outcomes in the criminal justice system. For example, if it is prosecutors' own understanding of themselves as quasi-judicial officials, rather than the law itself that discourages politicians from interfering with prosecutorial decision-making, reform efforts should seek to strengthen, rather than undermine, that self-understanding.

In choosing prosecutors rather than judges as the focus of this study, I have chosen to buck the trend of most comparative law and politics scholarship, which until recently, has focused primarily on judicial decision-making. In contrast to the vast scholarship which studies the decision-making processes of national high courts, this book details the decision-making practices of prosecutors who sit on the front-lines of Germany's criminal justice system. Ironically, while the bulk of scholarship has focused on judicial decision-making in high courts, before a case reaches the rarified chambers of a high court, actors on the ground have made dozens of discretionary decisions-many of which are unreviewable. As Kenneth Culp Davis (1976, p. 3) noted three decades ago:

> [T]the most injustice in the exercise of governmental power in cases involving identified parties probably occurs when officers who are not judges exercise unreviewed discretionary power without the kind of procedural protections that courts customarily provide . . . The strongest need and the greatest promise for improving the quality of justice to individual parties in the entire legal and governmental system are in the areas where decisions necessarily depend more upon discretion than upon rules and principles and where formal hearings and judicial review are mostly irrelevant.

1.8 Overview of the Book and Research Methods

The blueprint for the book proceeds as follows. Chapters 2 and 3 build on the introductory materials presented in this chapter and set the stage for the analysis that follows. While Chap. 2 details the history of the prosecution function, Chap. 3 explores the organizational culture of prosecution practice and explains why individuals become prosecutors, how prosecutors interpret their role, as well as the key skills that prosecutors believe are necessary to perform their jobs. Chapters 4–6 delve into mechanics of the investigation, charging, and trial processes in both minor and major crimes cases. While Chap. 4 focuses on the routines of practice in low-level crime cases, in Chap. 5, I detail the institutional mechanisms that are designed to circumscribe prosecutorial discretion in major crime cases. The chapter questions whether those controls promote efficiency at the expense of the system's normative goals. The chapter also sheds light on the decision-making processes in major crime cases and shows that decisions made in the investigation and charging stages of the criminal justice process are not narrowly prescribed by scientific legal reasoning processes but, but are constrained by a variety of organizational and law-based factors. Those factors include the definitions of the crimes themselves, collegial decision-making norms, as well as hierarchical review processes. Delving into the prosecution of a number of types of major crime cases, I demonstrate that the law defining these crimes simultaneously creates and circumscribes opportunities for discretionary decision-making. In Chap. 6, I examine a highly contested area of the criminal law in Germany, the enforcement of anti-corruption laws and other economic crimes. I show that although gaps in the law open the door to discretion, the complexity and length of the investigations themselves encourage prosecutors and judges to settle the cases. I highlight how factors beyond the simple growth of caseloads have led to the increasingly widespread use of "confession agreements." Although these agreements originally emerged in the shadow of the law, they have become the accepted mode of practice in white collar crime, corruption, and other major cases. Finally, to conclude this chapter, I show how differences in local legal cultures impact case handling and investigation practices and create extensive disparities in the implementation of the law

Chapter 7 takes the reader into the courtroom presenting a dynamic picture of prosecutors' courtroom practices. While analyzing how prosecutors chose to represent the state in three different rape cases, I argue that prosecutors perform the dance of "objectivity" differently depending on the facts of the case, their relationship with the court, and the strength of the evidence. The chapter probes the meaning of "objectivity" and "truth-finding" in the context of modern trial practice. In Chap. 8, I examine a long-neglected area of comparative criminal research, the prosecution of juvenile crime, and look at a myriad of forms of practices in juvenile departments throughout Germany demonstrating how local cultures influence the delivery of justice.

The contribution of this book is that it details empirical evidence which shows that, while German prosecutors are statutorily bound to follow the "objective" dictates of the law, in the majority of cases, their decision-making practices are shaped by organizational imperatives and the mindset of the prosecutors themselves. Drawing on interview data and participant observation studies of prosecutors, I examine the widespread discretionary authority that prosecutors possess with regard to their investigation and charging practices. In the book's core chapters, I detail the variety of discretionary choices that prosecutors possess in screening and prosecuting the cases that cross their desk. Using the voices of prosecutors themselves, I detail how resource constraints, relationships with police and the courts, and the "opportunity principle" have opened a wide door to discretionary decision-making practices.

Although the law permits prosecutors to depart from the norm of mandatory prosecution when handling low level crimes and juvenile offenses under Section 152 of the Criminal Procedure Code (StPO), during the past 20 years, prosecutors have nearly doubled the rate of discretionary case dismissal practices increasingly using penal orders that obviate the need for a trial and permit prosecutors to provisionally terminate criminal proceedings (Oberwittler and Höfer 2005). Moreover, although legal scholars have argued that the discretion in the system is restricted to low-level or misdemeanor crimes, the German definition of low-level crimes (*Vergehen*) is vastly more inclusive than the Anglo-American concept of misdemeanor crimes (Culp Davis 1976). As a result, comparative law scholars have grossly underestimated the number of crimes that German prosecutors may dispense with through informal settlement practices.[18]

Having identified the key variables that affect decision-making outside the courtroom, in the conclusion, I return to the system's inquisitorial roots and discuss the extent to which the system's normative goals still drive front line decision-making. I discuss the potential consequences that the German legal system may face if policy-makers and legal scholars fail to accept and confront the current realities of prosecutorial practice. The inordinate faith invested in the principal of mandatory prosecution places potential opportunities to reform prosecutorial practice at risk. In particular, the disjuncture between theory and practice threatens prosecutors' ability to achieve a standard of practice that conforms to the system's chief normative goal-namely to facilitate an objective search for the truth. In the concluding chapter, I return to the two questions raised at the start of the book: namely, (1) Does the law constrain prosecutorial discretion in the handling of major crime cases? And (2) in an age of tight resource constraints have German prosecutors lost their "objectivity"? Without spoiling the development of the book's argument, I will disclose that, to the surprise of few comparative law scholars, the answer to the first question is a qualified no. To start with, there are too many crimes currently classified under law as minor crimes to make the first inquiry as meaningful as it first appears. Second, the primary constraints on decision-making are situated, not in the law, but in the organization of the prosecution service.

The answer the second question is highly situation specific and depends on the mindset of the individual prosecutor, the resource levels of the office in which they work, and the impact that incentives and controls have on the decision-making process. While my research did uncover isolated cases in which political figures attempted to influence decision-making, the most pernicious evidence of politics in the system is the comparatively level of funding given to the judicial system. Resource constraints and the turn towards using efficiency-related metrics, more than any other factor, threaten to short-circuit the full-fledged search for truth envisioned by the system's founders.

I then proceed to ask whether the existence of wide-ranging discretion undermines the fairness of the system as well as its capacity to achieve justice. Because prosecutors perform an important gate-keeping function in the criminal justice

---

[18] Pursuant to §153 Nr. 2, prosecutors may use pre-trial agreements to dispose of any crime classified as a *Vergehen*. This category of crimes includes any crime which does not have a minimum prescribed sentence of at least 1 year of imprisonment. However, because many German crimes, which we might typically classify as felonies, such as some forms of rape and serious white collar crime, possess a possible minimum sentence of less than one year imprisonment, they are classified under German law as *Vergehen* or minor crimes. As Frase (2001, p. 22) confirms, very few nonviolent offenses are classified as *Vergehen*.

system, their decision-making practices play an instrumental role in defining a state's criminal justice policies. As the principle of mandatory prosecution continues to lose its ability to constrain prosecutorial discretion in Germany, local institutional practices are playing an increasingly central role in shaping the exercise of discretion. As long as policy-makers ignore the extent of prosecutorial discretion, little effort will be made to investigate both how local practices shape the implementation of the law as well as how the practices may support or undermine the law's normative goals.

Taking the discussion forward; I question whether the gap between the theory and practice of law in Germany is leading to "legitimacy deficit" in the criminal justice system. As discrepancies in how the law is applied in practice become public, they strengthen the public's belief in the fact that political considerations, rather than legal principles, guide prosecutorial decision-making. Recent media criticism of deals that the public prosecution office has struck with high profile, privileged defendants, such as former Chancellor Helmut Kohl and corporate executives such as former Volkswagen executive Peter Hartz, underscore this point. Given that a key foundation of Germany's post-war identity is founded on the citizenry's faith in the law based state or Rechtsstaat, the untethering of prosecutorial decision-making from structured legal guidelines threatens to undercut public confidence in the law and the state itself. I then explore the broader role that German prosecutors play in society before I draw concluding observations on the interaction between prosecutors, politics, and society in the final chapter and discuss possible directions for reform.

In the book's final chapter, I probe the implications that my research poses for reforming prosecution practice in Germany. In this chapter, I compare the factors which shape discretion in Germany with the factors driving discretion-making in the United States. I compare the shape of prosecutorial discretion in the both countries and address three questions: (1) to what extent, should discretion be accepted as an inevitable component of prosecutorial decision-making in Germany? (2) In what ways is discretion inadequately controlled? And (3) are there elements of best-practices related to the administration of justice in place in some offices which could be used as a model to improve the quality of the justice delivered by German prosecutors? I conclude by identifying questions that my research could not satisfactorily answer and offer suggestions for further inquiry.

Building on the law and society research tradition which explores the differences between law on the books and law in action, this book strengthens our comparative understanding of the role that prosecutors play as gatekeepers to the criminal justice system. Moreover, it is my hope that this project will broaden scholars' interest in Germany's criminal justice system and spur a deeper interest in the ongoing evolution of the civil law tradition.

Court Cases (German)

Federal Constitutional Court: BVerfG, 1 BvR 2378/98 of 2 March 2004.
Federal Constitutional Court: BVerfG, 1 BvR 357/05 of 5 February 2006.

German Law

German Code of Criminal Procedure

Sections: 152(2), 153, 153 Nr. 2, 153(1), 160(2), 172, 244, 244(2), 249, 252–260, 257, 296(2).

Reports/Statistics

Veritas Initiative. 2011. First Annual Report. Preventable Error: Prosecutorial Misconduct in California 2010. Santa Clara: Santa Clara University of Law. Available at http://www.veritasinitiative.org/wp-content/uploads/2011/03/ProsecutorialMisconduct_FirstAnnual_Final8.pdf. Last accessed on 1 June 2013.

Interviews

Appellate Judge Interview [22FE], 22 July 2004. Appellate Judge Interview [13MU], 10 April 2004.

References

Books, Articles and Online Publications

Alschuler, A. W. (1968). The prosecutor's role in plea bargaining. *University of Chicago Law Review, 36*, 50–112.

Asmus, H.-J. (1998). Der Staatsanwalt-ein bürokratischer Faktor in der Verbrechens Kontrolle. *Zeitschrift Für Soziologie, 17*(Heft 2), 117–118.

Bahners, P. (2009). Menschenwürde und Freiheitsrechte: Was unterscheidet das deutsche Grundgesetz und die Verfassung der Vereinigten Staaten? Donald Kommers, der beste Kenner, gibt Auskunft, *Frankfurter Allegemeine Zeitung*, 18 Mai.

Cohen, A. (2013). Prosecutors shouldn't be hiding evidence from defendants. *The Atlantic*, May 13

Culp Davis, K. (1976). *Discretionary justice in Europe and America*. Urbana: University of Illinois Press.

Dubber, M. D. (2005). The promise of German criminal law: a science of crime and punishment. *German Law Journal* 6, 1049–1051. http://www.germanlawjournal.com/pdfs/Vol106No07/PDF_Vol_6_No_07_1049-1073_Articles_Dubber.pdf. Accessed 22 Feb 2011.

Eisenberg, U., & Conen, S. (1998). §153 StPO: Legalitätsprinzip im gerichtsfreien Raum. *Neue Juristische Wochenschrift, 31*, 2241–2248.

Elsner, B., & Peters, J. (2006). The prosecution service function within the German criminal justice system. In J.-M. Jehle & M. Wade (Eds.), *Coping with overloaded criminal justice systems: The rise of prosecutorial power across Europe* (pp. 207–236). Berlin: Springer.

Erb, V. (2004). Absprachen im Strafverfahren als Quelle unbeherrschbarer Risiken für den Rechstaat. In *Recht Der Wirtschaft und der Arbeit in Europa: Gedächtnichsschrift Für Wolfgang Lomeyer* (pp. 743–758). GS W. Blomeyer.

Esposito, A. K., & Safferling, C. (2008). Report-recent case law of the Bundesgerichtshof (Federal Court of justice) [pdf], in Strafsachen (criminal law). *German Law Journal 9*, 683–710. http://www.germanlawjournal.com/pdfsvol09no05/PDF_Vol_09_No-05_683-710_Developments_Safferlling.pdf. Accessed 15 Nov 2012.

Felstiner, W. L. F. (1979). Plea contracts in West Germany. *Law and Society Review, 13*, 309–325.

Foster, N. (1996). *German legal system and laws*. Oxford: Oxford University Press.

Frase, R. (2001). Sentencing in Germany and the United States: Comparing Äpfel with Apples [pdf], Max Planck Institute. Available at http://www.iuscrim.mpg.de/verlag/Forschakutell/Frase-Endausdruck.pdf. Accessed 30 Nov 2006.

Geisler, C. (1999). Das Ermittlungsverfahren der Polizei und die Einstellung-Praxis der Staatsanwaltschaften: Bestandsaufnahme, Erfahrungen und Perspektiven.

Goldstein, A., & Marcus, M. (1977). The myth of judicial supervision in three "Inquisitorial" systems: France, Italy, and Germany. *Yale Law Journal, 87*, 240–283.

Goldstein, A., & Marcus, M. (1978). Comment on continental criminal procedure. *Yale Law Journal, 87*, 1570–1576.

Gordon, S., & Huber, G. (2009). The political economy of prosecution. *Annual Review of Law and Social Sciences, 5*, 135–159.

Hermann, J. (1974). The German prosecutor. In K. C. Davis (Ed.), *Discretionary justice in Europe and America*. Champaign, IL: University of Illinois.

Huysmans, J. (2004). Minding exceptions: The politics of insecurity and liberal democracy. *Contemporary Political Theory, 3*, 321–341.

Jescheck, H.-H. (1970). The discretionary powers of the prosecuting attorney in West Germany. *American Journal of Criminal Law, 18*, 508–517.

Kagan, R. A. (2001). *Adversarial legalism: The American way of law*. Cambridge: Harvard University Press.

Kommers, D., & Miller, R. (2012). *The constitutional jurisprudence of the Federal Republic of Germany* (3rd ed.). Durham: Duke University Press.

Langbein, J. H. (1979). Land without plea bargaining: How the Germans do it. *Michigan Law Review, 79*, 204–225.

Langbein, J. H. (1985). The German advantage in civil procedure. *University of Chicago Law Review, 52*, 823–866.

Langbein, J. H., & Weinreb, L. (1978). Continental criminal procedure: "Myth" and realty. *Yale Law Journal, 87*, 1549–1569.

Lepsius, O. (2007). Human dignity and the downing of aircraft: The German Federal Constitutional Court strikes down a prominent anti-terrorism provision in the new Air-Transport Security Act. *German Law Journal, 7*, 761–776.

Loughlin, M. (2010). *Foundations of public law*. Oxford: Oxford University Press.

Luban, D. (1989). *Lawyers and justice: An ethical study*. Princeton: Princeton University Press.

Luhmann, N. (1992). The coding of the legal system. In G. Teubner & A. Febbrajo (Eds.), *State, law and economy as autopoietic systems: regulation and autonomy in a new perspective* (pp. 145–186). Milan, Giuffre.

Ma, Y. (2002). Prosecutorial discretion and plea bargaining in the United States, France, Germany and Italy: A comparative perspective. *International Criminal Justice Law Review, 12*, 22–52.

Miller, F. W., & Remington, F. J. (1969). *Prosecution: The decision to charge a suspect with a crime*. Boston: Little, Brown.

Oberwittler, D., & Höfer, S. (2005). Crime and justice in Germany: An analysis of recent trends and research. *European Journal of Criminology, 2*, 465–508.

Pizzi, W. T. (1999). *Trials without truth: Why our system of criminal trials has become an expensive failure and what we need to do to rebuild it*. New York, NY: New York University Press.

Raz, J. (1979). *The authority of law: Essays on law and morality*. Oxford: Oxford University Press.

Rosenfeld, M. (2001). The rule of law and the legitimacy of constitutional democracy. *Southern California Law Review, 74*, 1307–1346.

Roxin, C. (1991). *Stravfverfahrensrecht: Ein Studienbuch*. Munich: Verlag CH Beck.

Rudin, J. B. (2011). The Supreme Court assumes errant prosecutors will be disciplined by their offices or the bar: Three case studies that prove that assumption wrong. *Fordham Law Review, 80*, 537–572.

Sessar, K. (1979). Prosecutorial discretion in Germany. In W. F. McDonald (Ed.), *The prosecutor* (pp. 255–276). Beverly Hills: Sage Publications.

Thaman, S. C. (2007). Plea-bargaining, negotiating confession and consensual resolution of criminal cases [pdf]. *Electronic Journal of Comparative Law*, 11(3), 1–54. Available at http://www.ejcl.org/113/article11-34.pdf. Last Accessed 26 July 2013.

Weigend, T. (2004). The prosecution service in the German administration of criminal justice. In P. J. P. Tak (Ed.), *Tasks and powers of the prosecution services in the EU Member States* (vol. 1, pp. 203–222). Nijmegen: Wolf Legal Publishers.

Weigend, T. (2008). The decay of the inquisitorial ideal: plea bargaining invades German criminal procedure. In J. Jackson, et al. (Eds.), *Crime, procedure and evidence in comparative and international context* (pp. 39–64). Oxford and Portland: Hart.

Weigend, T. (2010) Remarks at the Washington and Lee Law Symposium, Prosecutorial Power. A Transnational Workshop (April 2, 2010).

West, E. (October 2012). Court findings of prosecutorial misconduct claims in post-conviction appeals and civil suits among the first 225 DNA exoneration cases, *Innocence Project*. Available at http://www.innocenceproject.org/docs/2011/pmc_appeals_255_final_oct_2011.pdf. Last Accessed 27 July 2013.

Chapter 2
The Normative Vision of the Prosecution Service

2.1 Prosecutors and the Inquisitorial Tradition

One cannot understand the institutional mission of the German prosecution service without situating the creation of the service within the development of Germany's civil law tradition. That tradition has nurtured and shaped the institution's birth and purpose. Furthermore, unless we understand the role that law plays within the civil law world view, we cannot fully appreciate the depth and significance of scholars' present concerns about the prosecution service. Indeed, the current allegations that charge prosecutors with abandoning their search for the material truth in pursuit of efficiency, not only threaten the service's reputation, they also threaten the foundational pillars of Germany's civil law tradition.

For our purposes, a principal component of the civil law canon is that the law is code, rather than case-based, and has historically been resistant to interpretative development. The comprehensive legal codes, in use throughout Europe today, seek to closely define what actions constitute a criminal act, the applicable procedure, and the appropriate punishment. In theory, the codes leave little room for judicial interpretation. As a result of the limitations placed on the judicial role, in contrast to the Anglo-American tradition, the principal role of judges is to establish the facts of the case and to apply the appropriate code provisions. It is the duty of the legislature and legal scholars, rather than the judiciary, to draft and interpret the law.[1] Seen in this light, the fact that recent changes in German criminal law developed outside the legislative arena, challenges the preeminent role played by the Code of Criminal Procedure, the legislature's role, as well as the German legal creed that the law functions like a science.

While a handful of scholars have skillfully tracked the changes in the German Code of Criminal Procedure during the past two decades, it is important to

[1] "The Common and Civil Law Traditions," The Robbins Religious and Civil Law Collection. p. 1. Available online at http://www.law.berkeley.edu/library/robbins/CommonLawCivilLawTraditions.html. Accessed on 24 July 2013.

S.M. Boyne, *The German Prosecution Service*, DOI 10.1007/978-3-642-40928-8_2,

recognize that these changes are not mere technical corrections. They represent significant departures from Germany's civil law canon. The fact that the changes first appeared in practice before appearing in the Code, standing alone, is an anathema to civil law theorists. Indeed, Germany's turn towards abbreviated court proceedings and widening prosecutorial discretion challenge many of the cultural pillars which define the German legal tradition. To understand the nature of the threat posed by these changes, it is important to briefly probe the key assumptions of that tradition. As noted comparative legal scholars, John Merryman and Rogelio Perez-Perdomo, have written:

> A legal tradition, as the term implies is not a set of rules of law about contracts, corporations, and crimes, although such rules will almost always be in some sense a reflection of that tradition. Rather it is a set of deeply rooted, historically conditioned attitudes about the nature of law, about the role of law in the society and the polity, about the proper organization and operation of a legal system and about the way law is or should be made, applied, studied, perfected, and taught. The legal tradition relates the legal system to the culture of which it is a partial expression. It puts the legal system into cultural perspective (Merryman and Perez-Perdomo 1985, p. 2).

If one opened a German criminal law textbook 10 years ago in hopes of finding out the essential features of the prosecution service, one would learn that a key feature of the service was prosecutors' fidelity to the law. Consistent with scholars' understanding of prosecution practice at that time, the text would claim that prosecutors functioned with complete objectivity and that their decision-making practices reflected a scientific process. Moreover, the text would point to code sections that restricted prosecutorial decision-making as conclusive proof that prosecutors possessed limited decision-making discretion. Finally, the text would proclaim that that the roots of prosecutors' commitment to objectivity could be found in the history of Germany's civil law tradition. One implicit, but perhaps unstated, assumption running through the post-war portrayal of prosecutorial practice was a deep positivistic faith that the practice of law mirrored the dictates of the legal codes. A key corollary to this faith was the belief that law functioned as a science and that prosecutorial decision-making could be structured and controlled like a scientific process.

To this day, the German Code of Criminal Procedure attempts to define and mandate prosecutorial objectivity by requiring prosecutors to perform certain activities such as: investigating the facts for and against the suspect, summarizing the evidence for and against the accused during the main procedural hearing,[2] and permitting prosecutors to file an appeal on behalf of a defendant.[3] Indeed, in my extensive observations of prosecutorial practice, these code sections continue to shape courtroom practice.

Given that these code sections remain on the books, it is worthwhile to examine how the role of prosecutors came to be defined, not as a party that single-handedly

[2] §152(2) StPO.

[3] §296 StPO.

represented the state's interests, but as "second judges" committed to weighing the evidence in a neutral and objective manner. To answer that question, we need to examine the mission and institutional position of the prosecution service at the time of the institution's inception. Because the key pillars of Germany's civil law tradition and the structure of the criminal code came to fruition in the same time frame, it is fruitful to understand how the primordial elements of the code, the institution, and the legal tradition became interrelated.

2.2 The Birth of the German Civil Code

The birth of modern European law may be traced back to the foundation of ancient Roman law rediscovered by Italian legal scholars beginning in the eleventh century. Well after the Roman civilization had crumbled, the body of Roman texts that remained represented a detailed and reasoned body of wisdom. The thirst for that wisdom spread throughout Europe so, by the thirteenth century, students were flocking to Bologna. The law was not static as scholars continued to modify and interpret the texts to fit the conditions of the time. When these students returned to their native lands as their studies ended, their training in Italy enabled this common approach to the law to spread throughout the continent.

While European legal scholars continued to update the *Corpus iuris civilis* over the next several centuries, the Catholic Church also used Roman law in conjunction with religious texts to develop its own comprehensive system of law and governance. Indeed, a key step in the development of criminal law on the European continent was the development of canon law. In contrast to the feudal courts' use of adjudication methods such as trial by battle, the ecclesiastical courts were incubators for the development of reasoned court proceedings. The development of both civil and canon law became the foundation of a common body of legal thought in Europe. As one commentator has written "[t]he birth and evolution of the medieval civil law tradition based on Roman law was thus integral to European legal development."[4] When Roman law was reborn on European soil, it represented a significant step in the development of a comprehensive legal code.

Despite the existence of ecclesiastical courts, nation-states only made haphazard steps towards creating a central government and adopting standardized legal procedures. In Germany in particular, there was a patchwork quilt of legal jurisdictions with ecclesiastical courts applying canon law and judges in cities and towns seeking direction from local customs and the *jus commune* (Glendon et al. 1999, p. 27). Because the development of a central state administration in Germany lagged behind states such as France, customary law continued to flourish. Indeed, Germany's collection of principalities, kingdoms, and city states did not come together until 1871. By that time, German legal scholars had, by necessity, begun

[4] The Civil and Common Law Traditions, supra n 1, at 2.

to mix German customary law with Roman law and develop a unique German legal tradition.

The first systematic attempt to unify German law was the *Constitutio Criminalis Carolina* (Carolina) enacted in 1532 by Emperor Karl the V. Although the code did not completely usurp local customary law, it introduced a model system of procedure that sought to regulate the means by which judicial proof was gathered and evaluated (Langbein 1974b, p. 179). While the Carolina continued the practice of using of torture as a truth-finding tool, it also introduced a rudimentary notion of probable cause defined as a "legally sufficient indication" (Langbein 1974b, p. 180). As Germany moved closer to creating a central government administration, the building blocks of their legal tradition began to emerge.

A key development in the evolution of the civil law tradition was the emergence of state level civil codes. Reflecting the ideals of the Enlightenment period, law makers in France and Germany sought to create a system of law that was grounded on reason and would reinforce the state's socio-political objectives. Although these codes would eventually take the form of statutes enacted by an elected legislative body, the codes were fundamentally different in form and in orientation than subsequent statutory law enacted in common law countries. As Dainow describes:

> A code is not a list of special rules for particular occasions; it is, rather, a body of general principles carefully arranged and carefully integrated. A code achieves the highest level of generalization based on a scientific structure of classification. A code purports to be comprehensive and to encompass the entire subject matter, not in the details but in the principals, and to provide answers for questions which may arise (Dainow 1966–1967, p. 424).

It is important to note that these codes advanced divergent conceptions of the role that law would play in society. The most well-known of these codification efforts was the Code Napoleon adopted by France in 1804. Reflecting France's revolutionary aspirations, the code featured simplified, non-technical language that was designed to facilitate its' use as a citizen's handbook (Merryman and Perez-Perdomo 1985, p. 29). The legislation had to be "complete, coherent, and clear" because, according to the developing civil law tradition, the power to draft legislation was invested solely in the legislature. The authorities aimed to confine judicial power to the strict application of the law rather than its interpretation (Merryman and Perez-Perdomo 1985, p. 30). Moreover, the drafters believed that, by writing the law in clear terms, it would enable citizens to understand their rights and duties under the law (Apple and Deyling 1994, p. 18).

While the French Civil Code was widely admired throughout Europe in the early nineteenth century, in the aftermath of Napoleon's defeat, the prominent Heidelberg legal theorist A.F. Thibaut argued that, by developing and adopting a unified civil code, German legal theorists could encourage the state's diverse political entities to support German unification. As an advocate of prompt action, Thibaut claimed that the state could use the Prussian, French, and Austrian codes as a starting point (Glendon et al. 1999, p. 38). At the opposing end of the debate, the leading proponent of the historical school, Carl von Savigny, viewed the national law like a national language. Savigny claimed that the German code should reflect the state's unique national spirit. According to Savigny, the code should be a heavily researched endeavor that systematically reflected the historical sources of the law.

Savigny ultimately won the battle as the work on the German Civil Code began in 1874. It was promulgated in 1896, more than 20 years after the project commenced. According to Glendon, the technical precision of the final product, which included a special language employed throughout the document, had never been seen before in any prior legislative effort (Glendon et al. 1999, p. 40). According to Glendon et al. (1999, p. 40), the various parts of the code were cross-referenced to reflect a closed system of logic including a General Part which set forth the core concepts and principles. In contrast to the French civil code, which was rooted in secular natural law, the German Civil Code was based on an extensive, historical and scientific study of the existing German legal system (Merryman and Perez-Perdomo 1985, p. 32). Drafters of the German code aimed to create a body of law that legal theorists could study as if the law was a body of scientific data. In addition, by viewing the law as science, the leaders of the German codification effort believed that the uniformity of the codes would protect citizens from the arbitrary actions of the state.

In contrast to the straightforward French code that could be understood by citizens, the German code was the antithesis of a citizen's handbook. One key consequence of the Savigny's drive to create a legal science was that the development of a complex body of law fueled the growth of a professional judiciary as well as a symbiotic relationship between that judiciary and legal scholars. At times, even the judiciary required expert assistance to understand the law. Reflecting a developing belief that law was a scientific endeavor, the judges turned to law professors to write judicial opinions based on developed doctrine rather than rely on precedent. The complexity of the law and the reliance on law faculties to develop legal doctrine buttressed the premise that law was a complicated science inaccessible to the common citizen.

2.3 Judicial Power and the Creation of the Prosecution Service

While the complexity of the legal code accelerated the growth of the German judiciary's political power, a key reason why the judiciary amassed decisive political power dated back to 1815 when it severed its subservience to monarchical control back. As a result of their political independence, during the nineteenth century, German judges amassed and wielded considerable power that threatened the monarchy as well as the average citizen. Ultimately, it was the threat to the government posed by judicial power, combined with liberal concerns about judicial objectivity, which forged the unusual political coalition that led to the birth of the German prosecution service. Prior to the mid-nineteenth century, the German prosecution service did not exist.

The scope of a judicial power was not based merely on judge's independence but also stemmed from the breadth of their authority. Following the continental inquisitorial model, it was German judges alone who possessed the responsibility to investigate criminal accusations and to adjudicate guilt (Jackson 2007). Ironically, while the complexity of the law created a judicial class, the growth in institutional power ultimately led the state to create a prosecution service that was designed, in part, to serve as a check on the judicial power.

The growing power of the German judiciary reached its apex during the extensive period of social unrest in the mid-nineteenth century. In the eyes of political liberals at that time, the judiciary reacted to the social unrest by rebuffing the demands for societal justice and supported the existing political order In particular, as social unrest intensified, the judiciary viewed the political unrest through a law and order lens. As chief of the investigative process, judges adopted a proactive stance and initiated suits against democratic activists. Despite the fact that poverty drove much of the criminality of the period, judges continued to embrace a sharply retributive approach to crime.

The judiciary's elitist orientation attracted the ire of reformers who advocated the Enlightenment ideal of equality before the law. Riding a wave of expanding social unrest and dissent, liberal reformers began to focus their attention on the expansion of judicial power and its increasingly authoritarian character. Motivated by concerns about social justice, the reformers viewed the judiciary as a barrier to justice and accused judges of possessing a conviction mentality which developed during the case investigation process. Seeking to disperse state power, reformers proposed that the state create a prosecution service which was independent from the judiciary. By investing the prosecution service with the authority to supervise criminal investigations (Langbein 1974a, pp. 439, 446), the reformers hoped that the new institution would improve the objectivity of the judicial branch (Collin 2001). As Eberhard Siegismund points out, the liberal reformers who lobbied the King aimed to endow the prosecution office with a mandate towards objectivity:

> Hence the Prussian King was initially concerned only with disciplining the courts and affording the state interest in imposing punishment greater chances of enforcement. It was, however, the more liberal elements in the Berlin Ministry of Justice who succeeded in developing a conception for reform in 1845: according to this conception, the public prosecutor was not only to act in the state's interest but also to show equal concern for the defendant, i.e. for his defence. This was designed to obtain popular support for a novel institution, and to make it clear that the public prosecution office was now to be the custodian of the law, for the benefit of the defendant as well (Siegismund 2001, p. 1).

Ironically, it was the confluence of interests between liberal reformers, who sought to diffuse state power, and monarchal forces that sought to break the judiciary's grip, which led to the birth of the German prosecution service in 1847. While the reformers wanted to create a prosecution service that would conduct investigations guided by the law rather than politics (Jescheck 1970, p. 509), the forward-thinking ministers who advised King Fredrick Wilhelm IV aimed to preserve monarchal power by supporting minimalist "reform" (Collin 2001, p. 18). Additionally, the King's ministers viewed the concentration of power in an independent judicial branch as a potential threat to state power over the longer term. Although legal historians have long trumpeted the creation of the prosecution service as a liberal achievement which reflected reformist goals, the composition of the political alliance that spearheaded the institution's creation itself suggests the need for a more cautious interpretation. In fact, while the liberal reformers welcomed the prosecution service as an institution that would disperse state power, the monarchy hailed the new bureaucratic apparatus as an extension of executive power that could be tamed by ministerial control.

The expectations of the reform movement and the Ministers differed dramatically. Where the reformers sought to create an institution that would lack a conviction mentality and would be free to pursue cases in the public interest, monarchical interests sought to more effectively control political activity by bringing the investigative function under ministerial control. While the reformers sought to tame the judiciary's independence by vesting the prosecution service with the power to appeal lower court decisions, the government obtained a measure of judicial control. Most critically, by investing the prosecution service with a near monopoly on the charging function, the ministers intended to prevent judges from conducting their own investigations and initiating their own cases. Thus, while the birth of the prosecution service was celebrated as a step towards bounding state power within the confines of the law, in the short run, the new institution enabled the state to consolidate its' coercive powers.

From the start, the institutional placement of the prosecution service within the *Länder* level Ministries of Justice threatened to compromise prosecutors' independence and subjected the service to the bureaucratic prerogatives of the Ministries. In fact, it did not take long for the citizenry to realize that the locus of the prosecution service's loyalty was not to the people but to the state. That development should have come as no surprise as the first generation of Prussian prosecutors repeatedly equated the public interest with political ends (Schram 1969, p. 627). By investing the prosecution service with the obligation to prosecute crime, while subjecting it to the hierarchical control of the Ministry of Justice, the state created an institution that, at times, has owed its loyalty to competing masters.[5] The maxim that political reform often requires compromise to succeed played a key role in the prosecution service's ultimate institutional shape. In this case, the diverse elements of the political coalition that supported the creation of the prosecution service envisioned the institution both as an instrument of the state's coercive power as well as an instrument for justice. These divergent visions created an inherent tension in the service's mission and operating guidelines that continues to this day. As Jescheck has written:

> [T]he German prosecuting attorney's office was not only intended to take over the function of pressing criminal charges, but at the same time to guarantee the unstinting prosecution of

---

[5] §152 Nr. 2 StGB.

criminality, and, as an organ of judicial administration, to represent the state's will for justice (Jescheck 1970, p. 509).

2.4 The Drive to Depoliticize the Administration of Criminal Justice

The next critical step that occurred in the development in German criminal law and procedure occurred as a consequence of Germany's unification in 1871. In the aftermath of unification, Germany adopted a uniform criminal code (*Strafgesetzbuch*) and enacted legislation in 1871 that regulated the organization of courts and criminal procedure. This statutory scheme sought to standardize the administration of criminal justice throughout the former German territories as well as to depoliticize the decision-making process in criminal cases. The abuse of prosecutorial power by prosecutors, who had leveled charges against the regime's political opponents, prompted calls for further reform (Schram 1969, p. 627). While the establishment of the prosecution service diminished judicial authority, it did not protect the public from prosecutors' discretionary decision-making. This pivotal legal text continued to evolve in response to changing social conditions. For example, following the collapse of the Nazi government, the legislature revised the code adding new crimes to punish the incitement of racial hatred.

As the nineteenth century came to an end, the key ingredients of Germany's civil law tradition and legal institutions were in place. Chief among the attributes of that tradition was the belief that the law could function as a science. The responsibility for reforming the scientific code was vested in the legal academy and the legislature. Finally, by separating the investigative and adjudication functions of the legal system, liberal reformers hoped that the investigation process would be more objective and less political. The liberal reformers' goal to endow the judiciary with an objective lens, coupled with legal theorists' conviction that the law could embody a systematic scientific framework, created normative expectations that would eventually crystallize and come to define German criminal law and procedure.

2.5 Prosecutors and the *Rechtsstaat*

Sitting on the front lines of the criminal justice system, in the modern era, German prosecutors play a key role in maintaining the modern *Rechtsstaat*. While prosecutors are not immune from criticism, as an institution, the legitimacy that the prosecution service enjoys in part dates back to the goals of the institution's founders. Among the reformers' chief goals was to create an apolitical institution dedicated to operating within the boundaries of the law. Efforts to achieve that goal have continued through to the modern day. While a key goal of the post-war efforts to create the Basic Law was to ensure that the state protected human dignity, changes in the Code of Criminal Procedure hearken back to the original goals of the liberal reformers who created the service in the nineteenth century.

Most notably, legislators have sought to constrain prosecutorial discretion by seeking to structure the path of the investigation process in the statutory code. For example, statutory dictates charge German prosecutors with a mandate to investigate the "truth" and to file charges in all cases in which sufficient suspicion exists. Consistent with a positivist faith in the law's prescriptive force, the provision's drafters sought to banish prosecutorial discretion from the investigation and charging functions. By binding decision-makers to follow codified precepts, German legal theorists believed that the law could prohibit state interference in the administration of justice (Damaška 1981, pp. 119, 125). This attempt to mandate prosecution in all cases where sufficient suspicion existed was the first step in creating a criminal justice system that viewed the investigation process as a straight-forward process of collecting and classifying facts into the proper legal categories. Thus Savigny's claim that the law should function as a science has had an enduring impact on the German legal academy.

2.5.1 The Judicial Character of the Prosecution Function in the Twentieth Century

The collapse of Germany's Weimar government and the subsequent abandonment of the principle of legality by the National Socialist government led to a horrific abuse of the law that is well-documented elsewhere. Throughout the past seven decades of German history, law has played an instrumental role in forging German national unity and recasting the state's national identity. In the key transition periods following Germany's defeat in the Second World War and the triumphant period of German reunification, German leaders turned to the framework and language of the law to restructure the nation and to reframe the state's national identity. After the allied powers defeated the Third Reich, Germany's new leadership crafted the German Basic Law in a manner that aimed to firmly redefine the very definition of the state as a *Rechtsstaat* or rule of law state. During the reign of the Third Reich, political leaders, with the consent of much of the German judiciary, used the law instrumentally to advance the regime's political goals and to consolidate power. Post-war constitutional reforms aimed to rewrite the legacy of lawlessness created by the Third Reich's unchecked centralization of government power. In the post-war era, the new West German leadership was fervently committed to building a social democratic state firmly bounded by the rule of law. The legal foundations of the new state included a modern constitution that awarded a preeminent position to the principle of human dignity and endowed the state with the power to curb speech and political activity that threatened the state's democratic foundation. A crucial post-war reform was the establishment of the Federal Constitutional Court which is endowed with the authority to invalidate state action that contravenes the Basic Law. Germany's post-war *Grundgesetz* or Basic Law firmly redefined the purpose of the state as a *Rechtsstaat* or rule-of-law state. As a prerequisite to rejoining the international community, the new German state aimed to rededicate and strengthen its commitment to the rule of law. Indeed, Germany's (re)dedication to the rule of law in the postwar period played a symbolic role in recasting Germany's national identity and gave birth to the concept of constitutional patriotism.

While German constitutional law underwent a profound change in the post-war period, the roots of the state's legal culture possess continued relevance. In particular, the state's public law codes still aim to circumscribe judicial discretion and create a legal system that reveres the principle of legality. Germany's rededication to the continent's civil law tradition played a pivotal role in crafting the legal foundations of the post-war state. For many legal theorists, fidelity to the principle of legality is a key pillar of the *Rechtsstaat*. This formalistic view of the role of law in society reflects a philosophy of state authority in which the law sharply circumscribes state action. A central premise of the *Rechtsstaat* is that the law binds government action at all levels of governance. A second defining feature of the *Rechtsstaat*, which further defines this institutional separation of powers, is the prescriptive role played by the classic continental legal doctrine of legality. According to this doctrine, the legislative branch possesses the exclusive competence to define crimes and to prescribe criminal sanctions. Pursuant to German legal theorist's formalistic view of the role of law in society, it is the legislature, rather than the courts, that bears the sole responsibility for law-making. This division of state authority aims to enhance the law's predictability and to place a premium on legal certainty by preventing judges from "interpreting" the law.

2.5.2 A Commitment to the Principle of Mandatory Prosecution

With respect to the criminal justice system, lawmakers responded to the abuse of discretion by Nazi jurists by reinstating the principle of mandatory prosecution as well as several provisions that attempted to mandate prosecutorial objectivity. German criminal procedure law still attempts to mandate prosecutorial objectivity by requiring prosecutors to perform such activities as investigating the facts for and against the suspect and summarizing the evidence for and against the accused during the main procedural hearing. Other procedural provisions permit prosecutors to serve as a check on judicial discretion. For example, prosecutors may file an appeal on behalf of a defendant when the prosecutor believes that the defendant either is not guilty of the court's judgment or that the sentence imposed by the court is too harsh.[6]

[6] Prosecutors even possess the power to petition the court for an acquittal at the conclusion of a trial if they are not convinced that the evidence is legally sufficient to meet the standard of guilt. A prosecutor may also file an appeal on behalf of the accused. See §296 (2) StPO.

Echoing the positivist foundations of German law as well as an increasingly optimistic faith in the new constitutional order, German criminal law theorists praised the post-war orientation of the prosecution service. In numerous textbooks and legal commentaries, legal scholars maintained that German prosecution practice achieved the normative aspirations inscribed in the Code of Criminal Procedure. Reinforcing the German view that law functioned as a science, descriptions of prosecutorial decision-making portrayed a process in which prosecutors made decisions based on the law and facts from a neutral and detached perspective. The portrayal of legal decision-making as an impartial, neutral, and apolitical endeavor is consistent with the civil law tradition's strict separation of legislative and judicial powers. This neutrality stands at the core of the political legitimacy of the judicial branch and the prosecution service. To maintain that legitimacy, it is critical that decision outcomes are not seen as the end product of interpretive processes that serve as a cover for the decision-makers' policy preferences. According to one scholar, it is through their fidelity to the principle of legality, that German prosecutors are bound to pursue justice:

> [T]he German rule of compulsory prosecution of serious crime is no happenstance. The statutory standards, limitations, and remedies have been meticulously designed to fit the institutional structure and to serve the larger policies of the German criminal justice system. The rule is meant to achieve ends that are immensely important in the German tradition: treating like cases alike, obeying faithfully the legislative determination to characterize something as a serious crime, preventing political interference or other corruption from inhibiting prosecution, and more (Damaška 1981, p. 131).

This vision of the law and prosecutorial decision-making continues to reflect the German legal system's assumptions about the nature of truth itself. By the third quarter of the twentieth century, the function of German prosecutors came to reflect the key premises of Germany's own civil law tradition. In contrast to the adversarial system's assumption that the "truth" will emerge from a battle between advocates, the structure of the German system embraced the inquisitorial tradition's conviction that a neutral fact-finder can objectively discover the "truth." In contrast to the positivist nature of German criminal law theory, American criminal law theorists abandoned positivism's key premises in the early twentieth century and became highly skeptical of the premise that the criminal justice system could produce anything but a form of the "procedural truth" (Weigend 2003). Perhaps the most striking difference between the German and American criminal law theory is the fact that German theorists possess a firm conviction that a substantive truth exists and that the criminal justice process can be structured to find it.

Thus, a key purpose of the Criminal Procedure Code is to divine and prescribe a method for judges and prosecutors to find the truth. As noted earlier, a key premise of German legal theory is that the law itself is a science. Although prosecutors in America's party-based adversarial system may function like gladiators who aim to win the battle, the German system assumes that prosecutors function as legal scientists. Charged with leading the search for truth during the investigation process, prosecutors are entrusted, not with leading the effort to convict a suspect, but rather with uncovering all of the facts that are relevant for determining a suspect's guilt or innocence. Although, like their American counterparts, German prosecutors possess a near-monopoly on the state's charging power, the discretion that they possess in performing that function is intentionally more circumscribed (Jescheck 1970, pp. 508–509).

In key ways, the system's institutional structure aims to support the search for truth. Prosecutors and judges work in tandem to discover the truth. While prosecutors bear the ultimate responsibility for the investigation and charging functions, judges spearhead the truth-finding process at trial. On paper, at least, both institutions check and balance each other. To protect the independence of prosecutors and judges, after an initial probationary term, the occupants of both professions enjoy a lifetime appointment subject to the proviso that they do not break the law. In contrast to the majority of state prosecutors in the United States, who belong to locally-organized offices headed by an elected District Attorney, German prosecutors function as members of a hierarchically organized professional civil service. In addition to legal controls, prosecutors are bound by both *Länder* and local level bureaucratic decision-making controls that will be discussed in a later chapter.

2.6 Conclusion

The historical trajectory of the prosecution service is an important backdrop to understanding prosecutorial decision-making today. In my interviews with prosecutors, it was apparent that there is indeed an enduring cultural mindset that influences decision-making. While the drive towards efficiency and swift case-handling practices impacts day to day practice, these pressures have not completely erased prosecutors' commitment to objectivity. Understanding the face of that commitment is the subject to which I now turn.

Legislation

German Code of Criminal Procedure (StPO)
Sections: 152(2), 152 Nr. 2, 296, 296(2)

References

Books, Articles and Online Publications

Apple, J., & Deyling, R. (1994–1995). *A primer on the civil-law system* [pdf]. Federal Judicial Center. Available at http://www.fjc.gov/public/pdf.nsf/lookup/CivilLaw.pdf/$file/CivilLaw.pdf. Accessed 23 July 2013.

Collin, P. (2001). Die Geburt der Staatsanwaltschaft, in PreuBen, *Forum Historiaese Iuris* 12 [online] (12 März). Available at http://www.rewi.hu-berlin.de/online/fhi/articles/0103collin.
Dainow, J. (1966–1967). The civil law and common law: Some points of comparison. *American Journal of Comparative Law 15*, 419–435.
Damaška, M. (1981). The reality of prosecutorial discretion: Comments on a German monograph. *American Journal Comparative Law, 29*, 119–138 (Winter).
Glendon, M. A., Gordon, M. W., & Carozza, P. G. (1999). *Comparative legal traditions in a nutshell* (2nd ed.). St Paul: West Publishing.
Jackson, J. (2007). *The role of the public prosecution service within the administration of justice* [pdf]. Workshop on Human Rights and Pre-trial Procedures: Investigations, Arrest, and Pre-trial Detention, Cairo, 6–7 December 2007. Available at http://www.pogar.org/publications/arabinaiba/hr/cairo/roleprosescution-jackson-e.pdf.
Jescheck, H.-H. (1970). The discretionary powers of the prosecuting attorney in West Germany. *American Journal of Comparative Law, 18*, 508–517.
Langbein, J. H. (1974a). Controlling prosecutorial discretion in Germany. *University Chicago Law Review, 41*, 439–467.
Langbein, J. H. (1974b). *Prosecuting crime in the renaissance: England, German, France.* Cambridge: Harvard University Press.
Merryman, J., & Perez-Perdomo, R. (1985). *The civil law tradition: An introduction to the legal systems of Western Europe and Latin America* (3rd ed.). Stanford: Stanford University Press.
Schram, G. (1969). The obligation to prosecute in West Germany. *American Journal of Comparative Law, 17*, 627–632.
Siegismund, E. (2001). *The public prosecution office in Germany: Status, functions, and organization* [pdf]. Available at http://www.unafei.or.jp/english/pdf/PDF_rms/no60/ch03.pdf. Accessed 25 July 2013.
Weigend, T. (2003). Is the criminal process about truth? A German perspective. *Harvard Journal of Law and Public Policy, 26*, 157–173.

Chapter 3
The Organization of Prosecution

3.1 Basic Organization of the Prosecution Function

Germany's prosecution offices as well as its court system are organized on the state or *Länder* level and are subsumed within the state-level Ministries of Justice.[1] While the Minister of Justice at the state level is a political appointee, appointed by the state's Minister-President, prosecutors are career civil servants, who are protected from arbitrary dismissal after they complete a period of probationary service. An exception to that rule exists in four states, where the position of General Public Prosecutor (*Generalstaatsanwalt*) is a political appointee who serves at the pleasure of the Minister of Justice. Regardless of that fact, all prosecutors at the state level are members of a hierarchically ordered bureaucracy.

Because the prosecution service's bureaucratic structure is relatively flat, the decision-making practices which occur at the bottom of the organization play a central role in determining the extent to which the decision-making mirrors the system's theoretical assumptions (Lipsky 1980). Despite the fact that a strong hierarchical structure exists on paper, in terms of their daily decision-making, German prosecutions possess a great deal of decision-making authority. This discretion reflects the fact that governmental control of the prosecutorial service was relaxed in the 1970s (Blankenburg and Treiber 1985, p. 375).

The vast majority of prosecutors will never rise beyond the ground-level position of public prosecutor (*Staatsanwalt*). A small minority will become senior public prosecutors or departmental leaders (*Oberstaatsanwälte*). However, even that promotion takes typically 10–15 years to achieve and carries with it only a 4 % increase

[1] There is also a smaller federal prosecution office known as the Bundesanwaltschaft. However, their jurisdiction is limited to prosecuting serious offenses against the state such as high profile terrorism cases. Their primary mandate is to represent the State before the Federal Court of Appeals (Sect. 142 subs. 1 COA). The *Länder* prosecution services represent the state at the *Amtsgericht* (local court), *Landgericht* (district courts), and *Oberlandesgericht* (Higher Regional Court) Levels.

S.M. Boyne, *The German Prosecution Service*, DOI 10.1007/978-3-642-40928-8_3,

in pay. Each prosecutor's pay is primarily influenced by their years of service, rather than their rank. The fact that few interim career steps exist between the positions of public prosecutor and senior public prosecutor reflects the judicial service's desire to preserve the independent decision-making authority of prosecutors regarding case dispositions.[2] Once prosecutors satisfactorily complete a 2–3 year probationary period (*Probezeit*), they cannot be fired unless they commit a serious criminal offense. The individual who supervises the department heads is the chief office prosecutor who serves as the director of a prosecution office (*Leitender Oberstaatsanwalt*) and has risen through the civil service ranks. This individual reports to the highest prosecuting officer at the state level—the General Public Prosecutor.[3]

Because of this flat structure, the majority of the investigation and charging decisions are made at the public prosecutor level and much of the day to day supervision of those decisions is conducted at the senior prosecutor level. In Table 3.1 below, I have drawn a highly simplified organizational chart for a prosecutor's office that shows the various hierarchical levels in a prosecution office. As a point of comparison, the relatively mid-size prosecution office located in Koblenz, a city of 107,000 inhabitants, possesses nine departments. In the Koblenz office, there is one chief office prosecutor, ten senior public prosecutors, 42 public prosecutors and well over 100 auxiliary personnel (*Justiz* 2007). On the other hand, the prosecution department in the City–State of Berlin is comprised of 37 departments (*Staatsanwaltschaft* Berlin 2007) that employ approximately 300 prosecutors (*Justizzahlen in Berlin* 2007).

The institutional position of the prosecution service creates an interesting tension for prosecutors between their fidelity to the law and the demands of their organizational environment. A body of statutory law attempts to provide a roadmap for prosecutors to navigate these tensions and guide decision-making. As members of a hierarchically ordered bureaucratic apparatus, prosecutors are required by statute to implement the orders of their superiors. Moreover, because the political responsibility for the prosecution service is vested in the Ministry of Justice, the Minister may issue general rules and regulations which seek to guide prosecutorial decision-making. In his or her capacity as a member of the Land's governing party, the Minister possesses a so-called external right of instruction (*externale Weisungrecht*)—a general right to instruct the General Public Prosecutor in broad terms regarding how cases should be handled. Thus the Minister may decide, for example, that juvenile cases involving violence should receive more attention and direct that more prosecutors be assigned to handle those types of cases. The law aims to protect prosecutors' adherence to the legality

---

[2] Prosecutor Interview [9BU], 4 May 2005.

[3] The organization of prosecution offices parallels the organization of the courts. There is a *Generalstaatsanwalt* located at each of the 25 regional courts of appeal (*Oberlandesgerichte*). Some of the Länder possess more than one regional court of appeal. There are 116 district courts (*Landgerichte*) in Germany. Beneath the district courts are the *Amtsgerichte*.

Table 3.1 Simplified organizational chart for a prosecution office

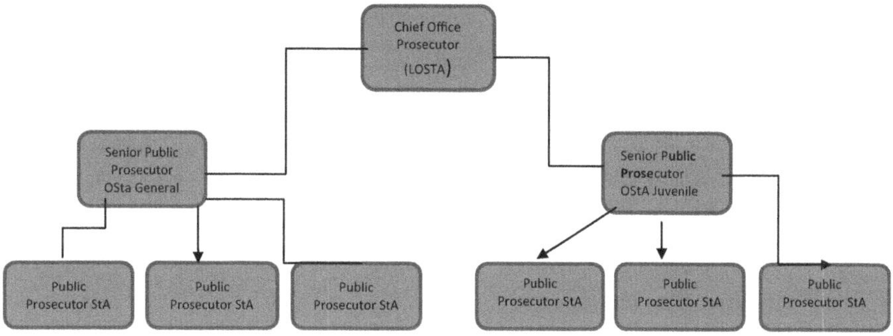

principle from hierarchical interference by prohibiting Ministers from issuing specific instructions to prosecutors regarding the handling of an indivdual case. In this regard, the Minister may not instruct a prosecutor to file charges against an innocent person nor dismiss charges that are supported by a sufficient factual basis. Nothing in the law however, prevents a Minister from ordering the supervising General Public Prosecutor to assign the case to another prosecutor.[4] The more informal means of influencing prosecutorial decision-making will be discussed later in the book.

Even though prosecutors are members of hierarchically structured organizations, one cannot ignore the fact they have also participated in a professional socialization process to earn their status as fully-trained lawyers (*Volljurist*). In order to understand the empirical arguments which stand at the heart of this book, it is important to briefly outline three aspects of the socialization and professionalization process of the German lawyers. These interrelated processes play a role in constructing the identity and outlook of German prosecutors. First, to achieve the status of a fully-trained lawyer, German law students participate in an educational and apprenticeship process designed to train all students to think "like a judge." Accordingly, law students are inculcated with a reasoning process that leads them to find the "objectively correct" answer to a legal problem (von Münch 2002). The structure of legal education narrowly emphasizes learning code and statute sections and reflects the contention that law is a science that must be taught by scholars (Künnecke 2006, p. 218). In contrast to American law students, who learn to view a legal problem from the dynamic perspective of an advocate's standpoint, German students do not learn to analyze legal problems through an adversarial lens which permits alternative paths to the truth (Korioth 2006, pp. 85, 94). As a result, the learning process not only inculcates an attitude that the "answer" can be found in the codes, but it also nurtures faith in the fact that the reasoning process will yield a "legally certain" answer. Reflective of Germany's civil law tradition, German law students are taught to view legal problems through the lens of a judge. The civil law tradition's construction of the judicial role and characterization of the

[4] §64 Par. 2 NBG (*Niedersächsisches Beamtengesetz*), §145 GVG (*Gerichtsverfassungsgesetz*).

decision-making process does not countenance a process in which judges are free to interpret ambiguous or unclear legislation (Merryman 1985, p. 36). As Sessar states:

> [While] [t]he German jurist would agree that not all deviant behavior which falls under penal law has to be punished, [they] would argue that [the] necessary screening should be accomplished legislatively (e.g., by transforming an offense into a petty, noncriminal infraction to be handled by administrative authorities, or by making prosecution dependent on the victim's formal motion) (Sessar 1979, p. 256).

3.2 Entering the Profession

For decades, German legal scholars have consistently portrayed German prosecutors as civil servants dedicated to the search for truth. Prosecutors perform a quasi-judicial role as they collect evidence both for and against a defendant. Legal textbooks portray prosecutors as dispassionate legal scientists who classify facts into neat legal categories by matching the case facts to fit a particular crime and to determine the appropriate punishment. We now know that this reliance on "the pursuit of truth" is simultaneously too vague to serve as a template for prosecutorial behavior as well as unrealistic given modern workloads. To bridge the gap between the portrait of German prosecutors found in legal texts and the characteristics of actual prosecutors, I asked current prosecutors why they choose to become prosecutors and how they would describe the ideal prosecutor. The answers to these questions give us an initial window into German prosecution practice.

3.2.1 Why Prosecution?

A German prosecutor is a paper pusher, a bureaucrat, a detective, a legal expert, and the leader of the investigation process. Protected by life-time job security, few prosecutors seek political careers. Unlike their American counterparts, they play a secondary role at trial and are likely to remain out of the limelight throughout the course of their entire careers. Burdened by ever-growing numbers of case files, many prosecutors are destined to spend a large part of their work days ensconced in a small office sifting through ever-growing mounds of case files.

Given this portrayal, why do so many top law graduates seek to enter the profession? Certainly, some individuals become prosecutors because the social standing of prosecutors has traditionally been high.[5] Others seek a stable career that will enable them to financially support their families as well as give them the time to raise children. Three prosecutors whom I interviewed had worked in private practice prior to joining the prosecution service and made the transition to work

[5] Prosecutor Interview [7SE], 5 April 2006.

more reasonable hours. As an example, one prosecutor who was now working on drug and homicide cases told me that she had worked as a lawyer in a large city handling insurance cases. She switched to the prosecution service because "the pace of the work [in private practice] was very fast and she had to work too many hours."[6] Another prosecutor, who had worked on civil suits involving construction disputes explained to me, that as a lawyer in private practice, he didn't have enough time to spend with his family.[7]

Once individuals enter the judicial service, some prefer to pursue a career as a judge because judges possess full decision-making freedom. Still, in those *Länder* where individuals are given a choice between the prosecution service and the judiciary, many individuals choose to pursue a career as a prosecutor. The chief reasons motivating this selection are a desire to work with a group of colleagues,[8] a preference for working exclusively in the criminal justice system, and perhaps most importantly, the ability to play an active role in the investigation process.[9] Indeed, one senior prosecutor told me that, although he had started his career as a judge and then rotated into the prosecution service, he had elected to remain a prosecutor because he enjoyed working closely with colleagues.[10] According to another senior prosecutor, a prime drawing point of working in the prosecution service for him was that the relationships between prosecutors are tighter and less hierarchical than the relationships between judges.[11] Another factor mentioned by a prosecutor was judges must always keep learning new law.[12] He was referring to the fact that jurists in the judicial ranks may rotate between positions in a variety of civil, as well as criminal, courts. Another department manager related to me that the principle of mandatory prosecution led him to pursue a career as a prosecutor rather than as a judge.[13] Other prosecutors stated that they were happy with their positions as prosecutors because their work hours were flexible. One male prosecutor told me that he enjoyed the fact that he had the flexibility to leave work early if his children were ill.[14]

Several prosecutors explained to me that it was the nature of the job itself that drew them to the prosecution service:

---

[6] Prosecutor Interview [4KD], 23 February 2006.

[7] Prosecutor Interview [4AJ], 2 February 2006.

[8] Many judges work in courts with a single professional judge, other courts include one professional judge and two lay judges. Although judges at the *Landgericht* level may work on a five judge panel, those panels are comprised of a presiding judge, two additional professional judges with differing levels of seniority, and two lay judges.

[9] Prosecutor Interview [13AS], 10 June 2004.

[10] Prosecutor Interview [13OI], 10 June 2004.

[11] Prosecutor Interview [13AS], 10 June 2004.

[12] Prosecutor Interview [9EG], 8 May 2006.

[13] Prosecutor Interview [13PR], 6 December 2005.

[14] Prosecutor Interview [4GG], 30 January 2006.

> I had studied law and I was interested in the legal truth. It was my impression that one could take more initiative as a prosecutor and, by taking that initiative, one could serve justice. That is the main reason that I chose [the prosecution service].[15]

> It is more interesting to be a prosecutor than a judge because the judge receives the file once it has already been put together. In most of the cases, the file is complete and the judge's only role is to present witnesses. [In contrast], the prosecutor stands in the middle of the action during the investigation. So, we get to work on every level [of the process]. We are also responsible for the execution of sentence.[16]

> I started here and I worked here for six months and then I had to go to another city... [where] I was a judge... who [approved] the arrest warrants, search warrants, [etc.]. Then I worked at an appeals court in civil law and after that [assignment] I had to decide what I wanted to do and I [thought] that I had had the best time in this [prosecution] office so I came back here.[17]

> During my externship experience, I decided that I preferred the combination of abstract, juridical activity and the practical nature of the job [as a prosecutor] over the job as a judge.[18]

> When I was in the sixth grade, I began to watch television programs where people came before a court. I decided that that's the career that I wanted to pursue. So I decided to study law and I wanted to become a family court judge. But after my legal studies, when I worked as an extern in a prosecution office, I enjoyed it so much that I decided to become a prosecutor.[19]

There are prosecutors in some *Länder* who would prefer to pursue a judicial career but cannot do so because of a dearth of openings. For example, the morale of one prosecutor took a hit on the day of our scheduled interview because she had just found out that the Ministry had offered an unadvertised judicial opening to another colleague. Stressed by her role as a single parent, a judicial position would have given her more flexible hours.

> I work to earn money. I skip the morning coffee meetings [with my colleagues] so that I can leave early to be home with my children. I would have applied for the judicial opening to decrease my daily commute and also because judges have more flexible work hours. The Ministry treats judges better and a judge does not need to work as hard [as a prosecutor].[20]

Whether a law student aims to pursue a career as a prosecutor, judge, or as an attorney, they receive the same general legal education. As a result everyone who seeks a career as a prosecutor or as a judge has been similarly trained. In all but a small number of cases, individuals begin their career as prosecutors or judges immediately after completion of their second state legal exam. All students who

[15] Prosecutor Interview [2BN], 16 July 2004.

[16] Prosecutor Interview [4AJ], 2 February 2006.

[17] Prosecutor Interview [13WT], 18 November 2005.

[18] Prosecutor Interview [2QM], 6 October 2005.

[19] Prosecutor Interview [19BS], 14 May 2008.

[20] Prosecutor Interview [6SB], 23 February 2006.

seek to pursue a legal career must first obtain an undergraduate legal education that lasts at least 4 years.[21] After completing that coursework, students must pass a first state exam in law before they can proceed to the second stage of the educational process. After that exam, aspiring lawyers participate in a 2-year apprenticeship rotation between different legal offices of their choosing and then take a second state exam (Korioth 2006). The individuals who score in the top 5–10 % among all test-takers the individuals taking the test have the best chance of obtaining a position in the judicial service.[22]

The structure of the hiring process for the judicial service reinforces the idea that prosecutors are judicial officers rather than advocates. Since the responsibility for the administration of the criminal justice system is primarily located at the *Länder* level, the application procedures and even the career paths differ from Land to Land. Although each Land is free to devise its own hiring processes, in the majority of the states, individuals are hired into a broadly defined judicial service which includes the prosecution, judicial, and ministerial functions rather than specifically as prosecutors or judges. During their probationary period, new hires often rotate between positions as a judge or prosecutor depending on the needs of the Ministry of Justice. In some states, at the end of the probationary period, individuals will choose or be assigned to a career track as a judge or as a prosecutor. As a result, even though an individual would prefer to serve as prosecutor or as a judge, he or she may be placed on the other career track due to the needs of the particular state. An alternative career ladder is present in *Länder* such as Bavaria and Sachsen-Anhalt where individuals will rotate throughout their careers between positions in the prosecution service, judiciary, and the Ministry of Justice. These different career paths reflect historical differences in the administration of justice as well as different perspectives of the prosecution and judicial roles. Those *Länder* that favor a continuing rotation of personnel into different functions believe that the rotation will encourage prosecutorial objectivity as well as foster the development of a wider perspective of the law.[23] In contrast, personnel policies that encourage jurists to specialize in the prosecution or the judicial services reflect the belief that the skills needed to succeed in each profession differ. As one General Prosecutor described the selection procedure in his Land:

> During the probationary period in this Land, each individual will spend time in a small court, a regional court, and also in a prosecutor's office. [Supervisors in] all three areas will evaluate the individual. The individual can also voice their preference. But the types of people who become judges are very different than those that become prosecutors. A judge is a person who carries a problem around with him and then looks at it and makes a decision. A prosecutor is a more active person who must take the initiative and think about possible courses of action.[24]

---

[21] Deutsches Richtergesetz [DRiG], Sept. 8, 1961; BGBl.I at 1665, §5 paragraph 1 (F.R.G.). Available at "*Gesetz* in internet." http://bundesrecht.juris.de.

[22] The judicial service encompasses positions in the prosecution function, the judiciary, and the Ministry of Justice.

[23] Prosecutor Interview [8HL], 25 May 2006.

[24] Prosecutor Interview [2BN], 16 July 2004.

Although one needs a top exam score to pass the first stage of the selection process, an applicant also must pass the interview process and possess a bit of luck. In some states, tight budgets mean that the Justice Ministries may hire less than a handful of new applicants each year.[25] The opportunities are particularly acute in the eastern states where declining populations and stagnant economies create few new openings and make it extraordinarily difficult to get hired.[26] In one large city prosecution office, almost 60 % of the new hires possess doctoral degrees even though those degrees are not a necessary prerequisite.[27] In most *Länder*, individuals in the Ministry of Justice or the office of a General Public Prosecutor will screen the applications and only interview applicants who scored in the top 10 % on the second state exam.[28] Beyond the exam scores, the hiring committee may review the written evaluations that an individual received during their externship rotations as well as the results of any written exams that a student may have taken during their legal studies. When I asked hiring committee members what qualities they looked for during the interview process, the answers included social competence,[29] decisiveness,[30] as well as a knowledge of economics.[31] During the interview members of the hiring committee typically question applicants about legal issues, recent court decisions, as well as their family situation.[32]

One consequence of the institutional closeness of the prosecution and judicial functions is that in many *Länder* one must be prepared to accept a position in either service. Although individual preferences may impact an individual's subsequent placement, individuals who become effective prosecutors share certain skill sets. Before we can evaluate the effectiveness of prosecution training programs, it is important to first understand the skill set that prosecutors must ideally possess or develop.

[25] Prosecutor Interview [7GC], 6 April 2006.

[26] Prosecutor Interview [7GC], 6 April 2006. See also Prosecutor Interview [9BU], 4 May 2005.

[27] Prosecutor Interview [9BU], 4 May 2005.

[28] Other states have a top 25 % score cutoff. Ministry Interview [13JM], 10 June 2004.

[29] Prosecutor Interview [2BN], 16 July 2004.

[30] Prosecutor Interview [11OT], 15 July 2004.

[31] Prosecutor Interview [11OT], 15 July 2004.

[32] One prosecutor told me that his hiring committee was impressed by the fact that he already had three children. Prosecutor Interview [4AJ], 2 February 2006.

3.2.2 The Ideal Prosecutor

At one end of the performance spectrum, there are some prosecutors who just sit in their offices like the prototypical bureaucrat and write orders that their assistants send to the police. Content to allow the police to perform the investigative work, they wait for the case files to reach their office for their review. Prosecutors in this mold view and perform their job in a formulistic fashion. When an order comes from above, they follow it without reflection and simply do the work that sits in front of them. They are paper pushers who move files from their "in box" to the "out box" and perform their jobs like workers on a factory line. In the courtroom, they follow the judge's direction and convey the impression of an impersonal bureaucrat whose job is to uphold society's respect for the law and no more.

To the extent that such prosecutors still exist, they are ill-equipped to deal with the modern practice of criminal law enforcement. The world of prosecution practice is now a place where organized crime syndicates pursue business opportunities across national borders and businessmen, who seek to profit from fraudulent transactions on a daily basis, create fictitious shell corporations to shield illegal financial transactions. It is a world in which criminals often effectively use modern technology to disguise their criminal endeavors. In short, it is a world in which prosecutors, who are not creative thinkers and are uncomfortable with taking the lead in complex investigations, cannot function effectively.

On the frontlines of modern prosecution practice in elite homicide, drug, and economic crime departments, the portrait of an ideal prosecutor continues to evolve. It is a job that differs vastly from the bureaucratic portrait described above. As one economic crimes, prosecutor shared with me:

> With this job, I don't sit behind my desk. I am always learning new things. The investigation methods are different. I need to make decisions at the start of a case about which way I will take the investigation. I work closely with the police and other investigation agencies and I like that. I go out with the police to conduct search warrants and conduct investigations.[33]

While descriptions of the ideal prosecutor may differ, my conversations with prosecutors across a variety of departments revealed a sought after core skill set, mindsets, and work practices. Although legal knowledge is a prerequisite for the job, a prosecutor must be much more than a detached legal scientist. Across the board, three critical characteristics emerged. First, a prosecutor must possess good communication skills and know how to work with people. Second, they must be able to work closely with the police to direct the course of an investigation. In the case investigation stage, prosecutors must be able to determine what the "*Sachverhalt*" is, in other words what are the critical facts of the case. As one senior prosecutor stated, "an important skill that prosecutors need is to [be able] to understand what is *Sachverhalt* ... The most difficult questions [in a case] are

[33] Prosecutor Interview [5XW], 19 January 2006.

factual, rather than, legal ones."[34] In describing a prosecutor's role in the investigation process, one child abuse prosecutor emphasized that "one cannot do the job just by the telephone." You must investigate the facts with the police, make sure that the child was heard, and that the investigation is also completed in a competent manner.

Finally, a prosecutor in a major crime departments in particular must be able to take the initiative.[35] He cannot be content to sit back and wait for files to reach his desk. He can intuitively determine how an investigation should proceed and how to complete an investigation file. The ideal prosecutor knows how to work with the police and knows when the state should use extraordinary legal measures such as search warrants to obtain evidence. As two prosecutors noted:

> I believe that the ideal prosecutor knows how to work with the police. Should the police interview the suspect or a witness? How should one com le a file (complete an investigation). What technical investigation tools are available to obtain evidence from the suspect? We have now an actual case in which a 9 year old girl was taken in a car and then raped in the woods and left on a bridge on the highway. Then one must ask what technical measures is it possible to use. But one must accommodate the child.[36]

> One cannot do this job just over the telephone. You must investigate facts with the police. One can influence the police investigation and make sure that the child was heard and that the investigation is completed in a competent manner.[37]

> The difference lies in how intelligent [one is] and how much initiative a prosecutor takes in the investigation. As a practical matter a prosecutor may ask, "Is the result of the investigation in order or are there holes in the investigation? What can I do to obtain a better result?" That is a core difference between a prosecutor who just follows the routine and a prosecutor who will take the initiative to reach a better result. The [better prosecutor] is one who thinks independently and then follows through with a thorough process. It is important that a good prosecutor has the strength and the possibility to seize the initiative.[38]

Effective prosecutors are able to lead complex investigations by deciding what steps the police should take. In making investigation decisions, they must understand how criminals think. At the same time, a prosecutor must also use commonsense and not go overboard in using his power by resorting too often to the use of extraordinary measures such as wiretapping. To guide their decision-making, a prosecutor must possess a sense of responsibility, an understanding of their societal role, and a larger understanding of their role. He must make level-headed decisions in pursuit of justice rather than convictions. The ideal prosecutor enjoys their work, is level-headed, and works well with the police. He is not driven by the quest to ensure that a suspect is found guilty. He must have a larger perspective of his job. It is not enough to simply do your duty. You must reflect on the impact of your

[34] Prosecutor Interview [5BC], 16 January 2006.

[35] Prosecutor Interview [12FG], 24 April 2006.

[36] Prosecutor Interview [13BR], 18 November 2005.

[37] Prosecutor Interview [12CJ], 29 November 2005.

[38] Prosecutor interview [2BN], 16 July 2004.

decision-making. What will be the effect of filing a charge against a suspect? What will be the effect of the sentence? You must have a clear self-understanding of the social consequences that your investigation will have on a suspect, or a business in an economic crimes case. To be a successful jurist, a prosecutor must often work in a hands on manner and take an active role in the investigation. He must conduct part of the investigation himself and be determined to get clear evidence. He should take pride in the investigation.

In the courtroom environment, a prosecutor serves as a check on judicial decision-making. His job is "not to exercise power but to work with the court to ensure that the investigation and proceeding comply with the rule of law."[39] As a prosecutor summarizes the evidence at the end of a main proceeding, the prosecutor must "analyze a case's legal aspects and make a convincing presentation" to the court.[40] One prosecutor described her courtroom role in these words, "my main objective in the main proceeding is to walk away from the proceeding and to know that I have been fair."[41] Other prosecutors, as well as an appellate judge, underscored the need for prosecutors to think independently in the courtroom, to monitor the judicial decision-making, and to be prepared to file an appeal when those decisions conflict with the law.[42] The number of interview comments that stressed the need for prosecutors to play an active role in the courtroom appeared to implicitly criticize those prosecutors who were content to play a more passive courtroom role. As one prosecutor stressed, "[p]rosecutors must be prepared to play an active role in the main proceeding and not remain silent. You must be able to represent the state's view of the law and take notice of the suspect's personality."[43]

In their descriptions of ideal prosecutorial practice, prosecutors noted that they faced two challenges in their jobs: handling a heavy workload and thinking independently while ensconced in a hierarchical bureaucracy. Although prosecutors need not triumph over defendants to succeed, they must successfully manage their workloads. In their decision-making in the case investigation stage, prosecutors must be able to determine what investigative measures will be the most productive, since time and resource constraints will limit the investigation.[44] As the stack of case files in a prosecutor's inbox grows, a prosecutor must be able to resolve cases quickly. This means intuitively determining what investigative measures are possible and then later pulling everything together quickly so that the judge, prosecutor, and the defense attorney can come to an agreement on the disposition of the case. The ability to manage work flow is particularly acute in departments that process a large number of every day crimes. Prosecutors who handle dozens of new

[39] Prosecutor Interview [16AG], 9 June 2008.

[40] Prosecutor Interview [7AG], 7 April 2006.

[41] Prosecutor Interview [5XW], 19 January 2006.

[42] Appellate Judge Interview [13MU], 10 April 2004.

[43] Prosecutor Interview [7GC], 6 April 2006.

[44] Prosecutor Interview [2QM], 6 October 2005.

case files each week must be able "to work the files." In practice this means that a prosecutor must make quick case disposition decisions and find ways to close cases quickly. In short, one must be able to "control" the flow of the files.[45]

There was a time when securing a position as a prosecutor meant that you could keep banker's hours. During that era, senior prosecutors left the office at 2:00 p.m. and junior prosecutors followed shortly thereafter. In many of the offices that I visited, that time had passed. In fact, a surprising number of prosecutors told me that they often had to work weekends to keep up with their workloads and to do a conscientious job. While the work hours of a prosecutor do not match those of a lawyer in a large firm practice, prosecutors must use their work hours judiciously to be effective. One of the most challenging constraints on prosecutorial decision-making is the workload itself. Even the most motivated prosecutor finds that in the course of their daily decision-making they must make compromises in the amount of work that they can devote to a single case.

Although prosecutors seemed to voice complaints about workload pressures almost as a matter of habit, the key point of contention was not the workload pressure, but rather the matter of prosecutorial independence. When I posed the question, "what qualities does an ideal prosecutor possess?" I expected interview subjects to detail a list of personal qualities and skills, yet a number of prosecutors responded to the question by stating that the ideal institutional position of a prosecutor would be similar to that enjoyed by German judges. That is prosecutors should be completely independent in their decision-making. Still, opinions about the need for more decision-making freedom and the degree of decision-making interference spanned a wide spectrum.

> The ideal prosecutor would be a prosecutor who was not beholden to the bureaucracy but instead possessed the independence of a judge. Although this is only possible on a theoretical level, the ideal prosecutor would not be constrained by the preferred work practices of their supervisor, but he would be fully free in his decision-making.[46]

> I am satisfied with the current system. Perhaps it would be better if prosecutors were a bit freer from the state, like a judge. We are civil servants. There are differences between judges and prosecutors. A judge is fully independent. In principle he is free to decide according to his conscience while we are still civil servants. That means that the General Public Prosecutor stands above us and the Minister of Justice stands above him. And they possess the power to give orders (*Weisungsbefugnis*). Perhaps it would be better if the prosecutors were treated like judges. In that case, we could do our jobs without the possibility of constraint from political influence. There is however very little political interference. In my sixteen years of service, I have never received such an order.[47]

> The fact that political influence is possible is a problem because it reflects badly on prosecutors. A defense attorney may ask a prosecutor in a main proceeding whether he has received an instruction on how to handle the case [from a superior]. Everyone in the

[45] Prosecutor Interview [2QM], 6 October 2005.

[46] Prosecutor Interview [19BS], 14 May 2008.

[47] Prosecutor Interview [19IC], 14 May 2008.

courtroom will become interested in his answer. Still, a prosecutor is free to make their own decisions in a particular case.[48]

It is impossible to identify the precise moment when prosecutors began to envision their role as something beyond that of a mere bureaucrat who simply followed orders. One might point to the period that followed the social revolution that began in 1968 and spanned the decade of the 1970s. In that decade a movement of younger prosecutors began publicly criticizing the prosecution service's dominant organizational culture. Consonant with a broader call for societal change, the organization alleged that the old ways of simple order following had led to catastrophic consequences for the judicial system as well as the country. In a widely read declaration, the movement called on prosecutors to dedicate themselves to doing good work rather than merely following orders. In key ways the cognitive revolution that the group called for has occurred as prosecutors no longer define themselves as mere bureaucrats. As one appellate judge noted, "the period where upper management can exercise complete control over the front line prosecutors is over."[49] It is also clear, that a measure of hierarchical control still exists. I will explore the extent of that control in a later chapter.

If an ideal prosecutor is indeed a person who takes the initiative and possesses excellent communication skills so that they can work effectively with the police, then the training and selection processes should support those goals. However, as I will discuss later, the method of training new prosecutors, which focuses on developing the art of writing instructions, perpetuates the idea that the prosecution function is a bureaucratic one. In fact, those department leaders who are comfortable with the bureaucratic practices continue to emphasize the practice of writing instructions in their office training programs. That gap between training and ideal practices is a key problem facing the prosecution service today. Although the organizational culture does not strongly perpetuate a bureaucratic vision of practice, the ongoing use of entrenched training practices hamstrings the development of new prosecutors who must learn the skills most critical to their success outside the formal training process.

3.2.3 *Learning the Craft: The Written Culture of Prosecution Practice*

They really put you in a room and you find a pile of files in the corner and during the first month you are still being monitored by your immediate boss, which in my case was [my department manager], so he looks at all the files I'm doing and corrects them and comes to me and speaks to me and says well I've changed this because I think this and this would make more sense but in the beginning I'm the one to look at the files first and nobody really teaches you how to handle it. . . . [W]hat we have is a complete folder with forms. So that gives you an idea of [questions that may be] similar to this and what you can do. They

[48] Prosecutor Interview [16PP], 30 April 2008.

[49] Appellate Judge Interview [13MU], 10 April 2004.

are also in the computer. We also get hard copies and then all colleagues recommend this book. It's a book that all of the *Staatsanwälte* (prosecutors) at least at the beginning have on their desk *Das Arbeitsgebiet des Staatsanwaltes* (The Work Activities of a Prosecutor).[50]

The process of learning how to function as a prosecutor is a process that is formally regulated by statute and takes an identical form throughout Germany. When an individual first enters the prosecution service, they will be assigned to a particular department. Typically, new prosecutors begin work in a general crimes department or a specialized department that only handles traffic crimes. Although the bulk of the cases in general crimes departments include simple cases of theft or assault for example, in some prosecution offices the general crimes department may also handle cases involving more serious crimes such as rape or even murder. The department structure of offices differs. Although all offices contain departments that specialize in the prosecution of certain crimes such as economic crimes or crimes involving state security, the particular array of specialized departments differs. In some offices, prosecutors may be assigned to a specialized department such as economic crimes but also carry a partial case load of general crimes cases. Most often however, a new prosecutor will be assigned an area of responsibility within the remit of general crime cases. For example, the prosecutor may be responsible for all general crimes cases in which the suspect's last name begins with a C or a D. The lead prosecutor (*Leitender Oberstaatsanwalt*) in each office typically adjusts the department assignments on a yearly basis. The assignments serve a twofold purpose. First they identify the contact person within the prosecution office that outside agencies should contact if the case they are working on falls within that person's area of responsibility. Second, it reinforces the principle of legality. By establishing in advance which person will be responsible for handling certain cases, it minimizes the opportunity for superiors to shape case outcomes by assigning particular cases to particular individuals as new cases enter the office.

Every new prosecutor begins their job by receiving an assignment to a particular area of responsibility. On a practical level that means that all active case files that fall within that area will cross the new prosecutor's desk. As the prosecutor sits at their desk, the first thing that is likely to grab their attention is a stack of red files sitting in their inbox. The files may represent cases at various stages of the criminal justice process. Without a doubt, the new prosecutor is intially at a loss to determine what to do with the files. The process of learning what to do with the files is supervised by an assigned mentor or perhaps the department manager. During the first couple of months, although the prosecutor may write an instruction in the file, the mentor must cosign every instruction before the file is even sent to another internal destination. As time goes on and the prosecutor's competence grows, the mentor will gradually decrease the degree of supervision and eventually, the prosecutor will earn the right to issue most instructions without a supervisor's oversight. This intensive apprenticeship process is much like learning a craft. The craft of writing instructions or documenting the work that needs to be done on the

[50] Prosecutor Interview [13BC], 8 December 2005.

file is a craft that can only be learned by doing it.[51] It is not a subject taught in the universities.

The craft of working the files is work that a prosecutor performs alone in his office. Unlike the prosecutor's performance in a main proceeding, it is work that is be subject to minimal controls. For that reason, it is important that the work that new prosecutors initially complete on the files is observed by a senior mentor. In fact, a considerable part of the daily routine of German prosecutors is devoted to reading and writing instructions in files. In Koetz and Feltes' (1996, p. 170) time-management study of prosecutors' work routines, the researchers concluded that prosecutors devoted over 30 % of their work hours to studying case files. If you add to that number the amount of time that prosecutors spend at their desk on other activities which require them to use the information contained in their files, such as drafting charging documents, that figure exceeds 50 % of their work hours. In consequence, a significant part of the time that a new prosecutor spends learning how to perform their job is devoted to learning how to record decisions and instructions in case files (Hohmann and Neubeck 1996). Although new prosecutors acquire a solid understanding of criminal law concepts during their university education, during their initiation into the prosecution service, they must learn an entirely new foreign language, "The Art of Issuing Instructions." Although form books exist which show young prosecutors how to write instructions, new prosecutors frequently learn how to write instructions by speaking with their colleagues or their assigned mentor. The time required to learn how to complete routine written paperwork was a common surprise to many of the new prosecutors whom I interviewed. The most difficult problem for a new *Staatsanwalt* is figuring out how to write a specific instruction and how to figure out where the file should be sent next. As one new prosecutor commiserated:

> I am just learning how to do this job so I have a great deal of work and [so I] must work from 8:30 in the morning until 7:00 p.m. at night. We have a special language that we must use when we are writing *Verfugüng* (instructions). [The form of] my instructions are getting better and better but during my [first week on the job] I asked myself if I had learned anything while studying for my first and second state exams.[52]

As a file crosses the prosecutor's desk, the variety of decisions that the prosecutor must make reflects the broad range of tasks associated with the prosecution function. Although the forms contained in each file may differ from Land to Land, the forms are relatively consistent as they reflect case decision-making practices. For example, a standard case history form found in files includes check off boxes for various types of background checks. These boxes include the national criminal database (*Bundeszentralauszug*), the transportation registry (*Verkehrsregistrierung*), and the pending criminal charges database (*Verfahrensregister*). When a prosecutor receives a new case file, the first step that the prosecutor will often take is to "order" his secretary to retrieve a suspect's history from those

[51] Prosecutor Interview [1DR], 15 March 2006.

[52] Prosecutor Interview [4EW], 2 February 2006.

databases. A prosecutor may decide to dismiss the current case if the suspect was facing more serious charges in another pending case. If the current case is a non-serious offense, the prosecutor may elect to dismiss the case if the suspect has no prior criminal history or offer the suspect a conditional dismissal.

When a prosecutor receives a new file in a typical misdemeanor or *Vergehen* file, it may trigger the prosecutor to issue a number of instructions (*Verfügung*). For example, in a file that I reviewed that included the charges of leaving the scene of an accident and giving a false statement to the police, the prosecutor had written the following instructions in the file:

1. Treat "witness A" also as a suspect because they lied to the police (Secretary/ Police).
2. Give the lawyer in the accompanying civil suit a copy of the file and ask him if he is going to serve as the suspect's counsel in the criminal case (Secretary).
3. Get the suspect's prior criminal records (Secretary).
4. Send the file to an accident reconstruction expert for analysis (Secretary).
5. Take the statement of a mentally challenged person who was at the scene (Police).

The character of those written instructions reflects the traditional written culture of a bureaucratic prosecution practice. Viewed from the perspective of a legal system in which the public visibility of sensational trials dominates the news, it may be difficult to understand why German prosecutors spend so much time "working the files." Even if we take into account the fact that many cases are settled outside courtrooms in the United States, an understanding of prosecutorial practice based on the American model would still underestimate the dominant role that file work plays in German prosecution practice. As a first step, it is critical to note that norms of practice require prosecutors to build a step by step record of their investigation and charging decisions. Moreover, the distribution of functions between courts and prosecution offices has elevated the role that case files play in the decision-making process for three critical reasons. First, because the court makes the decision to open a main proceeding on the basis of the material in the file rather than on the basis of an oral hearing, the contents of the case file play a critical role in determining whether or not a case will move forward. The case investigation file that prosecutors assemble is the same file that the court uses to decide whether or not to open a main proceeding. Although the information in the file is not evidence, standing alone, it is a complete catalogue of the investigation completed in a particular case as well as a window into the decisions made by the prosecutor, police, and other state agencies during the case investigation. To satisfy the evidentiary standard to open a main proceeding, the judge must, on the basis of the evidence collected in the file, be convinced that there is sufficient suspicion to believe that the accused has committed a criminal offense.[53] If the evidence in the file is insufficient, the judge can order the prosecution office to gather more

[53] §203 StGB.

evidence.[54] In addition, although it rarely occurs, a German judge may formally refuse to open a main proceeding on factual or legal grounds.[55]

As a result, the case file plays an important fact-finding role in the German system. In contrast, in the American system, in order to move a felony case from the charging stage to the trial stage, a prosecutor must present oral and physical evidence sufficient to establish "probable cause." Depending on the jurisdiction and procedural rules, this presentation must be made to a lower court judge in a preliminary hearing or to a grand jury. Regardless of the type of procedure employed, neither the magistrate judge nor the grand jury will reach their decision by reading the prosecution's case file. They will only consider the oral, written, and forensic evidence formally presented during the hearing. As a result, in the American criminal system, the need to document the investigation and decision-making process is far less compelling. In fact, given that a trial is a face-off between opposing parties, structural incentives weigh against the creation of transparent and richly documented investigation files.

Second, once a judge decides to open a main proceeding, the judge will use the file assembled by the prosecution service to determine which witnesses should testify and what evidence should be presented in the main proceeding. Since the presiding judge, rather than the prosecutor and defense attorney, bears the primary burden of summoning witnesses to court and directing their testimony, the information contained in the file itself can play an instrumental role in "binding" or forecasting the outcome of the trial itself. Finally, because prosecutors inscribe virtually every decision they make regarding a particular case in the case file, each file is a decision-making record. The catalog of written instructions inscribed in a file serve as a record that is intended to show that the process used by the state to investigate and prosecute the case was consistent with the rule of law.[56] Moreover, as I will explain in detail in a later chapter, departmental leaders, chief prosecutors, and even ministry officials may uses the files to monitor and evaluate the decisions made in a case.[57]

Although the flow of files ensures both that decisions are made and that those decisions can be subjected to hierarchical review, the nature of the file processing routines also promotes the system's norms of accountability and transparency. Given the preeminent role that files play in supporting the key function of prosecutors of building an investigation file, it is not surprising that prosecutors spend a large amount of time reading and documenting their decision-making in case files. Virtually every decision that a prosecutor makes regarding a particular case is inscribed in the file-from the simple instruction to a secretary to send the file to the defense attorney to an instruction directing the police to interview a particular

[54] §202 StGB.

[55] §204 StGB.

[56] Prosecutor Interview [12LH], 29 November 2005.

[57] See Prosecutor Interviews [13OI], 10 June 1984 and [13AS], 10 June 1984.

witness. This minutia of detail reflects the critical role that documentation plays in the daily work of a German prosecutor.

In small-to medium-sized prosecution offices, the emphasis on documenting instructions and then sending the file to another office is an inefficient way to communicate with other departments and agencies, especially when the target of the communication is the police:

> The system is too bureaucratic. Many department leaders operate in a bureaucratic manner because it is just safer to issue written orders. In order to resolve cases quickly, everything must come together . . . the defense attorney, the judge, [and] the police . . . This does not always happen. . . [However] in this department we have changed a lot. This department is [now] less bureaucratic than most [departments]. I have changed things. The police were doing all of the investigating and I have changed the system so that the prosecutors have begun to do more investigative work.[58]

The central role of that documentation plays in both directing and reflecting the work routines of German prosecutors is underscored by the following example which occurred during a case progress meeting that I attended held in *Freystadt*. The focus of the meeting was a major economic crime and corruption case. During this particular meeting, the two prosecutors met to exchange notes regarding what had transpired on the previous day of witness questioning. At one point in the discussion, one of the prosecutors raised the issue of whether or not it was necessary to write a note in the file stating that a potential witness had refused to give a statement in the case.[59] After a short discussion, the prosecutor's colleague recommended that she write a detailed note to the case file describing the specific circumstances surrounding the witness's refusal to provide a statement. After a moment's reflection, the prosecutor who had originally raised the issue replied, "*Na ja, Akten Klarheit=Akten Wahrheit*" (Clear files are truthful files).[60] This mnemonic serves as a reference point. It both teaches and reminds prosecutors of the importance of documenting the decisions and the actions they have taken in a particular case. When I queried the prosecutor about what this statement meant, she explained that everything in the case file must be transparent. If a prosecutor does not logically construct a case file, and by implication the case investigation, a judge or defense attorney may challenge the objectivity of the investigation procedures. In order to ensure that a defendant receives a fair trial, a defense lawyer must be able to trace the progress and logic of the investigation in the case file. Given that the aggressive cross-examination style of defense attorneys in the United States does not fit with the open-ended questioning that occurs in German proceedings, a defense attorney's right to review the file and trace the investigation process is critically important. What is more, there exists an implicit belief that the path to truth is paved by a clear, transparent, and logically sequential decision-making process. The norms of governmental administration

[58] Prosecutor Interview [5BC], 16 January 2006.
[59] Prosecutor Interview [1ZU], 15 March 2006.
[60] Prosecutor Interview [1ZU], 15 March 2006.

in Germany place a high value on transparent record keeping. As a result, prosecutors record virtually every decision related to a criminal case's investigation and prosecution in case files. For these reasons, documentation practices play a critical role in the administration of the justice in Germany. Not only do files function as records of routine decision-making, but they also play a determinative role in the construction of the "truth" in a criminal proceeding.[61] Moreover, from a research perspective, files serve as a form of ethnographic records of the inner workings of Germany's criminal justice system. It is impossible to accurately analyze the daily work of German prosecutors without understanding the relationship between prosecutors and their files.

3.2.4 Practice Routines

As resource constraints have risen, the mechanics of how work is organized in each particular prosecution office itself has become an important constraint on the thoroughness and timeliness of the case investigation process. Traditionally, prosecutors made a notation in the case file every time they made a decision on a case that required further action. The file was then routed to law enforcement, support staff, a court, or another agency for further work. Thus, if a prosecutor wanted a police officer to interview a particular witness, the prosecutor would inscribe that instruction in the case file and send the file to the officer. After the officer completed the interview, the officer would send the file back to the prosecutor handling the case. Although the practice of writing written instructions in the file creates a transparent record, the practice is inefficient and time consuming. For example, as part of my field work, I sat with prosecutors as they worked on their files. In one simple traffic accident case, the prosecutor read the accident report in the file and then wrote an instruction in the file to her secretary ordering her secretary to contact the police to gather additional evidence and to take a witness statement. In that case, the prosecutor delayed resolution of the case by resorting to the traditional method of issuing written orders. It is also evident that, reliance on the practice of issuing written orders may discourage prosecutors from conducting part of the investigation themselves. There is an increasing recognition within the prosecution service that the traditional method of working the case files is too bureaucratic. As one senior prosecutor noted:

> Too many colleagues just write a letter rather than going to the police and defense attorney with the file to get the case resolved. The problem is that [during their training period] prosecutors learn the system of writing instructions. Many prosecutors [just] want to work

[61] According to the German, Code of Criminal Procedure defense lawyers possess a right to inspect the same files which are made are available to the court (§147 StPO). This requirement exists in European law as well. According to Article 6 of the European Convention on Human Rights, defense counsel must have the opportunity to access the observations and evidence compiled by the prosecution.

> on files... Some prosecutors prefer to work abstractly and not deal directly with people. Rather than take the initiative, they just issue written orders. One must take an active role [to move a case forward.]
>
> When I took over this department, I changed the procedures ... The police were doing all of the investigations and I changed the system so that the prosecutors would do more of the investigative work. Once the investigation is complete the file must go to the court for a decision as to whether the court will open a main proceeding. In economic crime cases, the court may take six months to a year to reach a decision. Many last longer. If a suspect is in detention, the judge must set a reasonable date for the opening of the main proceeding.

The work practices that I observed in the 18 offices that I visited varied from an unrelenting dedication to the old, written practices to the use of specially designed software programs that helped prosecutors to map out and track complex financial investigations. The extent to which office practices are "bureaucratized" varies with the office history, local leadership, and financial constraints. It is difficult to draw a global conclusion regarding which offices have moved into the future and which remain stuck in the past. As one prosecutor in an office located in the former East Germany related to me, although he prefers to pick up the phone and speak with law enforcement officers, in some large cities in the western part of the country, the use of written instructions is still prevalent.

When prosecutors use written orders to communicate with law enforcement rather than picking up the phone or scheduling a face to face meeting, it slows down the investigation process and potentially limits the scope and complexity of the cases that the prosecutor can effectively investigate. Where investigations are particularly time sensitive, the use of slow bureaucratic communication practices may provide suspects with the time and opportunity to hide evidence of criminal activity. The use of tradition-based written orders also reflects a view of the prosecutor-law enforcement relationship as hierarchically ordered with the prosecutor in command. Whether a particular prosecutor views the investigation practice as simply issuing written orders versus working as a team with the police depends in large part on the preferences of the office and department leadership. To some extent, the nature of the criminal activity that is being investigated, as well as the relative resource levels of the prosecution and law enforcement offices, dictates the degree to which prosecutors are willing to cede control of the case investigation to the police.

In some complicated economic crimes cases, offices with specialized prosecution units will become intimately involved in planning the direction of the case investigation from day 1. Similarly, prosecutors in specialized sex crimes units may adopt the same proactive decision-making role. As soon as a sexual abuse case is reported, sex crimes prosecutors may take control of the victim interview process from the start-especially in cases involving child victims. With the vast majority of crimes however, a prosecutor will not become aware of a case until the police have completed the case investigation. Even in those cases however, the prosecutor assigned to the case may order the police to conduct additional investigation work on a case.

3.3 The Prosecution Function Through the Eyes of Prosecutors

Although the German Code of Criminal Procedure sets forth the prosecution service's "judicial" character, the nature of actual work practices, as a well as prosecutors' own attitudes towards their role and mission, strongly shape the role that prosecutors actually perform. A critical question is whether or not prosecutors possess the time, resources, and motivation to fulfill their obligation to ensure that the investigation process is conducted fairly.[62] While I will discuss the challenges that resource and time constraints create for prosecutors in greater detail in Chap. 4, this section aims to more fully show how prosecutors themselves view their role within the criminal justice system. Studying the voices of prosecutors themselves and noting the points where they both conform to and diverge from the normative definition of their role on the books, provides us insight into their routine everyday decision-making as well as their larger role within the German criminal justice system.

Viewed through the eyes of prosecutors, the role of a prosecutor extends beyond the duty to perform an objective investigation. It is also a role that continues to evolve. Although legal scholarship often highlights the fact that prosecutors perform a gate-keeping function, prosecutors themselves envision their role as a more multifaceted one that is simultaneously tightly tied to their statutorily defined duties. To begin to understand how prosecutors view their role I will detail how three prosecutors describe their role through their own voices.

> Q: What is the main role of a prosecutor?
>
> To clarify the facts. That is important. In this department, we prosecute sexual abuse against children and women whether or not the complainant wishes to pursue a criminal case. It is very important to bring the charges to the court so that everyone can see what happened, the suspect and all the involved parties. We must clarify and determine the facts because sometimes people lie. It is really important.[63]
>
> [Our main role is] to collect all of the evidence for the main proceeding. Not only the evidence that shows that the suspect is guilty but also the evidence that shows that a suspect is innocent. I take note of what the defense attorney says in the courtroom. If the suspect is sentenced, I make sure that the punishment is commensurable with the crime.[64]
>
> Our legal duty according to the German procedural rules is to clarify the evidence, to decide whether a set of facts is actionable as a crime and to decide whether or not to bring charges. Prosecutors must work with the police in the investigation stage. The nature of the relationship between police and prosecutors is different in each Land (state). That means that at certain stages of the investigation the prosecutor must supervise what the police are doing. The prosecutor guides the police investigation and we follow the case from the first moment of criminal suspicion through the court proceeding and through to the execution of the sentence.

---

[62] §160(2) StPO.

[63] Prosecutor Interview [5UD], 19 January 2006.

[64] Prosecutor Interview [12CJ], 29 November 2005.

> We have many cases and for that reason we carry a heavy caseload. Therefore it is natural that in many cases this affects how well a prosecutor can oversee the case investigation process. We put together the case file but in special areas of criminality we can no longer pursue additional lines of investigation because we lack the organizational resources to do so. In other areas, for example organized crime, it is different. The prosecutors are on the one hand beholden to bring the file to the court. That can happen very quickly. Sometimes it can take months and sometimes a year. The function of prosecutors is frequently restricted in the end to saying that was "okay" or to saying that there is something more [to be done on the file]. We are required to be objective, to be just, and to clarify the facts.[65]

What is remarkable about these answers is that they paint a picture of the prosecutorial role that is remarkably task specific. These descriptions contain no grand pronouncements about keeping society safe or getting criminals off the streets. As German prosecutors describe their function in society, they eschew descriptions of individual achievements. Notably absent from these descriptions are the use self-aggrandizing terms. Unlike American prosecutors, German prosecutors do not describe themselves as white knights or avenging angels (Suthers 2008, p. 1). Also absent from these descriptions of the prosecutorial function are portrayals of the criminal justice process itself as a crusade for justice or as a means to achieve vengeance on behalf of society. A German prosecutor does not "do battle" in the courtroom (Kroger 2008), put the criminal "away" (Rice 2010), or triumph over evil (Winerip 1985). Nor do German prosecutors boast about wielding the tools of power or achieving certain sentences.[66] While American prosecutors may define the role of a prosecutor as a function performed by individual personalities, with few exceptions, the German prosecutors that I interviewed did not ascribe any sense of individual agency to the performance of their duties. This lack of an instrumental identity and agency stems from a variety of factors. Chief among them is the fact that German prosecutors do not function as parties. As a result, prosecutors do not regard convictions as victories. A prosecutor does not function as a party that seeks to triumph over the opposing party, but rather as an anonymous part of a larger bureaucratic service dedicated to finding the "finding the truth" according to the dictates of the law. As a result, their self-identity is not cloaked in terms of individual agency, but rather as part of their larger function as co-partners with the judiciary. While prosecutors have acquired more control over case disposition decisions as the ambit of discretionary decision-making has expanded, prosecutors are reluctant to embrace descriptions of their role that are defined in the language of power. Underscoring this point, one prosecutor stated, "[n]othing would change in society whether or not I am the person who did this job."[67]

Indeed, since prosecutorial "success" is more likely to be measured in terms of the consistent performance of routine decision-making that takes place away from the public's eye, individual prosecutors themselves do not define their function in

---

[65] Prosecutor Interview [2QM], 6 October 2005.

[66] Prosecutor Interview [7GC], 6 April 2006.

[67] Prosecutor Interview [7GC], 6 April 2006.

terms of the exercise of power. In their interactions with police with few exceptions, prosecutors function in a collegial manner, giving advice and direction. In the courtroom, prosecutors and judges function more like colleagues than adversaries. Since the work of prosecutors is largely ensconced within these consensual decision-making processes, it is more difficult to attribute the system's outcomes to any sense of individual agency. I did find a few exceptions to this. For example, one prosecutor that I interviewed in an organized crime department regaled me with stories of his cases and explained to me that he only wanted prosecutors in his department who wanted to target the major criminals and not administrative types. Ironically, in the next breath, he told me that he did not want to work with prosecutors who were only out for themselves and did not want to work as a team.[68]

Lacking a sense of individual agency, German prosecutors are reluctant to link performance of their role to the exercise of power. As one prosecutor explained:

> I would not speak of power. Also I would not say that we [prosecutors] are more powerful than courts or that courts are more powerful than prosecutors. Rather, we work together. We both possess the goal to determine the facts in a manner consistent with the rule of law. I don't lose in court and I don't win in court. Personally, I believe that I co-manage the proceedings before the court. Also, when a suspect is acquitted, sometimes I, myself, will have argued in favor of a not-guilty verdict. That is a just outcome. It is also my job to work towards an acquittal. For that reason, I would not speak of power. From the perspective of the possibility to influence the criminal justice process, prosecutors have more opportunities to do so [than judges] because we are involved very early in the process. What we also decide here in the prosecution service is whether or not we [should] terminate a proceeding or bring it to the court, whether or not there is enough initial suspicion [to justify an investigation], and whether we should conditionally dismiss a case and impose a fine. And only about one-third of the cases that land on a prosecutor's desk even reach the court.
>
> To be sure, we have more opportunities to steer the direction of a case. When a case has been brought before the court, the court plays the decisive role in determining the suspect's sentence. In far as I can exert any influence before the court my influence comes through the charges that I propose, my closing argument, and at particular points in the proceeding, whether I can suggest that the court view the evidence in a certain way. However, the court will make the final decision about the sentence. But I would not speak of power. The relationship between the court and the prosecution office ... is not a hierarchical relationship.[69]

Because the law charges prosecutors with the duty to view cases through a judge's independent lens while they must function as part of a hierarchically organized bureaucratic civil service, there is an inherent conflict in their position. Prosecutors must serve the law while being accountable to the state level Ministry of Justice. Ironically, the inherent tension in the position that prosecutors occupy in the criminal justice system is also reflected in the layouts of courtrooms throughout Germany. In some of the courtrooms that I visited, the prosecutor sat on the same elevated bench as the judicial panel but off to the side of the panel itself. In other

---

[68] Prosecutor Interview [1CK], 13 March 2006.

[69] Prosecutor Interview [16AG], 9 June 2008.

courtrooms, the prosecutor sat a table on par with the defense attorney. When I asked a senior prosecutor about the different courtroom layouts, he told me that the fact that prosecutors sit on the same level as judges in many older courtrooms, reflects a conception of the prosecution function as a part of the judicial function. In contrast, the position of prosecutors in the more modern courtrooms reflected a vision of the prosecution service, not as an organ of the judiciary, but rather as an organ of justice.[70]

Many prosecutors that I interviewed viewed themselves as civil servants whose main function was to gather and view the facts of a case through a judicial lens. In describing their role, they emphasized the fact that they possessed education identical to that possessed by judges.[71] In addition, many stressed the point that whether an individual becomes a judge or a prosecutor often reflects a twist of fate rather than a one's interests and abilities. Moreover, the pay that judges and prosecutors receive is identical.[72]

We can learn more about the self-identity of prosecutors by examining prosecutors' "source of job satisfaction." When I asked prosecutors to name a case that they were proud of, a number of prosecutors spoke with pride about their ability to research and apply the law in a new way. For example, one prosecutor mentioned that she had opened an investigation into a sexual assault allegation that had occurred during the time that East Germany was under communist control. Because the crime had occurred during the DDR time, the crime had to be prosecuted under the criminal law in effect at that time. Although it was difficult to prosecute an old case, the prosecutor said that she was "very happy with the sentence."[73] This same prosecutor stated that it also made her quite happy to dismiss cases when drug addicted defendants successfully completed a treatment program.[74] Another prosecutor spoke with pride about writing a journal article in which he criticized a decision made by the court because it was incorrect under the law.[75] Evocative of legal scholars' idealized description of prosecutors as legal scientists, another prosecutor described the work that he had done researching an appeal that required detailed research on a jurisdictional question in which higher courts had reached divergent opinions.[76]

In sum, the organizational position of German prosecutors and their daily decision-making routines shape their understanding of their role in the criminal justice system. While prosecutors may occasionally speak with pride about particular case outcomes, most prosecutors are not driven by a desire, either to exercise the levers of power, or to notch convictions or harsh sentences. At first cut then,

[70] Prosecutor Interview [5BC], 16 January 2006.

[71] See, e.g., Prosecutor Interview [16AG], 9 June 2008.

[72] Justice Ministry Interview [12CR], 2 December 2006.

[73] Prosecutor Interview [6SB], 23 February 2006.

[74] Prosecutor Interview [6SB], 23 February 2006

[75] Prosecutor Interview [13WT], 18 November 2005.

[76] Prosecutor Interview [4AJ], 2 February 2006.

the factors that influence German prosecutors' job satisfaction are consistent with the law's normative goals. It remains to be seen whether prosecutors' daily work routines match the normative vision of their role as objective decision-makers dedicated to the search for truth. It is to that question, that I now turn.

Legislation

Code of Criminal Procedure (StPO)

§147, 160(2)

Code of Criminal Law (StGB)

§202, 203, 204

Other Laws

Sect. 142 subs. 1 Constitution of Courts Act (Gerichtsverfassungsgesetz, GVG).

Sect. 145

Section 64 Nr. 2 Niedersachsen Civil Service Law (Niedersächsisches Beamtengesetz, NBG)

German Law on Judges (Deutsches Richtergesetz, DRiG) Sept. 8, 1961, BGBl. I at 1665, § 5 para. 1 (F.R.G)

International Conventions

Article 6 of the European Convention on Human Rights

Interviews

Prosecutor Interview [9BU], 4 May 2005

Prosecutor Interview [7SE], 5 April 2006

Prosecutor Interview [4KD], 2 February 2006

Prosecutor Interview [4AJ], 2 February 2006

Prosecutor Interview [130I], 10 June 2004
Prosecutor Interview [13AS], 10 June 2004
Prosecutor Interview [2BN], 16 July 2004
Prosecutor Interview [13WT], 18 November 2005
Prosecutor Interview [2QM], 6 October 2005
Prosecutor Interview [19BS], 14 May 2008
Prosecutor Interview [6SB], 23 February 2006
Prosecutor Interview [4GG], 30 January 2006
Prosecutor Interview [8HL], 25 May 2006
Prosecutor Interview [2BN], 16 July 2004
Prosecutor Interview [7GC], 6 April 2006
Prosecutor Interview [11OT], 15 July 2004
Prosecutor Interview [5XW], 19 January 2006
Prosecutor Interview [5BC], 16 January 2006
Prosecutor Interview [12FG], 24 April 2006
Prosecutor Interview [13BR], 18 November 2005
Prosecutor Interview [12CJ], 29 November 2005
Prosecutor Interview [16AG], 9 June 2008
Prosecutor Interview [7AG], 7 April 2006
Prosecutor Interview [19IC], 14 May 2008
Prosecutor Interview [16PP], 30 April 2008
Prosecutor Interview [13BC], 8 December 2005
Prosecutor Interview [1DR], 15 March 2006
Prosecutor Interview [4EW], 2 February 2006
Prosecutor Interview [12LH], 29 November 2005
Prosecutor Interview [1ZU], 15 March 2006
Prosecutor Interview [5UD], 19 January 2006
Prosecutor Interview [1CK], 13 March 2006
Appellate Judge Interview [13MU], 10 April 2004
Justice Ministry Interview [12CR], 2 December 2006

References

Books, Articles and Online Publications

Blankenburg, E., & Treiber, H. (1985). The establishment of the public prosecutor's office in Germany. *International Journal of the Sociology of Law*, *12*, 375–391.

Hohmann, B., & Neubeck, G. (1996). *Zur Tätigkeit des Staatsanwalts*. Dresden: Sächsischen Staatsministerium der Justiz.

Justizzahlen in Berlin. (2007). *Berlin*: *Senatsverwaltung Für Justiz* [pdf]. Available at http://www.berlin.de/imperia/md/content/senatsverwaltungen/justiz/aktuell/justizzahlen_2005_2007.pdf. Accessed 28 June 2008.

Koetz, A. G., & Feltes, T. (1996). *Organisation Der Staatsanwaltschaften*. Köln: Bundesanzeiger Verlag GmbH.

Korioth, S. (2006). Legal education in Germany Today. *Wisconsin International Law Journal, 24*, 85–108.

Kroger, J. (2008). *Convictions: A prosecutor's battles against MAFIA killers, drug kingpins, and Enron thieves*. New York: Farrar, Straus and Giroux.

Künnecke, M. (2006). The accountability and independence of judges: German perspectives. In G. Canivet, M. Andenas, & D. Fairgrieve (Eds.), *Independence, accountability, and the judiciary* (pp. 217–231). London: British Institute of International and Comparative Law.

Lipsky, M. (1980). *Street level bureaucracy: Dilemmas of individuals in public services*. New York: Russell Sage.

Merryman, J. (1985). *The civil law tradition*. Stanford: Stanford University Press.

Rice, L. I. (2010). A case for reform: Paul Butler '86 used to put people away – Now he wants to set them free. *Harvard Law Bulletin* (Summer). Available at http://law.harvard.edu/news/bulletin/2010/summer/cn_03.php. Accessed Aug 2013.

Sessar, K. (1979). Prosecutorial discretion in Germany. In W. McDonald (Ed.), *The prosecutor* (pp. 255–276). Beverly Hills: Sage Publications.

Staatsanwaltschaft Berlin Website, Senatsverwaltung für Justiz. Available at http://www.berlin.de/sen/justiz/strafverfolgung/sta/index.html. Last Accessed 23 July 2007.

Suthers, J. W. (2008). *No higher calling, no greater responsibility: A prosecutor makes his case*. Golden, CO: Fulcrum Publishing.

Von Münch, I. (2002). *Legal education and the legal profession in Germany*. Baden-Baden: Nomos Verlag.

Winerip, M. (1985). High profile prosecutor, *New York Times Magazine*, June 9, 1985. Available at http://query.nytimes.com/gst/fullpage.html?res=9903E3DAA35755C0A963948260. Accessed 19 July 2013.

Chapter 4
Everyday Practice and Low-Level Crime

4.1 Introduction

The average German prosecutor who practices before the *Amtsgericht* [lower level criminal court] must process 1000 cases per year. That averages out to 4–5 cases per day. Because of the burden of this case load, a prosecutor's first question when he approaches a case is: "Shall I dismiss the case?"
-Ministry of Justice Official[1]

At least 50% of the cases that our economic crimes department must handle now are general crime or juvenile cases that belong to the other departments. The major crime departments here now have no time to work on their special cases because if you come back from a search warrant, you have all these general crime cases to deal with.
-Department leader[2]

I work in a department with three prosecutors and two paralegals. I handle 170–200 cases per month. That works out to 45 per week and 11 per day. Of these 11 cases, I will dismiss 6 cases each day.
-Paralegal working in a General Crimes Department[3]

[W]hat I have to do most of the time is to work on these files and we don't do too many investigations on our own. But it's different [in each department]. For example, if you work in organized crime, you do not have so many files. In our department, you have a lot of files as you can see. If you have only a few files, maybe you can do some investigations on your own... I do [investigative work] only on very special cases ... but in normal cases I don't. It's too much work. Sometimes if you want to file an accusation against someone, you have to listen to what [they have to say]. Normally, I let the police do this... The same with a search warrant. I only do it in special cases. Normally, I don't do it.
-Prosecutor in an Environmental Crimes Department[4]

---

[1] Justice Ministry Official [9CK], 4 May 2006.

[2] Prosecutor Interview [10BJ], 26 June 2006.

[3] Prosecutor Interview [10ED], 28 June 2006.

[4] Prosecutor Interview [13WT], 18 November 2005.

S.M. Boyne, *The German Prosecution Service*, DOI 10.1007/978-3-642-40928-8_4,

In this chapter, I explore the discretionary decision-making practices which guide how prosecutors handle every day, low-level crime.[5] I begin first by laying out for the reader the range of discretionary case disposition options that German prosecutors possess. I then detail the enormous role that discretionary decision-making plays in the German criminal justice system and argue that many scholars, who have misunderstood the types of cases that qualify as minor crimes under German law, have downplayed the extent of prosecutorial discretion.

After showing that prosecutorial discretion is widespread, I address a more intriguing issue, namely, what factors shape everyday prosecution practice? Here, I explore German prosecutors' own understandings of the nature of their work practices, their decision-making processes, as well as the discretionary choices that they make. By examining the actual work routines of prosecutors who handle low-level crime, I show how norms of practice influence and shape decision-making. In the course of this analysis I probe how the organizational constraints within which prosecutors operate differentially impact decision-making. In particular, because the organizational environment establishes resource levels, shapes incentives, and reinforces norms of conduct, it affects how prosecutors implement the law. I conclude this chapter by asking whether or not the discretionary choices made by prosecutors advance the system's normative goals. The most important question addressed in this chapter is not whether widespread discretion exists, but rather whether or not that discretion is being exercised judiciously. The normative premise underlying the German criminal justice system is that prosecutors and judges can work together to discover the "truth." With prosecutors supervising the investigation function and judges structuring the presentation of evidence and the questioning of witnesses at trial, legal scholars have traditionally regarded the court's final judgment is the logical result of a process leading towards the truth. However, the vast majority of cases are disposed of long before the evidence is fully presented before a court. Through their ability to dispose of cases and impose sanctions largely free from meaningful oversight, prosecutors perform a quasi-judicial function. The degree of prosecutorial discretion that German prosecutors now possess is not particularly striking when compared to American prosecutors. However, the incentives that drive disposition practices, in particular the need for efficiency challenge the system's underlying normative premises. Before I examine those incentives and their impact on daily decision-making, it will be helpful to describe the expansion of discretionary disposition practices that has occurred during the past 30 years.

---

[5] I use the term "every day" crime to apply to crimes classified in the German system as a low-level offense or *Vergehen*.

4.2 The Growth of Discretion

Beginning in the 1970s, repeated amendments to German Code of Criminal Procedure began to dramatically widen prosecutorial discretion by creating a number of disposition practices that short-circuit the full criminal procedure process. Ironically, while the growing scope of prosecutorial discretion is a modern phenomenon, the German prosecution service has possessed the ability to dismiss cases for economic or official reasons since its creation (Collin 2001, p. 4). However, the use of the principle of opportunity (or discretionary non-prosecution) in German criminal procedural law was, until recently, largely restricted to cases involving petty crimes. As mentioned earlier, the principle of legality has been bedrock principle framing prosecutorial decision-making. Indeed, until very recently, German scholars have pointed to the principle of legality as the defining principle of prosecution practice. As Hans-Heinrich Jescheck stated in 1970:

> Whether a suspect in America is charged with a crime, and indeed with what crime, lies within the discretion of the public prosecutor. He may refrain from pressing charges at all, and sometimes even has the power to suspend a trial already underway. The situation is quite different in Germany. Instead of sweeping discretionary power, the German prosecutor is bound by the "*Legalitatsprinzip*" or "legality principle," under which he is obligated to bring an action in all non-petty cases, whenever he is able to prove his case in court. The prosecutor can even be compelled to file charges by a formal judicial proceeding brought by the victim of the crime. Furthermore, the "legality principle" absolutely prohibits the authorities from bargaining with the defense attorney for reduction of charges in exchange for a guilty plea (Jescheck 1970, p. 56).

In some of my interviews with high ranking prosecution officials, the interviewees maintained that the guiding principle of German prosecution practice was the principle of legality.[6] While one must be careful to stake a claim on the basis of two interviews, those particular interviews illustrated to me that the picture of practice presented to outsiders at the top of the hierarchy is different from that presented by front-line practitioners. The statistics presented above further press this point. In sum, the daily decision-making processes of front-line prosecutors, Lipsky's "street level bureaucrats," rather than the scholarly writings of legal theorists determine the actual course of case dispositions. While the German legislature has widened prosecutors' opportunities for discretion, legislative reforms have often followed, rather than anticipated, changes in practice. The most compelling argument for this assertion is the fact that the legislature rather belatedly enacted legislation which sanctioned the practice of "confession bargaining." Even though reports that prosecutors were engaging in bargaining began to emerge in the 1970s, the legislature failed to sanction the process for nearly three decades.[7] With respect to the alternative disposition options currently available to prosecutors through sections 153 (1) and 153 (a–d) StPO, an argument

[6] Prosecutor Interview [11OT], 15 July 2005 and Prosecutor Interview [13PR], 6 December 2005.

[7] Federal Court of Justice NJW 2005, 1440f.

could be made that, if those options were not available to prosecutors, there would be an increase in the number of cases dismissed for reasons of insufficient evidence under Section 170(2). As I pointed out in the introduction, the rising crime rates Germany experienced between 1975 and 1983 initially fueled the expansion of prosecutorial discretion (Heinz 2006). During the past two decades, however, crime rates have stabilized with a slight increase occurring after 2002 (Jehle 2005, p. 12).

Yet, during this same period, prosecutors' use of informal sanctions has dramatically increased, rising from a rate of 36.3 % in 1981 to 55.7 % in 2004 (Heinz 2006). The increasing use of informal sanctions, not only signals a rise in prosecutorial discretion, but a shift in sanctioning authority as well. Since it is primarily prosecutors, rather than judges, who establish the informal sanctions, the move towards their increasing use, has increased prosecutors' control over the sanctioning process. As I will show in Chapter 8's discussion of corruption cases, it is no longer true that the law confines the exercise of that discretion to cases where there is little public interest in prosecuting. As Heinz describes:

> At the beginning of the 80s, just short of two thirds of all the informal sanctions were pronounced through the prosecution; this portion has grown to about 85.0 %. In 2004, there were about 839,000 people whose proceedings were discharged by the prosecution in accordance with Sections 153, 153a, 153b of the Code of Criminal Procedure and Section 45 of the Act on Juvenile Courts and about 934,000 people were either formally sanctioned or their proceedings were discharged by the court in accordance with Sections 153, 153a, 153b of the Code of Criminal Procedure and Section 47 of the Act on Juvenile Courts. That means that 47.3 % of all informal and formal sanctions were imposed by the prosecution (Heinz 2006, Sect. 1.2).

In the modern era, the daily realities of prosecutorial practice, in particular the need to handle larger caseloads without a concomitant increase in staff, began to strain prosecutors' ability to handle their case loads effectively in the 1960s. It was during that era that the need for a modern formulation of the Opportunity Principle (*Opportunitätsprinzip*) first became apparent. It was then that the prosecution service first confronted a shortfall in its' ability to process mass crimes (Albrecht 2000, p. 246). Seeking to ensure that prosecutors concentrated their efforts on mid-level and serious crime, the German legislature introduced Section 153 of the Criminal Procedure Code (Treiber 1980, p. 446). That procedural change allows prosecutors to dismiss minor cases when the guilt of the suspect is minimal and there is no public interest in prosecution. The type of case that might fit under Section 153(1) would be a minor case of shoplifting committed by a first offender.[8] When a prosecutor dismisses a case under this provision, it constitutes an outright dismissal of the case. In other words, there are no penal consequences for the defendant. Critically, most of the dismissals under this provision are never reviewed by a court as the court only reviews those cases in which the

[8] Justice Ministry Interview [9CK], 4 May 2006.

mandatory minimum sentence exceeds a 5 day fine or involves significant damage.[9] The introduction of Section 153 of the Code of Criminal Procedure, by itself, did not ostensibly undercut the efficacy of the principle of mandatory prosecution as the purpose of the principle is not to mandate that prosecutors prosecute every single offense. Rather, as Zappalá (2006, p. 209) explains, the "purpose of mandatory prosecution is to avoid prosecutorial decisions which are not made on either: (i) legal grounds or (ii) the hierarchy of values predetermined by the legislature" (Zappalá 2006). Accordingly, by enacting Section 153 StPO, the legislature merely declared that prosecutors should not devote their time to handling petty crimes.

This policy change coincided with efforts to decriminalize a large percentage of less severe crimes. In 1969, Germany decriminalized a large number of motor vehicle and administrative law violations, reclassifying those offenses as administrative violations. This trend towards decriminalization continued in 1975 when the legislature abolished the category of crimes known as petty misdemeanors and reclassified the bulk of those crimes as petty infractions. As part of this reform effort, Germany embraced a trend towards replacing most sentences of imprisonment with the imposition of fines (Sessar 1979, p. 247). Further growth in the scope of prosecutorial discretion occurred in the mid-1970s when the enactment of Section 153(a) StPO opened the door for prosecutors to dismiss cases involving minor guilt provided that the suspect agreed to a set of conditions. The enactment of this provision enabled prosecutors to dismiss a wider range of "minor" crimes by securing the suspect's consent to a minimal sanction. Under this provision, to merit a dismissal of the case, a suspect must agree to pay a fine, perform community service, compensate the victim, and/or assume other related responsibilities. In cases where this provision is in play, prosecutors will typically review the investigation file and then send a letter to the suspect or their lawyer proposing the specific terms of the dismissal. Incongruous with the theory of limited discretion, a prosecutor is theoretically free to recommend a fine or length of community service of any amount subject to a constitutional prohibition against disproportionate punishment (Albrecht 2000, p. 247). In practice, prosecution offices have developed internal standards which guide prosecutorial decision-making in this area. For example, in petty property cases the prosecutor may be allowed to terminate proceedings on their own authority during the case investigation stage.[10]

---

[9] See § 153 Nr.1 StPO. Under the "day fine" system which Germany adopted from Swedish practice, fines are calculated progressively, i.e. the more income one earns, the higher the fine. A fine for a certain crime is first assessed in terms of a specific number of days. Then the prosecutor estimates the defendant's income from the information the defendant has provided to the police and calculates the appropriate value of the fine per day. Thus while two defendants who are charged with a crime may be assessed a similar punishment of a 5 day fine, the amount of the fine will differ according to their estimated income levels.

[10] According to Germany's Code of Criminal Procedure, if a prosecutor believes that there is sufficient evidence to warrant holding a trial in a case, the prosecutor will send the investigation file to the court with a petition to open a main proceeding. The court will then review the file and

On its face, this modification seems to be an insignificant one. However, by investing prosecutors with the power to impose punishment on the defendant without judicial review, it shifted some of the law's sanctioning power from the court to prosecutors (Geisler 1999). The legislature continued to sanction and widen this shift in authority when it enacted the "Act to Reduce the Burden of Justice Administration." Under the terms of this Act, the legislature eliminated the requirement in §153(a) StPO that the suspect's guilt level could not rise above the level of "minimal" guilt. Under terms of the amendment, in order for a case to qualify for a disposition under this provision, the gravity of the accused's guilt simply could not be an obstacle to abandoning prosecution of the case (Eser 1996). In that same Act, the legislature also loosened the qualifications for case dismissals under §153(1) StPO. Under the Act, cases eligible for a dismissal now include all offenses and misdemeanors that do not qualify for an enhanced minimum penalty and which have minor consequences. As a result of these changes, prosecutors now possess the ability to dismiss, not only misdemeanor cases, but also mid-level crimes (Eser 1996, p. 344). Defenders of the practice of discretionary dismissals claim that because citizens may request an administrative and judicial review of dismissal decisions, the Act deters prosecutors from filing discourages frivolous dismissals (Jescheck 1970). In addition, individuals may prosecute their own cases in a narrow class of cases involving private interests.[11]

The discretionary disposition options do not stop there. Prosecutors may also use the penal order procedure to efficiently dispose of more serious crimes where the potential sentencing exposure does not exceed 1 year imprisonment. This procedure, which is detailed in Sections 407–412 StPO, is a separate procedure from the dismissal procedure envisioned by Section 153 (a)(2) StPO. Under the penal order procedure, prosecutors must seek a judge's concurrence to dispense with a main proceeding. In cases where a prosecutor decides that the crime merits a suspended sentence to be served on probation or a fine, the prosecutor will send the file to the court for approval. Proponents of the procedure argue that the judiciary effectively monitors the issuance of penal orders because a judge must approve the proposed disposition. (Jescheck 1970, p. 516). Moreover, the suspect himself may reject the penal order and request that the court hold a main proceeding. However, this judicial oversight mechanism may merely provide the appearance of judicial control rather than effective oversight. Given that many judges are themselves struggling with burgeoning case loads, it is in a judge's interest to approve a

determine whether the evidentiary standard for opening a main proceeding has been met. Although a main proceeding has a similar outcome to a trial in the United States (i.e. the court will enter a determination of the defendant's guilt or innocence), there are significant procedural differences. In recognition of those differences, I will continue to refer to that stage of the proceedings as a main proceeding rather than as a trial.

[11] Pursuant to §374 StPO, an aggrieved party may initiate prosecutions in cases involving trespass, defamation, violation of the privacy of correspondence, bodily injury, threat, taking or offering a bribe in a business transaction, criminal damage to property, certain criminal offenses related to unfair competition, and a range of other offenses related to trademark, patent, and copyright infringement.

prosecutor's penal order application as a rejected application may then appear on the court's crowded docket. Indeed, a judge in one large city told me that he could review 70 routine cases in 15 min-an average of one case every 13 seconds. Given their own workloads, it may be presumptuous to assume that judges carefully review and deliberate over applications for penal orders. As Felstiner (1979) reported:

> If the prosecutor has decided to use a penal order, he sends the file to the judge. Although the prosecutor's review may be perfunctory, the penal order is a prosecutorial instrument, and the judicial review tends to be even more cursory (312–313).

In fact, a judge will deny only deny a penal order if he finds something out of the ordinary—a psychologically disturbed defendant, a problem too complicated to be captured on paper, a difficult family situation, an offender with a history, or a defendant who appears to contest the facts. In 1976, the judicial denial rate was less than 1 % (Felstiner 1979, pp. 312–313). The low rejection rate reported by Felstiner has been substantiated by Elsner and Peters' (2006, p. 217) study.

A second criticism of the penal order process is that, although a suspect is free to reject an order, the "order" on its' face is coercive. Although penal orders resemble plea agreements, unless a defense attorney has initiated the procedure by proposing that a prosecutor resolve a case with a penal order, the order is a one-sided exchange. Defenders of the practice, such as Langbein, assert that the practice is neither coercive nor unjust because the practice is limited to non-imprisonable misdemeanors and there is no implicit threat of a longer sentence if the suspect rejects the offer (Langbein 1979, p. 78). As the range of discretionary dispositional practices has increased, the number of cases resolved short of a full search for the truth has diminished. As can be seen from the chart below, in 2006, prosecutors filed charges in only 11.5 % of the cases that crossed their desk (Table 4.1).[12] In 38.4 %, prosecutors disposed of the case using one of the informal disposition means at their disposal including an unconditional dismissal, a conditional dismissal, and a penal order.[13] In effect then, in almost 40 % of the cases that prosecutors review, it is the prosecutor who determines that, although a crime has probably been committed, the case either warrants no punishment or it warrants a punishment determined by the prosecutor with scant judicial review.

Faced with the growing complexity and global reach of certain forms of criminality such as white-collar crime, as well as severe resource constraints, prosecutors have developed coping practices that allow them to quickly dispose of "low-level" crimes. In response to this development, some commentators have suggested that the opportunity principle has overtaken the principle of legality as the predominant principle governing everyday decision-making (Erb 1999). By solely looking at case outcome data, it is impossible to determine how prosecutors make choices among different outcomes as well as to determine the degree of latitude that

---

[12] Statistics of the Public Prosecution Offices (2006). German Federal Statistical Office, Wiesbaden (Table 4.1).

[13] Id.

Table 4.1 Disposition of preliminary proceedings (2006)[a]

Status of the case and method of settlement	Number of cases	Percentage
New cases	4,914,335	
Completed preliminary proceedings	4,876,989	
Method of disposition		
Indictment	560,427	11.5
Application for penal order [Sect. 407 StPO]	581,713	11.9
Conditional dismissal [Sect. 153a StPO]	241,102	4.9
Unconditional dismissal [Sect. 153(1) StPO]	1,053,645	21.6
Insufficient evidence [Sect. 170 (2) StPO]	1,293,152	26.5
Death of accused, lack of criminal responsibility	8,652	0.2
Other disposition[b]	1,138,299	23.3

[a]2006 Statistics of the Public Prosecution Offices, published by the German Federal Statistical Office, Wiesbaden

[b]Including proceedings passed on to other Public Prosecution Offices (n = 202,173), to an administrative authority (regarding regulatory offences; n = 232,716), in connection with another matter (n = 350,906), provisional termination (n = 112,180), recommendation that private proceedings be brought (n = 174,038), application for securing proceedings (n = 535), applications for simplified juvenile proceedings (n = 17,099), applications for summary or securing proceedings (n = 527), applications for simplified juvenile proceedings (n = 19,336), applications for summary decisions (n = 27,540)

prosecutors possess in individual cases. Moreover, output based conclusions ignore the fact that case outcomes are the product a series of choices and the end result of many incremental steps. To understand why the range of prosecutorial discretion has exploded, it is important to look beyond the disposition categories imposed by the law and examine prosecutors' daily decision-making routines. In the area of "low-level" crimes, a key line of inquiry is the extent to which prosecutors' daily decision-making is of a routine nature that may be equated with the processing of a repetitious case load. To the extent that decision-making is mechanical and routine and dictated by organizational work patterns, it undercuts the thesis that prosecutors possess significant unbridled discretion.

4.3 Defining Minor Crimes

According to the German Criminal Code, a crime qualifies as a *Vergehen* (low-level crime) as long as the minimum sentence for the crime prescribed by statute falls below 1 year of imprisonment. The classification of crimes into felonies and misdemeanors in the Anglo-American system denotes a difference in the crime's severity as well as the corresponding level of punishment. Because German legal scholars view law as a science, the classification level of a crime carries with it an additional level of meaning as well. As Dubber (2005) points out, the taxonomical quality of German criminal law lends itself to a certain formalism in which arguments are frequently resolved through means of a classification process. This reliance on formalism asserts itself in discussions regarding the prevalence of

Table 4.2 Partial list of *Vergehen* (minor crimes)

Name of crime	Criminal code section (StGB)
Assault against organs and representatives of foreign states	Sect. 102
Obstruction of an election	Sect. 107
Freeing of prisoners	Sect. 120
Bribery of Members of Parliament	Sect. 108e
Providing support to a terrorist organization	Sect. 129a(3)
Sexual abuse of children under 14	Sect. 176(1)[a]
Rape	Sect. 177[b]
Trafficking in human beings	Sect. 180b
Homicide by request	Sect. 216
Negligent homicide	Sect. 222
Dangerous bodily injury	Sect. 224
Burglary of a dwelling	Sect. 244
Receiving stolen property	Sect. 259
Fraud	Sect. 263

[a]Forms of sexual abuse which fall under this provision include "sexual acts on a person under 14 years of age" which do not involve penetration, are not committed by more than one person, do not place the child in danger of serious health damage or substantial impairment of his physical or emotional development, or involve a perpetrator with a prior similar conviction within the previous 5 years. See §176(1) StGB for a list of the acts that qualify as *Vergehen*

[b]Cases of rape which do not qualify as *Verbrechen* include, for example, rape which is especially degrading or is committed by more than one offender. See §177 (2) StGB

discretion in the German criminal justice system when defenders of the principle of legality claim that to the extent that discretion exists, it is limited to the disposition of low-level crimes. By implication, proponents of this argument maintain that, although discretionary decision-making exists, it impacts the system's quest for truth inconsequentially. In terms of the gross number of crimes committed on an annual basis, my estimate of the percent of crimes that qualify as *Vergehen* (low-level crimes) exceeds 85 %. A partial list of crimes which are typically classified as felonies in the United States but which fall under the category of *Vergehen* (low-level crimes) in Germany include the criminal acts listed above (Table 4.2).

From this partial list, we can see that the proposition that prosecutorial discretion is restricted to "low level" crimes, even if it is true, does not prove that prosecutorial discretion is limited in scope. The full impact that prosecutorial decision-making has on case dispositions is reflected in the fact that only 12 % of the cases opened by the public prosecutor's office culminate in an indictment resolved through a main proceeding (Nestler 2004, p. 109). Indeed as Elsner and Peters (2006, p. 211) has concluded, the proportion of cases that end with a full trial is very low. The import of this statistic is that the judiciary rarely conducts a full review of the facts of a case in a German courtroom. As a result, in the vast majority of cases, prosecutorial decisions shape, if not determine, case outcomes. This funneling process begins with the decision to dismiss a case on the grounds of insufficient evidence or inadequate suspicion pursuant to Section 170 (2) StPO. This occurs in approximately 27 % of the cases (Elsner and Peters 2006, p. 210). Of the remaining cases, prosecutors dismiss over 20 % of the cases on the grounds of minor guilt and minor public interest without imposing formal sanctions.[14] In these cases, the court's consent is required only if the offender faces more than the minimum penalty. While a disposition falling under this provision is not entered in Germany's central criminal register, it is noted in the prosecution service's register. As a result, the statistics are accessible to other government agencies. While an offender has not been convicted of a crime in the formal sense, a record has been made that carries with it a presumption of guilt. Moreover offenders possess no recourse to object to the process. In the case of conditional dismissals under Section 153a, a suspect must consent to and fulfill the conditions which the prosecutor proposes before the prosecutor will dismiss the case. The individual states (*Länder*) have enacted guidelines that dictate the circumstances under which prosecutors may dispose of cases using Sections 153 (1) and 153 (a) StPO. The effectiveness of those guidelines is discussed below.

4.4 The Pressure of Organizational Imperatives

4.4.1 The Mindset of Practice

> If this would by my room, you would find furniture over there... On one side you would find the remark "entrance" and on the other side "exit." And this is the perspective of a good public prosecutor. That what is coming in today has to be finished.[15]

In prosecution offices, as in other workplaces, the daily rhythm of practice dominates decision-making routines. As I witnessed prosecutorial work routines and interviewed prosecutors, it became evident that the daily flow of case files into the offices of individual prosecutors plays an instrumental role in structuring daily decision-making. The character of each day is profoundly shaped by the flow of files as the flow of work itself crafts the nature of the work pressure confronting prosecutors. If you were to visit any state prosecution office in Germany today and silently observe work practices, you would be struck by the way that the flow of case files appears to dominate the nature of the work. The important role that file processing routines play in defining the nature of prosecutorial decision-making in Germany is underscored by the following excerpt taken from a prosecution manual:

> Your function at the prosecution office is to handle the new files coming into the prosecution office, to work with the files, and to make decisions in the investigation proceeding. At the beginning you will think that you have in front of you insolvable problems. Do not

[14] §153 Nr. 1 StPO.

[15] Appellate Judge Interview [22FE], 22 July 2004.

doubt that after a few weeks it will become significantly easier to cope with the daily file processing and to make decisions in the investigation processes (Hohmann and Neubeck 1996).

Because a prosecutor makes decisions and undertakes actions while he or she is embedded in an organization, a prosecutor's ability to function in an objective manner is not only determined by the individual's mindset, but by organizational norms, practices, resources, and inter-institutional relationships. The routine file processing practices themselves provide a frame of reference for the decisions that prosecutors make. In the next three subsections, I will explore the constitutive role that statistical controls, bureaucratic work routines, and the organization of practice play in shaping decision-making with respect to low-level crimes.

4.4.2 The Drive for Efficiency

When a prosecutor receives a new file, one of the first actions that a prosecutor takes is to determine the potential charge that the suspect faces. The purpose of that initial decision is not to determine the law that applies to the case, but rather to determine the amount of time that the prosecutor should spend resolving the case. To determine that number, a prosecutor will turn to a "*Sachgebietsschlüssel*" chart that lists the all of crimes and the number of hours that the average prosecutor will ideally spend resolving the case. As one prosecutor who was describing the mechanics of creating a new case file described to me:

This is very special. It's called *Sachgebietsschlüssel*. It's a new law in Germany that we have to give these Sachgebietsschlüssel for every crime, yes because they have decided for special subjects they have decided that for special subjects, you have only, this case should end, for example, in 20 hours. You have to [complete] work [on]this case in 20 hours. So for every case we have these *Sachgebietsschlüssel* and for every crime there other [average amounts of time] that you have to spend on the case. For example, I can show you [taking out a multi-page chart]. This is the *Sachgebietsschlüssel* for the crime of *Körperverletzung* (criminal assault), you understand *Körperverletzung*? If I punch you. If I hit you . . . For every *Körperverletzung*, you have 80 minutes, for a normal case, and you have to finish the case [in 80 minutes].

Q: So this applies to all of Deutschland?

Yes it's all of Deutschland. For example, you see there's a difference. If you work with adults you have 80 minutes. If you work with children, *Jugendliche*, they are between 14 and 18. And between 18 and 21, we say *Heranwachsende* and in some cases, they can, they get treated like *Jugendliche*. And you have only 49 minutes for the case. . If you are an *Amtsanwält* (paralegal) you have 56 minutes, less than a *Staatsanwalt* (public prosecutor), because they think if an *Amtsanwält* (paralegal) works on this case, it's not such a difficult case, it's an easier one... [I]f you think about it, we say it's really ridiculous. You can't handle a case this way. For example, *Kapitalverbrechen*. . .for example, murder, [under the guidelines you have] 1200 minutes for such case. But if you have a very complicated case, it can last, months, years. The reason why they have[created this system is], because in Germany, as you heard, the state does not have enough money, that is the main reason, so they want to, yes, save money...[16]

[16] Prosecutor Interview [13WT], 18 November 2005.

Although a case's particular *Sachgebietsschlüssel* does not per se prohibit a prosecutor from devoting more time to a case than is listed in the chart, administrators use the data to determine a particular office's productivity. Perhaps equally important, because a prosecutor must consult and make note of the *Sachgebietsschlüssel* every time a new case is opened, the number provides an internal reference point that frames further decision-making in that case. When prosecutors sit at their desks and look at the stack of files that require their attention, they cannot ignore the pressure of time and resource constraints. While many legal norms may structure decision-making in an indeterminate manner, the numerical indicators of a prosecutor's case processing efficiency set a crystal clear reference point. For this reason, the goal in handling many of the low level crime cases is to uncover a sufficient factual basis to determine whether the case should be dismissed, sent to another agency, settled out of court, or brought to court only as a last resort.

Efforts to cut spending on the state level have created workload pressures for prosecutors that were not present two to three decades earlier. As a whole, prosecutors are working longer hours than their predecessors did. Because high caseloads are prevalent in "general crimes" departments, it is not uncommon for new prosecutors to work extra hours to stay on top of their caseloads.[17] Anecdotal evidence suggests that this is a significant change from the workload stress that existed 20 years ago. The increased use of accounting systems to monitor office productivity levels and frozen staffing levels contribute to workload pressure. In an effort to efficiently allocate personnel among various prosecution offices, states (*Länder*) throughout Germany have adopted different systems to estimate office workload rates. Although *Länder* level Ministries of Justice have traditionally used task assignment codes or "*Sachgebietsschlüssel*" as guidelines to estimate the average time that it takes a prosecutor to complete a certain task, during the past two decades, the numbers have become key management tools.

Ironically, to modernize the guidelines, the states (*Länder*) hired prominent accounting firms to conduct time-management studies of prosecutors' work. The most common systems in use today are the MESTA and PEBB§Y systems. Ministry officials use the systems primarily to allocate personnel resources based on each office's case volume.[18] Unsurprisingly, these time management guidelines have drawn fire from prosecutors who claim that the guidelines underestimate the complexity of the decision-making process. According to these systems, each particular type of crime is allocated an average required case processing time. That figure purportedly represents the amount of time, on average, that a prosecutor needs to complete an investigation, draft the charges, and appear in court on a case. Based on the number of cases that an office actually handles in a year, ministry officials use the guidelines to estimate each office's productivity level and staffing

[17] Prosecutor Interview [4GG], 21 January 2006.

[18] Ministry Interview [9RR], 30 June 2006.

requirements. According to one prosecutor, the system attempts to apply the logic of product manufacturing controls used in the business world to legal decision-making.

> For example . . . during my studies, I worked in a company, to finance my education. They have the same [type of system]. If you have to make a product, they will say, for this product, for example, you have one hour [to make the product]. I think that a prosecution office is a totally different [environment than a factory]. But [the administration] created the system. This is the reason why I have to write down the *Sachgebietsschlüssel* (code) [into the file].[19]

The daily flow of case files impacts whether or not a prosecutor has time to take an active role in a particular case investigation. With the exception of prosecutors who work in capital crimes or serious economic crime departments, the bulk of German prosecutors are responsible for large numbers of case files. The crush of case files is most severe in the "general crimes" departments where prosecutors on average receive 120 new cases per month.[20] A somewhat humorous exchange which illustrates this point occurred when I met with a senior prosecutor in one prosecution office to schedule the participant observation periods. At the start of the meeting I provided him with a list of research activities I would like to schedule. One of the items included on my list was: "meetings with prosecutors in departments which routinely process large numbers of files." When the prosecutor read this item, he laughed and remarked: "There are no prosecutors here who do not work on large numbers of files."[21] The pressure of high caseloads is strongest at the lower court or *Amtsgericht*[22] level as, on average, a German prosecutor who primarily handles *Amtsgericht* level cases will typically handle 1,000 case files per year. In the bulk of the offices that I visited and in the interviews that I conducted, prosecutors consistently reiterated the point that prosecutors, who must handle large numbers of case files, have little time to devote to case investigation. The three prosecutors quoted below, who are based in three different offices, each describe an onerous case load:

> Q: What is a typical day? What is your workload like?
>
> A typical day-I start work at 8:30. I come here in my office and here in my *Eingang* (in box), there are all the files from the following day that I have to work out . . . In my department, I think, on average, every day, twenty files and so I've got to work these files. . . [W]hat I have to do most [of the] time is work on these files . . . [W]e don't make so many [sic] investigations on our own. Most investigations [are conducted by] the police. But it's different. For example if you [work in] organized crime, you don't have so [many] files. In our department, you see, you have a lot of files. . . If you have only a few files, maybe you

[19] Prosecutor Interview [13WT], 18 November 2005.

[20] Prosecutor Interview [12BX], 25 April 2006.

[21] Prosecutor Interview [9BU], 4 May 2005.

[22] The *Amtsgericht* level includes two "first instance" venues for cases involving adults. A single "*Strafrichter*" or criminal judge sitting alone can hear cases involving possible a possible criminal sanction of up to 2 years imprisonment. The "*Schöffengericht*", which includes one professional judge and two lay judges, is competent to hear cases involving a potential sentence of up to 4 years imprisonment. Cases which involve potential sentences of 4 years or more imprisonment begin at the *Landgericht* level. See §§ 24, 25, 74 GVG.

> can make some investigations on your own. I always do these things only in very special cases ... But in normal cases- I don't. It's too much work. Sometimes if, as I told you, if you want to accuse someone, you have to hear [what he has to say] before you accuse him. Normally I let the police do this too but ... some prosecutors do it on their own. They think it's better if they do it ... I only do it in special cases. Normally I don't do it.[23]

> I worked for four months in *Steinau*[24] in the general crimes unit. You can't do a good job [there] on these cases unless you work ten to twelve hours per day. There are [only] fifteen prosecutors working in *Steinau*... [So] everyone must handle two hundred cases per month and work weekends to get through their workload.[25]

> [During] my last two months in the drug crimes department I have had 110 new cases per month. Before that I routinely had 55 new cases per month. This includes both small and big cases ... *Jauer* is known as the "cavalry of justice." This office gets results [and] we have fewer open cases ... We have a more pragmatic perspective on cases. For example, if [we] have a case with seven crimes [we] are more willing to concentrate on a small number of crimes to pursue and to drop the rest of the charges.[26]

In more leanly staffed offices, the pressure of high caseloads is not restricted to prosecutors who work in the so-called "general crimes" departments. As an example, a department leader of a drug trafficking and money laundering case department told me that the six prosecutors in his department between them handled 3,800 cases in 2005.[27] While she assigns the less complicated cases to the department's less experienced prosecutors, on average, each prosecutor in the department handles more than 600 cases per year.[28]

Workload pressures create a different decision-making logic than the one represented by legal scholars. As envisioned by theorists, the legal decision-making process is a logical, almost formulaic, procedure, in which the decision-maker classifies the facts of a case under the appropriate legal headings. German legal scholars in particular have long maintained that the law, rather than organizational incentives and daily work routines, is the primary factor that shapes a prosecutor's decision-making. For example, in describing the prosecutorial function, Joachim Hermann stated that a prosecutor "does not act as an administrator trying to attain practical goals; instead his function is limited to the judicial task of applying the provisions of the Penal Code to the facts of the case" (Hermann 1976, p. 18). According to German Criminal Procedure Code, the prosecution office will begin an investigation when it receives information about a suspected criminal offense.[29] At that point, the prosecutor assigned to the case will then review the information and decide how to proceed. To be sure the initial decisions that a prosecutor will make upon receiving a new case will entail a series of legal judgments. Those initial

---

[23] Prosecutor Interview [13WT], 18 November 2005.

[24] *Steinau* and all other place names that appear in italics are pseudonyms.

[25] Prosecutor Interview [12AE], 28 November 2005.

[26] Prosecutor Interview [7WK], 5 April 2006.

[27] Prosecutor Interview [1CK], 13 March 2006.

[28] Prosecutor Interview [1CK], 13 March 2006.

[29] § 160 Nr. 1 StPO.

decisions will include: 1) Is the behavior criminally punishable? 2) Do time considerations bar punishment? And, finally 3) Does the crime fall within the jurisdictional authority of this particular prosecution office and this particular prosecutor? As a prosecutor evaluates the case facts to answer these questions however, workload pressures create incentives for prosecutors to answer the questions in a manner that will get the case off their desk. As a result, the default answers to these questions (which are written in italics) may look like this:

1) Is the behavior criminally punishable?	*Can the case be dismissed?*
2) Is a conditional dismissal possible?	*Is a penal order appropriate?*
3) Is punishment bared by time considerations?	*So I may dismiss the case?*
4) Does the crime fall within my competence?	*So I can assign it to another agency or another prosecution office?*

As I observed prosecutors make routine case decisions, I witnessed many prosecutors who handle general crime cases employ this type of efficiency driven decision-making. Organizational incentives, inefficient case handling practices, and the organization structures themselves fuel this decision-making dynamic. In the next three subsections, I will explore the impact created by each of these factors.

4.4.3 Efficiency and Work Routines

> My daily work consists of bringing this pile of records into this pile.
> -German Prosecutor[30]
> [Pointing to the stacks of files in the in-box and the out-box on her desk]

The pressure to efficiently handle caseloads while ensuring that cases are investigated adequately and objectively is a critical tension intrinsic to German prosecution practice. In assessing the impact that case loads have on decision-making, it is important to understand the extent to which a prosecutor's daily time is consumed by routine, rather than deliberative, decision-making. Because routine case-processing duties demand so much time, it can be difficult for a new prosecutor to find the time to think about how to respond to more complex legal issues.[31] Increasing workload pressures and the drive for efficiency mean that file review processes are no longer as thorough and precise as before.[32] The pressure to "move" cases originates in the monthly statistical reports used by department leaders. These reports show department managers exactly how many new cases a prosecutor is carrying, how many cases each prosecutor has closed, as well as the average

[30] Prosecutor Interview [3TW], 8 November 2005.

[31] Prosecutor Interview [4EW], 2 February 2006.

[32] Prosecutor Interview [7VG], 3 April 2006.

amount of time that a prosecutor keeps a case open. The statistical guidelines do not force a prosecutor to have a stopwatch at their desk and to track how much time they can spend on a particular case. Instead the guidelines exert a more insidious impact on prosecutorial decision-making. Because prosecution offices track the number of cases for each crime that the office handles on a monthly basis, administrators can use the statistics to determine staffing levels in particular departments and in particular offices. In this way, the system forces prosecutors to work efficiently. In other words, if a prosecutor does not wish to work extra hours, they must treat their case handling decisions as a zero-sum game. If you spend extra time on an investigation in one particular case, there will be pressure to handle the next case more expeditiously. Workload pressures encourage some prosecutors to try and game the system. For example, one attorney told me that when he worked in a prosecution office as a law student, the prosecutor that he worked for would place a stack of easily resolvable cases in reserve behind his desk. He would then move those cases in a month when he had to handle a number of complex cases. That procedure enabled him to maintain good case processing numbers as the less time-intensive files averaged out with the more complex cases.[33]

A prosecutor's ability to efficiently manage their workload is not only a key measure of their job performance, but it also affects their promotion potential.[34] Because prosecutors have little control over the flow of files into their offices, if a prosecutor fails to make the decisions required to move files forward in the process, files will accumulate quickly. The presence of multiple stacks of files in a prosecutor's office may become a visible flag that the production line is not running smoothly. The statistical systems track how long a particular case has been open as well as the total number of open cases assigned to a particular prosecutor. While some cases will inevitably take longer to resolve, supervisors closely monitor the average time that individual prosecutors require to resolve cases.[35] The emphasis on numerical measures, however, does not mean that efficiency is the sole focus of managerial oversight. When looking at the average case investigation time, for example, it is better for a prosecutor to fall near the average than at either end of the spectrum. If a prosecutor closes cases in less than a month for a particular month, while the department average is 2.5 months, it may indicate that the prosecutor is not ordering or conducting any investigation at all on his cases. In this sense, the numbers serve as a guideline that signals potential problem areas. Similarly, when those same numbers indicate that a prosecutor is not keeping up with the department's workload, the department manager will attempt to find out what is happening. As one department manager explained:

> [If you don't handle pressure] . . . then you sit and you will be here all night and that can also happen . . . [W]e have every month a list for all prosecutors where they [can] see their oldest cases and I watch three or four times a month in our computer system where I can see how many cases came in, how many cases the prosecutor has completed. . . And then I watch

[33] Attorney Interview [9QO], 16 July 2006.

[34] Prosecutor Interview [16PP], 30 April 2008.

[35] Prosecutor Interview [16PP], 30 April 2008.

> how many cases are in every *Dezernat* (individual area or responsibility) at the end of the month and when, for example, there's one coming up to two hundred, I go to him, talk to him, and ask where are the problems, how we can help and so (on) and then we try to catch the problem but basically every prosecutor is working (with) his own decisions.[36]

There are however, legitimate reasons why a backlog occurs. A prosecutor may have stacks of new cases piled up in their office simply because she was assigned to handle too many days of courtroom duty in a particular month. Perhaps some of the new cases were more complex than normal. Where it is clear that the source of the problem is not the prosecutor's effort level, the department manager may adjust incoming caseloads to even out the workload. Although the focus on the numbers seems to indicate that efficiency is the primary focus of administrative oversight, the focus on the investigation length also carries a certain legal significance. If cases take too long to investigate, it is also more difficult for prosecutors, according to German law, to recommend a stiffer sentence as, courts will view the length of the investigation as a burden on the defendant that needs to be weighed in the defendant's favor at sentencing. As one department manager related:

> Every prosecutor knows by himself that if he has too many cases, he cannot handle them anymore so it's very important for him to keep the amount of cases low. It is also [true] that most of the colleagues have a natural feeling for justice and that brings you often, in most cases, to the right decision. You have to show them the right way. And everybody here is clear that if you have [a] case too long, you [will] not get the same high punishments any more. So the best [thing] is to handle the case here [for] only a short time and then to bring it to the court.[37]

The nature of the workload and the decision-making practices in the "specialized crimes" departments (*Sonderabteilungen*) differ from those in the general crime departments. For example, in contrast to general crimes prosecutors, prosecutors who handle economic crimes or corruption cases may receive only 15 new cases per month. There may be a substantial disparity between the complexity levels of new cases. For example, of these fifteen new cases, ten cases may be dispensed of with a simple conditional dismissal (*einstellen*), four may require further investigation, and one case may require the prosecutor to draft a complaint. The character of the charges themselves thus strongly influences decision-making routines. Whatever their department, prosecutors must be able to prioritize cases and quickly determine what cases can be disposed of informally. Prosecutors who cannot move files quickly will attract the negative attention of their superiors.[38] To avoid attracting that attention, prosecutors must, by necessity, develop ways to prioritize their work.

Case management is essentially a zero-sum game. If you want to conduct a thorough investigation in a more complicated case, you have to "find" that time by quickly processing a number of other cases. Many of the prosecutors whom I observed used different methods to organize their work. These methods allowed

---

[36] Prosecutor Interview [12BX], 25 April 2006.

[37] Prosecutor Interview [12BX], 25 April 2006.

[38] Prosecutor Interview [16PP], 30 April 2008.

them to differentiate between decisions on cases that they needed to ponder, those decisions that were extremely time-sensitive, and those actions that could be made quickly with little thought. While I observed prosecutors going through the stack of files sitting in their in-box for the day, many prosecutors would first evaluate whether or not the action required on the case was routine work that could be done quickly with little deliberation. On the other end of the spectrum, prosecutors might set the "complicated" decisions to the side and inform me that they were going to think about the case over the weekend, talk to a colleague, or research case decisions and legal commentaries before reaching a decision. One prosecutor with 8 years of experience, who worked on sexual crimes, juvenile, and some drug cases, divided her pending work into these piles:

1. New cases that came from the police that require a review within a short period of time but require some thought.
2. Files involving recent arrests and other procedural questions that require an immediate decision that can be made quickly.
3. Routine file maintenance cases that require a signature or a new follow-up date.
4. Case questions involving legal research or more complicated investigation decisions.[39]

Organization-based file processing systems, such as the use of different file colors, perform a signaling function that allows administrative assistants to flag certain time-sensitive decisions. For example, in this particular office, cases in which the suspect was in custody were flagged with a yellow file cover. In other offices that I visited, administrative assistants used post-it notes to flag case files that required a prosecutor's immediate attention. When I entered the office of a prosecutor who had worked for less than a year, I immediately noticed that he had developed his own time management system. The wall above his bookshelf was decorated with a series of post it notes indicating the types of decisions that were required in the files stacked below each post-it note.[40] The high number of case files that prosecutors in many departments must regularly handle force prosecutors to prioritize decision-making. At the same time, prosecutors do not make every decision swiftly. Those prosecutors who can organize their work efficiently find the time to deliberate about the more important and complicated decisions. Despite the pressure to be productive, prosecutors need not always sacrifice case investigations nor forego researching more complicated legal questions. Whether a prosecutor can carve out that time is a function, not only of a prosecutor's own initiative level, but also the extent to which a particular office's investigation and case handling procedures have broken free from traditional bureaucratic practices. It is to those practices that I now turn.

[39] Prosecutor Interview [6SB], 23 February 2006.

[40] Prosecutor Interview [4EW], 2 February 2006.

4.5 Bureaucratic Practices

A key organization-based factor in German prosecution offices that affects how prosecutors approach their work is the degree of bureaucratization in a particular office. For my purposes here, I will examine a particular type of bureaucratic practice, namely the use of written orders as a case management practice. Without a doubt, when prosecutors document each action that has been taken in a particular case in the file, it promotes transparency. It enables a prosecutor's colleagues and superiors, as well as the court, to review the prosecutor's work on the case and serves as a decision-making record. One senior official in the Ministry of Justice defended the practice of using written instructions as a practice necessary to preserve a case's decision-making trail. He also maintained that it was more efficient to send an instruction to the police rather than to play phone tag with a particular officer.[41] In addition, in an era in which department managers and top office prosecutors have appeared to concentrate their oversight efforts on the pursuit of efficiency, file documentation practices help to support informal collegial control practices. The following example supports this proposition.

Because files contain a record of a case's progress, when a new colleague takes over a case, that colleague may elect to discuss his or her assessment of the quality of the prior work completed on the file with other colleagues. This informal performance monitoring system can undercut one's reputation within an office. Since offices may adjust prosecutors' areas of responsibility on an annual basis, the transfer of files between prosecutors occurs regularly. In addition, when a colleague is ill or goes on vacation, another prosecutor must cover his or her workload. For these reasons, a prosecutor's decision-making practices are transparent, not only to their superiors, but also to their colleagues. A conversion that I witnessed during a coffee break in *Strehlen* illustrates how a prosecutor may damage their reputation by attempting to dodge file work. During a morning coffee break, in which a group of young prosecutors routinely participated, one prosecutor started complaining about the cases that she had inherited from another prosecutor. In December of the prior year, after prosecutor in the office had learned whether or not they would soon be transferred to a different department, her colleague delayed action on every single file which had crossed her desk. To avoid working, she had simply inscribed the same instruction in every file: "Please return file to this office for review in exactly one month." Thus, instead of making an effort to clear cases, the prosecutor had simply postponed all work on the files assigned to that section until the new prosecutor inherited the case load.[42] In this way, she was able to ensure that files did not accumulate in her office despite the fact that she had effectively ceased working. As this exchange of gossip indicates, informal communication networks socialize new prosecutors and help to articulate standards of acceptable performance.

---

[41] Ministry Interview [9CK], 4 May 2006.

[42] Prosecutor Interview [4GG], 30 January 2006.

But the value of documentation practices has been perhaps overplayed. Although defense attorneys are entitled to receive a copy of the file, they do not receive a copy of the *Handakte*, a sub-file that contains key information about the case. Specifically, it includes a copy of the complaint, comments written by the prosecutor, important evidence in the case, a record of cases pending in other districts, as well as the defendant's prior history, and the prosecutor's sentencing recommendation.[43] Although the court will receive information about a defendant's history, the prosecution office also does not provide a copy of the *Handakte* to the court.[44] In addition, when a supervisor reviews a prosecutor's work on a case, typically they will only review the material in the *Handakte*. According to one prosecutor, 90 % of the information in a case file is never reviewed by a supervisor.[45] Given these facts, the role that file documentation practices play in promoting transparency has been overplayed.

There are also significant disadvantages to using these extensive documentation procedures. A key drawback is the amount of time that prosecutors must devote to simply writing instructions. On a practical level, file documentation requirements mandate that prosecutors spend considerable time inscribing written instructions in files. This practice contributes to the work load and time pressures of practice. In turn, the crush of case processing demands places a premium on individuals who can make decisions quickly. When I asked prosecutors what type of skills it took to succeed, "decision-making ability" or "*Entscheidungsfähigkeit*" frequently topped the list.[46]

A second disadvantage is that the use of archaic documentation practices itself is often linked to the use of out-dated criminal investigation practices. For example, in one small city that I visited, prosecutors use written instructions to communicate with police during the investigation stage of a case when it might be quicker to simply pick up the phone. In offices that rely heavily on the use of written instructions to communicate with the police, other government agencies, and defense counsel, reliance on written communications may slow the investigation process. When new prosecutors in these offices are trained to write instructions to initiate action, they discover that they may work on a case at arm's length and minimize their contact with other people.[47] While this method of working on cases is bureaucratically "correct," it stifles individual initiative. Examples of such written orders that I found in my review of case files include the following orders (Table 4.3).

---

[43] Prosecutor Interview [13EU], 6 December 2005; Prosecutor Interview [5BC], 16 January 2006; and Prosecutor Interview [12CO], 24 April 2006.

[44] Prosecutor Interview [4EW], 2 February 2006.

[45] Prosecutor Interview [4GG], 30 December 2006.

[46] Prosecutor Interview [7AG], 7 April 2006.

[47] Prosecutor Interview [5BC], 16 January 2006.

Table 4.3 Sample file orders collected from actual case files

Instruction written in file	Potential charge(s)
Send the file back to the police and tell them to interview witness "X"	Aggravated assault
Send a letter to suspect "X" and ask them to come into the prosecutor's office to be interviewed	Driving a mini-bike without a license
Treat this witness as a suspect and give me the file back in 1 month	Leaving the scene of an accident
Make a copy of the file for the lawyer in the accompanying civil suit and ask him if he is going to serve as the defense attorney in the criminal case. Give me the file back in 2 months	Leaving the scene of an accident

Even if one could argue that the file documentation practices further the goal of promoting transparency, the practice of writing instructions may get a file off a prosecutor's desk while undermining the achievement of other goals. In some files that I reviewed the practice of issuing written orders prolonged the length of a case investigation and delayed charging decisions. For example, in one simple robbery case where a young man allegedly tried to rob an elderly woman, the orders in the file included the following:

1/2/	Case opened by the police
1/28/	Victim statement taken by the police
3/4/	Witness Statement
3/23/	Attempt to interview defendant
3/23/	File sent to prosecution office for action.
4/9/	Prosecutor's Instructions: 1. Send a letter to the witness who did not appear at the police station asking him to give a statement. 2. Return file to me in one month for follow-up
5/3/	Witness again says that he knows nothing
7/12/	Prosecutor's Instructions:
7/24/	Prosecutor's Instruction (*Hagau*) 1. Assess a 100 Euro fine against the witness for not appearing to give a statement.
7/27/	Prosecutor's Instruction (*Hagau*) 1. Witness states that he cannot appear for a statement because he works at a bank. Also, he forgot about the appointment. 2. *Hagau* sends the file back to the original prosecutor because the witness works in the city where the prosecutor is situated.
8/25/	Witness statement: The victim cried out for help and he caught the suspect.
9/7/	Prosecutor's Instruction 1. Close investigation. 2. File charges.

In this case, the prosecutor took 8 months to close a simple robbery case. While the thoroughness of the investigation is praiseworthy and comports with the system's goal of finding the truth, the length of the investigation undermines the state's ability to impose a swift sanction that might encourage the young offender turn around his life. In this case, the bureaucratic practice of issuing written instructions to different agencies prolonged the investigation of a case that was not factually complex.

The practice of issuing written instructions developed during a time when prosecutors' caseloads were lighter and the majority of crimes were not as complicated as some of the more sophisticated economic crimes being committed today. In prosecution offices that are staffed by department leaders who are not interested in developing new methods of practice, the practice of issuing written instructions continues to be passed down to new prosecutors that join the office each year. Although some departments and even entire prosecution offices have found ways to reform bureaucratic practices, the old ways of organizing work practices generate a familiar sense of security to department managers in many departments. Due to the entrenched nature of bureaucratic practices, often the impetus for change must come from the higher levels of leadership.[48] The range of decision-making controls will be explored in the next chapter.

4.6 The Organization of General Crimes Work

In many prosecution offices throughout Germany, the majority of low-level crimes are handled by attorneys located in "General Crimes" department. The types of cases that fall within their purview is determined by the lead office prosecutor in each office. As I described above, the stereotypical work routine of a prosecutor assigned to this department is dominated by the reading and writing of file instructions. In their routine case investigations, these prosecutors have little contact with the police. Because the repetitive nature of the work on low level crimes cases may lead to boredom and frustration, ministry officials and prosecutors themselves have led calls for organizational reforms.

For example, one senior prosecutor complained to me that the cases which are less complex from an evidentiary and legal standpoint should be delegated to paralegals.[49] He noted that many of the decisions made by prosecutors in many low level crime cases is similar in complexity to the work performed by skilled laborers. Motivated by these concerns, some prosecution offices do use paralegals to process cases such as routine traffic matters and shoplifting cases. In one such

[48] As one department manager explained:

> Our current Justice Minister was a judge for ten years. He is a good person and he is better than his predecessor. He has eliminated many of the bureaucratic practices. He visits each office once per year, not to give orders, but to drink beer and talk. You can say anything to him ... While it is clear that everyone must do their job, he has improved working conditions. For example- he made sure that everyone had an internet connection and that they have new computers. Prosecutor Interview [7GC], 6 April 2006.

[49] Prosecutor Interview [7VG], 3 April 2006.

department, the department was staffed by three prosecutors and two paralegals. One of the paralegals whom I interviewed handled 170–200 cases per month, an average of 11 cases per day.[50] On an average day, he would typically dismiss six cases and file charges in the remaining five cases.[51] In this particular office, the office's computer system supported expedited decision making as prosecutors and paralegals could simply use a computerized form to open case files and the send the file quickly to the court to set a hearing date.[52] As this paralegal described the procedure:

> We use the computer to draw up and print out the charges and then the file will go to the court within two days and the court will set a date for a hearing relatively quickly. If a suspect committed a simple theft today, we could have a hearing next Wednesday. But most of the cases are set two or three weeks later... .With other cases, it is more difficult. If the police call me this morning and report that a crime was committed last night, the police can hold the suspect until the end of the tomorrow. We must in the meantime, file the charges. When the suspect has a prior case that may still be pending before another court . . . we must make a phone call to find out the status of the prior charges.[53]

In that particular prosecution office located in the former East Germany, the office uses these accelerated case disposition procedures to dispose of over 3,000 routine cases per year.[54] When a new case comes into the office that involves a simple crime, the department leader will review the case to see if the defendant has already admitted culpability. In cases that meet those criteria, she will ask the court to set a hearing date within two weeks. According to § 417 StPO, the prosecutor may file an application for an expedited disposition:

> In proceedings before the criminal court judge and the court with lay judges the public prosecution office shall file an application, in writing or orally, for a decision to be taken in an accelerated procedure if, given the simple factual situation or the clarity of the evidence, the case is appropriate for an immediate hearing.

When the case comes to court, the court will ask the defendant if she is willing to consent to the use of an accelerated procedure. If the defendant declines, the court will rest the case for a full main proceeding. If the defendant consents however, the court will quickly dispense with the case. The prosecution will not attempt to investigate the case prior to the hearing. Nor will they file formal charges. Instead, the prosecutor will simply recite the charges orally at the beginning of the hearing. In addition, the presiding judge may elect just to read the case record or written

---

[50] Paralegal Interview [10ED], 28 June 2006.

[51] Paralegal Interview [10ED], 28 June 2006.

[52] Offices that do not regularly use expedited decision procedures may also use computerized charging forms that can be accessed by paralegals to file charges in simple cases such as the failure to pay a bus fare. Prosecutor Interview [4 GG], 30 January 2006.

[53] Id.

[54] The procedures are delineated in §§417–420 StPO.

statements in the file, rather than to hear evidence in the case.[55] The decision as to how much evidence will be presented lies with the court and not with the prosecution (Wade et al. 2008, p. 137). Although defendants are entitled to counsel in cases where there is a potential imprisonment of at least 6 months, if the defendant consents to the use of the accelerated procedure, she cannot contest the court's disposition of the case. When a defendant consents to the procedure however, the court cannot impose a prison sentence of greater than 1 year. One drawback to the procedure is that court-appointed defense attorneys, motivated by the desire to make a quick profit, may be too willing to advise their clients to use the procedure. According to one prosecutor many defense attorneys like the procedure because they can earn their normal fee even though the case takes only 5 minutes to resolve.[56] A second drawback is that, when a prosecutor's caseload becomes particularly oppressive, the objectivity of the decision-making process may be compromised.[57]

Rather than confine general crime cases to a single department, other prosecution offices have elected to distribute those cases beyond a single department. In one office for example, each prosecutor handles a case load that contains 50 % general crimes cases and 50 % specialized cases that are concentrated in a particular area of responsibility such as environmental crimes or crimes involving state officials. While this new division of labor distributes the workload more equitably, it creates a different type of work load pressure as prosecutors may rush through general crimes cases in order to devote more time to the more interesting cases.[58] In another office that I visited, one of the senior administrators stacked the general crimes cases in piles and distributed them throughout the office so that on 1 day each month, the office as a whole processed a large number of general crimes cases.[59] This file management system, not only ensures that the low level crime cases are handled expeditiously, but it also helps each prosecutor to improve their performance according to productivity measures. By resolving a large number of cases quickly 1 day each month, prosecutors can devote more time to serious cases the rest of the month and still score high marks according to case processing related statistical measures.

The fact that prosecution offices throughout Germany are experimenting with new organizational forms to minimize the boredom of prosecutors assigned to general crimes departments is a positive development. In certain low level crime cases, it can also be prudent for prosecution offices to use paralegals and expedited procedures to resolve cases expeditiously. One issue that remains unanswered however is whether prosecutors, in pursuit of efficiency, have sacrificed their

[55] §420 StPO.

[56] Prosecutor Interview [10SK], 21 June 2006.

[57] Paralegal Interview [10ED], 28 June 2006.

[58] Prosecutor Interview [4GG], 30 January 2006.

[59] Prosecutor Interview [16PP], 30 April 2008.

duty to supervise or conduct objective investigation in cases which are in the public interest to prosecute.

Legislation

Code of Criminal Procedure (StPO)

Sections 153, 153(a), 153(a)(1), 153(1), 170, 170(2), 407–412, 417

Code of Criminal Law (StGB)

Sections 102, 107, 120 108(e), 129(a)(3), 176(1), 177, 177(2), 180(b), 216, 222, 224, 244, 259, 263

Interviews

Prosecutor Interview [9CK], 4 May 2006
Prosecutor Interview [10BJ], 26 June 2006
Prosecutor Interview [10Ed], 28 June 2006
Prosecutor Interview [13WT], 18 November 2005
Prosecutor Interview [11OT], 15 July 2005
Prosecutor Interview [13PR], 6 December 2005
Prosecutor Interview [4GG], 21 January 2006
Prosecutor Interview [9RR], 30 June 2006
Prosecutor Interview [12BX], 25 April 2006
Prosecutor Interview [9BU], 4 May 2005
Prosecutor Interview [12AE], 28 November 2005
Prosecutor Interview [7WK], 5 April 2006
Prosecutor Interview [1CK], 13 March 2006
Prosecutor Interview [3TW], 8 November 2005
Prosecutor Interview [4EW], 2 February 2006
Prosecutor Interview [7VG], 3 April 2006
Prosecutor Interview [16PP], 30 April 2008
Prosecutor Interview [12BX], 25 April 2006
Prosecutor Interview [6SB], 23 February 2006
Prosecutor Interview [13EU], 6 December 2005
Prosecutor Interview [5BC], 16 January 2006
Prosecutor Interview [12CO], 24 April 2006

Prosecutor Interview [7AG], 7 April 2006
Prosecutor Interview [7GC], 6 April 2006
Paralegal Interview [10ED], 28 June 2006
Attorney Interview [9QO], 16 July, 2006
Appellate Judge Interview [22FE], 22 July 2004
Justice Ministry Official [9CK], 4 May 2006

References

Books, Articles and Online Publications

Albrecht, H.-J. (2000). Criminal prosecution developments, trends and open questions in the Federal Republic of Germany. *European Journal of Crime, Criminal Law and Criminal Justice, 8*, 245–256.

Collin, P. (2001). Die Geburt der Staatsanwaltschaft, in PreBen, *Forum Historiaese Iuris* (12 März). Available at http://fhi.rg.mpg.de/articles/0103collin.htm. Accessed 3 Aug 2013.

Dubber, M. D. (2005). The promise of German criminal law: A science of crime and punishment. *German Law Journal, 6*, 1049–1071.

Elsner, B., & Peters, J. (2006). The prosecution service function within the German criminal justice system. In J.-M. Jehle & M. Wade (Eds.), *Coping With overloaded criminal justice systems: The rise of prosecutorial power across Europe* (pp. 207–236). Berlin: Springer.

Erb, V. (1999). Legalitäts und Opportunitätsgrundsatz als normative Prinzipien. In C. Geisler (Ed.), *Das Ermittlungsverhalfen der Polizei und die Einstellungspraxis der Staatsanwaltschaften* ed. Reihe Kriminologie und Praxis Wiesbaden: Schriftenreihe für Wolfgang Blomeyer. Berlin: Dunker and Homblot.

Eser, A. (1996). The acceleration of criminal proceedings and the rights of the accused: Comparative observations as to the reform of criminal procedure in Europe. *Maastricht Journal of European and Comparative Law, 3*, 341–370.

Felstiner, W. L. F. (1979). Plea contracts in West Germany. *Law & Society Review, 13*, 309–325.

Geisler, C. (1999). *Das Ermittlungsverfahren der Polizei und die Einstellung-Praxis der Staatsanwaltschaften: Bestandsaufnahme, Erfahrungen und Perspektiven*. Wiesbaden: Kiminologische Zentralstelle eV.

Heinz, W. (2006). *Penal sanctions and sanctioning practice in the Federal Republic of Germany, The Konstanz repository on crime and sanctioning, 1882–2004*. Konstanz: Konstanzer Inventar Sanktionsforschung (KIS).

Hermann, J. (1976). The German prosecutor. In K. Culp Davis (Ed.), *Discretionary justice in Europe and America* (pp. 16–74). Urbana: University of Illinois Press.

Hohmann, B., & Neubeck, G. (1996). *Zur Tätigkeit des Staatsanwalts*. Dresden: Sächsischen Staatsministerium der Justiz.

Jehle, J.-M. (2005). *Criminal justice in Germany: Facts and figures* (4th ed.). Berlin: Federal Ministry of Justice.

Jescheck, H.-H. (1970). Principles of German criminal procedure in comparison with American law. *Virginia Law Review, 56*, 239–253.

Langbein, J. H. (1979). Land without plea bargaining: How the Germans do it. *Michigan Law Review, 78*, 204–225.

Nestler, C. (2004). Sentencing in Germany. *Buffalo Criminal Law Review, 7*, 109–138.

Sessar, K. (1979). Prosecutorial discretion in Germany. In W. McDonald (Ed.), *The prosecutor* (pp. 255–276). Beverly Hills: Sage Publications.

Treiber, H. (1980). Die Macht der Routine oder Was Geschiet nach dem Inkrafttreten eines Reform-Gesetzes Zur Implementierungspraxis der §§ 153, 153a StPO beim Bagatelldiebstahl. In K. Lüderseen & F. Sacks (Eds.), *Vom Nutzen und Nachteil der Sozial Wissenschaften Für das Strafrecht* (pp. 444–478). Frankfurt/Main: Zweiter Teilbd.

Wade, M., Smit, P., & Aubusson de Cavarlay, B. (2008). The prosecution role where courts decide cases. *European Journal of Criminal Policy Research, 14*, 133–143.

Zappalá, S. (2006). The German federal prosecutor's decision not to prosecute a former Uzbeck Minister: Missed opportunity or prosecutorial wisdom? *Journal of International Criminal Justice, 3*, 602–622.

Chapter 5
Discretion and Major Crimes

5.1 The Principle of Mandatory Prosecution and Major Crime Cases

To this point, this book has detailed how the expansion of prosecutorial discretion in the disposition of low-level crimes has challenged the sacred norm of the "principle of legality." I have shown how concerns for efficiency, in an era of tight fiscal constraints, have widened the ambit of discretionary case handling practices both, in practice, as well as under the law. As I will detail in Chap. 7, the legislature has also exempted the treatment of delinquent juvenile acts from a strict application of the "principle of legality" according to which prosecutors must initiate action against all criminal acts where sufficient evidence exists to warrant prosecution.[1]

If we judge the efficacy of German efforts to limit discretion by the volume of cases in which the law prohibits discretion, one would have to conclude that Germany has long since abandoned its' fidelity to the principle of mandatory prosecution. In terms their frequency, the number of low-level and juvenile crimes in Germany dramatically trumps the incidence of major crimes.[2] Seen from this perspective alone, the claim that the "principle of legality" dominates German prosecutorial practice, on its face, overstates the reality of both the state of the law as well as actual practice. Still, given the widespread acknowledgment that the U.S. system produces uneven and unjust outcomes, if the German system's normative claims hold true with respect to major crimes, that would be a significant achievement. While critics of recent changes in the German system have focused their ire on the introduction of confession bargaining, one cannot determine that development's significance without determining whether concerns about efficiency

[1] § 152 StPO.

[2] Because of incongruities between the procedure used in collecting police statistics and prosecution statistics, as well as the number of cases dismissed or diverted, it is difficult to state precisely what percent of cases handled by German prosecutors qualify as major crimes.

S.M. Boyne, *The German Prosecution Service*, DOI 10.1007/978-3-642-40928-8_5,

have undermined the handling of serious cases. In particular, one must determine whether the impact of that practice has undermined prosecutors' commitment to objectivity across the board. If prosecutors are no longer committed to fulfilling that mandate, the resulting state of affairs would call into question the depth of Germany's commitment to a founding principle of the *Rechtsstaat*. For many legal theorists, fidelity to the principle of legality is a key pillar of the *Rechtsstaat*.[3] To be sure, this formalistic view of prosecutorial decision-making as a rule-following endeavor is consistent with the continental legal tradition's view of the role of criminal law itself. By narrowing the ambit of discretionary decision-making, the principle of legality "is supposed to shield citizens against the dangers of arbitrary application of public power, and unlawful restriction of their rights and liberties" (Claes and Krolikowski 2010, p. 60). Ultimately, the key metric for evaluating prosecutorial decision-making is not whether the law completely constrains discretion, but rather whether prosecutors exercise that discretion in an arbitrary and unjust manner.

5.2 The Incidence of Major Crimes

To what extent does prosecution practice focus on the prosecution of major crime cases? In terms of their sheer number, low-level crimes far outpace major crimes. The significance of that difference for the daily routines of prosecutors is hard to state with precision. Because of the funneling effect that occurs with case referrals and dispositions to the public prosecution offices, it is difficult to compare the time that prosecutors expend on major crime cases as opposed to minor crimes cases in absolute numerical terms. According to the German Federal Office of Statistics (*Statistische Bundesamt*), in 2011, the courts convicted a total of 807,800 individuals of crimes. The vast majority of those "convictions," 72 %, resulted only in a fine (*Statistische Bundesamt*).

In Germany, as in other western democracies, there is a diminishing funnel effect between the number of incidents of crime reported to police and prosecution offices and the number of cases actually filed by prosecutors. For example, in 2003, only 12 % of the cases reviewed by prosecutors culminated in the filing of a criminal charge (Jehle 2005). The fact that a charge is filed however, does not mean that the charge necessarily involved a major crime. It only means that the prosecutor decided not to dispose of the case with a penal order[4] or elected to terminate the case on the grounds that the offender's guilt was minor and there was no public interest in prosecution.[5] Given, that individuals convicted of a major

[3] GG Article 20(3).

[4] *See* §§ 407–412 StPO.

[5] *See* §§ 153 et al. StPO.

Table 5.1 German criminal sentences (*Statistisches Bundesmant*, 2013)

Term of imprisonment	As of March 31, each year 2010	2011	2012
Less than 3 months	6,238	6,165	5,852
3 months up to 1 year	19,803	19,876	19,180
Over 1 year up to 5 years	26,564	26,273	25,680
Over 5 years up to 15 years	5,504	5,201	4,864
Life Imprisonment[a]	2,584	2,552	2,497

[a]Includes preventative detention

crime are not eligible for these milder sanctioning schemes, we can assume that, at maximum, the percentage of major cases does not exceed 12 %.[6]

In 2011, the number of individuals who were sentenced to a term of confinement, including preventative detention, totaled 58,073 individuals out of roughly 800,000 incidents of crime (*Statistisches Bundesamt*).[7] Using the numbers for 2011, about 7.3 % of the criminal cases filed with German courts resulted in the defendant receiving a sentence involving some type of confinement. The length of confinement included in the sentences may be seen above (Table 5.1).

When we consider the total volume of major crime cases, it is important to note that, by definition, an individual convicted of a major crime (*Verbrechen*) cannot be punished solely with a fine, nor can their prison sentence be suspended if it exceeds a 2 year period. However, the number of individuals sentenced to confinement includes individuals sentenced for violations of so-called minor offenses. There are a large number of crimes for which a sentence including imprisonment is possible but they do not require a judge to impose a minimum term of imprisonment of 1 year. For example, an individual convicted of Election Fraud contrary to Section 107a may receive a sentence ranging from a fine up to a 5 year prison sentence. In addition, even in cases where an individual has been convicted of a major crime (*Verbrechen*), one can avoid prison by receiving a sentence of probation of between one and 3 years.[8] Still, measured on a volume basis, the number of major crime cases handled by prosecutors runs under 10 % of the total cases handled.

On the basis of these statistics as well as prior reports of criminality, it is apparent that without out a doubt, in comparison with their American colleagues,

[6] The ratio of cases in which charges were filed to those cases that were disposed of via a penal order or other form of prosecutorial dismissal [i.e. penal orders, *Einstellungen* (dismissals/deferrals)] with conditions and without conditions, the percentage of cases in which charges were filed approaches 23 %. This calculation is based on the figures provided in STATISTISCHES BUNDESAMT: DEUTSCHLAND. *Rechtspflege*: *Staatsanwaltschaften 2004*, at 24. The number of cases in which charges were filed in 2004 was 588,851. The total cases which were disposed of via penal code totaled 623,021, a dismissal with conditions 265,317, and dismissals without condition 1,087,722. The calculation should be considered only as an approximation.

[7] Because some cases may be filed in 1 year and adjudicated in the following year, one cannot use the number of cases filed in criminal courts in a particular year as the denominator.

[8] § 59 (1) StGB.

German judges impose non-custodial sanctions on non-violent offenders with far greater frequency (Frase 2001). Even when an individual is convicted of violating a particularly heinous crime, such as murder, the maximum term of imprisonment is a life sentence. Consistent with the German legal culture's faith in the belief that most offenders may be rehabilitated, offenders, after serving a 15 year period, must be given the opportunity of parole.[9] Another notable difference with American law is that the German Constitution prohibits the death penalty.[10]

5.3 The Societal Significance of Major Crime

Despite the relative infrequency of major crimes in Germany, a public prosecutor's response to serious crimes performs a crucial societal function. In terms of the broader system of governance, prosecutors play a key role, not only in preserving the social order by prosecuting criminals, but also in maintaining citizens' confidence in the legal order. The Code of Criminal Procedure, in particular, the principle of legality, attempts to suborn politics to the dictates of the law. By requiring prosecutors to file charges in all cases where sufficient suspicion of criminality exists, the principle seeks to ensure that no one is exempt from reach of the criminal law. In this respect, prosecutors' role as "second judges" speaks to the tradition's aspiration that prosecutors will view the merits of each case through a neutral lens. The obligation to prosecute seeks to ensure that prosecutors enforce the law uniformly and that their decision-making is free from political influence. According to Glanert (2008), this vision of the law reflects the civil law tradition's "nomothetic" or rule-based conception legal knowledge in which the law itself, if rigorously applied, can solve any legal question free of political influence or the impact of resource constraints.

Though the law permits prosecutors to employ a wide range of disposition practices in minor crime cases, the categorization of certain crimes as major crimes (*Verbrechen*) aims to ensure that prosecutors investigate and prosecute all serious lawbreakers. To this end the classification of an act as a major crime reflects the legislature's assessment of the importance of the protected interest that the criminal law seeks to safeguard. Thus, a sanction's severity reflects both the act's normative weight, as well as the legislature's desire to ensure that the court's sanction will reflect the weight of the legally protected interest (Dubber 2005).

[9] § 38(2) StGB. A separate provision allows for the extended detention of individuals who pose a security risk.
[10] GG Art. 102.

5.4 Defining Prosecutorial Objectivity

Given that prosecutors will inevitably possess some measure of discretion in their daily decision-making, the key question to be asked is whether German prosecutors perform their duties in an objective manner. More specifically, what does "objective" decision-making require prosecutors to do? When the prosecutor reviews an investigation file compiled by law enforcement, what actions should the prosecutor take to investigate the facts in favor of the accused? When the prosecutor handles an investigation from start to finish, must he or she find a witness who will speak favorably on the suspect's behalf? Is the standard that a prosecutor must leave no stone unturned? When one attempts to define objectivity using a range of concrete practice activities, the term's subjectivity becomes more apparent. Although several code sections seek to mandate that prosecutors view a case objectively, those code sections simply cannot "operationalize" objectivity at each step of the process. For example a prosecutor, who has failed to interview a potentially exculpatory eyewitness prior to trial, may stand up in the courtroom near the close of the case and, by stating a handful of minor points in the defendant's favor, comply with the code. The law's limited ability to define what "objectivity" means, like the Code's inability to legislate away discretion, underscores the limits of using the law alone to prescribe bureaucratic decision-making.

While the concept of objectivity plays a key role in defining German prosecutors' institutional identity, the extent to which this normative mandate actually influences decision-making varies. Although statutory requirements may force prosecutors to, at minimum, pay lip service to objectivity, the level of reflexivity mandated by the law is limited. It is not only the law's open texture that opens the door to indeterminacy, the fluid and non-formulaic nature of the investigation process itself creates a variety of discretionary choices. Because of the complexities of human nature, the fact gathering process is not formulaic. As supervisors of the investigation process, prosecutors make a variety of decisions that decisively influence a case's forward trajectory. For example, prosecutors may fail to take the initiative and elect not to nudge law enforcement thoroughly investigate a case. Rather than encouraging law enforcement to find sufficient facts to justify the filing of a case, in some instances, prosecutors may elect to close out an investigation or to pursue only minor charges. In other cases, prosecutors might have to take up the reigns of the investigation itself to ensure that the investigation is complete. Thus, the degree of dedication of an individual prosecutor may determinatively affect case outcomes.

Most importantly, individual prosecutors view the extent of their mandate to be objective differently. Some prosecutors believe that they can satisfy their duty to be objective simply by making a charging decision that is not likely to be overturned by their supervisor or the General Prosecutor's Office (GStA). Beyond the goal posts set by statutory requirements, a prosecutor's degree of individual motivation, coupled with organizational incentives, shape the degree to which a prosecutor strives to decide cases objectively. Other prosecutors interpret their duty more expansively and believe that the duty to weigh evidence objectively extends to the main proceeding stage where they are required to play an active role by carefully weighing the credibility of all witnesses in the courtroom.[11] Since there is no precise definition of objective decision-making, measuring compliance is a subjective process.

Indeed, in my interviews of German prosecutors, some prosecutors would point to the fact that they had performed certain actions as conclusive proof that German prosecutors did, in fact, make objective decisions. Yet, standing alone, these minimal requirements cannot ensure that prosecutors comply with the principle of objectivity. In fact, one could argue that these requirements have become mere ritualized manifestations of objectivity. As one might expect, individual prosecutors' commitment to objectivity vary. While some prosecutors are content to define compliance with carefully dotting their "I's" and cross their "t's", others embrace and are committed to honoring a more expansive interpretation of objectivity.

Without a doubt, it is much easier to define the type of case handling processes that undermine the quest for equality. Certainly, when a political figure picks up the phone and tells a prosecutor to recommend a sentence in a particular case that falls outside community norms, we can agree that the outcome sought would conflict with the system's goals. In other situations however, it is not clear that the prosecutor's behavior violates the spirit of the norm of objectivity. For example, if a prosecutor, out of sheer laziness, refuses to gather further evidence to supplement the police investigation when the investigation is incomplete, we might conclude that the prosecutor is negligent, but not that they are acting in a biased manner.

The fact that objectivity cannot be quantified and is susceptible to disagreement and interpretation may lead prosecutors to subordinate their commitment to objectivity to other goals such maintaining collegiality and achieving efficiency. Critically, although the norm of objectivity is inscribed in statutory directives, the true impact of that norm depends upon the extent to which it is embedded in prosecutors' work practices. Since a prosecutor makes decisions and undertakes actions while he or she is embedded in a multilevel organization, a prosecutor's ability to function in an objective manner is driven not only by an individual's mindset, but perhaps more importantly, by organizational practices.

At the same time, the norm of objectivity is not a completely vacuous reference point. While legal rules may not guarantee uniform compliance with the principle's intent, because the norm has become an integral part of the prosecution service's identity, the norm does guide consensual decision-making processes. Most critically, the norm's significance may be seen in the fact that German prosecutors do not view themselves as zealous party advocates. While the norm of objectivity may be an imperfect guide to decision-making, it plays a constitutive role in reinforcing prosecutors' institutional identity.

[11] Public Prosecutor Interview [4AJ], 6 February 2006.

5.5 The Organization of Prosecution and the Creation of Decision-making Norms

Prosecutorial decision-making does not occur in a vacuum. Because prosecutors are embedded in institutions with norms, expectations, and resource constraints, the range of the decision-making options that are available to prosecutors are bounded, not only by the law, but also by institutional practices and behavioral norms. While the particular mix of restraints that bind decision-making in the investigation and prosecution stages of a proceeding may vary, German prosecutors do not operate with complete autonomy. Throughout the course of my participant observation studies, I observed that the intensity of hierarchical control varied from *Land* to *Land*, from office to office, and even between departments in the same offices. The constellation of formal and informal methods of control in effect at each level of the bureaucracy shaped not only the degree of latitude, but, in some cases how that latitude should be exercised.

By divesting the primary authority to prosecute and punish crime to the *Länder*, the founders of the post-war German state opened the door to Land to Land variations in prosecution policies and priorities. In this section, I detail the dominant institutional factors that shape prosecutorial behavior.

5.5.1 Authority Versus Independence at the State Level

> If you go from a position as a judge to the prosecution service your mind will not adapt to the change. You cannot carry the same perspective of objectivity with you. You cannot bring an isolated free standing mind with you. Rather, [in a prosecution office] your mind is captured by the collegial culture... You are [now] embedded in a culture of control.[12]

> The General Public Prosecutor stands above us and the Minister of Justice stands above him. And they possess the power to give orders (*Weisungsbefugnis*). Perhaps it would be better if the prosecutors were treated like judges. In that case, we could do our jobs without the possibility of constraint from political influence. There is, however, very little political interference. In my sixteen years of service, I have never received such an order.[13]

The hierarchical structure that prosecutors must work within establishes its own decision-making norms. To understand how the organization of the prosecution service impacts prosecutorial decision-making, one must first understand how prosecution offices are structured. Germany's prosecution offices, as well as the court system, are organized on the *Land*-level and are subsumed under state-level Ministries of Justice. Although federal legislative bodies draft and enact changes in

[12] Appellate Judge Interview [13MU], 10 April 2004.

[13] Prosecutor Interview [19IC], 14 May 2008.

the German Codes of Criminal Law and Procedure, the federal government relies on the *Länder* to implement the law and to manage the criminal justice system.

Though there is a Federal Prosecutor's Office, known as the *Bundesanwaltschaft*, the footprint of that federal office is quite small. Their primary mandate is to represent the State before the Federal Court of Appeals. In addition to appellate work, the federal prosecutor's office handles cases involving espionage, terrorism, treason, and genocide. For our purposes here, it is important to note that federal prosecutors belong to an independent hierarchy and, as such, do not possess supervisory authority over Land-level prosecutors. According to (Foster and Sule 2010), only about 20 % of federal prosecutors litigate courtroom cases. Although the potential for jurisdictional infighting exists, in the majority of the case handoffs between the Land and federal prosecutors, the parties discuss and effectuate the hand off via informal channels. Where the parties cannot negotiate an amicable hand off, the dispute will be decided by a higher authority. When a Land prosecution office hands off a case to the federal prosecution office, the hand off is memorialized via a formal, written procedure. The procedure requires the parties to agree that the opinions of federal prosecutors within their jurisdiction carry the day.

It is the state level Ministries of Justice, through the regional prosecution offices, which bear the brunt of the authority for investigating and prosecuting crime. In terms of the hierarchy of the courts, the Land prosecution services represent the state at the *Amtsgericht* (local court), *Landgericht* (district courts), and *Oberlandesgericht* (Higher Regional Court) Levels. The Federal Prosecutor represents the state in the *Bundesgerichtshof* (Federal Court of Justice). The state-level Ministries of Justice supervise the prosecution service, the judicial system, as well as the correctional system at the *Land* level. Within the Land-level executive branch, it is the Minister of Justice who ultimately sits atop the prosecution service.

As we begin to assess the impact that politics might play in prosecutorial decision-making it is important to recognize that the Minister of Justice at the *Land* level is a political appointee who is subject to pressure from other cabinet ministers as well as from the political party which he or she represents. To the extent to which the various *Land* governments throughout Germany are dominated by members of different political parties, a particular party's attitudes towards the criminal justice system may shape ministerial policies. For example, the conservative Christian Socialist Union, which has long ruled over Bavaria politics, views the criminal justice system through a different lens than the Green Party led alliance that took control of the state legislature (*Landtag*) in Baden-Württemberg in the 2011 elections. The fact that the Minister of Justice is a political figure charged with following the party's mandate, on paper, poses an existential threat to prosecutorial objectivity. Even if we push to the side concerns about improper influence in an individual case, it is apparent that the policies developed at the top of the prosecutorial chain of command influence the delivery of justice on the front lines. Even policies—such as the staffing levels of individual offices and departments—which on their face appear to be apolitical, may be the product of political platforms. For example, if a department head within the prosecution office seeks to fight corruption, he or she cannot do so single-handedly. To succeed, the department head must secure the support of the lead office prosecutor and adequate resources from the Ministry of Justice.

In the German parliamentary form of government, the *Land*-level ministers also serve as members of the parliament. The justice ministers are not elected independently, but rather report to the legislature at the *Land* level. Since the General Public Prosecutors in Germany do not stand for election, their political legitimacy stems from the fact that they report to the Minister of Justice at the *Land* level and that the Minister of Justice is accountable to the legislature. As a result of the fact that General Public Prosecutors do not possess any independent political legitimacy, they are ultimately beholden to the state level Minister of Justice. Given the hierarchical nature of this relationship, policies developed at the ministry level influence how prosecutors administer justice.

Pfeiffer and Wetzel's (1996) study, which examined the rates of imprisonment throughout Germany in the period of the early 1990s, confirmed this thesis. The study sought to identify the source of the strong disparity in the sentencing and case handling practices between the neighboring German states of *Niedersachsen* and *Schleswig-Holstein*. The researchers discovered that the primary reason why there was a strong disparity between the neighboring states stemmed from the differences in the perspectives between the Ministers of Justice in both states. In particular, the top prosecutor in the latter state was a liberal criminologist with a university research background. Accordingly, one of the *Niedersachsen* Minister's key policy directives was to ensure that only the most serious cases were litigated in court. Under this new policy, the number of cases resulting in informal disposition increased and judges sent only the most serious defendants from the cases that they saw in court to prison.

One of the most contentious powers that the Justice Minister possesses is the power to issue instructions to the Office of the Public Prosecutor. According to the so-called *Weisungsrecht*, the Ministry may issue general instructions that direct prosecutors to handle groups of cases according to a particular policy.[14] These general instructions cannot direct a prosecutor to handle a particular case in a certain way and are designed to ensure that the Ministry is responsive to the legislature (*Landtag*). Nevertheless, according to several prosecutors whom I interviewed, a practice of issuing informal instructions to prosecutors exists. These instructions often pertain to cases involving political crimes.[15]

Despite the political orientation of the Ministries at the Land-level, prosecutors and judges are career civil servants. Their status as civil servants protects them from arbitrary dismissal after they complete a period of probationary service. However, the path of a prosecutor's career will be influenced by the staffing needs and personnel policies established at the Ministry level. Most importantly, the structure

[14] Second Leading Office Prosecutor Interview [16PP], 11 May 2006.

[15] Second Leading Office Prosecutor Interview [16PP], 11 May 2006.

of state-level personnel policies opens the door to the exercise of political influence.[16] In some states, during the period of probationary service, individuals will rotate between positions in the judiciary and the prosecution service. At the end of the training period, depending on staffing needs, they will be assigned to either the prosecution or judicial service where they will remain throughout their career. However, in states such as Bavaria and Saxony, prosecutors, judges, and ministry officials rotate through different positions every 3 years. On its face, this policy appears to promote more objective decision-making as each individual is able to acquire experience in the different facets of the criminal justice system. However, because Ministry officials determine a prosecutor's subsequent placement opportunities, they have the power to reward decision-making with particular promotion opportunities. Promotions decisions are made according to state-level policies which, in some cases, may undercut a prosecutor's decision-making freedom. Transfer decisions are not always made according to fair and impartial procedures.[17] Conversely, the Ministry may discourage the aggressive prosecution of public figures by "promoting" a prosecutor, who aggressively prosecutes such cases, to a position as a low-level judge. The possibility of influence undercuts prosecutors' decision-making freedom.

5.5.2 Regional Oversight

Below the ministry level, responsibility for the prosecution service is divided into regions, the seat of which is often a city which has been a historical seat of power.[18] At the regional level, General Public Prosecutors (*General Staatsanwälte*) oversee all of the local prosecution offices.[19] The majority of General Public Prosecutors are also career civil servants. In four states however, those positions are staffed with political appointees made by the Land-level Ministries of Justice.[20]

Individual prosecution offices are headed by leading senior prosecutors (*Leitende Oberstaatsanwälte*) (LOSTA) who have risen through the civil service ranks and have the power to set office policies. Most offices are organized along department lines with different departments managing different types of crime. As a general rule, the departments are headed by senior public prosecutors who make case assignments and possess oversight responsibility over the departments as a

[16] Senior Public Prosecutor [8HL], 25 May 2006.

[17] Senior Public Prosecutor Interview [8AQ], 26 May 2006.

[18] Sect. 142 (1) COA.

[19] Sect. 142 (1) COA.

[20] The organization of prosecution offices parallels the organization of the courts. There is a *Generalstaatsanwalt* located at each of the 25 regional courts of appeal (*Oberlandesgerichte*). Some of the *Länder* possess more than one regional court of appeal. There are 116 district courts (*Landgerichte*) in Germany. Beneath those courts are the *Amtsgerichte*.

whole. To be eligible for promotion to the position of department manager, prosecutors must typically complete a rotation at the General Public Prosecutor's Office. During that rotation, their primary role is to review appeals filed by victims who have contested case dismissals. By removing potential department leaders from their home office and temporarily placing them in a regional office, the training aims to ensure that all department managers in a particular judicial district possess a uniform view of the control function. Moreover, the focus of this oversight is to identify potential violations of the principle of mandatory prosecution. Senior officials use the training not only to assess an individual's work ethic, but also to reinforce policies designed to constrain discretion.

5.5.3 Office Leadership and Mandatory Reporting Requirements

The leadership style of the lead prosecutor in each office (*LOSTA*) determines the extent and form of organizational controls that exist within a particular prosecution office. The top prosecutor may choose to exercise control by setting certain statistical standards of performance as well as by establishing case review protocols for certain types of cases. The LOSTA possesses the power to decide what type of case decisions will require his or her approval. They may also draft charging guidelines to give prosecutors more specific direction. In one office that I visited for example, the LOSTA required that prosecutors send all cases involving a murder or serious drug charges to his office for review at periodic intervals.[21] If the prosecutor received the case file back with a green cross written on the file cover, the prosecutor knew that the LOSTA wanted to meet with him or her about the case. In another office, the LOSTA required prosecutors to obtain his approval before they filed cases in the higher level courts (*Landgerichte*) which hear cases involving serious criminality. According to one department manager, that directive is designed to ensure that the prosecutor has drafted a charging document that accurately reflects the investigation findings.[22]

In all prosecution offices, prosecutors are required to pen regular reports which are sent up the chain of command. Those reports detail the progress that has been made on key cases—usually cases that will appear in the media as well as major crimes cases. The primary purpose of this reporting requirement is to keep the top leadership abreast of case developments so that managers can respond to inquiries about important cases. These reporting requirements not only force prosecutors to pay particular attention to key cases, but they also open the door to more intense scrutiny and second-guessing by supervisors. However, German law attempts to shield prosecutors from hierarchical influence that steps outside the boundaries of the law.

[21] Senior Prosecutor Interview [13AS], 10 June 2004.

[22] Senior Prosecutor Interview [2QM], 6 November 2005.

Accordingly, a supervisor may only review a prosecutor's file decisions to ensure that they comply with legal requirements. A supervisor may not order a prosecutor to file a charge that the prosecutor does not think is supported by evidence.

Officials in the state-level Ministries of Justice may also require prosecutors to report high profile cases to the Ministry so that the Minister is not caught off guard by inquiries from the press. In one office that I visited, the LOSTA gave prosecutors a remarkable degree of free reign and even delegated personnel decisions to department managers.

Despite the fact that a strong hierarchical structure exists on paper, in terms of their daily decision-making, German prosecutors possess a great deal of decision-making authority. While the leadership philosophy of the individuals at the top of the institutional hierarchy may determine the extent of that discretion, two factors weigh against the strong exercise of hierarchical control. First, the prosecution service is not immune from larger societal forces. As a result of the wave of social change that swept Germany in the 1970s, prosecutors' self-concept changed. A large group of prosecutors organized themselves during those turbulent years and challenged the service's culture of obedience and subservience. As a result of the group's activities and changing societal conditions, the amount of hierarchical interference in prosecutorial decision-making has decreased.[23] However, ongoing concerns about political influence have led the German Judges and Prosecutors Association (*Deutscher Richterbund*) to call on the legislature to abolish the Minster's right to issue instructions.[24]

The prosecution service's relatively flat structure is a second factor that weighs against oppressive hierarchical control. Although a small minority of prosecutors, after ten to 15 years of service, will become senior public prosecutors or departmental leaders (*Oberstaatsanwälte*) most prosecutors will never rise beyond the ground-level position of public prosecutor (*Staatsanwalt*). The dearth of interim career steps between the positions of public prosecutor and senior public prosecutor is intentional and reflects the judicial service's desire to preserve the prosecutors' independent decision-making authority.[25] As a result of this variance in leadership practices, the extent of decision-making freedom may vary from department to department. The range of leadership styles is reflected in the following comments:

> [In this district], there are no controls on the case dismissal rates. For the bulk of prosecutorial decision-making, there are effectively no controls since [prosecutors dismiss a high percentage of cases].[26]

> [T]he LOSTA can issue guidelines, but he cannot control all of the finer points of decision-making."[27]

---

[23] Appellate Judge Interview [13MU], 10 April 2004.

[24] Deputy Leading Office Prosecutor Interview [16PP], 30 April 2008.

[25] Senior Prosecutor Interview [9BU], 4 May 2005.

[26] Justice Ministry Official [9RR], 6 May 2006.

[27] Senior Prosecutor Interview [25ST], 16 April 2008.

> If a prosecutor has made a mistake on the file, there will be a phone call.[28]

> The identity of the LOSTA has a large impact on the organizational culture. [In this office] it is very collegial. He doesn't get involved in managing the cases. He believes that the prosecutor, who is handling the case, knows the most about the case and should manage it individually. The individual prosecutors have a lot of decision-making room. Also the LOSTA protects our backs against the Ministry of Justice and the General Public Prosecutor. This is not the usual practice in Germany.[29]

Every prosecution office is organized along department lines. The larger the office, the more specialized the departments. Thus, a large office is likely to have a specialized department that handles sexual assault cases, while in a smaller office, those crimes may be handled by prosecutors who handle a range of cases. Each department is typically headed by a department leader who has typically reached the senior prosecutor level. Department leaders are the primary focal point of the day to day supervision of prosecutorial decision-making. It is the department leader who decides how much latitude individual prosecutors will possess with respect to sentencing recommendation guidelines. Early in their career, many prosecutors consult their department head on every big case that crosses their desk.[30] Office policies and a department manager's own leadership style determine the degree of supervisory control as well as whether or not the control is exercised through formal or informal mechanisms. The standard operating procedures of a particular office generate behavioral expectations and notions of "appropriate behavior." Both institutional, office, and department norms constrain decision-making. As two different department managers related:

> [Our] system of control is mostly informal. Within my department we all know each other very well ... Everyone knows their job. No one likes to control and no one wants to be controlled. Every case that goes to the LOSTA [for review] must first cross my desk and I can look at it. All of the new cases first come to me ... I also review all the cases that come back from court.[31]

> Every day there are conversations between prosecutors and department managers. The department manager might say, 'My opinion is....' These conversations occur in the spirit of collegiality rather than of supervision.[32]

On a more routine level, department managers may control the decision-making within their departments by reviewing cases to determine whether the facts of a case satisfy the specific legal requirements of a crime. If the prosecutor and the department manager disagree on whether there are sufficient facts to send the case to the court, a department manager may reassign the case to another prosecutor.[33]

[28] Public Prosecutor Interview [13WT], 18 November 2005.

[29] Public Prosecutor Interview [7WK], 5 April 2006.

[30] Public Prosecutor Interview [8AR], 23 May 2006.

[31] Senior Prosecutor Interview [25IFG], 16 April 2008.

[32] Deputy Leading Office Prosecutor [16PP], 11 May 2006.

[33] Deputy Leading Office Prosecutor [16PP], 11 May 2006.

5.6 The Push for Efficiency

Despite the fact that the principle of mandatory prosecution encourages prosecutors to file charges in all cases in which there is sufficient evidence to believe that a crime had been committed, staffing levels at all levels impose workload limits. It stands to reason that in offices with higher per capita caseloads, resource constraints will force prosecutors to dismiss and resolve cases well short of an extensive truth finding process. In states facing tighter resource constraints, prosecutors must not only weigh case facts, but also consider whether or not they have the time and resources to prosecute each case. As Jackson (2004, p. 115) concluded:

> [W]hatever the formal powers granted to prosecutors, the degree to which they become involved in the process of investigating individual cases and making a detailed assessment of the strength of the evidence will depend on the resources available to them and the manner in which their offices are organized.

As financial constraints have become more onerous, the primary focus of managerial oversight of prosecutorial decision-making has shifted. Controls designed to reinforce the norm of objectivity have been pushed aside in favor of efficiency-related metrics that emphasize the efficient processing of cases. Pressured by political parties and other members of state level cabinets, Justice Ministers throughout Germany at the state level have adopted a system of metrics that evaluate the work of judges and prosecutors using economic measures that emphasize efficient case closure rates. This system of metrics, known as the PEBB§Y system, has perhaps had the most instrumental impact on oversight practices-shifting the focus from a quality-based performance evaluation system to efficiency-related metrics. Christoph Frank, the Chairman of the German Judges Association (Frank 2009, p. 99) has written, "[c]ourt practice is continually drifting apart from the Principle of Legality to make decisions based on opportunity and go against the system and endanger the postulate of justice."

The push for efficiency extends from the Ministry level down to department managers where department managers must evaluate their department's performance using metrics typically used by factory managers rather than by judicial officials. The chief means of control are the case processing reports that inform department managers and office leaders how many files a prosecutor has open, how many cases have been closed, as well as how long particular cases have remained open. The statistics help department managers to flag particular cases that may be languishing during the investigation stage. When a particular case has remained open too long, the department manager will inquire why the investigation is taking too long.[34] In addition, if a particular prosecutor's average investigation length lags behind the other prosecutors in that department, the supervisor may speak with the prosecutor and examine a prosecutor's work habits and investigation procedures. The use of metrics such as the average investigation length does not, on its face, undermine prosecutors' ability to find the truth. Moreover, in some cases, the impact

---

[34] Public Prosecutor Interview [7GC], 6 April 2006.

might be a positive one if it encouraged a prosecutor, who might be spending too much time reading the morning paper, to be more productive. Yet, there is a point at which efficiency-based metrics may indeed subtly encourage prosecutors to seek to cut short an investigation and reach an agreement with the defense.

The higher the stack of pending cases that an individual prosecutor has in her in box, the more willing a prosecutor will be to resolve the case with a "confession agreement."[35] Part of the pressure to resolve cases short of a main proceeding is that the structure of the procedures involved themselves. Although a prosecutor in the United States may file a complaint supported by the bare minimum of facts, the formal requirements of German procedure impose more rigid demands on German prosecutors. For example, even the process of drafting the document that prosecutors must file with the court to open a proceeding is more difficult than in the United States. As one prosecutor noted:

> The '*wesentliche Ermittlungen*' (key investigation facts)is complicated and difficult to write. You must use the past tense when you write about the facts that you think are true and then use the perfect tense when you write about why you think the facts are true.[36]

The desire to move cases can lead prosecutors to dismiss or deal cases short of a full investigation. High workload pressures force a particular office's decision-making practices to shift in favor of increased case dismissals. As one senior prosecutor shared with me, "in our office we dismiss cases that would be charged in a smaller city in this same district."[37] The crush of workload pressures may, not only short circuit the truth-finding process, but they may also undercut the ability of the top leadership in the prosecution service to put their own imprint on decision-making practices. As one prosecutor related:

> [I]t is difficult to imagine what parts of the job a General Prosecutor might be able to change. Prosecutors are independent in one sense but they are not independent of the fact that they must handle a certain number of cases. The chief prosecutor has little ability to change anything because the fact that many prosecutors have too many cases to handle is the dominant factor that determines the nature of prosecutor's work practices.[38]

Indeed, one former judge explained to me that when prosecutors, besieged by high case loads, first review a new case, their first decision is to determine whether there are grounds to dismiss the case.[39] The ever-present pressure to clear cases may subtly encourage a prosecutor to dismiss a case rather than to direct the police to investigate the case further. One might imagine that a prosecutor may look at the size of the stack in their in-box when making that decision. On some days, the crush of work will tilt the decision in favor of a dismissal. A simple logic favors dismissals—a dismissed case is unlikely to return to the prosecutor's in-box,

[35] Leading Office Prosecutor Interview [2BN], 16 July 2004.

[36] Public Prosecutor Interview [13WT], 18 November 2005.

[37] General Prosecutor Interview [11OT], 15 July 2004.

[38] Public Prosecutor Interview [12CJ], 29 November 2005.

[39] Justice Ministry Official [9CK], 4 May 2006.

however an investigation order will only temporarily get the file off his desk.[40] It is at this point that the law's indeterminacy and prosecutorial discretion converge. By failing to gather the facts necessary to classify a case as a serious crime, a prosecutor may ensure that he or she has a full range of case dismissal options available. For example, if a serious charge of theft requires that the value of the property stolen equal a certain amount, by failing to seek an appraisal, a prosecutor may ensure that a potential major crime will fall into the minor crime category. Thus, workload pressures weigh against conducting extensive evidence gathering to obtain facts that may weigh either in favor of or against a suspect's guilt. Eyeing productivity guidelines and current office case loads, one deputy office leader told me that, according to the guidelines, prosecutors in his office had to settle routine cases every three minutes to meet the Ministry's objectives.[41]

It is inherently difficult to compare workload pressures across prosecution offices. Although it is easy to compare case loads, simple numerical comparisons do not capture the cases' factual and legal complexity. Although the observation of workload pressures may be inherently subjective, in some offices that I visited, the pressures seemed particularly acute and the level of job stress was very high. In these offices, it was not unusual for prosecutors to work weekends to reduce caseloads. As one senior prosecutor commented:

> It is a system of exploitation of the good guys. This is the main problem that we will have for the next few years but our chief cannot see this. In the last three to four years, we have had three prosecutors quit because of the workload.[42]

One procedural check on a prosecutor's decision to dismiss a case exists. Pursuant to the Code of Criminal Procedure, the victim in a criminal case may challenge a prosecutor's decision to dismiss a case. Once a victim initiates that process, the department manager must review the work conducted in the case and determine whether the investigation was adequate. That decision may also be reviewed by prosecutors in the General Public Prosecutor's Office. According to one senior prosecutor, the efficacy of this review process rests with the department leader's willingness to review the investigation with an open-mind.[43]

Concluding a deal is one way to resolve and perhaps, shortcut, this evidentiary uncertainty. Indeed, the pressure generated by limited resources originally led prosecutors to begin using confession agreements well before courts and legislators had authorized the practice. It is remarkable that judges and prosecutors in a civil law system readily traversed statutory directories and adopted procedural practices

---

40 Senior Paralegal Interview [10ED], 28 June 2006.

41 Deputy Leading Office Prosecutor Interview [16PP], 30 April 2008.

42 Senior Prosecutor Interview [10BJ], 26 June 2006.

43 Senior Prosecutor Interview [7GC], 6 April 2006.

outside the formal boundaries of the law for at least a decade. This development demonstrates how the realities of practice on the ground can readily usurp the formal requirements of the law. At the same time, it is important to note that deal-making may not uniformly undermine the truth-finding process. Finding the truth in the context of a criminal proceeding is often a difficult process. In the face of evidentiary uncertainty, striking a deal may be viewed simultaneously as a step towards objectivity and truth (the defendant is certainly guilty of what they are confessing to) as well as a step away from objectivity and truth (the suspect may be guilty of more).

5.7 The Front Lines of Change

Sensing that increasing caseloads are undermining the prosecution service's collective dedication to the principle of objectivity, many top office prosecutors have reorganized the distribution of routine work. These reform efforts attempt to preserve prosecutors' ability to function as neutral fact-finders by separating routine casework that requires scant reflection from the handling more complex cases that draw on prosecutors' deliberative thought processes, legal knowledge, and investigation skills. Traditionally, the bulk of routine cases are assigned to prosecutors housed in the so-called "general crimes" departments. Prosecutors situated in other departments such as low level economic crimes also often handle case loads that contain a high percentage of routine crime. While this format enables prosecutors in specialized departments to hone the investigation skills necessary to handle their particular criminal caseload, the increasingly onerous caseloads found in general crimes departments have often forced prosecutors to adopt decision-making practices that mirror those used on factory production lines.

In the past decade, prosecution offices have attempted to more equitably distribute low level crimes cases. Those reorganization plans have included:

1. Requiring every prosecutor in the office to devote 1 day/month to working through stacks of general crimes cases.
2. Reducing the size of the general crimes department and requiring prosecutors in specialized units to devote 50 % of their time to general crime cases.
3. Hiring paralegals to handle routine cases
4. Making use of accelerated case disposition practices.

The proliferation of these reform efforts underscores the fact that, at the bureaucracy's top levels, officials remain committed to the principle of mandatory prosecution and concerned about job burnout. However, although these reforms are well-intentioned, there are few effective safeguards in place that ensure that prosecutor has conducted a thorough investigation and viewed the evidence from both sides of the case. As a result, it is difficult to evaluate whether or not these reforms have improved prosecutorial decision-making in non-routine cases. Although officials from the General Public Prosecutor's offices in the past conducted surprise random file reviews in local offices, in the course of my field work, I was unable to locate a single region in which that review process was currently functioning. In fact, in my interviews with prosecutors, the necessity of being productive ran head to head with prosecutors' commitment to objectivity. As one prosecutor who worked in an economic crimes department noted, "in determining who is going to be promoted, it is more important that a person has been productive than that they have done good work."[44]

5.8 Political Interference

Although German law attempts to shield prosecutors from political pressure, from time to time, supervisors seek to interfere with prosecutorial decision-making. This form of control is less frequently exercised, but more insidious, than productivity-based incentives. Here again, the federal legislature has sought to minimize political influence through several legal mandates. Chief among those mandates is the requirement that the top office prosecutor annually draft an office plan that clearly delineates which cases each prosecutor will handle depending on the type of case and the first letter of the defendant's last name. For example, the plan could assign a particular prosecutor all general crimes cases where the suspect's name ends with A–K. This legal directive seeks to prevent the top prosecutor from steering particular cases to specific prosecutors in an attempt to affect case outcomes.

Absent conducting a large scale empirical study, it is impossible to determine how often higher ups attempt to influence prosecutors' decisions in individual cases. Based on my formal and informal interaction with prosecutors during the period of my study, I can say with confidence that, in most states, political pressure is not a routine occurrence. On the other hand, the majority of the more experienced prosecutors with whom I spoke were able to name at least one case in which someone in the chain of command had orally suggested that the prosecutor take the case in a different direction. Some of the prosecutors reported that, in some cases in which they had experienced pressure to handle a case in a certain way, the General Public Prosecutor or the Leading Offfice Prosecutor was trying to quiet public outrage.[45]

A number of prosecutors related to me instances in which they had received "informal" instructions from their superiors. This type of influence occurs more frequently in political and economic crime cases where politicians in the ministries may try to manipulate case outcomes.[46] However, a significant number of prosecutors reported to me that a superior had never issued an instruction on how to handle a case. In addition, one General Public Prosecutor asserted to me that no

[44] Public Prosecutor Interview [12FG], 24 April 2006.

[45] Senior Public Prosecutor Interview [5BC], 26 January 2006.

[46] Senior Public Prosecutor Interview [16PP], 30 April 2008.

Minister would ever attempt to influence the outcome of a case for political reasons.[47] He argued that such an attempt would carry extreme political risk because, if the media discovered that the Minister was attempting to exert such influence, there would be immediate calls for the Minister to resign. A prosecutor's own degree of self-confidence plays a definitive role in determining whether that prosecutor will bend to political pressure. As one senior prosecutor stated:

> Although [law professors] say that we are the most objective civil servants in the world, there is a definite hierarchical influence on decision-making. But I think it is very small. It comes in the form of instructions. However, when the instruction is not right, I can ignore the order. I don't know how the influence works in [the more] political departments. There is little interference in the murder department . . . In all prosecution offices, prosecutors are required to write regular reports for the chain of command detailing the progress that has been made on cases that frequently appear in the media.[48]

Although prosecutors enjoy lifetime employment after a 3 year probationary period, personnel policies do not protect prosecutors from being transferred to a less desirable department if they ignore directives from above. In addition, because all prosecutors who seek a promotion to the level of senior public prosecutor must serve a rotation in the General Public Prosecutor's Office, prosecutors who are eligible for promotion might be more willing to follow the General Public Prosecutor's directives. In states such as Bavaria where government attorneys are transferred between positions in the judiciary, prosecution, and administration every 3 years, an errant decision made during one rotation may affect your future placement. The most famous example of this is the prosecutor who filed charges against the former Chancellor Helmut Kohl, who found himself "promoted" to a position of family court judge in a small German town. Although the original prosecutor filed charges at the major crime level against the former Chancellor, the case ultimately was dismissed under Sect. 153a of the Code of Criminal Procedure. This provision allows the court to dismiss minor cases that are not in the public interest to prosecute. According to German law, the fact that a crime is classified as a major crime (*Verbrechen*) in theory restricts a prosecutor's decision-making latitude preventing the prosecutor from dismissing major crimes. Per German law, the primary opportunity that prosecutors possess to suspend prosecution is limited to cases where non-prosecution is in the public interest or the suspect's guilt is of a minor nature.[49] According to Miller (2001), it is widely acknowledged that the government's failure to prosecute Kohl stretched the boundaries of circumstances under which non-prosecution might be in the public interest.

Nevertheless, prosecutors' institutional identity and status, most notably their fidelity to the principle of mandatory prosecution serves as an important bulwark against political influence. In the course of my participant observation studies, I

[47] General Public Prosecutor Interview [11OT], 15 July 2004.

[48] Senior Public Prosecutor Interview [10FF], 28 June 2006.

[49] §153a StPO.

discovered ample evidence that there are prosecutors who, do in fact, invoke the principle of legality as a shield against political pressure. Many prosecutors shared with me examples of cases where they had invoked the principle of mandatory prosecution to protect themselves from political pressure to dismiss certain cases. In describing one case, a prosecutor explained:

> In the beginning of the investigation, it came to our attention that the former Minister had accepted [campaign] donations. We brought the case to court even though the Ministry was displeased. The original court dismissed the charges. We then filed an appeal and the charges were reinstated.[50]

5.9 Relational Norms

In their daily decision-making, a prosecutor's actions extend beyond the suspect and victims connected to a particular case to a prosecutor's colleagues as well as other institutional players. The desire to preserve friendly relationships and satisfy expectations affects prosecutorial decision-making. Within work groups or departments, a prosecutor's desire to conform to norms of acceptable behavior regulates his or her decision-making. Certainly many norms, such as those that encourage prosecutors to work diligently, support a prosecutor's willingness to investigate and prosecute cases with an objective mindset. In other instances however, a prosecutor's desire to preserve collegiality may constrain a prosecutor's willingness to reopen an investigation initiated by a colleague. This restraint is most visible in cases where one prosecutor supervised the investigation process and a different prosecutor handles the main proceeding. In those cases, the prosecutor who takes the case to court will be extremely reluctant to conduct further investigation in the case or to request that the court dismiss the case. According to one prosecutor that I interviewed, second guessing a colleague in open court may trigger a transfer to another department.[51] In this sense, the scope of actions that an individual prosecutor may take to discover the truth is restricted by a case's procedural stage and the need to preserve institutional cohesion. Decisions made by other prosecutors earlier in the process may create a path dependent logic that subsequent prosecutors are reluctant to change at the expense of damaging collegial relationships. Thus informal norms of acceptable behavior have the power to trump the formal requirements of the law. The two primary types of relational norms facing prosecutors include collegial norms and inter-institutional norms.

[50] Senior Public Prosecutor Interview [10FF], 28 June 2006.

[51] Public Prosecutor Interview [12CJ], 29 November 2005.

5.9.1 Collegial Norms

Despite the prosecution service's hierarchical structure, most often decision-making on the front-lines of practice is shaped by collegial norms rather than than from directives issued from above. These informal conversations between colleagues, which occur on a daily basis, guide prosecutorial decision-making. Through face-to-face and informal group conversations more experienced prosecutors transmit local norms of practice to their less experienced colleagues. Collegial conversations serve as the primary mechanism through which prosecutors learn how to interpret and apply the law. That learning process never ends. To the extent that my research could discern best practices, those practices were reflected in the frequency with which my interviews were interrupted by other prosecutors wanting to discuss the direction they should take in a particular case. It is through these frequent exchanges of knowledge that localized understandings of justice develop. As Hildebrant (2007, p. 64) postulates:

> [A] tradition is a bran-tub of information on how to perceive the world and do things. This information comes to us from past actions, decisions, tests and has to be translated into present actions by those that draw on it. A legal tradition is the bran-tub of information that is mined by those that adhere to it, to decide how to act. While acting they add information, but to motivate new actions this new information will again have to be translated to the new situation. A legal tradition is strong and vulnerable.

In this sense, one outcome of the increased opportunities for discretion may be that prosecutors must rely more and more on their colleagues for advice on how to negotiate the uncertainties in the law. The process of "learning by doing" may be one of the most important institutional factors that reinforces prosecutors' support of institutional norms. In the vast majority of cases, the most influential factor that structures decision-making is not hierarchical directives and instructions, but rather prosecutors' shared understandings of practice and justice.

> You cannot learn what the "*Objectivitätsprinzip*" (principle of objectivity) means in your university studies. You learn it on the job... This develops with practice-the more cases you handle. Most importantly you will have conversations with your colleagues about what the sentence should be-how high or low the punishment ... [One's] knowledge about how much evidence is enough develops over time and through conversations. Sometimes I must put a break on young prosecutors. I had a young colleague who had been with the BKA, the federal police. He worked really quickly with the cases but he was too eager to get arrest warrants and search warrants. You have to learn objectivity by handling many cases.[52]

While the law prescribes broad sentencing ranges for specific crimes, norms of local practice may establish a more specific range. Differences in local case disposition practices explain why cases that may be regularly dismissed in Berlin find a way to court in Bavaria. Local norms of practice develop and are transmitted through consensual decision-making processes that occur on the individual and group level. When a prosecutor approaches a department manager for advice, the

[52] Senior Public Prosecutor Interview [1DR], 15 March 2006.

conversation may not be a top-down transmission. Instead, the manager and the prosecutor may jointly tease out a solution to the question. Regular coffee breaks that occur on a daily basis in prosecution offices throughout Germany play a critical role in building and transmitting consensual norms. In the course of my field research, I regularly joined in these breaks and observed prosecutors exchange opinions of how certain cases should be handled. The breakdown of the coffee groups varies between offices. The groups may break down along lines of experience, departmental affiliation, or personal preferences. The coffee meetings are an important vehicle that promotes organizational cohesion and learning. When the meetings include prosecutors from different departments, the meetings offer a vehicle for dissipating the isolation of new prosecutors located in large bureaucratic organizations. It also is a key horizontal means of communication in an organizational structure which may be managed in a very hierarchical manner. The information shared between colleagues on case-related questions offer a forum for exchanging information on oral practices that are not found in code books. They also transmit organizational expectations of productivity.

The nature of the cases that a particular department handles may also affect the department's cohesion. For example, in drug or state security departments, the use of enhanced investigation practices often creates a special camaraderie among department members and a shared outlook about how cases should be prosecuted. Where a department becomes tight knit, the norms and standards adopted by a particular department may boost department morale, particularly in cases where the department manager protects the decision-making of prosecutors in the department.[53] One prosecutor candidly shared with me that she had been transferred out of the drug crimes department because her supervisor told her that she had the wrong perspective (*Einsichtstellung*) for the drug department.[54] The nature of the caseload that a particular department handles may shape prosecutors' work practices. In drug departments for example, the prosecutors work closely with the police from the initial suspicion that a crime is being or has been committed onwards. Because the police cannot install a wiretap or search property without a warrant, the police must work in tandem with the prosecution office. This tight camaraderie between the police and the prosecutor's office can undercut a prosecutor's willingness to act as a check on police behavior. The initial task of catching a suspect in the act of making a drug deal may also focus the prosecutor's attention on acquiring evidence of guilt in a particular case. Drug prosecutors' symbiotic relationship with the police, in conjunction with a prosecutor's early involvement in the case investigation, may undercut a prosecutor's ability to step back and evaluate the evidence objectively. As a result, a stiffer pro-conviction, tough on crime philosophy often develops in drug prosecution units.

[53] Public Prosecutor Interview [6SB], 23 February 2006.

[54] Public Prosecutor [4BI], 3 April 2006.

Anecdotal evidence supports this proposition. In the course of speaking with a young prosecutor about on-the-job learning, the prosecutor explained to me that, on one particular day, she had been asked to handle a sentencing hearing on drug case in addition to her normal caseload to be handled in court. The prosecutor relied on her own sense of a fair outcome in the case. When the prosecutor returned to the office, a senior prosecutor from the drug department admonished her for proposing a sentence that was too lenient. Although she had relied on her own department's sentencing practices, the drug crimes, department played by a different set of rules. The shared sense of mission within particular departments is not unique to drug departments. A number of prosecutors spoke fondly of the fact that the prosecutors in their department shared a common vision and a special camaraderie. As one prosecutor noted:

> The three of us in the State Security department handle cases the same way. We work together well. Our department manager strictly oversees the cases that are dismissed as well as charging decisions so that we apply the law consistently.[55]

Department managers may implement specific case handling policies with an aim to achieving specific justice-related objectives. For example, one specialized regional economic crimes department adopted a practice in which the prosecutors aimed to hold all suspects in pre-trial detention. Since the bulk of their suspects possessed white collar crime backgrounds, the department manager believed that a few months of confinement would lead a suspect to confess to at least a part of the charged criminal activity.[56] Since judges must approve requests for pre-trial confinement, the department was only able to successfully implement the policy because several judges at the regional court level also possessed punitive attitudes towards white collar criminality and supported the practice. In that instance, one might argue that a common way of viewing white collar crime represented a shared "culture" between the prosecution and the judiciary. At the same time, despite judicial approval of the practice, the policy appears to reflect a more adversarial and less objective approach to the prosecution of those cases.

5.9.2 Institutional Relationships

Prosecutors and judges in Germany are products of the same system of legal education and aspirants for both positions enter the judicial service directly out of law school. After a 3 year rotation between positions, individuals in the state ministries of justice will assign individuals to either a judicial or a prosecutorial position based upon the state's needs. As a result of this common training and their shared mission of implementing the law objectively, prosecutors and judges possess

[55] Prosecutor Interview [12LH], 29 November 2005.

[56] Senior Prosecutor Interview [10BJ], 26 June 2006.

a similar outlook towards the role of law in society. While the common vision of the law shared by prosecutors and judges is a strong factor facilitating inter-institutional cooperation, prosecutors and judges also possess a joint interest in clearing the docket. The structure of the judicial system itself also facilitates cooperation. While prosecutors in the American system are considered to be a party, the role of a German prosecutor has been equated with the role of a second judge. As a result of that role definition, judges and prosecutors may confer prior to the main proceeding outside of the defense attorney's presence. Ex parte communications with the court by the prosecution or the defense are not barred in Germany because the court does not act as a referee between parties. Where the court senses an opportunity to close a case short of a full proceeding, judges may directly contact a defense attorney for example to see if the defendant would be amenable to an agreement or a dismissal with an agreement to pay a fine. Similar to the interactions between the prosecutor and the judge, the primary factor driving inter-institutional cooperation is the court's desire to clear cases.

In many cities, there is a strong norm of cooperation between the prosecution office and the judiciary. Strategic considerations drive this cooperation. Although the institutions are designed to act as a check on each other's decision-making, the shared norms and interests of the players may undermine the efficacy of that accountability mechanism. As a general rule, the extent of cooperation between judges and prosecutors is greater in smaller cities where it is easier to develop trusting relationships. In cities where close, tight–knit relationships exist, there is a potential to resolve cases more quickly because the prosecutor and judge have had the time to develop trust each other's judgment.[57] In some instances, this mutual trust may prompt a prosecutor to discuss a case with the presiding judge prior to the main proceeding and discuss a way to quickly resolve a case. Because the judge and prosecutor know and trust each other, they trust each other's judgment. In some cases, the adjudication process moves along behind closed doors.

What happens to the principle of legality when judges become involved in a case's resolution at an early stage in the criminal justice process? In particular, what impact does the involvement of independent judges have on the truth-finding process when judges take an active role in encouraging "confession agreements?" In those cases where a judge contacts a prosecutor after reading the investigation file and inquires about the prospects for settling a case, it would be naive to expect that the prosecutor will insist on taking the case forward and holding a full main proceeding to discover the truth. In effect, the requirement that the judges participate in the conclusion of confession agreements may actually help to further undermine the principle of legality. In short, where judges, who are motivated to reduce their own caseloads, actively suggest that a "confession agreement" should be in play in a particular case, judicial involvement helps to undermine, rather than support, the principle of legality.

[57] Senior Prosecutor Interview [5BC], 16 January 2006.

Key decisions may take place in the shadows of public courtrooms. In some cases, the judge and prosecutor may "stage" a courtroom conflict in an effort to convince a suspect that the court's position is a reasonable one. One prosecutor explained to me that the prosecutor will often recommend a stiffer sentence than the court is inclined to impose. In cases where the court elects to impose a more lenient sentence that the one recommended by the prosecutor, a defendant is less likely to appeal the court's ruling when the court appears to be more reasonable than the prosecution.[58] To courtroom observers, the judge's decision appears to check the prosecutor's will for justice. Yet, the participants may simply be performing a scripted outcome, in part, to "sell" the appearance of judicial moderation. While I am not suggesting that this practice is widespread, the practice demonstrates that the close working relationship between prosecutors and judges may undermine the judiciary's ability to act as a check on prosecutorial decision-making.

5.10 Conclusion

In an effort to check the power of the central government, the founders of modern Germany assigned the task of prosecution and the administration of justice largely to the *Land* level. By subjecting prosecutorial decision-making to executive control, the federal structure of prosecution practice and the organization of the prosecution function itself ensure that organizational imperatives will influence the delivery of justice at multiple levels Within prosecution offices, the identity of the chief office prosecutor sets the tone for the office and the degree of commitment to more detailed decision-making guidelines (*Richtlinien*) that may exist at the *Land* or regional levels. Although the law is malleable, management may establish more detailed case handling guidelines at the office and department level as well. In the present environment however, the most consistent pressure is not the pressure to handle a case in a certain way, but rather not to let the case sit open for a longer period than the department's norm. To be sure, the relatively flat structure of the service and the protection of lifetime tenure grant prosecutors considerable latitude. The fact that few prosecutors are promoted to senior prosecutor (department manager) drastically eliminates the lure that career incentives may play in shaping decision-making. However, in those states, in which prosecutors do not remain in the prosecution service for the course of their career, the door to more pernicious influence may be open. In theory, the fact that high-level Ministry officials determine the rotation assignments of prosecutors, judges, and lower level Ministry officials in some states threatens prosecutors' decision-making latitude and objectivity. Regardless of whether the federal legislature ever eliminates the practice of issuing instructions, at minimum, the Land-level legislatures in the so-called

[58] Prosecutor Interview [3TW], 8 November 2005.

"rotating" states should revisit their rotation policies to preserve prosecutor's decision-making objectivity.

Legislation

Basic Law of the Federal Republic of Germany

Article 20(3)
Article 102

Code of Criminal Procedure (StPO)

§152
§407-412
§153
§153a

Code of Criminal Law (StGB)

§59(1)
§38(2)

Other Laws

Sect. 142 subs. 1 Constitution of Courts Act

Reports/Statistics

Wetzels, P. & Pfeiffer, C. 1996. *Regionale Unterschiede der Kriminalitätsbelastung in Westdeutschland: Zur Kontroverse um ein Nord-Süd-Gefälle der Kriminalität*. Forschungsberichte Nr. 52Hannover: KFN.

Statistisches Bundesamt: Deutschland, *Rechtspflege: Staatsanwaltchaften* 2004.

Interviews

Appellate Judge Interview [13MU], 10 April 2004
Deputy Leading Office Prosecutor Interview [16PP], 30 April 2008
Deputy Leading Office Prosecutor Interview [16PP], 11 May 2006
General Prosecutor Interview [11OT], 15 July 2004
Justice Ministry Official Interview [9RR], 6 May 2006
Justice Ministry Official Interview [9CK], 4 May 2006
Leading Office Prosecutor Interview [2BN], 16 July 2004
Public Prosecutor Interview [4AJ], 6 February 2006
Public Prosecutor Interview [13WT], 18 November 2005
Public Prosecutor Interview [7WK], 5 April 2006
Public Prosecutor Interview [8AR], 23 May 2006
Public Prosecutor Interview [7GC], 6 April 2006
Public Prosecutor Interview [12CJ], 29 November 2005
Public Prosecutor Interview [12FG], 24 April 2006
Public Prosecutor Interview [6SB], 23 February 2006
Public Prosecutor Interview [4BI], 3 April 2006
Prosecutor Interview [19IC], 14 May 2008
Prosecutor Interview [12LH], 29 November 2005
Prosecutor Interview [3TW], 8 November 2005
Second Leading Office Prosecutor Interview [16PP], 11 May 2006
Senior Paralegal Interview [10ED], 28 June 2006
Senior Prosecutor Interview [13AS], 10 June 2004
Senior Prosecutor Interview [2QM], 6 November 2005
Senior Prosecutor Interview [25ST], 16 April 2008
Senior Prosecutor Interview [25IFG], 16 April 2008
Senior Prosecutor Interview [10BJ], 26 June 2006
Senior Prosecutor Interview [7GC], 6 April 2006
Senior Prosecutor Interview [5BC], 16 January 2006
Senior Public Prosecutor Interview [8HL], 25 May 2006
Senior Public Prosecutor Interview [8AQ], 26 May 2006
Senior Public Prosecutor Interview [5BC], 26 January 2006
Senior Public Prosecutor Interview [16PP], 30 April 2008
Senior Public Prosecutor Interview [10FF], 28 June 2006
Senior Public Prosecutor Interview [1DR], 15 March 2006

References

Books, Articles and Online Publications

Claes, E., & Krolikowski, M. (2010). The limits of legality in the criminal law. In E. Claes, W. Devroe, & B. Kreisbilck (Eds.), *Facing the limits of the law* (pp. 89–107). New York: Springer.

Dubber, M. D. (2005). The promise of German criminal law: A science of crime and punishment. *German Law Journal, 6*, 1049–1071.

Foster, N., & Sule, S. (2010). *German legal system and laws* (4th ed.). New York: Oxford University Press.

Frank, C. (2009). Judicial self-governance: A role model for Germany. In P. Albrecht & S. J. Thomas (Eds.), *Strengthen the judiciary's independence in Europe*. Cambridge: Intersentia.

Frase, R. (2001). *Sentencing in Germany and the United States: Comparing Äpfel with Apples*, Max Planck Institute. Available at http://www.juscrim.mpg.de/verlag/Forschaktuell/Frase-Endausdruck.pdf.

Glanert, S. (2008). Speaking language to law: The case of Europe. *Legal Studies, 28*(2), 161–171.

Hildebrant, M. (2007). European criminal law and criminal identity. *Criminal Law and Philosophy, 1*, 57–78.

Jackson, J. (2004). The effect of legal culture and proof in decisions to prosecute. *Law, Probability, and Risk, 3*, 109–131.

Jehle, J.-M. (2005). *Criminal justice in Germany: Facts and figures* (4th ed.). Berlin: Federal Ministry of Justice.

Miller, R., (2001). Germany's Party Finance Scandal "Ends" With Kohl's Plea Bargain and Too Many Unanswered Questions. *German Law Journal*, (15 March 2001). Available at www.germanlawjournal.com/article.php?id=60

Chapter 6
A Closer Look at Discretion: The Prosecution of Serious Economic Crimes

Everyone in our society thinks it's not so bad-this type of crime.
-Economic Crimes Prosecutor[1]

6.1 Introduction

While the last chapter described how organizational factors shaped the prosecution of major crimes in general terms, in this chapter I explore how nuances in the criminal law, combined with organizational factors, impact decision-making. In focusing on the prosecution of serious economic crimes, I demonstrate how organizational priorities and resource allocations impact prosecution rates. By creating groups of prosecutors with specialized expertise, some states have made a strategic choice to prioritize the prosecution of serious economic crime and corruption. In many of those specialized departments, prosecutors create work routines which reflect a shared approach to practice that, in some cases, is shared by the investigative team itself. Due to the complexity of many economic crimes, prosecutors must find ways to successfully work in joint investigation teams across agency lines. To succeed in this environment, during the investigation process, many prosecutors have had to abandon work practices of the past which reflected prosecutors' strict hierarchical control of the investigation's progress. In the most effective units, prosecutors no longer inscribe a written order in a file and then wait a day for a file to be delivered to law enforcement. Instead these prosecutors must meet with investigators face-to-face, use email, or pick up the phone to steer and coordinate the course of investigation on a daily basis. Despite that coordination, in some cases, these investigations may last several years.

The field of economic crimes and corruption is a particularly interesting one to examine as European integration and the globalization of financial markets have

[1] Senior Prosecutor Interview [8HL], 25 May 2006.

S.M. Boyne, *The German Prosecution Service*, DOI 10.1007/978-3-642-40928-8_6,

created large-scale opportunities for corruption on a global scale. At the same time, up until 1997 when Germany became a signatory to the OECD Convention, German enforcement efforts failed to discourage businesses from greasing the wheels of business at both home and abroad (Goel and Jo 2012, p. 4).

Despite the fact that the German government is now publicly committed to fighting corruption and economic crime, the bulk of these cases are settled outside the public eye. Indeed, it is the legislature's framing of economic crimes itself, in particular the categorization of many economic crimes as misdemeanors, which opens the door to the use of confession bargaining practices in these cases. The complexity of the evidence which prosecutors must collect, the time-intensive nature of the investigation process, and the financial resources at defendants' disposal also act to encourage settlement practices and discourage prosecutors from asking courts to open a main proceeding. While a central premise of the German system of justice is that the law grants prosecutors discretion only with respect to minor crime cases, in the case of economic crimes, some of these so-called "minor" crimes significantly impact the societal order and citizens' respect for the law.

6.2 Economic Crimes: Complexity and Change

In economic crime and corruption cases a key problem that prosecutors face is that the globalization of financial networks has dramatically complicated the investigation of economic crimes. At the same time, many of the criminal laws that define economic offenses such as fraud were drafted and enacted in the late nineteenth century before the advent of global capital markets became inter-connected with sophisticated technology. Furthermore, many prosecution offices, as well as the courts, are using case handling procedures that were designed to handle lighter caseloads and less sophisticated evidence. Consequently, neither institution has been prepared to efficiently investigate and adjudicate these cases.

With globalization, the opportunities for corruption have greatly increased. In Germany, the visibility of the country's corruption problem became apparent when Germany became a signatory to the Organization for Economic Cooperation and Development ("OECD") Convention in 1997. A key factor spurring Germany's fight against corruption is the fact that, as a party to the OECD's Anti-Bribery Convention (1997) and related documents, the government is obligated under international law to strengthen the investigation and prosecution of corrupt practices.[2] Not only are the G-8 countries signatories to the convention, but another 29 countries are as well. A key challenge that Germany faced when it signed on to the convention is that many German firms had grown accustomed to using bribes as

[2] The Convention on Combating Bribery of Foreign Public Officials in International Business Transactions (21 November 1997).

a standard business practice (Kreutzer 2002)—one seen as necessary to succeed in global markets. Moreover, the titans of business typically enjoyed cozy relationships with politicians, up to and including the German Chancellor. According to a March 2012 article in the *New York Times*, the public's tolerance for business as usual is changing.

Although cases involving serious economic crimes may take years to investigate, the actual number of cases under investigation is comparatively small. In the OECD Working Group's Phase 3 Report (March 2011) to Germany reported that government prosecutors were currently pursuing 176 active cases and 43 investigations. In the period between 2003 and 2011, according to the working group, "Germany's enforcement has increased steadily and resulted in a significant number of prosecutions and sanctions imposed in foreign bribery-related cases against individuals" (OECD Phase 3 Report 2011, 5). The actual number of instances of corruption reported to the police has increased precipitously, rising 148 % between 2009 and 2010, from 6,354 to 15,746 cases (BKA 2011, pp. 7–8).

The word "corruption" may entail a wide variety of behaviors, which in some countries, are merely considered the price of doing business. It includes, for example, the following representative examples:

- A case where a company purchasing agent demands bribes in exchange for supply contracts.
- Cases in which pharmaceutical companies pay doctors to prescribe their medications.
- Pay offs made to government officials in exchange for the awarding of government construction and services contracts.
- The supervisory board member of a bankrupt company fails to exercise due diligence and discover that the company had made several sham transactions.

To bring Germany into compliance with the OECD, practices which were once a common feature of the business landscape, have gradually become illegal. For example, prior to the late 1990s, the law permitted German companies to treat bribes paid to foreign officials as tax deductable (Dougherty 2007). That is no longer the case.

Although the crimes typically handled by an economic crimes department handle may run the gamut from fraud, tax-evasion, to illegal check-writing, the key corruption-related provisions were not enacted until the Anti-Corruption Act of 1997 (*Gesetz zur Bekämpfung der Korruption*).[3] The primary sections of the German criminal code, which focus on charges involving corruption and bribery, are listed below (Table 6.1):

The criminal code treats corruption in the public sector under separate code sections than corrupt practices in the commercial arena. A public official "who

[3] *Gesetz zur Bekämpfung der Korruption* [KorrBekG] [Anti-Corruption Act], STRAFGESETZBUCH [STGB] [PENAL CODE], August 19, 1997, BUNDESGESETZBLATT [BGBL.] I §§ 331–35 (Ger.).

Table 6.1 German code sections: bribery and corruption

Code section	Language
§ 108b, § 108e StGB	Bribery of voters/members of parliament
§ 299 StGB	Taking and giving bribes in commercial transactions
§ 300 StGB	"Especially Serious" (aggravated) taking and giving bribes in commercial transactions
§ 331 StGB	Taking a benefit/bribe
§ 332 StGB	Taking bribes as an incentive to violating one's official duties
§ 333 StGB	Granting an undue advantage/bribe
§ 334 StGB	Giving bribes as an incentive to the recipient's violating his official duties
§ 335 StGB	"Serious" corruption (aggravated cases)

demands, allows himself to be promised or accepts a benefit for himself or for a third person in return for the fact that he performed or will in the future perform an official act" will face a penalty not exceeding 3 years or a fine.[4] If the offense rises to the "serious" level, the potential sentence runs from 6 months to 5 years.[5] In "especially serious" cases, the potential term of imprisonment ranges from 1 to 10 years.[6]

Despite the new Act, the state of the German law in this subfield is not without problems. For example, although the problem of influence-peddling in the halls of elected legislatures is a global problem, Germany's law prohibiting bribery of a member of parliament is so narrowly defined that it is effectively impossible to prosecute. The law requires that the state show that the "gift" can be linked to a specific vote or election behavior.[7]

Another problem with the code sections is that the categories between a "normal" violation, a serious violation, and an "especially serious" violation appear to be quite fluid. For example, according to Section 335(2) StGB, the law defines "especially serious" cases as in which: (1) the offense relates to a major benefit; (2) there have been ongoing payments or (3) "the perpetrator acts on a commercial basis or as a member of a gang whose purpose is the continued commission of such offences." Depending on the facts introduced in court, the payments involved may or may not have been ongoing or the collection of individuals involved may have acted with another purpose in mind.

With respect to commercial transactions, the regulations define the concept of a "benefit" quite broadly and includes modest gifts, hospitality, donations to charity, and even business contracts "which benefit the recipient materially or immaterially and to which the recipient has no legal claim (Interior Ministry 2011, p. 9)." Pursuant to Section 299 StGB, the maximum penalty is 3 years imprisonment or

[4] §332(1) StGB.

[5] § 332(1)–(2)StGB.

[6] § 335(1)(a).

[7] §108e StGB.

a fine.[8] As I will discuss below in Sect. 6.8, where the minimum sentence falls below 1 year of imprisonment, prosecutors may dismiss the case using Section 153 (a) StPO sparing the defendant the possibility of serving a prison sentence. This latitude gives prosecutors substantial discretion in the disposition of economic crime cases.

6.3 The Organization of Prosecution as Politics

Given that prosecution offices possess limited resources, at the management level, senior officials must decide what crimes prosecutors will target. In this sense, the very process of distributing organizational resources can be construed as a political decision. For example, in Chap. 8, I will show how increased media attention concerning violent juvenile offenders led some prosecution offices to create specialized repeat offender units. In the eastern states in particular, rates of right-wing extremist related crime has led some prosecution offices to establish special units designed to counter that form of criminality. In addition to creating departments with a specific focus, Ministries of Justice on the state or *Land* level frequently create special regional offices with particular competencies to coordinate prosecutions among several prosecution offices (*Schwerpunktsstaatsanwaltschaften*).

For example, there are specialized regional departments dedicated to the prosecution of organized crime in Celle in the state of Niedersachsen, Gera in the state of Thüringia, and Frankfurt am Oder in Brandenburg. Specialized prosecution competencies can dramatically increase law enforcement effectiveness. As one example, in the area of organized crime, in 2004 German police conducted 620 investigations of organized crime-related offenses involving 11,380 suspects (*Bundeskriminalamt* 2005, 10). Of the 620 organized crime investigations conducted in 2004, 72.3 % of the case investigations were conducted by specialized prosecution units that focus on organized crime or by prosecutors in charge of specialized offices (2005, 12). This pattern of success has led the media and victim rights groups to call for the creation of specialized units with other types of crime as well.

The creation of specialized units can increase prosecutorial effectiveness in complex crime cases where interagency cooperation is necessary to successfully investigate and prosecute crime. Ironically, in the area of corruption, where Germany faces an ongoing challenge (Amies 2004a; Von Hawranek 2006; Parkin 2007; Thomas Sims 2007) state and local prosecution offices have been reluctant to create specialized prosecution units. One reason for this reluctance is that many prosecution offices have, to date, created so many specialized departments that prosecutors in "general crimes" departments are overburdened and the prosecution of so-called "normal" crimes has suffered.[9]

[8] §299 StGB.

[9] Land Level Ministry of Justice Official [9RR], 30 June 2006.

As far back as 2001, the nonprofit organization, Transparency International (Wiehen 2001), strongly advocated that the *Land*-level Ministers of Justice create specialized departments to prosecute corruption and serious economic crime:

> The so-called "*Schwerpunktstaatsanwaltschaften*" [specialized units of prosecutors who handle corruption and economic crime cases] have proved their value; but at this time [2001] there are only 7 of them in existence (Munich, Frankfurt, Wuppertal, Neuruppin, Hamburg, Hannover, and Kiel), and it appears that even they are not nearly adequately provided with staff and other financial and technical resources. Generally, more prosecutors, with specialized knowledge and experience about economic crime, and better (dedicated) police support are called for. A number of municipalities have established task forces and control groups against corruption, but recent experience in Frankfurt and Munich shows again, that inadequate staff resources easily render such units ineffective.

Because each state is responsible for funding and administering the state level criminal justice systems, the priority which states assign to funding and staffing corruption units varies. A 2010 report by Transparency International-Germany, which examined Germany's compliance with OECD implementation, criticized the fact that the resource levels among prosecution offices varied widely. The report singled out the Munich prosecutor's office as being significantly better equipped to prosecute corruption cases. In speaking of the changes to the Munich office, Dr. Hansjörg Eishorst of Transparency International stated to *Amies* (2004b):

> We now have more tools to investigate corruption and more people to carry out investigations. On one particular day in the Munich investigation, there were 100 people working on the case. A few years back, there weren't even 100 investigators in Germany.

It is also clear that the creation of those units positively impacts the prosecution of economic crimes. Between 1994 and September 2002, Munich's Anti-Corruption department secured a conviction in over 50 % of the cases they investigated (OECD 2004). Furthermore, the total number of convictions during that period totaled 683 cases with only two acquittals (2004, 32). Where a specialized department enjoys the benefit of strong leadership, the department may achieve a strong conviction record, rather than a legacy of dismissals and soft deals.

Where regional districts have failed to create specialized units or to adequately staff such units once they have been created, prosecutors often cannot adequately investigate cases. As a result, prosecutors may lack sufficient evidence to argue in favor of higher sanctions, there may not be enough evidence to file the case with the court, and, in some cases, prosecutors may not even initiate an investigation although the requisite level of initial suspicion exists. Because prosecutors possess insufficient resources to investigate cases involving corruption and white-collar crime, it may also cause investigation delays leading to milder punishments. The problem is so severe that, in a 2005 opinion, Germany's Federal Court of Justice criticized the government for devoting insufficient resources to the prosecution of economic crimes cases. In the case at issue, the Court held that the defendant's punishment had to be lowered because the case investigation had taken too much time.[10] The Court went on to state that it felt compelled to comment that, too often in complex economic crimes and corruption cases, courts cannot satisfactorily punish the defendant because the state lacked resources sufficient to conduct an adequate investigation.[11] Pursuant to Germany's obligation under the European Convention on Human Rights,[12] German courts must consider the period during which a suspect is under investigation as a burden on the defendant that courts must weigh during sentencing process.

A 2007 article in *The Economist* highlighted the work of Frankfurt's corruption department, and its department head at the time, senior prosecutor Wolfgang Schaupensteiner:

> The overworked Frankfurt attorney, who calls himself the 'truffle pig' because he unearths crimes but then has few resources to process them, is handling a string of prominent cases... But he knows of far more cases than he is able to pursue. He is aware, for example, of an international web of dummy companies used for tax evasion, but going after it would spread his team too thin. And when he does catch criminals, the result is often a plea-bargain and a reduced sentence, to save time. 'Not much of a deterrent,' says Mr. von Blomberg [a representative from the non-profit organization Transparency International] 'That's reality,' snorts the truffle pig (Economist 2006).

According to a 2006 report released by the non-profit organization Transparency International, in six states (*Länder*) the responsibility for corruption cases is still assigned to prosecutors located at the regional court level (Löhe 2006). These states have yet to create centralized prosecution corruption units despite the fact that the units that have been created have made remarkable advances (Löhe 2006). In the state of Lower Saxony (*Niedersachen*) for example, prior to the creation of a centralized corruption unit in 1995, prosecutors pursued only 50 cases of corruption. By 1999, that number had climbed to 189 cases. While overworked corruption departments located at the regional level in Frankfurt and Munich have spearheaded some high-profile prosecutions, according to Transparency International, the Ministries of Justice in the states of Hessen and Bavaria have so far failed to establish centralized, well-staffed corruption units at the state or Land level. The Ministries have argued that corruption cases are best handled at the regional level and that current caseloads do not warrant the dedication of additional resources. In some respects, however, this argument is a circular one.

Until states dedicate sufficient resources to fight corruption, prosecutors must, in essence, ration their resources and target only the most egregious or winnable cases. In fact, the Organization for Economic Cooperation and Development's (OECD)

---

[10] BGH 5 StR 268/05 (2 Dezember 2005) (LG Köln).

[11] Id. at 20. The original German language in the decision reads: In diesem Zusammenhang sieht der Senat Anlass zu folgender Anmerkung. Nach der Erfahrung des Senats kommt es bei einer Vielzahl von großen Wirtschaftsstrafverfahren dazu, dass eine dem Unrechtsgehalt schwerwiegender Korruptions- und Steuerhinterziehungsdelikte adäqute Bestrafung allein deswegen nicht erfolgen kann, weil für diegebotenen Aufklärung derart komplexer Sachverhalte keine ausreichenden justiziellen Resourcen zur Verfügung stehen.

[12] Art. 6 (1) European Convention on Human Rights.

2004 report, which evaluated Germany's compliance with the Anti-Bribery Convention, highlighted the resource deficiencies that German prosecutors face:

> One specialized-unit chief prosecutor noted that severe resource problems limit the activity of the unit to managing its existing case loads, which include cases of domestic bribery. He stated that the unit operates with insufficient human resources, and although there have been a small number of staff supports from the Land ministry of justice; it remains insufficiently staffed to undertake further investigation and trial responsibilities. He cited an example where he and two other staff members alone handle a case involving approximately 100 companies and 250 suspects.

The debate concerning the resources devoted to the fight against corruption cannot be divorced from the larger resource crisis facing German prosecutors. Unless governments at the state level increase the total number of prosecutors, the decision to create special centralized corruption units will necessarily trigger zero-sum staffing consequences at the inter-department levels. In an era of fixed budgets, the act of adding prosecutors to certain departments will by necessity increase workload pressures and, most probably, dismissal rates in other departments. In recent times, the budgets of the Ministries of Justice within German states have been treated as distant step-cousins. Ironically, because law enforcement budgets are part of the more politically prominent Ministries of the Interior, those budgets in many states have grown, while the judicial and prosecution functions lag behind. The disparity between the growth of the judicial and investigative budgets creates a backlog of investigative cases that prosecutors and courts lack the resources to effectively handle. Nor has the problem of workload pressures and resources been distributed equally across all prosecution offices, as some of the *Länder* are in a stronger financial position.

Unfortunately, it is inherently difficult to compare workload pressures across prosecution offices. Numerous problems develop when one attempts to use statistical data to assess the comparative intensity of workload pressures. While the observation of workload pressures may be inherently subjective, at the same time, in some offices that I visited, the pressures seemed particularly acute and the level of job stress noticeably high. As one senior prosecutor commiserated:

> They are losing 20% of the new hires who are going to law firms. Prosecutors who begin their careers now must work harder for less money ... When someone leaves; it takes at least six months to fill the position. The General Public Prosecutor will advertise an opening. They will receive ten to twelve applications for the position from persons with excellent exam results. The General Public Prosecutor will only interview only one person and will accept him ... Then it takes another six to seven months to hire them. They will take advantage of the time lag to save money in the Ministry of Justice.[13]

[13] Senior Prosecutor Interview [10BJ], 26 June 2006.

6.4 Loopholes in the Law

Germany's commitment to strengthening enforcement of economic crimes in general and corruption, in particular, has sharply increased during the past decade. Some of these changes have occurred in response to the ongoing site visits by the members of the OECD working group. For example, in response to criticism from members of the OECD working group that visited Germany in 2003, Germany undertook a concerted effort to strengthen reporting requirements of the tax authorities regarding acts of suspected bribery. As the result of that effort, reports of suspected incidents of bribery by tax and revenue authorities increased (2011, 53). In other areas of the law however, the OECD Working Group has not been so sanguine about German efforts.

Most critically, in their 2011 (OECD 70) report, the Working Group stated that "the level of sanctions applied to both legal and natural persons may not always be fully effective, proportionate and dissuasive, and a limited number of legal persons have so far been held liable and sanctioned in cases of foreign bribery in Germany." There are a number of weaknesses in German law. To begin, a key weakness exists with the legislature's definition of bribery-related cases involving legal persons rather than individuals. Because of that definition and classification, in these cases, the principle of mandatory prosecution does not apply (OECD 2011, 41). As a result, German prosecutors are not required under the criminal law to investigate "suspicious facts indicating a potential criminal offence and, if applicable, initiate an investigation in order to decide whether public charges are to be filed (41)." When a bribery case involves a legal person, the Administrative Offenses Act (*Ordnungswidrigkeitengesetz*), applies rather than the criminal law. Under German administrative law, when a corporation is fined, it cannot be forced to also forfeiture proceeds.

6.5 Specialized Expertise and Routines of Practice

Throughout Germany, the bulk of serious economic crimes cases are handled by economic crimes departments. According to the Constitution of Courts Act, all bribery and corruption cases, which require that a prosecutor possess specialized expertise in economics, should be assigned to specially-constituted departments and prosecuted in complex economic crimes courts (*Wirtschaftsstrafkammern bei den Landgerichten*).[14] To date however, German state, has created specialized departments and courts in every region within its boundaries. As one example, in the German state of Baden-Württemberg, there are specialized units in only two of the state's 17 district courts—at Mannheim and Stuttgart. According to one senior prosecutor, each of those departments contains 20–25 economic crimes prosecutors Hornung (2010, p. 46). Although every local prosecution office has its own

---

[14] Constitution of Courts Act, §74c .par. 1 n 5 and 6.

prosecutors who prosecute economic crime cases, where specialized units exist, local offices may elect to send the most complex cases to the specialized offices. According to Hornung (2010, p. 46), a senior economic crimes prosecutor in Freiburg, Germany, their unit sends 2–3 cases per year to Mannheim, while the Freiburg office handles small and medium level corruption cases involving bribes of approximately 100,00–150,000 €.

The increasing specialized nature of these departments as well as the nature of complex economic crimes cases themselves has raised the bar in terms of prosecutors' requisite work skills. While in smaller prosecution offices, economic and corruption-related cases may be handled by a single department, in larger offices these cases are typically split between several separate departments. For example, in one office that I visited, the specialized economic crimes department consisted of 13 prosecutors—two of whom ranked at the department manager level. The department only handled large cases in which the damages ran into the millions of euros. As a result, these particular department managers often seek prosecutors who possess specialized skills to fill department openings. The interview excerpts below indicate the range of skills needed to succeed in these departments.

> [To qualify to work in this department] you must have a special competence in tax law or the ability to read balance sheets... It is not everyone's cup of tea to work on these cases as when you go home at the end of the day, all your work is not done. You do not feel that quick feeling of accomplishment here that you feel in the general crimes department. A single case in this department may take two to three years to close. One can say that the psychological pressure in this department is higher than in other department. [In fact] sometimes people come to this department and after three weeks they want to go back to the general crimes department... You must fit into the team [here] and be able to sit down with your colleagues and discuss ideas ... When we have an opening in the department we look for a level-headed person who will fit into the team.[15]

> In our office, [the department leaders] cannot choose which prosecutors they would like to have in their department. If there is an opening in your department and you know that a person in another department is applying for a promotion, you can call them up and tell them to apply for the opening but, usually, you have little choice ...[And] because you cannot change a person's personality, you have to accept it. For example, you can have a person who is an excellent jurist and examines cases in detail. They can solve complicated legal problems and will file every possible charge in a case but their thoroughness will take more time. In contrast, you may have a prosecutor who has more of a 'rough cut.' They will handle a case quickly and conduct good suspect interviews. I have a person like that now. He always is able to get a confession when he goes with the police to interview suspects.[16]

> On the job, you need to understand files. The most important job skill is not identifying the legal issues, but rather how to reconcile conflicting testimony. How to determine what is the truth and what is a lie. The biggest mistakes that prosecutors make are the practical decisions about the facts of a case. And it is these decisions that prosecutors typically make alone. Because economic crimes cases often take a year or two to investigate and are very complicated, a prosecutor should have five years of experience before joining this

[15] Senior Prosecutor Interview [1ZU], 15 March 2006.

[16] Senior Prosecutor Interview [8HL], 25 May 2006.

department. In addition, one must possess a lot of patience to assemble the evidence in these cases.[17]

6.6 Initiating an Investigation (*Anfangsverdacht*)

In a typical corruption case, the first inkling that prosecutors may receive that a business executive has paid a bribe is often flagged by the tax authorities. For instance, an initial business audit may reveal a pattern of unusual payments such as unexplained payments for services. At this stage of suspicion, the tax authorities may widen their investigation examining a firm's banking records. Alternatively, a whistle-blower might walk into a prosecutor's office or the police department, bringing with them copy of an invoice or other evidence that services are being provided on a *quid pro quo* basis. The goal of the investigation will be to collect enough information to substantiate the initial suspicion and to meet the evidentiary burden necessary to open a main proceeding. Pursuant to the principle of legality, prosecutors may not open an official investigation until this standard is satisfied.[18] Nor can prosecutors commence investigations on the basis of unsubstantiated second-hand rumors of illegal payoffs. They may, however, pursue claims of bribery allegations published initially in the media (Hornung 2010, p. 47).

Although I found some prosecutors in major crimes departments who investigated economic crime cases on their own, in the larger departments in particular, prosecutors work closely with an investigative team. In the majority of cases prosecuted in Germany, the case will start with a police investigation, and after a certain amount of investigation has been completed, the case will be sent to the prosecution office. In economic crime and corruption cases, the nature of the cases themselves, requires that prosecutors, members of law enforcement, and other agencies work together from the start. In most cases, the prosecutors work hand in hand with members of the local law enforcement. In the larger cities, the law enforcement members of this team have completed specialized training in financial investigations. By necessity, these investigations require individuals with knowledge of accounting, financial balance sheets, and electronic banking. In contrast to the United States, the German equivalent of the FBI, the BKA (*Bundeskriminalamt*) plays only a very minor coordinating function in fighting high-level corruption (Hornung 2010, p. 46). The bulk of the law enforcement expertise with respect to economic crimes and corruption cases is found at the regional levels. For example, according to Hornung (2010, p. 46), in the German state of Baden-Württemberg , the Regional Criminal Investigation Departments (RCID) each have two specialized divisions-one of which normally deals almost exclusively with corruption cases.

---

[17] Senior Prosecutor Interview [5BC], 16 January 2006.

[18] Sect. 160 (1) StPO states: "As soon as the public prosecution office obtains knowledge of a suspected criminal offense either through a criminal information or by other means, it shall investigate the facts to decide whether public charges are to be preferred."

In an attempt to understand the level of investigative support and expertise that is required to investigate economic crimes and corruption cases, I interviewed a police officer who specialized in the investigation of financial crimes. He related to me that he had received a full year of specialized training in economic crimes that included rotations through various departments.[19] At the time, he had spent 7 years, out of his total career of 8 years in this department. His experience level is not atypical in that department as he told me that his colleagues each possess between 6 and 10 years experience.[20]

Depending on the facts of the case, an investigation team may also include individuals from other government agencies such as the tax (*Finanzamt*) and labor administrations. Indeed, one case investigation meeting, which I observed, was held at the regional offices of the *Finanzamt*. Depending on the organization of a particular prosecution office, prosecutors may also delegate cases involving less than 100,000 euros to paralegals (*Amtsanwälte*). The ranks of the paralegals as well as the tax officials typically include graduates of technical schools who have completed specialized continuing education classes.[21]

In a standard investigation involving corruption charges, the initial information may then lead prosecutors to then examine the tax records and bills for a circle of individuals surrounding the primary suspect who may be connected through financial transactions. Given that prosecutors must be adept at sifting through financial and accounting reports, it is easy to understand how quickly a prosecutor in a general crimes department might be stymied in when she is first faced with building a serious economic crime case. If prosecutors can meet the initial suspicion standard at this point in the process, they will typically seek the court's permission to obtain search warrants on the homes and businesses of the primary suspects. The specialized prosecution departments, which I observed, do not rely on the archaic practice of writing instructions to the police within the file and then sending the file back to the police to direct the police at each successive stage of the investigation. Indeed, the tax official with whom I spoke, told me that he talked with the senior prosecutor in charge of the department two to three times a day to coordinate game plans.[22] He elaborated further:

> It is easier [however] to work with each other face-to-face. Because the complexity of the work, we cannot do all the communication by phone. We need to review paper [evidence] in person. . . . Every day we have a to-do list for the investigation . . . We also communicate by email.[23]

During the meeting that I observed, members of the team showed me a large flow chart detailing the flow of illicit funds in an ongoing investigation. Using a specialized software program, both the investigators and prosecutors could log in and

---

[19] Police Officer [26AE], 27 January 2006.

[20] Police Officer [26AE], 27 January 2006.

[21] Tax Administration Official [26AD], 25 January 2006.

[22] Tax Administration Official [26AD], 25 January 2006.

[23] Tax Administration Official [26AD], 25 January 2006.

catalog evidence into the program so that each member of the team was up-to-date on the latest developments in the case.

While prosecutors normally possess wide latitude in choosing investigation tactics, according to German law, in economic crime and corruption cases, up until 2008, the law did not allow prosecutors to use wire intercepts in the investigation of economic crimes. Indeed, until the 2008 revision, law enforcement could only intercept and record communications in investigations involving for a limited range of offenses including: murder, manslaughter, genocide, extortion, robbery, drug offenses, bribery of a public official and money laundering.[24] Pursuant to the 2008 revision, law enforcement is now permitted to use wiretap technologies in the investigation of corruption and bribery cases provided that they have obtained a warrant from a judge.[25]

Individual prosecution offices may employ their own preferred methods of pursuing investigations. For example, one prosecutor told me that her unit attempts to use the element of surprise by simultaneously searching the homes and offices of multiple suspects. In investigations run by this unit, a prosecutor will accompany each and every search team and attempt to take statements from the defendants at the time of the search. However, while the element of surprise may help prosecutors secure "admissions" at the time of the search, prosecutors must also be careful to use only those investigation measures that are proportionate and necessary under German law.[26]

Because corruption and serious economic crimes cases demand considerable resources as well as time, typically a prosecutor cannot handle a caseload of more than 15–20 cases. Moreover, prosecutors face procedural hurdles in prosecuting economic crimes cases. A key hurdle is simply finding the time and expertise to collate the data collected in a serious economic crimes case. The data in a single case may run to 10,000 pages.[27] Although specialized software programs, which help prosecutors and financial specialists, organize case data, exist, the price of these software programs is often beyond the reach of an office budget.[28]

It is easy to underestimate the complexity and scope of these cases. In the one case related to me by a tax department official, the investigation commenced in 1997 when the department received an initial piece of information regarding the defendant. It was not until 2002, that the tax authority had collected sufficient information to permit the prosecutor's office to form an investigation team-including four tax officials and four police officers. During the investigation's first phase, the team executed over thirty search warrants and placed five individuals in pre-trial detention. In order to track down the whereabouts of the suspects, the team asked four additional prosecution offices for assistance in the investigation. The scope of

---

[24] §100(c) (3) StPO. The new provision may be found at §100(a)(2)(1)(t) StPO.

[25] Law on the Revision of Telecommunications Monitoring and other Covert Investigation Measures and implementing Directive 2006/24/EC113 of 21 December 2007.

[26] Senior Prosecutor Interview [1ZU], 25 May 2006.

[27] Senior Prosecutor Interview [5BC], 16 January 2006.

[28] Senior Prosecutor Interview [6FE], 21 July 2006.

the case eventually required the team to use the services of ten different tax fraud investigation offices. The group continued investigating until 2005 when the court determined that they had gathered sufficient evidence open the main proceeding. By that time, the total losses well exceeded 3 million euros with another 5–6 million euros in collateral damages.[29]

The complexity of that investigation points to another important issue in the German criminal justice system, namely the nature of the working relationship between the police and the prosecution offices. Traditionally, the law has treated prosecutors as the chief of the investigation process. As police departments have begun to develop specialized competencies during a period in which prosecutors relative workloads have steadily increased, the nature of the relationship has become more symbiotic. This is especially true with respect to legally complex crimes as well as drug cases which require that a prosecutor's involvement in the early stage of an investigation where prosecutors assist officers in obtaining search warrants. A key inquiry is how relational factors between the parties affect the investigation. It is worthwhile to look at how that interaction works in the context of a specific investigation. In one case meeting that I witnessed, the case meeting involved an allegation of illegal dumping of construction material. The local newspaper had reported the dumping on the previous day. The meeting began with several police officers telling the prosecutor that they had interviewed one witness, but the witness professed to know nothing. The prosecutor listened patiently and finally instructed the police to reinterrogate the witness and specifically ask him: Who in the company had done the packing? Who had done the selling? Why was there no longer any contaminated material on the premises?[30] The prosecutor continued the discussion by reminding the officers of the specific type of evidence that the team would need to bring before the court. While the case itself was not factually complex, everyone in the room knew that the owner of the facility was politically connected to the Land level government. At first glance, one might be tempted to conclude that the interaction in this case had proceeded along stereotypical lines with the prosecutor "educating" the police about the evidence needed to secure a conviction. However, faced with the case's potential political implications, one must be careful to attribute the officers' floundering to a lack of legal training. In fact, after the meeting, the prosecutor in charge of the case related to me that, in working with the police, "it is easier if I make the decisions, it takes the political pressure off of them."[31]

In addition to resource constraints, economic crimes' prosecutors must also overcome the problems inherent in working with foreign officials. While money and people may easily traverse national boundaries within Europe, procedural rules in other countries make it difficult and time-consuming for prosecutors to obtain documentary evidence located abroad. To accomplish this task, prosecutors must

[29] Tax Administration Official [26AD], 25 January 2006.

[30] Case Meeting Observation, 26 January 2006.

[31] Senior Prosecutor Interview [5BC], 16 January 2006.

often work through diplomatic, rather than law enforcement, channels. Those procedures take time and lengthen an already difficult investigation process. In addition, there may be dozens of potential defendants and shell corporations involved in any case involving an extensive web of cross-border financial transactions. To avoid facing off against dozens of defense attorneys in a single case, prosecutors are often forced to limit the number of individuals they pursue criminally.[32]

6.7 Pretrial Detention of Suspects

The use of pre-trial detention to hold suspects prior to trial is a key strategy employed by economic crimes' prosecutors. On a regular basis, prosecutors will attempt to hold a suspect in a white collar crime case in pre-trial detention to prevent the suspect from destroying evidence or talking to potential witnesses.[33] According to statute however, courts may only order a suspect's arrest if the accused is "strongly suspected of the offense," there is a ground to support the arrest, and the arrest is not "disproportionate to the case's significance."[34] Despite the fact that a suspect's pre-trial detention may facilitate the completion of the case investigation, higher level courts vigilantly monitor detention decisions. Not only must courts approve the initial detention decision, but the higher regional court (*Oberlandesgericht*) will conduct a mandatory review of detention decisions at the 6 month mark.

According to the Criminal Procedure Code, an individual may not be held in pre-trial detention longer than 6 months unless the complexity of the investigation or another important reason justifies the suspect's continued detention.[35] At this point, unless prosecutors demonstrate that they are continuing to make progress on the investigation, the court will release the defendant. Courts may not order pre-trial detention when the detention is considered to be disproportionate to the severity of the offense and the likely punishment.[36] Many of the economic crimes prosecutors

[32] Senior Prosecutor Interview [1ZU], 25 May 2006.

[33] Senior Prosecutor Interview [8AQ], 22 May 2006; Senior Prosecutor Interview [8HL], 24 May 2006.

[34] Sect. 112 StGB. According to Sect. 112 (2):

> A ground for arrest shall exist if on the basis of certain facts: 1. it is established that the accused is fled or hiding; 2) considering the circumstances of the individual case, there is a risk that the accused will evade the criminal proceedings (risk of flight); or 3. the accused's conduct gives rise to the strong suspicion that he will a) destroy, alter, remove, suppress, or falsify evidence, b) improperly influence coaccused, witnesses, or experts, or c) cause others to do so, and if, therefore the danger exists that establishment of the truth will be made more difficult (risk of tampering with evidence).

[35] Sect. 121 (1) StGB.

[36] Sect. 122 (1) 2 StGB.

with whom I spoke stated that this standard is a difficult one to meet.[37] Faced with these restrictions, prosecutors must carefully pursue only those cases that warrant an investment of investigative resources. Since prosecutors must direct the case investigation process on an ongoing basis and stay on top of the progress of the investigation, they can only realistically pursue a limited number of cases. Moreover, because the likely sanction will continue to decrease as the investigation continues to run its course, prosecutors have an incentive to investigate only those cases that they can investigate and prosecute within a tight time frame.

6.8 Filing Charges

Within the ambit of corrupt business practices, the sparsely worded German criminal code does not always precisely define what actions violate the law. Where the federal legislature has been unwilling or unable to modernize the law, prosecutors have used the law's ambiguity to their advantage to target corrupt business practices. For example, in several cases, prominent German businessmen have been charged with violations of offenses such as "breach of trust" (*Untreue*) which have traditionally been used to prosecute small-time embezzlers.[38] However, prosecutors face hurdles here as well. A frequent charge at issue in economic crimes cases is the charge of "breach of trust" contrary to Section 266 StGB. In order to violate the breach of trust provision, an individual must act intentionally. Several prosecutors stated that it is difficult to convict a suspect on these charges because the state must show that the suspect was aware of his or her fiduciary duties, that he or she breached those duties, and that they knew that the actions would financially disadvantage a firm.[39]

The evidentiary difficulties surrounding the element of intent demonstrate that the decision to prosecute breach of trust violations is not necessarily a straightforward one. Moreover, the skilled defense attorneys that white-collar criminals are often able to hire have proven to be adept at exploiting legal ambiguities. For example, to cast doubts on the issue of intent, individuals charged with breach of trust may claim that they relied on the advice of their consultants in making the

[37] *See, e.g.*, Group Leader Prosecutor Interview [8FN], 26 May 2006; Group Leader Prosecutor Interview [8DE], 26 May 2006.

[38] According to Section 266, the offense of "Breach of Trust" trust is defined as:

> Whoever abuses the power accorded him by statute, by commission of a public authority or legal transaction to dispose of assets of another or to obligate another, or violates the duty to safeguard the property interests of another incumbent upon him by reason of statute, commission of a public authority, legal transaction or fiduciary relationship, and thereby causes detriment to the person, whose property interest he was responsible for, shall be punished with imprisonment for not more than five years or a fine.

[39] Group Leader Prosecutor Interview [8FN], 26 May 2006.

decision at issue. Given that resources are limited, prosecutors shy away from filing charges when obtaining a conviction appears uncertain.

> [In this climate] we will only file charges if we are convinced that the court will find the suspect guilty without reasonable doubt. If there is doubt and the actions could have transpired in a different way, we will not file charges. We must be able to collect enough evidence to [sway] the judge. In these cases, sometimes the source of the information we have collected turns out to be a suspect's business competitor. In these cases we will drop the case during the investigation stage. . If we cannot trust the witness more than the suspect, we will not file charges. In other cases, we cannot file charges because documents have been destroyed.[40]

> I have worked in several other departments in this office. In other departments there is more pressure to clear cases quickly. When you receive many new cases each day you do not have a long time to think about the legal issues in a case, to consult the legal commentaries and deliberate about whether the facts constitute a fraud or a breach of fiduciary duty. There is a tendency with some prosecutors to dispose of cases involving fraud with a penal order even though in reality the case may qualify as a breach of fiduciary duty. And because the judges also have a lot of work, they will simply approve the penal order. In economic crimes cases, the position of the prosecutor is weakening. They may dismiss cases even when there are damages involved. In cases where there was a possibility of the fine, the case is not investigated in a fully objective manner. That is not the way we are trained but that is how the law is practiced. The small cases are disposed of quickly and the system ... functions well. But in the large economic crimes cases involving large damages and the loss of assets, cases fall under the table and the legal consequences are not always proportionate.[41]

While some prosecutors may be reluctant to file cases absent a strong case, a handful of economic crimes and corruption prosecutors seem determined to redefine the law's legal boundaries to combat corrupt business practices. The myriad of ways in which prosecutors are attempting to extend criminal liability in this area can be can be seen in the following excerpts of media reports of cases in which prosecutors initiated investigations into and sometimes filed "breach of trust" charges.

> For a man about to go on trial for a crime that could send him to prison for ten years, Josef Ackermann, CEO of Deutsche Bank, seems remarkably calm ... In one of the most bizarre attacks on the corporate excesses of the 1990s, German prosecutors have charged Ackermann, 55, and five others with *Untreue*, or breach of trust, for their actions as executives or members of the board of Mannesmann, a German telecommunications company. Their alleged crime: unlawfully granting $56 million in appreciation awards and accelerated pensions to Mannesmann executives, including $15 million to former CEO Klaus Esser, after Britain's Vodafone agreed to acquire the company in a hostile $163 billion takeover in February 2000 (Guyon 2004).

> Prosecutors brought charges Thursday against a second suspect in a corruption scandal at Volkswagen, accusing a federal lawmaker and former employee representative of involve-

[40] Senior Prosecutor Interview [8AQ], 26 May 2006.

[41] Prosecutor Interview [9CR], 14 June 2006.

ment in events that featured prostitutes. Hans-Jürgen Uhl stands accused of being an accessory to breach of trust over his alleged participation in events in Barcelona and Seoul in 2001 "during the course of which the services of prostitutes allegedly were called upon," prosecutors in Braunschweig said in a statement... The investigation revolves around whether VW managers and members of its employee council received illegal privileges, including lavish foreign trips paid for by the company... Prosecutors said they suspect Uhl knew that Klaus-Joachim Gebauer, a former personnel executive, would improperly charge the costs of the events to Volkswagen... [Former Volkswagen personnel Chief Peter Hartz] was charged by prosecutors in November with 44 counts of breach of trust (AP 2007).

The former German Chancellor, Helmut Kohl, will not be prosecuted for accepting illegal political donations worth two million marks ($1m) while he was in office. A court in Bonn agreed that prosecutors should abandon their 14-month investigation of Mr. Kohl and the secret donations to his party, the Christian Democratic Union (CDU). Mr. Kohl will pay a fine of 300,000 marks ($142,000), but will not be left with a criminal record... He admitted breaking rules on the funding of political parties, but rejected accusations that he accepted the donations in return for political favours ... The investigation into Mr. Kohl for a suspected offence of breach of trust was officially called off for lack of evidence. The presiding judge said the decision had been taken because there was still no clear prospect of the case leading to a successful prosecution (BBC 2001).

While interpreting the law inventively has long been a prosecutorial tradition in common law jurisdictions, scholars have yet to researched the prevalence and implications of the use of similar strategies by prosecutors in civil code jurisdictions. In some respects, the statutory structure and content of economic crime laws in Germany invites prosecutors to push the boundaries of the law. Take, for example, the "Mannesman trial" which was billed by one reporter for the Financial Times (2004) as the "biggest criminal trial in German corporate history." In the 2004 trial, German prosecutors filed breach of fiduciary duty charges against six former directors of the large German telecommunications and engineering firm, Mannesman AG. The key legal issue in the case was whether or not the firm's directors had breached their fiduciary duties when they approved bonus awards and pension enhancements to eighteen executives after the executors approved the firm's takeover. Because the case's central legal issue was whether or not the payments were "appropriate," in an article in the *Financial Times* (2004, 13), business analysts accused prosecutors of over-reaching and of putting the free market itself on trial.

The impetus behind the analysts' attacks was the fact that, by filing criminal charges against the executives, prosecutors sought to use the criminal justice system, rather than the market, to determine what constituted an "appropriate" compensation level. Unsurprisingly, this issue is not directly addressed in the statutory definition of breach of fiduciary duty defined in Section 266 StGB. Instead, the actions which constitute a breach in this context can only be understood if one reads the German Stock Corporation Act which, according to Maier (2006, p. 604), itself provides no precise criteria for determining what constitutes an appropriate compensation level. Section 87(1)(i) of the Act states:

> When determining the total remuneration of individual executive directors, the supervisory board. . .must ensure that total remuneration is kept in appropriate relation to the tasks of the executive director and the state of the company (Kolla 2004, p. 830).

Further complicating the legal issues at stake in the case was the fact that, what was at issue in the case was not the size of the executive's contracted salaries, but rather the bonus payments which Mannesmann directors agreed to pay out after the firm was taken over by Vodafone. While supplemental compensation payments are not per se illegal, prosecutors argued that the payments violated the law because they were designed to persuade executives to drop their resistance to the takeover bid (*Deutsche Welle* 2006). After a protracted legal battle, prosecutors agreed to accept a plea in the case but not until after the Federal Court of Justice had crafted new law and the defendants agreed to pay large fines to the state. As one editorial written by Karl Zawadsky, a business editor for *Deutsche Welle* (2006) stated:

> [T]he trial sensitized high-paid executives to the concepts of service versus self-service. Or so we hope. In any case future wrongdoers are not going to find it so easy to dodge charges by claiming they weren't aware their actions were illegal. The trial did its part to prop up the stability of the law. But given that it also seems to officially sanction defendants buying their way out of justice, it still leaves a bad taste in the mouth.

The fact that the charge of breach of fiduciary duty itself is not classified as a major crime underscores the wide scope of discretion that prosecutors possess in handling major cases. Although the crime does not fall under the definitional rubric of a major crime, prosecutors may allege that the violation rises to the level of "an especially serious case." In these circumstances the potential criminal liability increases to a period of imprisonment between 6 months and 10 years and may include extraordinary fines. Pursuant to Section 263, a case may qualify as an especially serious case if the perpetrator:

> 1. acts professionally or as a member of a gang which has combined for the continued commission of falsification of documents or fraud; 2. causes an asset loss of great magnitude or by the continued commission of fraud acts with the intent of placing a large number of human beings in danger of loss of assets; 3. places another person in financial need; 4. abuses his powers or his position as a public official; or feigns an insured event after he or another have, to this end, set fire to a thing of significant value or destroyed it, in whole or in part, through the setting of a fire or caused the sinking or wrecking of a ship.

Prosecutors possess additional latitude in their decision to offer reduced sentences to cooperating witnesses. Although cooperating defendants often receive a reduced sentence in exchange for their testimony, prosecutors may not promise cooperating defendants that they will receive a specific disposition in exchange for their confession. In order to prevent the appearance that a "deal" has been made, some prosecutors will write a specific notation in the case file sent to the court noting that, at the time of the suspect's confession, they informed the suspect that the prosecution office would recommend that the suspect receive the typical sentence for that offense.[42] In essence, this notation rises to the level of a legal

[42] Senior Prosecutor Interview [8HL], 24 May 2006.

fiction as it is a backhanded way for the prosecutor's office to ask the court to negotiate a deal. In a 2010 position paper, Dr. Sebastian Wolf, Transparency International-Germany (2010) criticized the legislation that sanctioned deals noting that, as a result of deals:

> The gathering of evidence can be seriously reduced, investigations which might lead (specifically in corruption cases) to further cases are immediately stopped and cases are not tried in public any longer.

Although there is no supposedly quid pro quo agreement underlying a deal, a defendant who confesses almost invariably will receive a lighter sentence because judges must consider the defendant's guilt as one factor in the sentencing process. According to Sect. 46 (I) StGB "the guilt of the perpetrator is the foundation for determining punishment."[43] In the context of sentencing, Streng (2007, p. 155) maintains that the offender's guilt is based on characteristics that existed both preceding and following the act. As a result, cooperating defendants invariably expect that they will receive a lighter sentence as consideration for their confession. The existence of a confession can decisively influence case outcomes as it may be impossible to obtain a conviction without the cooperation of an inside witness.[44] When one considers that there is still widespread denial throughout Germany regarding the use of "confession agreements" in major crime cases, the fact that a prosecutors and judges have choreographed semi-scripted dance of practices to perpetuate their use is a testament to the ongoing disconnect that exists between theory and practice. Moreover, the parallel development of apparently "transparent" notation practices that, in essence, serve as a cover for behind the scenes deal-making, is a troublesome omen for those scholars who continue to harbor any belief that the law, in major crime cases, effectively contains prosecutorial discretion.

6.9 Confession Bargaining and Disposition Practices

The complexity and cost of an investigation, standing alone, encourages prosecutors to settle economic crimes cases well short of an investigation's end. In addition, many white collar defendants can afford to hire a well-funded defense team. Because the law is ambiguous and particularly subject to interpretation with regard to economic crimes, by filing motion after motion, defense attorneys, may test a prosecutor's ability to keep up the defense's attempts to question the legal aspects of a case. A case in point, in a case involving illegal payments received by the laboratory chief of a university hospital, the list of defendants included: the laboratory chief, his asset managers, and two chief executive officers of manufacturing companies. When describing the case, one prosecutor detailed

[43] Sect. 46(I) StGB.

[44] Senior Prosecutor Interview [8HL], 24 May 2006.

Table 6.2 Bribery cases—prosecution data (March 2011 to March 2013)

Dismissals for lack of grounds	33
Sanctions against individuals/legal persons	21

Source: Germany: Follow-up to the Phase 3 Report & Recommendations (2013, 3)

that, in the pre-trial phase, the four defense attorneys filed extensive briefs of over one hundred pages long denying that their clients were criminally liable (Hornung 49) and challenging of aspects of the government's case. In a report prepared for a regional OECD conference, Hornung (49) related:

> They claimed, firstly, that the credit contracts were intended to be real credit contracts with an existing repayment obligation, secondly, that the credits were given for mere personal reasons (from friends to a friend) with no link whatsoever with the professional situation of the accused, thirdly, that the laboratory section chief had not divulged any secret and market-relevant information concerning the immediate business rivals of the Northern German manufacturer, and fourthly, that the contracts were legally concluded outside the public tender rules.

In hopes of securing some level of punishment without spending a decade investigating a case, many prosecutors and courts look to "deals" to resolve economic crime cases. The fact that a crime qualifies as a major crime (*Verbrechen*) in theory restricts the latitude that prosecutors and courts possess to conclude deals with defendants in the most serious cases. Moreover, according to the law, the primary opportunity that prosecutors possess to suspend prosecution is limited to cases where non-prosecution is in the public interest or the suspect's guilt is of a minor nature.[45] A significant problem under German law is that the legislature has elected to classify several of the key crimes in this field, namely—foreign bribery, commercial bribery and breach of trust as minor crimes or misdemeanors under German law. As long as the case is so classified, prosecutors may defer prosecution under Section 153(a) StPO or craft a written judgment which will be issued by the court without a hearing under Section 407 StPO. Under those provisions, there will be no main hearing or full presentation of evidence. Indeed, one can say with certitude that, with respect to bribery cases, the majority of "convictions" are secured through deals. In Germany's follow-up report to the OECD's Phase 3 report (April 2013, 3), the members of the group reported the following case dispositions listed above[46] (Table 6.2).

In more than three quarters (78 %) of the cases resulting in a sanction, the court imposed the sanction following a settlement under section 153a StGB (2013, 3). It is important to note that in the 21 cases resulting in legal sanctions, courts sanctioned a total of 141 individuals. The charges fell into the categories detailed below (Table 6.3). In the time period prior to March 2011, courts sanctioned 69 individuals, with 35 of those individuals receiving a sanction pursuant to a Section 153a agreement—a "settlement rate" slightly exceeding 50 % (2013, 3).

[45] Sect. 153a StPO.

[46] More than one individual may be charged in a single case.

Table 6.3 Bribery charges in sanctioned cases (March 2011 to March 2013)

Bribery of a foreign public official	43
Commercial bribery	80
Breach of trust/tax evasion	18

Source: Germany: Follow-up to the Phase 3 Report & Recommendations (2013, 3)

It is evident that German prosecutors and judges have accelerated their efforts to prosecute bribery and corruption cases pursuant to the OECD convention. It is also evident that the recent prosecution of Siemens AG, which resulted in the company paying a fine of over 600 million euros to the government, has earned the country widespread praise for its' anti-corruption efforts (Rubenfeld 2011). However, it will take a sustained record of achievement to erase the memory of the state's failure to hold former Chancellor Helmut Kohl accountable for his improper handling of campaign donations. Although the sentencing guidelines used in some states define the circumstances under which a prosecutor may suspend the prosecution of a case, it is widely acknowledged that the adjudication of the Kohl case stretched the boundaries of circumstances under which non-prosecution might be in the public interest.

One of the most egregious parts of the case is that although the former Chancellor admitted funneling over 1 million dollars of illegal campaign donations into secret accounts, he refused to name the sources of those donations (Wyatt 2000). Despite that refusal, the court allowed Kohl to pay a large fine and escape a conviction by invoking Section 153a of the Criminal Procedure Code. One wonders whether prosecutors afford drug dealers the same disposition option if they do not name their suppliers or promise to cooperate. According to a BBC report (2001), the case's lenient disposition spurred members of German opposition parties to charge that prosecutors closed the investigation because they "lacked political courage." The procedural path that prosecutors as well as the court used to terminate the investigation was unusual given the weight of the allegations and amount of the public interest in the case. These circumstances ultimately provoked the Bavarian parliament to conduct investigative hearings. During the hearings, the original prosecutor on the case testified that the Justice Ministry had issued instructions to him telling him how to handle the case.[47] In response to this disclosure, the criticism of the case widened to include the judicial branch itself. The editors of the German Law Journal (2001) commented:

> The crux of the path taken by the Regional Criminal Court is that it leaves the widely interested public both disappointed and clueless as to the message that the Court actually wished to make. The bottom-line being that Mr. Kohl was neither indicted, convicted nor acquitted ... [Because] the decision to take this route is delegated to the discretion of the prosecution and the Court, there is room for concerns for reasons of equality, control and judicial review . . .[W]hile this might seem unproblematic from a pragmatist's perspective, those more concerned with the *rule-of-law* might be much more skeptical of the architecture and scope of the procedure.

[47] Second Office Prosecutor [16PP], 30 April 2008.

Ironically, Germany's OECD site visit occurred after the resolution of the Kohl case. Unsurprisingly the Visiting Experts, who conducted the site visit, sharply criticized prosecutors' broad discretionary power to effectively dismiss charges under §153a StPO and identified that provision as being an impediment to creating an effective bribery prosecution record (OECD 2004, 43). Moreover, the OECD's legal examiners recommended that Germany implement guidelines that would uniformly define what constellation of facts constituted a "minor case" in the context of Sect 153a StGB (43). The German government responded by seeking to "clarify" the definition of "public interest" in the context of corruption cases. As the 2003 OECD report stated:

> The German authorities state that in cases of corruption, it can be assumed that there is a public interest in a criminal prosecution. Also, they refer to no. 260 of the 'Guidelines for Criminal Proceedings and Proceedings to Impose a Regulatory Fine" (RiStBV), which are nation-wide uniform instructions binding on the public prosecution offices that expressly state such a position for the offense of private to private bribery (section 299, Criminal Code)...
>
> The German authorities state that the public interest could be mitigated in cases that are not particularly serious but are difficult or complex, necessitating excessive lengthy proceedings. A judge stated, during the on-site visit, that in certain cases potentially long proceedings could mitigate the 'public interest' and could lead to the application of an informal fine under section 153a. In making such a determination, she considered factors such as what sanction would be appropriate for the particular case and whether lengthy proceedings were warranted due to the nature of the case.

Another source of decision-making latitude available to prosecutors is their ability to offer defendants a term of probation rather than imprisonment. When a defendant is facing a potential sentence that includes a 2-year period of imprisonment or less, the prosecutor's ability to recommend probation, rather than imprisonment, increases a prosecutor's ability to settle a case as the typical defendants in these cases are highly averse to serving time.[48] The 2-year sentence serves as a cutoff point as it is at or below that point that a court has the discretion to sentence the defendant to a period of probation rather than prison. For many economic crimes prosecutors, their primary objective is not to obtain a long prison sentence:

> Every person who is sent to prison costs the state money. In these [difficult] times, we must save money. It is better for the state when a defendant receives a sentence involving probation and a fine. [Most economic crimes defendants] are used to living in luxury. We tell them that we could give them prison. The defense attorney will threaten to make the main proceeding last a long time and [we know] that the defense attorney will make money from [the length of the trial].[49]
>
> Sentencing decisions are difficult for both prosecutors and judges. As I have become older; I have adopted a milder attitude towards sentencing. However what is important in a

[48] Senior Prosecutor Interview [1ZU], 15 March 2006.

[49] Senior Prosecutor Interview [1ZU], 15 March 2006.

> particular case is that the punishment is imposed quickly rather than that it is severe. For me it is important to file the charges themselves.[50]

At the same time, the possibility that a probated sentence may result does not mean that prosecutors will necessary forgo the option of recommending incarceration in white collar crime cases. For example, in one hearing in a case involving the environmental crime of the illegal dumping of asbestos, the senior prosecutor recommended that the court impose an 8 month prison sentence. The court agreed. The crimes involved in this case included violations of these statutes:

- § 326 StGB [Unauthorized Dealing with Dangerous Wastes]
- § 327 StGB [Unauthorized Operation of Facilities]

According to the provisions of Section 326 (1) StGB, in the case of a "substantial deviation from the proscribed or authorized procedure," the court may sentence a defendant to a prison term of not more than 5 years or a fine. In the alternative, if a person acts "negligently," the potential sentence may include a term of imprisonment for not more than 3 years or a fine [Paragraph 5 (1)]; or imprisonment for not more than 1 year or a fine [Paragraph 5 (2)].

The progress that a case makes in court varies greatly depending on the dedication, competence level, and workload of the courts. For example, one senior prosecutor shared with me that at one time their department had faced a substantial backlog of cases filed at the court. When the Ministry appointed a new judge to that court who possessed a tough attitude toward economic crime, the judge quickly cleared out the backlog. The prosecutor describes the change in procedure instituted by the court: "From the beginning of the process onward, the judge takes over the case and adopts a hard line and everyone knows that the cases will be handled a certain way."[51] That particular experience appeared to be an outlier. Several prosecutors from a collection of offices across Germany told me that it can take courts between 6 months to 2 years to review an investigation file and decide whether or not to open a main proceeding.[52] During one interview with an economic crimes prosecutor, when I questioned the prosecutor about court backlogs, he pointed to six tiers of bookshelves which contained the evidence collected to date in a single case. Given the complex task of tracing financial transactions, the documentary evidence compiled in a single file may be daunting to both courts and prosecutors.

Given the resource strain on both courts and prosecution offices, there is a willingness among judges and prosecutors to resolve cases short of a complete presentation of the evidence. In some cases, the judge will contact defense counsel and ask whether or not the suspect is willing to make a deal.[53] In most cases, the

---

[50] Senior Prosecutor Interview [5BC], 16 January 2006.

[51] Senior Prosecutor Interview [10BJ], 26 June 2006.

[52] Prosecutor Interview [13BR], 18 November 2005; Prosecutor Interview [12AE], 28 November 2005; and Senior Prosecutor Interview [5BC], 16 January 2006.

[53] Senior Prosecutor Interview [5BC], 16 January 2006.

prosecutor will inform the court as well as the defense what her bottom line is for a sentence in a particular case.[54] This may be communicated in terms of a range, for example, a prison sentence of 6–12 months. In complicated cases, the agreement may be contingent on the fact that the prosecutor will not have to complete the case investigation. However, even where the defendant makes a confession in court, the court will typically listen to testimony from other witnesses in the case as well because the judge must consider the defendant's "guiltiness" in the sentencing decision. Even where the defense agrees to the proposal, the defendant still possesses the right to challenge the court's verdict.

Judicial involvement in resolving cases before a main proceeding raises the question of the impact that this involvement may have on prosecutorial decision-making. To understand this point, it is necessary to briefly discuss the role of the German judiciary in the sentencing process. The established theoretical framework that serves as the foundation of German sentencing philosophy does not tether judicial decision-making to mandatory sentencing guidelines. While the discretionary decisions made by prosecutors have redefined the principle of mandatory prosecution in practice, the theoretical considerations that underlie sentencing practices also have caused judges to view efforts to limit discretion with disdain. As a result, the force of the principle of mandatory prosecution during the main proceeding is being undercut today, not only by prosecutorial practice, but also indirectly by judicial practices. According to Streng (2007), pursuant to a key German theory of sentencing known as the *Spielraum* or "leeway" theory, judges possess considerable decision-making latitude. In its most basic form this principle grants judges substantial leeway to work hand-in-hand with prosecutors to shape outcomes.

> The *Spielraum*-theory is based on the proposition that the judge establishes a specific framework for the individual guilt derived from the general statutory provisions. Within this margin the judge then takes account of utilitarian, or as Germans prefer to say preventive aims, avoiding both overstepping and under-shooting the guilt of the accused. At its core the theory is based on equity, and is bounded with few concise criteria. One could go so far as to call this method a 'black-box-model' of judicial decision-making (155).

> In contrast to a technocratic or an authoritarian criminal law system the judge in our law system relies on values which are coined by his social and professional personality. Under this perception of his role the German judge thus demands a wide sentencing range, from which he is free to choose a just and fair sanction in accordance to his persuasion. Mandatory sentencing guidelines would contradict this self-conception of judges (154).

6.10 Prosecutorial Independence & Corruption

> Is the truth so terrible that Helmut Kohl places his word of honor above the German Constitution? (Gabi Bauer -TV Anchor NDR, 2000)

---

[54] Senior Prosecutor Interview [5BC], 16 January 2006.

The stakes involved in major crimes cases create incentives for political actors to sway the decision-making process. Whenever a leading politician or prominent business person faces criminal charges, often the most serious consequences in play are not the criminal charges themselves, but rather the suspect's loss of prestige and social standing. By filing charges in corruption cases, prosecutors may challenge the distribution of power in a society. Consequently, political actors invariably will try to the influence the outcome. As the interview excerpts below indicate, even if prosecutors never receive a written instruction from their superiors regarding a case, numerous informal control mechanisms exist. At the same time, it would be inaccurate to describe the German prosecutors who handle these high stakes cases as bureaucrats who simply implement their superiors' prerogatives. Many of the prosecutors who serve in these departments strive to preserve their independence and to apply the law equally regardless of a suspect's power and wealth. Consequently, in the high stakes cases, prosecutorial decision-making is neither completing constrained, nor completely insulated from, hierarchical influence.

> My goal in these cases is two-fold. First, I target the profit that companies make as a result of these illegal transactions; Second, I try to recover the actual amount of the bribe ... When I was handling a case several years ago, a person from the General Public Prosecutor's Office would visit my office [while the case was pending] and ask me why I was seeking such a high punishment. I told her that I wanted to make an example to show that it was unacceptable for businesses to give bribes.[55]

> The pressure on me right now comes from the Ministry. We must write weekly reports for them. [They want to know] what the basis is for filing the charges, when will the investigation be completed? I have never experienced pressure before [in my fifteen year career]... We are also having difficulties meeting time deadlines because we need to secure evidence from other countries. However, the press is our ally in this case. The Ministry of Justice would not dare to issue an instruction in this case because the press is so involved with following the case.[56]

> From time to time, the newspapers will find something out. For example, one of the Ministers received a bribe from a foreign firm. The bank notified the prosecution office because of the size of the bank deposit. Another Minister found out about the investigation and tipped off the suspect before we could execute a search warrant. [When this information came out], the Minister resigned but the General Public Prosecutor decided that the phone tip-off did not violate the law... At this point, the case will be difficult to prove ... In Germany we can only guarantee a 'sort of justice.' No system is perfect.[57]

---

[55] Senior Prosecutor Interview [8HL], 2 May 2006.

[56] Senior Prosecutor Interview [1ZU], 15 March 2006.

[57] Senior Prosecutor Interview [10BJ], 26 June 2006.

6.11 Conclusion

The strides taken by the German government to enforce anti-bribery laws are remarkable. In areas of the country where the regional authority has created specialized prosecution units which work in tandem with qualified members of law enforcement, prosecution rates have dramatically improved. Unfortunately, many areas of the country lack the resources and training to target corruption and economic crime. The decision to create a specialized prosecution unit itself is a political decision typically made at the Ministry level. Despite this stepped up enforcement, prosecutors possess considerable decision-making latitude in prosecuting the majority of these cases. Given the complexity of the investigation process, limits on time and resources, and the prospect of dealing with a well-funded defense effort, many prosecutors choose to make "deals" in these cases. Although, one can find instances where political pressure may have affected prosecution efforts, those cases are very rare.

Legislation

Code of Criminal Procedure (StPO)

§100(a)(2)(1)(t)
§100(c)(3)
§153a
§160(1)

Code of Criminal Law (StGB)

§46(1)
§108e
§112
§112(2)
§121(1)
§122(1)2
§266
§299
§332(1)
§332(1)–(2)
§335(1)(a)

European Convention on Human Rights

Article 6 (1)

Other Laws

BGH 5 StR 268/05 (2 Dezember 2005) (LG Köln).

German Stock Corporation Act. Section 87(1)(i).

Law on the Revision of Telecommunications Monitoring and other Covert Investigation Measures and Implementing Directive 2006/24/EC113 of 21, December 2007.

Gestez zur Bekämpfung der Korruption [*KorrBekG*] [Anti-Corruption Act], *Strafgestezbuch* [StGB] [Penal Code], August 19, 1997, *Bundesgestezblatt* [BGBL], 1 at 2038 §§331-35 (Ger.)

Constitution of Courts Acat, §74c, par. 1 n5 and 6.

Reports/Statistics

Bundesrepublix Deutschalnd, Bundesministerium Des Innern [Federal Ministry of the Interior], 2001. Private Sector/Federal Administration Anti-Corruption Initiative, Answers to Frequently Asked Questions about Accepting Gifts, Hospitality, or Other Benefits 9. Available at: <http://bmi.bund.de/SharedDocs/Downloads/EN/Themen/OED_Verwaltung/Korruption/initiativkreis_korruptionspraevention2.pdf?_blob=publicatoinFile>.

Bundeskriminaltamt, 2005. Situation Report – Organised Crime in the Federal Republic of Germany. (June) Available at: <www.bka.de/lagebericht/ok/2004kf/lagebild_ok_2004_kurzlage_englisch.pdf>.

Bundesrepublik Deutschland [Federal Republic of German], Bundeskriminalamt [Federal Criminal Office], Korruption: Bundeslagebild 2010 [Corruption: The Federal Picture 2010] (2011) Available at: <http://www.bka.de/nn_193376/DE/Publikationen/JahresberichteUndLagebilder/Korruption/korruption__node.html?__nnn=true>.

Organization for Economic Cooperation and Development (OECD), Working Group on Bribery in International Business Transactions, Phase 3 Evaluation of Germany position paper – on-site visit on 23 September 2010. Available at: <http://www.transparency.de/Position-Paper.1735.0.html?&no_cache=1&sword_list%5B55D=prosecutors>. [Accessed on 31 July 2013].

Organization for Economic Cooperation and Development (OECD), Working Group on Bribery, Phase 3 Report on Implementing the OECD Anti-Bribery

Convention in Germany (March 2011), Available at: <http://www.oecd.org/germany/Germanyphase3reportEN.pdf>.

Organization for Economic Cooperation and Development (OECD), 2012 Data Enforcement of the Anti-Bribery Convention (June 2013). Available at: <http://www.oecd.org/daf/anti-bribery/WorkingGrouponBribery_2012EnforcementData.pdf>.

Organization for Economic Cooperation and Development (OECD), 2004. Implementing the OECD Anti-Bribery Convention Report on Germany (Complete Edition, *OECD Governance*, Volume 2003, Number 27, (Sept.).

Interviews

Case Meeting Observation, 26 January 2006

Group Leader Prosecutor Interview [8FN], 26 May 2006

Group Leader Prosecutor Interview [8DE], 26 may 2006

Land Level Ministry of Justice Official [9RR], 30 June 2006

Police Officer [26AE], 27 January 2006

Prosecutor Interview [9CR], 14 June 2006

Prosecutor Interview [10BJ], 26 June 2006

Prosecutor Interview [13BR], 18 November 2005

Prosecutor Interview [12AE], 28 November 2005

Second Office Prosecutor [16PP], 30 April 2008

Senior Prosecutor Interview [8HL], 24–25 May 2006

Senior Prosecutor Interview [10BJ], 26 June 2006

Senior Prosecutor Interview [1ZU], 15 March 2006/25 May 2006

Senior Prosecutor Interview [5BC], 16 January 2006

Senior Prosecutor Interview [6FE], 21 July 2006

Senior Prosecutor Interview [8AQ], 26 May 2006

Tax Administration Official [26AD], 25 January 2006

References

Books, Articles and Online Publications

Amies, N. (2004a). How corrupt is Germany? *Deutsche Welle*, 16 March. Available at http://www.dworld.de/dw/article/0,1564,1144554,00.html.

Amies, N. (2004b). How corrupt is Germany. *Deutsche Welle* (16 Mar 2004). Available at http://www.dw.de/how-corrupt-is-germany/a-1144554.

Associated Press. (2007). German charged in Volkswagen corruption inquiry, *International Herald Tribune*, 4 January. Available at http://www.iht.com/articles/2007/01/04/business/vw.php.

BBC NEWS (2001). Kohl charges dropped. http://news.bbc.co.uk/2/hi/europe/1198301.stm (March 2, 2001).

Bundesministerium des Innern (2011). Private sector/federal administration anti-corruption initiative, 13 August. http://www.bmi.bund.de/SharedDocs/Downloads/EN/Themen/OED_Verwaltung/Korruption/initiativkreis_korruptionspraevention2.pdf?__blob=publicationFile

Cohen, R. (2000). Suicide of a party official is tied to German scandal, *New York Times*, 21 January. Available at http://www.globalpolicy.org/nations/corrupt/kohl15.htm.

Dempsey, J. (2012). Germany cleans up its politics, 19 March. Available at http://www.nytimes.com/2012/03/20/world/europe/20iht-letter20html?_r=0. Accessed 2 Aug 2013.

Deutsche Welle. (2006). Prosecutors agree to drop charges in Mannesmann trial, 24 November. Available at http://www.dw-world.de/dw/article/0,2144,2247880,00.html.

Dougherty, C. (2007). Germany takes aim at corporate corruption, *International Herald Tribune*. Available at http://www.nytime.com/2007/02/114/business/worldbusiness/14iht-scandal.4596099.html.

Germany's Party Finance Scandal "Ends" With Kohl's Plea Bargain and Too Many Unanswered Questions. 2001. *German Law Journal*, *5*:2 (15 March). Available at http://www.germanlawjournal.com/article.php?id=60.

Goel, A. & Jo, M. Y. (2012). Recent anti-corruption developments in Germany. In A. Goel (Ed.), *International anti-bribery and corruption trends and developments* (pp. 2–52). Available at http://www.ropesgray.com/biographies/g/~/media/Files/articles/2012/05/201205321_ABC_Book.ashx. Accessed 1 Aug 2013.

Guyon, J. (2004). The trials of Josef Ackerman, *Fortune*, 26 January 2004. Available at http://money.cnn.com/magazines/forture/fortune_archive/2004/01/26/358833/index.htm.

Hornung, R. (2010). *The Baden-Wurttemberg example*. Germany: Organization for Economic Cooperation and Development (OECD) Anti-Corruption Network for Eastern Europe and Central Asia

Horsley, W. (2001). Kohl's legacy: burnished or tarnished? *British Broadcasting Company*, 2 March. Available at http://news.bbc.co.uk/1/hi/world/europe/1199032.stm.

Jenkins, P. (2004). Germany on trial. *Financial Times*, 15 January. Available at http://search.ft.com/iab?queryText=Patrick%20Jenkins%20Germany%20on%20Trial&aje=true&id=040114007034&location=http53A%2F%2Fsearch.ft.com%2FtArticle%3FqueryText%DPatrick+Jenkins+Germany+on+Trial%26aje%3Dtrue%26id53D040114007034&referer=http%3A%2F%2Fsearch.ft.com% 2Fsearch%3FqueryText%3DPatrick+Jenkins+Germany+on+Trial.

Kohl Charges Dropped. (2001). *British Broadcasting Company*, 2 March. Available at http://news.bbc.co.uk/2/hi/europe/1198301.stm.

Kolla, P. (2004). The Mannesmann trial and the role of the courts. *German Law Journal*, *5*:829–847. Available at: http://www.germanlawjournal.com/index.php?pageID=11&artID=460.

Kreutzer, C. (2002). Interview: Deutschland ist keine Bananenrepublik, *FRANKFURTER ALLGEMEINE ZEITUNG*, 19 March. Available at http://www.faz.net/aktuell/gesellschaft/interview-deutschland-ist-keine-bananenrepublik-149119.html.

Löhe, M. G. (2006). *Ressourcen der Korruptionsbekämpfung in Deutschland*. Berlin: Transparency International Deutschland. Available at http://www.transparency.de/fileadmin/pdfs/Themen/Justiz/justizielle_ressourcen_2007_FINAL.pdf. Accessed 5 Aug 2013.

Maier, S. (2006). A close look at the Mannesmann trial. *German Law Journal*, *7*:603–610. Available at http://www.germanlawjournal.com/index.php?pageID=11&artID=735.

Munchau, W. (2004). Market economics is in the dock in Germany, *Financial Times* (US Edition), 26 January.

OECD Governance (2004). *Implementing the OECD Anti-Bribery Convention Report on Germany* (Complete Edition), vol. 2003, p. 27.

OECD Anti-Corruption Network for Eastern Europe and Central Asia. (2010). In Proceedings of the seminar on effective means of investigation and prosecution of corruption (expert seminar),

National Anti-Corruption Directorate of Romania, Bucharest, 20–22 October 2010. Available at http://www.oecd.org/corruption/acn/47588859.pdf. Accessed 31 July 2013.
Parkin, B. (2007). German state fires aide as Grime probe nears Merkel Government, *Bloomberg. Com*, 13 June.
Rubenfeld, S. (2011). German's anti-bribery efforts get high marks from OECD, *Wall Street Journal*, 23 March. Available at http://blogs.wsj.com/corruption-currents/2011/03/23/germanys-anti-bribery-efforts-get-high-marks-from-oecd/tab/print.
Staff Writer. (2006). Dogmeat and the truffle pig, *The Economist*, 7 September. Available at http://www.economist.com/business/displaystory.cfm?story_id=7887902. Accessed 5 Aug 2013.
Streng, F. (2007). Sentencing in Germany: Basic questions and new developments. *German Law Journal, 8*, 153–172.
Teil, R. (2007). Zu wenige Staatsanwälte, zu viel Korruption: Eine_bersicht von Transparency International, *TRANSPARENCY INTERNATIONAL DEUTSCHLAND e.V.* Available at http://www.transparency.de/Zu-wenige-Staatsanwaelte-zu.440.98.html.
Thomas Sims, G. (2007). Germany rethinks board structure after corruption scandals, *International Herald Tribune*, 5 April. Available at http://iht.com/articles/2007/04/05/news/board.php.
Von Hawranek, D. (2006). Schmutz und Schund, *Der Spiegel* [online]. 27 March. Available online at http://www.spiegel.de/spiegel/print/d-46421534.html. Accessed 5 Aug 2013.
Wiehen, M. H. (2001) Submission of TI Deutschland to GRECO regarding the evaluation of anti-corruption activities in Germany, *Transparency International Deutsches Chapter, e.V.*, 21 September. Available at www.transparency.de/fileadmin/pdfs/30.83.00Submission18.9.01.pdf.
Wyatt, C. (2000). Analysis: German political tremors spread, *British Broadcasting Company*, 14 January. Available at http://news.bbc.co.uk/1/hi/world/europe/1199032.stm.
Zawadsky, K. (2006). Bought justice at Mannesmann trial still taught lessons, *Editorial Opinion*, 29, November. Available at http://www.dw-world.de/dw/article/o,2144,2252960,00.html.

Chapter 7
The Many Faces of Objectivity in the Courtroom

> The score may be the same . . . but if the instruments and players are not, the legal music will sound differently (Edwards 1997, p. 853).

7.1 Introduction

While prior research studies of the German prosecution function have emphasized how bureaucratic organizational practices have shaped the prosecutorial behavior during the case investigation stage, those studies shed little light on prosecutorial decision-making in the courtroom (Asmus 1988). In this chapter I explore that gap and examine whether prosecutors' courtroom decisions reflect their duty to be objective fact-finders. I argue that prosecutors interpret and perform their duty to function as second judges differently and those differences impact the outcome of the truth-finding process. That research argues that bureaucratic practices undermine prosecutors' application of the principle of legality, as prosecutors besieged with a crushing case load, must adopt efficient case-closing strategies (Blankenburg and Steffen 1978). While that research has broken important ground, it not only fails

Portions of this chapter appeared previously in the Washington and Lee Law Review: Shawn Marie Boyne, *Uncertainty and the Search for Truth at Trial: Defining Prosecutorial "Objectivity" in German Sexual Assault Cases*, 67 Wash. & Lee L. Rev. 1287 (2010). I thank the editors of the law review for permission to republish those sections.

S.M. Boyne, *The German Prosecution Service*, DOI 10.1007/978-3-642-40928-8_7,

to explain what happens in the courtroom, but it also ignores a key part of prosecutorial practice in major crime cases.

This chapter explores that gap. In particular I examine the decisions that prosecutors make in the courtroom and argue that how prosecutors both view and perform their duty to function as second judges impacts the outcome of the truth-finding process. Using data gathered from interviews and participant observation studies, I show how consensual decision-making norms often determinatively shape both the nature and rigor of the truth-finding process. The bulk of the chapter traces and analyzes the role played by prosecutors in three sexual assault trials. By closely examining decision-making at trial I show how prosecutors translate their duty to view the evidence objectively into a myriad of observable courtroom practices.[1]

7.2 Why Rape?

Rape cases offer us a unique lens through which to view the nature of objectivity. Prosecutors in both adversarial and inquisitorial systems play a gate-keeping role (Hermann 1976, p. 24). Through their discretionary decision-making, prosecutors determine what claims will proceed to trial (Hermann 1976, pp. 23–28). In the context of rape cases that role is particularly contested. The trajectory of a rape case is strongly shaped by the prosecutor's appraisal of witness credibility (Estrich 1988). Because the crime of rape typically occurs in private, the search for truth often focuses on the testimony of the victim and the suspect (Asmus 1988, p. 43). In cases in which the physical evidence is inconclusive, a prosecutor's assessment of witness credibility is often dispositive (Asmus 1988, p. 42).

In the United States, a large percentage of reported rape cases never reach the trial stage (Bryden and Lengnick 1997). Many victims of rape never report the crime out of fear of being stigmatized by the "fact-finding" process; victims also fear facing hostility from the police, prosecutors, and juries (Estrich 1988, pp. 1–5). Prosecutors are often reluctant to file charges in rape cases and even less likely to bring those cases to trial unless there is a high certainty that a jury will return a guilty verdict (Estrich 1988, pp. 8–9). The cases that do proceed to trial may be motivated by political reasons (Herbert 2009). In the absence of compelling physical evidence rape cases may be difficult to prosecute given that the crime often occurs in private and the issue of consent is often contested (Bryden and Lengnick 1997, pp. 1316–1317).

At first blush one might expect that German prosecutors, who do not view their role in adversarial terms, would be less reluctant to file rape cases than their American counterparts. The fact that professional judges, rather than lay juries, dominate the fact-finding process would seem to make the process less intimidating

[1] I observed these trials during an extended period of field research conducted in Germany between 2005 and 2008.

for victims (Bryden and Lengnick 1997, p. 1196). Moreover, rape victims in German courts need not struggle to conform their testimony to the strict evidentiary guidelines that bind testimony given in American courts (Pizzi and Perron 1996). Witnesses in German courts may speak in a narrative form, which would be considered unresponsive in American courtrooms (Pizzi and Perron 1996). Additionally, because German law allows victims the right to be represented by a collateral prosecutor (*Nebenklager*) at trial, one would expect that victims' rights would be more protected than in a system in which no lawyer is appointed to protect the victim's specific interests (Pizzi and Perron 1996, p. 59). Given these procedural differences, one would expect German courtrooms to be friendlier to rape victims. As a result, one might expect that victims would be more willing to report the crime and cooperate in the prosecution.

Thought experiments can not tell us how German prosecutors wrestle with conflicting evidence and assess witness credibility in the courtroom (Lovett and Kelly 2009). Indeed, many key questions have remained unanswered. How do German prosecutors translate their duty to be objective in rape cases that go to trial? Do they ask the court to acquit a suspect when they doubt the victim's credibility? By examining prosecutorial decision-making during rape trials we can understand more fully how German prosecutors interpret their duty to view the evidence objectively and whether their function as a "second judge" shapes their decision-making at trial. Moreover, by examining prosecutorial decision-making in cases in which the credibility of the victim, witnesses, and defendant is often extremely contested, we are offered a unique window into the truth-finding role of a German prosecutor. It is my contention that, in cases in which the facts are particularly uncertain, consensual decision-making norms between prosecutors and judges drive prosecutorial behavior.

In Sect. 7.3 I introduce the reader to the basic function of German prosecutors in the main proceeding. I continue to lay the groundwork for the analysis that follows in Sect. 7.4 where I discuss the importance of the prosecutor's relationship with the presiding judge in the main proceeding and suggest three different stances that prosecutors may take during the main proceeding vis-à-vis the presiding judge. Drawing on interview data and participant observation studies of German prosecutors, I argue that a prosecutor's daily decision-making practices help to construct his or her working "definition" of objectivity and that that definition is "situationally contingent." In the rest of the chapter, I draw on participant-observation studies of three different main proceedings to show how these different relational stances between the prosecutor and the court shape the construction of objectivity. Finally, in the chapter's conclusion I argue that, while the law creates and partially defines the duty of objectivity, prosecutors interpret and enact the full meaning of objectivity through their daily decision-making.

7.3 The Prosecution Function in the Main Proceeding

Consistent with their function as "second judges," prosecutors do not present the case against the defendant during the main proceeding.[2] Unlike an adversary proceeding in which prosecutors bear the evidentiary burden of presenting evidence against the accused, in German courtrooms the presiding judge bears the responsibility of conducting the hearing, examining the defendant, and taking evidence.[3]

The judicial composition of each court varies with the level of the proceeding. At the *Amtsgericht* (local court) level, which adjudicates minor criminal cases where the punishment runs up to 2 years imprisonment, a single judge takes charge of the proceedings. Above the local court is the *Schöffengericht* level which uses a panel of one professional and two lay judges. The three-judge panels hear cases involving potential sentences of up to 4 years imprisonment.[4] The most serious criminal cases are adjudicated at the regional court or *Landgericht* level. Those courts typically include a panel of three professional judges and two lay judges.[5]

Before a main proceeding is even scheduled, the judge will read the investigation file compiled by the prosecution office and use that file to determine whether there is sufficient evidence to open a main proceeding.[6] If the court decides that sufficient evidence exists, the court will control how to structure the presentation of evidence (Langbein 1977). As each witness is called to the stand, the judge or panel of judges will initiate the questioning and then inquire whether the prosecutor and the defense attorney have additional questions.[7] Consistent with the prosecutor's obligation to be objective, a prosecutor may present evidence that favors the accused (Jescheck 1970; Foster 1996). At the close of the presentation of evidence, the prosecutor will summarize the evidence for and against the defendant and recommend a specific disposition given his or her factual and legal appraisal of the case.[8] In accord with their duties under the principle of legality, prosecutors are free to recommend that the court acquit a suspect (Hannich 2008). In addition to the provisions of the Code of Criminal Procedure, prosecutors are required to follow other guidelines as well. For example, the procedures for recommending an acquittal are detailed in the Guidelines for Criminal and Fine Proceedings (*Richtlinien Für Das Strafverfahren und Das Bußgeldvergahren* [RiStBV] §§138, 139).

Under German law the sentencing hearing is not a separate proceeding.[9] Instead, at the conclusion of the presentation of evidence, the judge or judges will adjourn to deliberate simultaneously about the verdict and sentence. Perhaps the most striking

[2] §§243, 244 StPO.

[3] §238(1) StPO.

[4] §§28, 29 GVG.

[5] §§74–76 GVG.

[6] §199 StPO.

[7] §240 StPO.

[8] §258(1) StPO.

[9] §160 StPO.

difference between American and German prosecution practice is that, in contrast with American practice, the majority of German prosecutors do not regard convictions as victories and acquittals as losses (Damaška 1981).

7.4 Relational Constraints

Whether one envisions a prosecutor making a decision to file charges, posing a certain question to a witness on the stand, or proffering a sentencing recommendation to the court, it is evident that a prosecutor's institutional role factors into his or her daily decision-making. Although judges need not confirm a prosecutor's decision not to prosecute petty offenses under Section 153 of the *Strafprozessordnung* (StPO), they perform a checking function with respect to some key prosecutorial decisions as they must approve the termination of proceedings in minor crime cases under Section 153(a) StPO. Moreover, after reviewing the investigative file collected by the prosecution service, it is the judge's prerogative to decide whether or not to open a main proceeding.[10]

In stark contrast to criminal practice in the United States, the negotiation of plea agreements in Germany involves the court (Turner 2009). In fact, in some instances judges will even initiate the plea negotiation process by contacting the prosecutor or defense attorney to explore whether the case may be resolved short of a full main proceeding.[11] Judges and prosecutors depend to a certain extent on preserving the relationship between the two institutions to keep the wheels of justice moving. Where judges do not believe that a case file contains sufficient evidence to open a main proceeding, they will privately send the file back to the prosecutor's office for more investigation.[12] In some cases, there may even be a degree of implicit collusion involved in the relationship. For example, if a citizen lodges a meritless charge against another citizen, it is common for the prosecutor to send the application to open the main proceeding to the court but then telephone the judge and request that she deny the application.[13] Thus, while German law expects prosecutors to function as second judges; they are second judges who do not act fully independently of the judiciary.

Although procedural rules reinforce the prosecutor's role as a second judge, those procedures standing alone do not guarantee that a prosecutor will take an active role in looking for the truth. For example, while a prosecutor may comply with the procedural rule that requires prosecutors to summarize the facts for and against the accused, that rule does not require a prosecutor to pose questions to witnesses and actually resolve factual ambiguities.[14] It is thus possible for a

[10] §199 StPO.

[11] Prosecutor Interview [6SB], 23 February 2006.

[12] Ministry of Justice Interview [9CK], 4 May 2006.

[13] Public Prosecutor Interview [4GG], 30 January 2006.

[14] §293(1) StPO.

prosecutor to comply on a superficial level with the duty of objectivity by participating in certain procedures that have become mere ritualized manifestations of that duty.

While statutory mandates force prosecutors to pay lip service to objectivity, the level of reflexivity mandated by the law is limited. In fact, in my interviews prosecutors would point to the fact that they had summarized the evidence in favor of the accused at the conclusion of trial—supporting the contention that German prosecutors did indeed view the case through an objective lens.[15] Nonetheless, a prosecutor's minimal compliance with ritualized procedural requirements may not move the truth-finding process forward.

From an empirical standpoint it cannot be said that a prosecutor functions as a "second judge" on the basis of a single prosecutorial decision. For example, a prosecutor who merely summarizes the evidence presented at trial cannot be said to function objectively if the prosecutor failed to order the police to pursue potentially exculpatory evidence. Discovering the meaning of objectivity in practice requires going beyond a mere checklist evaluation of prosecutorial practices. In an effort to bring the analysis of prosecutorial objectivity beyond mere conformity with procedural requirements, in the next sections I explore the relational stance that a prosecutor takes vis-à-vis the presiding judge in a courtroom. Since the presiding judge organizes the presentation of evidence and initiates the questioning of witnesses at trial, a prosecutor's stance in the courtroom is necessarily a reactive one.[16] It is the presiding judge who sets the tone for the main proceeding and the prosecutor must decide how to position herself in relation to the role that the judge plays in the courtroom.[17] The ambiguous nature of the prosecutor's role is reflected in courtroom architecture throughout Germany.[18] In some courtrooms, the prosecutor takes a seat adjacent to and level with the judge or judicial panel. In other courtrooms, the prosecutor sits at a table that is separate from the judicial bench and on par with the defense counsel's seat in the courtroom. According to one senior prosecutor, older courtrooms tend to conform to the former style which reflected a

[15] Participant Observation [3TW], 9 November 2005. I observed the conclusion of a main proceeding in a fraud case involving two female defendants who had ordered a number of products online but never paid for the products. In the prosecutor's final argument, the prosecutor pointed out that the value of the fraud committed had been relatively small and that the merchandise ordered were gifts for one of the defendant's children. The prosecutor also mentioned that both defendants had confessed and that they had expressed remorse. The prosecutor then moved on to point out that the main points against the defendants were that their criminal behavior reflected a certain level of initiative and intelligence. For example, the defendants had put false names on their mailboxes that corresponded to the aliases that the suspects had used to order the merchandise.

[16] Public Prosecutor Interview [8AR], 23 May 2006.

[17] Appellate Judge Interview [18UE], 24 June 2004.

[18] Senior Prosecutor Interview [5BC], 16 January 2006.

view of the prosecutor as an "organ of the judiciary," the new courtrooms which conform to the later style reflect a view of the prosecutor as an "organ of justice."[19]

As one prosecutor described it, "the prosecutor's task in the courtroom is a difficult one."[20] Before making a recommendation that the court should convict or acquit a defendant, a prosecutor's main task is to "clarify the facts of the case."[21] Given this role it is erroneous to say that a prosecutor has a completely disinterested stake in the main proceeding. The particular actions that a prosecutor might take to accomplish that task may differ depending on their own level of initiative as well as the clarity of the evidence presented. According to one experienced prosecutor:

> [I] listen to the evidence presented in the main proceeding . . . I then must summarize the evidence at the end of the proceeding and explain why I believe whether a certain charge has been proven or not. I will state whether [I think] a witness has lied and whether or not they have told the truth . . . I will state why a witness is credible [or not].[22]

At the outset, it should be noted that procedural factors encourage cooperation between judges and prosecutors. It is the prosecutor's office that supervises the collection of evidence, documents that evidence in written form, and presents that written file to the court.[23] Therefore, both judge and prosecutor enter the main proceeding having formed preliminary assessments of the case based on a shared body of evidence. This shared decision-making lens is dramatically different from the lens possessed by American jurors, who serve as fact-finders in the courtroom and are likely to be unfamiliar with the evidence that will be presented in court prior to trial.

There is a second procedural factor that encourages cooperation. Because the prosecutor functions as a "second judge" rather than as a party, it is perfectly legitimate for a judge to speak with a prosecutor without communicating with the defense attorney.[24] In fact it is a common practice for a judge and a prosecutor to speak before a proceeding to get a sense of the other's view of the case. Since most criminal cases do not present complicated legal issues, the court's attention during the main proceeding is focused primarily on collecting facts and determining an appropriate sentence (Machura 2001). The pre-trial conversations allow judges and prosecutors to determine points of agreement and disagreement prior to the presentation of evidence. They may also identify areas in which the evidence is conflicting and uncertain. These conversations are more likely to occur when either the judge or the prosecutor is relatively inexperienced and either or both would like to ameliorate the decision-making uncertainty that comes with inexperience.

From a normative perspective, a German prosecutor should ideally enter the trial with an open mind. According to an appellate judge I interviewed, when a prosecutor

---

19 Senior Prosecutor Interview [5BC], 16 January 2006.

20 Appellate Judge Interview [18UE], 24 June 2004.

21 Public Prosecutor Interview [5DK], 19 January 2006.

22 Public Prosecutor Interview [12CJ], 19 November 2005.

23 §§158–77 StPO.

24 Ministry of Justice Interview [9CK], 4 May 2006.

expresses a public opinion prior to trial that he or she is convinced that a suspect is guilty, it violates the duty of objectivity.[25] Commitment to this duty is underscored by the fact that German prosecutors do not meet with the witnesses prior to trial to shape their testimony or to convince a jury of the defendant's guilt.[26] Ideally a prosecutor should approach the trial with an open mind. The structure of questioning in German courtrooms supports this unrehearsed style. Unlike American procedure, the form of the questions and answers is less regulated.[27] Witnesses often give long narrative answers which American attorneys would consider to be unresponsive. This unregulated style, coupled with the lack of witness preparation, makes the presentation of evidence at trial less certain. According to one prosecutor, even though a prosecutor may have presented the court with a thick file, the facts that are "revealed" at trial may change your opinion of the case.[28] The fact that the judge structures the presentation of evidence at trial and conducts most of the questioning, combined with this less constrained structure of evidence presentation, gives the prosecutor the opportunity to view the evidence from a more objective standpoint.

Because most of the evidence-collection process is dominated by the police, a prosecutor may have prepared the case file and filed charges without ever meeting a single witness. In this circumstance, the courtroom hearing may give the prosecutor his or her first opportunity to size up the credibility of the witnesses as well as the defendant's demeanor. In sexual assault cases, which may turn on the credibility of the victim and the defendant, there may be more factual uncertainty at the outset of trial than in other types of cases. It is possible to theorize that in, sexual assault cases, German prosecutors may possess a more open mind toward the evidence than in other types of cases. Additionally, they may be more inclined to adopt a less biased stance towards the testimony presented at trial (Grande 2008). In the United States, on the other hand, the a prosecutor's opinion is largely set in stone before the trial. The trial is a play designed to "show" those facts to the jury (Gershman 2002). Evaluating and weighing the evidence in rape cases can be difficult for prosecutors when the case comes down to the suspect's word versus the victim's word.

These procedural differences between the unstructured presentation of testimony in German courtrooms and the rigid evidentiary rules in American courtrooms reflect different normative visions of the path to "truth." As Elisabetta Grande has pointed out, in "the Continental world, neutrality is still considered attainable in the criminal process" and officials are still charged with searching for the objective rather than an "interpretive" truth (Grande 2008, p. 155). The alchemy of justice is not achieved through strict reliance on a fair process, but rather through a neutral search for a substantive truth (Grande 2008). Viewed from this perspective, the prosecutor's duty of objectivity in the German system requires that prosecutors make a more robust commitment to discovering the objective truth.

---

[25] Appellate Judge Interview [13MU], 10 April 2004.

[26] Public Prosecutor Interview [3TW], 8 November 2005.

[27] §239 StPO.

[28] Public Prosecutor Interview [12CJ], 29 November 2005.

Where German prosecutors start to show an adversarial face in a certain case, the judge may discount their opinion.[29] As one Justice Ministry official related to me, when prosecutors from a certain prosecution office began to acquire a reputation for recommending harsh sentences in the courtroom, the judges stopped treating the prosecutors as second judges, whose opinion should be considered with the deference accorded to a colleague, and instead discounted their opinion as a party opinion.[30]

7.5 A Proposed Model of Prosecutorial Behavior at Trial

For analytical purposes one might imagine three different stances that a prosecutor might adopt towards the judge's presentation of evidence in the main proceeding. First, a prosecutor might elect to play an *acquiescent role* in the courtroom in which he or she asks few questions of the witnesses and is content to allow the court's presentation of evidence to stand on its own. Second, a prosecutor might play a *supportive role* in the courtroom by asking questions and making arguments that support the judge's understanding of the case. Finally, a prosecutor might disagree with the judge's conclusion of the case and play an *independent role* in the courtroom.

To some extent these categories oversimplify prosecutorial decision-making because a prosecutor's actions may not fit neatly into a single category. However, these categories are useful analytical constructs because they allow us to categorize prosecutorial behavior and create a richer description of how prosecutors interpret their duty to function as second judges. They are a useful starting point that will allow us begin to identify factors which may influence a prosecutor's trial strategy. To the extent that these factors are institution based, understanding those factors will shed light on how organizational factors shape prosecutorial objectivity. To that end, it is useful to define three different potential trial strategies.

In postulating what an *acquiescent trial strategy* might look like, one might include the following behaviors:

1. The prosecutor chooses not to ask questions that might provide more detail into the nature of the events which have transpired.
2. The prosecutor takes no active steps to challenge witness credibility.
3. The prosecutor does not attempt to acquire background information on the defendant's life circumstances.

---

29 Ministry of Justice Interview [9CK], 4 May 2006.

30 Ministry of Justice Interview [9CK], 4 May 2006.

4. The prosecutor does not petition the court to fill in evidentiary gaps in the evidence.
5. Although the prosecutor is not convinced that the suspect is guilty, the prosecutor would recommend that the court convict the defendant if the court is leaning towards conviction.

In postulating what a *supportive trial strategy* might look like, one might include the following behaviors:

1. The prosecutor takes the initiative to determine what the judge's view of the evidence is prior to the commencement of the main proceeding.
2. The prosecutor plays an active role in questioning the witnesses, but asks questions that attempt to fill in the gaps in the judge's theory of the case.
3. The prosecutor recommends a sentence that will provide the court with a reference point for its' own sentencing decision.[31]

Finally, in categorizing the trial behaviors of a prosecutor who plays an *independent role*, those behaviors might include

1. The prosecutor reaches an independent opinion of witness credibility and states that opinion in the final argument to the court.
2. The prosecutor argues in favor of acquittal when the court seeks to convict or argues in favor of conviction when the court believes that the evidence is insufficient.
3. The prosecutor poses provocative questions to test witness credibility.
4. The prosecutor suggests that the court obtain further evidence such as calling additional witnesses to testify.

It is important to note that, although a prosecutor may elect to act independently of the judge, a judge may independently concur with the prosecutor's assessment of the case. This scenario may represent the ideal script from a normative perspective—the two institutions, acting independently of each other, reach the same legal conclusion. In this spirit one prosecutor stated that:

> [My] satisfaction comes from making a decision about a case that the court concurs in. When the court agrees with my recommendation I feel that I have fulfilled my duty. I am not satisfied and can get annoyed when the judges ignore my recommendations and make decisions that I think are incorrect.[32]

[31] As one former judge explained to me, in some cases, at first glance it may look like there is disagreement between the sentencing recommendation made by the prosecutor and the judges, but the prosecutor for strategic reasons will recommend a sentence that is more severe than the sentence that the court will impose. By inflating his or her sentencing recommendation, the prosecutor may be trying to increase the likelihood that the defendant will not file an appeal. The greater the difference between the judge's final determination and the prosecutor's recommendation, the likelier it is that the defendant will not challenge the sentence by filing an appeal. Ministry of Justice Interview [9CK], 4 May 2006.

[32] Public Prosecutor Interview [5DK], 19 January 2006.

7.6 The Construction of Prosecutorial Objectivity: A Look at Three Cases

7.6.1 Overview

The German Code of Criminal Procedure defines a minimal set of bench-line parameters designed to ensure that prosecutors function as neutral and objective second judges in the courtroom. In this section I examine the decisions made by three prosecutors in three different sexual assault cases in order to understand how prosecutors interpret this duty. I have purposely selected three cases in which the "truth" was difficult to determine in order to highlight the complex range of prosecutorial behavior in the courtroom. Although the task of evaluating the evidence may be straightforward, there are many cases in which the evidence conflicts. These cases offer a rich opportunity to see how prosecutors navigate an uncertain truth-finding process.

It is important to note that the definition of rape in German criminal law makes the prosecution of rape cases more difficult. In the words of one sexual crimes prosecutor, the definition of rape under German law is "archaic" because the victim's lack of consent is not sufficient.[33] The court must find that the suspect used force or a serious threat to effectuate the crime.[34] The threat must refer to a loss of life or a serious injury.[35] While some courts have shown their willingness to interpret the requirement of force liberally, this requirement represents a hurdle that is not found today in many other Western countries.[36] This requirement, coupled with the fact that the evidence in sexual assault cases may be conflicting and subject to interpretation, often means that the central question facing prosecutors is whether or not the victim is a credible witness. While prosecutors in some jurisdictions commonly rely on reports prepared by expert witnesses to evaluate a victim's credibility,[37] in other jurisdictions prosecutors will retain expert witnesses only if the victim is extremely young or suffers from a mental disorder.[38]

---

[33] Public Prosecutor Interview [8PT], 23 May 2006.

[34] Public Prosecutor Interview [8PT], 23 May 2006.

[35] *See* §177 StGB which states: "Whoever coerces another person 1) with force; 2) by a threat of imminent danger to life or limb; or 3) by exploiting a situation in which the victim is unprotected and at the mercy of the perpetrator's influence, to suffer the commission of sexual acts of the perpetrator or a third person on himself or to commit them on the perpetrator or a third person shall be punished."

[36] Public Prosecutor Interview [8PT], 23 May 2006.

[37] Public Prosecutor Interview [7CX], 7 April 2006.

[38] Public Prosecutor Interview [8AR], 23 May 2006.

7.6.2 Case One: Rosenberg

In the first case, the investigating prosecutor charged a Latvian national with forcibly raping a woman and stealing her purse in a large German city (*Rosenberg*).[39] The case was handled at trial by a prosecutor who does not normally handle sexual assault cases. Prior to trial, the trial prosecutor contacted the prosecutor who had directed the investigation and was told that an appropriate sentence in the case would be 3 years. According to the complaint in the case file, the defendant attacked a woman behind a public restroom on the city's pedestrian mall.[40] The investigating prosecutor had alleged that the suspect had violated the statute prohibiting assault with bodily injury,[41] Section 177, in part, defines the crime of rape in the following terms:

(1) Whoever coerces another person:

1. with force;
2. by a threat of imminent danger to live or limb; or
3. by exploiting a situation in which the victim is unprotected and at the mercy of the perpetrator's influence, to suffer the commission of sexual acts of the perpetrator or a third person on himself or to commit them on the perpetrator or a third person, shall be punished with imprisonment for not less than one year.

According to the facts stated in the complaint, the suspect hit Frau H. on the back of her head with his fist, forced Frau H. to have anal intercourse with him, and finally took Frau H.'s pocketbook which contained her keys and money before leaving the crime scene.[42] While the police investigation revealed that the victim was in a blackout at the time of the alleged rape, the officers took statements from two other witnesses. One was a Turkish gentleman who, for cultural reasons, was extremely reluctant to describe what he observed in open court. The second was an elderly woman who witnessed the defendant leaving the crime scene.

In accord with German criminal procedure the prosecutor read the complaint in open court to commence the trial. The judge then began questioning the defendant about his personal circumstances. Although he was not required to do so, at this time the defendant elected to tell the judge his account of the events. When the defendant began to tell the judge what happened in general terms, the judge stepped in and posed specific questions to the defendant. The defendant related to the court that he was a Latvian resident and currently separated from his wife. At the time of his arrest, he was traveling through Germany on his way to France to look for work. He proceeded to tell the court that on the date in question he had been drinking with six to eight people when a young woman approached the group. The suspect

[39] Public Prosecutor Interview [13WT], 18 November 2005.

[40] *See* Participant Observation [13WT], 8 December 2005.

[41] *See* §223 StGB which states: "(1) whoever physically maltreats or harms the health of another person, shall be punished with imprisonment for not more than five years or a fine. (2) an attempt shall be punishable."

[42] Participant Observation [13WT], 8 December 2005.

claimed that the young woman propositioned two other men in the group before she walked up to him, put her key in his pocket, and told him that she wanted to go with him to her house. The suspect followed the young woman willingly out of the bar, walking with her along the pedestrian walkway until they reached the public toilet facilities. At that point, Frau H. lifted up her shirt and kissed him. They proceeded to have consensual sex. During the defendant's entire testimony, the prosecutor only posed a single question to the defendant—namely, whether he had struck the victim on the back of her head.

The first witness to take the stand was the alleged victim, Frau H. According to the complaint, the victim was a 27 year-old unemployed woman, living on government support in a small town on the city outskirts. The judge's initial questioning proceeded as follows[43]:

Judge:	*On the fifth of September there were charges made. We heard from Mr. S. Now we would like to hear from you what happened.*
Frau H.:	*I went to the police …*

Only a few minutes into Frau H.'s testimony, the prosecutor interrupted:

Prosecutor:	*Have you been drinking today? I can smell alcohol.*
Frau H.:	*Yes. I had 2–3 vodkas this morning. I was nervous.*

At this interesting juncture, the defense attorney alleged that the witness was incapable of testifying because in her impaired condition she could not understand the importance of telling the truth. However, the judge, hearing no objection from the prosecutor, allowed the questioning to proceed. As the victim continued to testify it became apparent that she remembered little from the event:

Judge:	*Can you describe him?*
Frau H.:	*Thin. Tall … the defendant is now bigger.*
Judge:	*We have photos in the file. Please come forward and look at them.*
Frau H.:	[Pointing to a picture of the suspect in the file]. *He kissed me … I am not sure.*
Judge:	*Do you remember identifying the suspect to the police?*
Frau H.:	*I went to the police* [voice trails off].
Judge:	*The suspect has a good memory. We need to know the truth. The suspect said that you kissed and you gave him your key and that you wanted to take him to your apartment. We have photos from the crime scene that you can look at. Do you remember these steps?* [Judge points to a photo].
Frau H.:	[No response].
Judge:	*The suspect said that you pulled up your t-shirt and walked arm in arm. Then you went behind the toilet and removed your pants.*
Frau H.:	*I was at the toilet. It hurt.*
Judge:	*What happened here?* [The judge points to a photo in the file of the public restroom].

(continued)

[43] As the proceedings were not recorded or taped, I compiled the "transcript" from my handwritten notes recorded in court during the proceeding.

Frau H.:	*I tried to take my purse. I can't remember. I was drunk* [She begins to cry]. *I can't say clearly. I didn't give anyone my key. He lifted my t-shirt and took my pocketbook away. I'm sure he took my purse ....*
Defense:	*He took your money away? Was it consensual intercourse?*
Frau H.:	[Crying].
Judge:	*You are only here as a witness. We just want to know what the truth is. Did it take a long time or was it a short time? ... It is important that you tell us what you remember. You have a duty to tell the truth. Did he hit or force you?*
Prosecutor:	*Can you remember the steps?*
Frau H.:	*There was pressure on my head and pain. My purse was gone. He pulled it away from my arm.*
Prosecutor:	*Do you know that or do you suspect that?*
Frau H.:	*I was so drunk that I could not stand. I tried to push him away. What could it have been?*
Judge:	*I believe that you are trying to be objective .... Are there further questions?*
Frau H.:	*I can definitely say that he took my purse away.*

These excerpts illustrate the critical role that the presiding judge plays in leading the fact-finding process at trial and suggest that the prosecutor acted as a neutral fact-finder during Frau H.'s questioning. It was the prosecutor, rather than the defense attorney or the judge, who first raised the issue of the victim's competency to testify. During the trial the prosecutor continued to press the victim, adopting an almost confrontational stance. For example, while the prosecutor tried to ascertain whether or not the rape was committed forcibly, he probed the accuracy of victim's memory. The tone of the questions that he posed to the victim was not the tone of a supportive advocate; rather, he adopted the tone of an individual determined to test the victim's credibility.

Because the prosecutor had not personally supervised the case investigation, he faced an additional challenge at trial when it became evident there were several witnesses cited in the police report whom the police never elected to interview. Prior to trial, neither the investigating prosecutor, nor the judge, nor the defense attorney deemed it necessary to attempt to locate these individuals. By the time that this prosecutor was assigned to handle the court hearing, the investigative file had already been sent to the court.[44] The trial prosecutor himself had only read the prosecution office's thin court file (*Handakte*), which did not contain all of the evidence collected in the case.[45] It was also surprising that the investigating prosecutor had not petitioned the court to appoint an expert witness.[46] German prosecutors frequently ask the court to hire a psychological expert witness in cases in which the credibility of the victim may be questioned.[47]

Given that the defendant's testimony was evasive and the victim's testimony inconclusive, the chances for obtaining a conviction in the case rested on the

[44] Public Prosecutor Interview [13WT], 18 November 2005.

[45] Public Prosecutor Interview [13WT], 18 November 2005.

[46] Public Prosecutor Interview [7CX], 7 April 2006.

[47] Public Prosecutor Interview [24AZ], 10 April 2008.

remaining witnesses.[48] The key remaining witness was a Turkish gentleman who had previously told the police that he had witnessed a rape. Unfortunately, when it came time for him to testify in court, the witness was extremely reticent. In the excerpt below, both the judge and the prosecutor press the witness to explain what he had seen. Additionally, the prosecutor invokes the full power of the state by threatening to file charges against the witness to force him to reveal the truth. In this capacity, the prosecutor not only supported the judge's efforts but he played the role of the "bad cop." Within the context of his quasi-judicial role, the prosecutor has room to play the heavy hand.

Judge:	*What can you say about how the woman appeared? Was she drunk?*
Witness:	*The girl was very drunk. She was in his arms . . . I don't know if it was rape . . .*
Judge:	*You only need to say what you saw. You don't need to say if you think it was a criminal act.* [The judge begins reading part of the witness's prior statement to the police]. "*The man had pushed the woman against the wall. He grabbed her arm and then lifted her clothes high.*"
Witness:	*That is correct.*
Judge:	*I believe you. We just need to know what happened.*
Witness:	*I told the police that I saw a crime.*
Judge:	*I don't expect you to say whether or not it was a rape. What really happened?* [The Judge continues reading from the witness's prior statement given to the police]. "*He put his hands on her breasts. He left by himself with her pocketbook.*"
	What did you see of the rape? A rape occurs when someone has sex with force.
Witness:	*Yes.*
Judge:	*You told the police more than you are saying here. You don't need to be ashamed to say these things. Just say what you saw. Just tell us about the crime. In Germany it is a crime.* [The Judge continues reading the file]. "*He kissed her on the breasts.*"
Witness:	*Yes. That is normal.*
Judge:	*No, that is not normal.* [Emphatically].
Witness:	*I am a foreigner.*
Judge:	*You have lived in Germany for ten years. How often have you seen this on the street? Three months is not so long [The incident had been reported three months before this trial date]. What can you remember? What did you see after he kissed her on the breast?*
Witness:	*He licked and kissed the breast.*
Judge:	*How was the woman standing?*
Witness:	*Her back was on the toilet. It was a rape.*
Judge:	[Reading from the witness's prior statement to the police]. "*The man pushed the woman's arms away. He opened his pants and took his penis out and pushed her head ....*"
Witness:	*I can't say.*
Prosecutor:	[With raised voice]. "*Stop playing with us and tell us what you know.*" [Slamming his fist onto the table]. "*I can charge you with a crime . . . the failure to report a rape.*"
Witness:	*I am not a child.*
Judge:	*Just tell us what you saw.*

(continued)

[48] Public Prosecutor Interview [13WT], 18 November 2005.

Witness: *"I saw him take her arm ... he grabbed her breast and pushed her head. I can't remember more ... he went away."*

Finally, in the following excerpt extracted from the prosecutor's concluding statement, the prosecutor weighs the inconsistencies in the testimony presented during the proceeding. Because none of the witnesses who testified had stated that the defendant had used violence while raping the victim, and in response to the suggestion of the presiding judge, the prosecutor elected not to argue that the case qualified as a rape under the definition provided in Section 177. After the trial, the prosecutor explained that obtaining a conviction under Section 177 was precluded by the fact that the victim had made conflicting statements about the use of force.[49] At one point Frau H. testified that the defendant had forcefully hit her head against the wall- later in her testimony she contradicted that statement.

Prosecutor: *What crime do we have here? It is not clear how much alcohol the victim consumed. The defendant himself said he met the victim and talked to her and that she had been drinking. We know that they went to the public toilet. He kissed her. He pushed her against the wall. There was intercourse with force. The case is difficult ... the victim cried out. The defendant left the area with the victim's purse.*

The defendant has denied that he stole the victim's purse. But one witness said that she saw the defendant leave by himself with the purse. The victim lives in [*another town*]. *Why would a person* [*from another town*] *give a person in Rosenberg her apartment key? That makes no sense.*

We cannot believe that the defendant did not look in the victim's purse. We also know from Herr D. that the victim was very drunk. She probably has an alcohol problem. We know she was pushed against the wall ... the victim was helpless. One witness said that it was unusual to see a person so drunk.

What is the legal conclusion? The defendant pressed the victim's head against the floor. The victim was very drunk. He hurt her when he pushed her against the wall. There is the objective evidence that she had pain, there was bleeding, and she was helpless. However, it was not a forcible rape under Section 177 ... but a crime under Section 179 [sexual abuse of persons incapable of resisting].[50] *The taking away of the purse constitutes robbery under Section 249.*

As to the matter of culpability ... I do not understand why the defendant did not say that he had made a mistake, he had been drinking. The suspect was not so drunk that he did not know what he was doing.

Because the victim was so drunk, Section 179 applies. The minimum punishment for this crime is two years. The normal punishment is a range between two and fifteen years. I recommend a punishment of three years.

[49] Public Prosecutor Interview [13WT], 18 November 2005.

[50] *See* §179 StGB. Section 179 states: (1) whoever abuses another person who is incapable of resisting; 1) because of a mental or emotional illness or disability, including an addiction or because of a profound consciousness disorder ... Imprisonment for no less than one year shall be imposed, if: the perpetrator completes an act of sexual intercourse or similar sexual actions with the victim, which are combined with a penetration of the body, or allows them to be committed on himself by the victim.

After a short period of deliberation, the panel of one professional judge and two lay judges announced their verdict. The panel found the defendant guilty of the crimes of sexual abuse of a person incapable of resisting as well as theft. The court immediately sentenced the defendant to a term of imprisonment of 2 years and 6 months on the ground that the minimum punishment for a charge of sexual abuse was a 2 year sentence. According to the court, the case qualified as a case of serious abuse under the statute. For that reason, the court had the authority to impose a sentence totaling 15 years of incarceration.

In this case, the prosecutor defined his role not as an advocate arguing for a conviction on the highest possible charge, but rather as a second judge whose role was to neutrally weigh the evidence presented by the court. In line with his duty to weigh the evidence objectively, the prosecutor asked the victim whether she had been drinking the day of the trial.[51] While the prosecutor could have remained silent, the prosecutor's actions may have merely preempted a likely comment from the defense or the court. Because the prosecutor confronted the victim about her alcohol consumption and threatened to file charges against a witness if he did not tell the whole truth, one might be tempted to conclude that the prosecutor adopted an *independent trial strategy*. By performing an inquisitive fact-finding role, the prosecutor did not function like an interested party. However, the prosecutor's demeanor and language did not project the image of a dispassionate fact-finder; rather, it mirrored the role of a spokesman for the state's quest for truth.

Because the prosecutor in this case aggressively questioned the witnesses, his trial strategy does not fall into the *acquiescent* category. Based on his aggressive challenge to the victim's testimony in the case, it might be tempting to categorize his strategy as being *independent*. However, in other key respects, the prosecutor did *not* act in a manner that was independent of the presiding judge. Despite the evidentiary gaps, the prosecutor did not suggest that the court call additional witnesses to testify. It is possible that one of those witnesses may have observed the suspect use force against the victim. The prosecutor could have challenged the victim's competence to testify. For these reasons, the prosecutor did not act with complete independence. His actions, by design or accident, supported and reinforced the judge's perspective of the case. Moreover, the prosecutor conformed to the investigating colleague's expectations, agreed with his recommendation that the suspect should be found criminally liable, and concurred with his colleague's sentencing recommendation. For these reasons, the prosecutor's strategy in this case was largely *supportive* of the presiding judge's perspective of the evidence.

[51] Public Prosecutor Interview [13WT], 18 November 2005.

7.6.3 *Case Two: Schneekopf*

The second trial involves a serious sexual abuse of a child.[52] Because the proceedings involved a child, I have changed many of the case's descriptive details to further protect the victim's anonymity. In this case, a middle aged family man was accused of sexually abusing an 11-year-old child.[53] Prior to the incident, the suspect and the victim's family frequently attended the same social events. Because the victim was a child, prior to trial the judge appointed an expert witness who was charged with interviewing the victim and evaluating her credibility. According to the expert, the victim was telling the truth. While the defense attorney hired his own expert witness, that witness did not attack the victim's credibility but rather challenged the procedures that the court's expert used to formulate his evaluation.

In contrast to the first case, a collateral attorney (*Nebenklager*) appeared in court to represent the victim's interests during the proceedings.[54] The main proceeding began with the judge questioning the defendant about his personal circumstances. At the time of the hearing, the defendant stated that he was 35 years old, happily married, and employed in a good position with a government agency. After giving his personal information, the defendant informed the court that he wished to testify about the events in question. The defendant proceeded to testify that, on the date of the alleged incident, he and his wife hosted a neighborhood party where the defendant consumed alcohol with his guests. As the party was winding down, the defendant spotted the victim, who was a local neighbor, standing outside. The victim told him that she had lost her house key. Since it was too late to go home, the defendant invited her inside his house. The defendant proceeded to tell the court that his wife had asked him to sleep in the living room because he snores after he drinks alcohol. At this point in the proceeding the judge began to interrupt the defendant and ask specific questions about the events in question. The defendant

---

[52] Punishment for a serious sexual abuse of a child is codified in §176a of the StGB (defining punishment for sexual abuse of children That section provides:

(1) The sexual abuse of children shall be punished with imprisonment for no less than one year in cases under Section 176 subsections (1) and (2), if:

1. a person over eighteen years of age completes an act of sexual intercourse or similar sexual acts with the child, which are combined with a penetration of the body, or allows them to be committed on himself by the child;
2. the act is committed jointly by more than one person;
3. the perpetrator by the act places the child in danger of serious health damage or substantial impairment of his physical or emotional development; or
4. the perpetrator has undergone a final judgment of conviction for such a crime within the previous five years ...

(2) In less serious cases under subsection (1), imprisonment from three months to five years shall be imposed, in less serious cases under subsection (2), imprisonment from one year to ten years.

[53] Participant Observation [4AJ], 1 February 2006.

[54] §395 StPO.

continued to testify, telling the court that both he and the victim slept on separate couches in the living room. He then testified that when they woke up in the morning, nothing abnormal had occurred. After the defendant finished his account, the judge gently confronted him and reminded him that he should testify honestly. At this point the prosecutor took over the questioning. In the excerpt below, the prosecutor asks the defendant about a prior allegation made against the defendant by the victim's father.

Prosecutor:	*The victim's father said that you also touched his other daughter's leg at a birthday party, is this true?*
Defendant:	*I don't know.*
Judge:	*Do you remember what happened at the birthday party?*
Defendant:	*I was sitting next to a girl and merely pinched her near her waist.*
Prosecutor:	*What clothing were you wearing when you went to sleep?*
Defendant:	*Boxer shorts.*
Prosecutor:	*One of your neighbors told the police that you are usually a friendly person except when you are drunk. Then you try to touch women. Is this true?*
Defendant:	*I have no reply.*
Prosecutor:	*Did you see the victim after the night of the alleged incident?*
Defendant:	*No. I never talked to her about this event. My relationship with her did not change until she talked to her mother about it.*

After the prosecutor concluded his questioning, the collateral prosecutor had this exchange with the defendant:

Collateral P:	*Was there another room in your house that the victim could have slept in?*
Defendant:	*No.*
Collateral P:	*I don't believe your story but you want to stick with it.*[55]

At this point in the hearing the judge announced that the court would take a short break so that the attorneys, the prosecutor, and the presiding professional judge could meet in the judge's chambers to discuss the possibility of a plea. In the cases I observed, conferences like this were not unusual frequently. The parties then adjourned to the judge's chambers and the defense attorney began the discussion by stating that the defendant would only accept a punishment of less than 1 year. The defense counsel stressed that the defendant would lose his job in the armed forces if the defendant received a more severe sentence. Counsel proposed that the defendant admit that he only touched the girl and that the court impose a sentence of less than 1 year.[56] The prosecutor immediately and categorically rejected the offer:

[55] While this statement would undoubtedly draw an objection in an American court because it is not a question, German procedural rules permit a wider range of questioning practices. *See* §136 (a) StPO (delineating the boundaries of questioning broadly).

[56] A 1 year sentence would apply only if the court found the defendant guilty of the less serious offense. *See* StGB §176a (mandating a minimum 2-year sentence for aggravated child abuse).

> I cannot agree to a different criminal act because *that is not what happened in this case*. The minimum penalty for this crime is two years. It is not my job to worry about the defendant's job; the burden is on the defendant to start a new career.

The prosecutor's stance underscores a key difference between American plea bargaining practices and the German practice of "confession bargaining." In the German system, the constitutional principles of fair trial and guilt (Turner 2009, p. 89) in theory limit the parameters of the bargaining process. Those limits aim to preserve the key elements of an inquisitorial system's truth-finding process.[57] After this exchange, the collateral prosecutor stated that she would not agree to the deal either because it would send a signal to the victim that the court did not believe her. Moreover, the advocate reminded defense counsel that, if the defendant were to insist on going forward with the trial, the defendant could receive a prison sentence of more than 4 years. After the defense counsel consulted with his client, the defendant rejected the deal.

At this point in the case, in a private conversation, the prosecutor related to me that because the defendant's testimony had been so inconsistent, it was likely that the defendant had lied. Ironically, when the victim in the case took the stand it quickly became apparent that her testimony was also problematic. In response to open-ended questioning from the court, the victim testified initially that she had simply fallen asleep on the couch and then woke up the next morning. The judge then shifted to a more focused, but still gentle, questioning technique attempting to prod the victim forward by reading excerpts from the victim's prior statement. While the victim then confirmed her initial allegations, she then alleged that the defendant had actually penetrated her. In her prior statement the victim had maintained that the defendant had only touched her private parts. The judge greeted this new allegation with skepticism and told the victim that this new revelation would make the court's decision difficult. The judge specifically told the victim: "We must determine what happened. There are two possibilities. First, nothing more happened than you said before. Second, the defendant's actions went further."

After the prosecutor and collateral attorney concluded questioning the victim, the defendant's attorney submitted his questions to the judge who, under German law, decided which questions she would ask the victim.[58] In addition, the judge may decide whether the other attorneys may directly question the victim. In some jurisdictions, the prosecutor, collateral prosecutor, and the defense attorney will type the questions that they would like the court to pose to the victim into a computer.[59] However, if a judge refuses to pose a question requested by one of

---

[57] *See Bundesgerichtshof* [BGH] [Federal Court of Justice] 3 March 2005, 50 *Entscheidungen des Bundesgerichtshofs in Strafsachen* [BGHSt] 40, 48 (holding that plea bargains are generally permissible under German law).

[58] In cases involving the testimony of children under the age of 16, the judge screens the defense attorney's questions and then may decide which questions will be permitted as well as whether the judge or the defense attorney shall pose those questions to the child. *See*, §241(a) StPO (granting the judge the authority to screen potential questions posed to witnesses under the age of 16).

[59] Public Prosecutor Interview [8AR], 23 May 2006.

the attorneys, the refusal may create an appellate issue.[60] Even in cases involving adult victims, the judge is obliged to intervene to stop the cross-examination if the attorney's interrogation becomes too aggressive.[61]

The challenge of finding the truth increased when the facts in the victim's testimony shifted on the stand. One of the two lay judges actually began to shake her head as the victim was testifying. After the victim's testimony concluded, the court announced another break. At this point the prosecutor related to me: "I am no longer convinced that the defendant is guilty. The victim has told three different versions of what happened ... This latest allegation is completely new ... I cannot argue that the suspect is guilty unless I am *convinced* that the allegations are true."[62] When the proceedings resumed, the judge read out loud a section of the Code of Criminal Procedure in open court that detailed the potential penalties that the defendant would face if he was convicted in the district court (*Landgericht*). In choosing to do so, it seemed clear that the judge was trying to convince the defendant to confess. If the defendant elected to seek a retrial at the higher court level he could face a sentence that exceeded 4 years of imprisonment. Because the current local court (*Amtsgericht*) was limited to imposing a sentence of less than 4 years, the judge hinted that it would be a wise decision for the defendant to confess.[63] The defendant and his counsel left the courtroom to once again discuss the possibility of a confession agreement. During the break the prosecutor related to me: "I am still concerned about whether the victim is telling the truth or not. Now it is apparent that she told the psychologist that she had never injured herself and yet on the stand she testified that she had injured herself. There are too many inconsistencies."[64] The judge then called the prosecutor into her chambers and asked him what he thought about the evidence so far. Because the judge had subtly suggested that the defendant confess, it was evident at this point that the judge was leaning

---

[60] Public Prosecutor Interview [8AR], 23 May 2006.

[61] *See*, §241(2) StPO (allowing the presiding judge to reject an inappropriate or irrelevant question).

[62] Public Prosecutor Interview [4AJ], 1 February 2006.

[63] The jurisdiction of the *Amtsgericht* is specified in sections 21 and 24 of the German Code on Court Constitution, while the jurisdiction of the *Landgericht* is specified in §74. *See generally* GVG, §§21–21(j), 24, 74–74(f) (regulating the jurisdiction of the *Amtsgericht* and the *Landgericht*). It is currently an undecided issue in German law as to whether rape cases may be filed directly into the *Landgericht* or regional court, bypassing the local court (*Amtsgericht*). Public Prosecutor Interview [4AJ], 1 February 2006. The prosecutor who tried the case told me that he would have filed the case directly into the *Landgericht* and that prosecutor who initially filed the case in the local court may have made that choice because it was easier for him to do so. However filing the case in the local court places an extra burden on the victim. Because defendants in local court (*Amtsgericht*) cases have the right to de novo appeal, the victim may have to testify in two proceedings. Regional Court (*Landgericht*) trials typically take longer than local court (*Amtsgericht*) proceedings as the court is likely to take testimony from all of the available witnesses. The reason for this is that there is only one level of appeal from cases heard at the regional court (*Landgericht*) level—an appeal to the Federal Criminal Court challenging legal issues in the case.

[64] Public Prosecutor Interview [4AJ], 1 February 2006.

towards convicting the defendant. Despite that fact, the prosecutor informed the court that he could not argue that the defendant was guilty. The prosecutor's potential pursuit of an *independent trial strategy* drew a look of concern on the judge's face and the meeting ended.

After the defendant and his attorney returned to the court room, the defense attorney stated that his client wanted the trial to continue. At this point, the prosecutor requested that the court take the testimony of the victim's teacher. By suggesting that the court call an additional witness to the stand, the prosecutor took an affirmative step towards clarifying the facts in the case and playing a potentially independent truth-finding role.

On the stand, the teacher testified that the victim had approached her after class one day crying. When she asked the victim what was wrong, the victim told her that her neighbor had sexually touched her. This new evidence corroborated the victim's initial account of the incident and appeared to tip the scales against the defendant.

After this witness departed from the stand, the collateral prosecutor directly addressed the defendant in open court informing him that, in her opinion, the witness was extremely credible. The victim advocate proceeded to tell the defendant that, the longer the trial lasted, the more it would traumatize the victim. In closing, she suggested that if the defendant continued to call the victim a liar, it would further traumatize the victim. These comments highlighted the collateral prosecutor's role as a party acting on the victim's behalf and led the defense attorney to request a meeting in chambers. The judge began the meeting by stating outright that she believed that the defendant was guilty. In contrast to the American plea bargaining process, in which the judge merely confirms or rejects an agreement negotiated between the prosecution and the defense, the court's leadership role in the "confession bargaining" process represents a distinct difference between the roles of the players in the two systems. Since the presiding judge in the German system structures the presentation of evidence and dominates the questioning process, the judge has a stake in moving the case toward a resolution. Until this point in the case, it was the collateral prosecutor and the presiding judge who exerted pressure on the defendant to confess. That pressure eventually swayed the defendant.

After a discussion between all of the participants, everyone settled on a recommended sentence of 2 years of probation. When the parties returned to court, the defendant admitted that he had abused the victim. Consistent with German practice, the admission was accepted as part of the trial testimony itself, rather than as the basis for a free-standing plea.[65] The confession was followed by the attorneys' closing statements. In his closing, the prosecutor complied with his statutory duty to cite the factors that weighed both in favor of and against the defendant by stating:

> The range of sentences for this charge is from 2 to 15 years. I recommend two years of probation. On the one hand, the crime is severe. On the other hand, because the defendant has admitted committing the crime, he can get treatment . . . The defendant has two children

[65] Public Prosecutor Interview [4AJ], 1 February 2006.

of his own. In addition, he is going to lose his job as well as his pension . . . There were also problems with the victim's account of what happened. We heard different versions of the story.

After the final arguments concluded, the presiding judge retired to "deliberate" with the two lay judges. In theory, the lay judges could have outvoted the professional judge and refused to accept the agreement (Machura 2001, pp. 461–463). That did not happen here. When the judges returned to the court room the presiding judge announced that the defendant had been found guilty and that the court had decided to impose a 2 year suspended sentence with certain other conditions.

What does prosecutorial objectivity mean in this case? First, on the basis of the prosecutor's questioning, it appears that the prosecutor tested the credibility of both the victim and the defendant. In this respect, the prosecutor appeared open to the possibility that neither side was telling the truth. Second, while the prosecutor did not serve as the victim's advocate, he was not the defendant's advocate either. Although he privately voiced his doubts to the presiding judge and collateral prosecutor, he did not voice his doubts publicly until a deal had been struck. Interestingly, the collateral prosecutor was the driving force behind the deal. The presence of the collateral party, in effect, enabled the prosecutor to remain neutral. It was the collateral prosecutor, as well as the presiding judge, who continued to confront the defendant in order to sway the defendant to admit his guilt. While, during the trial the prosecutor and the judge disagreed as to whether the evidentiary burden had been satisfied, the collateral prosecutor and the judge were able to use the teacher's corroborating testimony to push the defendant towards a confession. It was a confession that came with a reduced sentence of probation rather than imprisonment. This reduction in sentence is common in rape cases adjudicated in German courts when witness credibility is at issue.[66]

The dynamic of the proceeding is an interesting one that calls into question the ability of analysts to draw bright line distinctions between the roles played by the different actors in the case. While the judge hinted that the defendant could face a higher imprisonment level if he insisted on pursuing the case further, the collateral prosecutor continued to stress the trauma that the process was causing the victim. During this exchange, the prosecutor stayed on the sidelines. Once the negotiations over the deal had commenced, however, the prosecutor set a bottom line for the sentence that cost the defendant his employment. It would have been interesting to see whether the prosecutor would have actually recommended an acquittal had the trial continued. In essence, while the prosecutor viewed the evidence through an objective lens, he stayed in the background while other participants steered the trial towards an agreement. He did, however, set a bottom line for a recommended sentence even before he was convinced that sufficient evidence existed to show guilt. When an agreement was in sight, the prosecutor represented the state and the

[66] Public Prosecutor Interview [13WT], 18 November 2005 (noting that it is often difficult to be certain who is telling the truth in rape cases because you must often weigh the victim's word against the defendant's word).

law's interest by refusing to redefine the crime to allow the defendant to protect his job. Although the prosecutor acted independently of the presiding judge throughout most of the main proceeding, when the scales of credibility tipped towards the victim, the prosecutor joined in confirming the confession agreement.

While the prosecutor pursued an *independent strategy*, one could argue that the role played by the collateral prosecutor both created the space that allowed him to voice his doubts as well as narrowed his decision-making options once the other players convinced the defendant to confess. It is not clear, however, in what sense the trial represented an objective search for the truth. The active role that the presiding judge played in trying to effectuate a deal raises a question as to whether the judge's desire to conclude the case colored her own objectivity.

From the prosecutor's perspective, "confession agreements" may be seen not merely as time-saving, but also as a means of reducing evidentiary uncertainty. When the evidence presented in the courtroom is indeterminate, a prosecutor who is charged with the duty to view that evidence through an "objective," rather than an adversarial, lens may be in a more uncertain decision-making position. While a prosecutor in an adversarial system may simply argue for a conviction and leave the outcome up to the jury, the decision-making posture of German prosecutors is more ambiguous. As one prosecutor in a money-laundering trial related to me, "conflicts in witness testimony make me uncomfortable."[67] By agreeing to a "confession agreement," a prosecutor can minimize the uncertainty of the fact-finding process. Although the suspect's confession may confirm the suspect's guilt, that level of guilt may be diminished by a less-than truthful confession. In essence, the confession may be viewed as a move towards the truth, but it is not necessarily "the truth." In this light a prosecutor is willing to accept a confession agreement when the degree of movement towards the truth outweighs the degree of guilt confirmed by the sentence. Viewed from this perspective, these agreements do not necessarily short-circuit the truth-finding process, but rather help the system achieve some level of justice. Against an uncertain evidentiary backdrop, the interrelationships between the courtroom actors, not only affect the delivery of justice, but also delineate the extent to which the truth-finding process is an objective one.

7.6.4 Case Three: Strehlen[68]

In this final case, the interrelationship between the presiding judge and the defense attorneys complicated the prosecutor's willingness to perform a robust fact-finding role in the courtroom. Moreover, as in the *Rosenberg* case, the trial prosecutor did

[67] Public Prosecutor Interview [5DK], 19 January 2006.

[68] *Strehlen* is a fictitious name that I have assigned to the city where the proceeding was held.

not supervise the investigation conducted in the case.[69] These factors dramatically shaped the courtroom's decision-making dynamic.

In 2008, the state charged two 18-year-old young men with seriously abusing a child under the age of 14—a major crime (*Verbrechen*) under German law.[70] In contrast to the other case-studies discussed in this chapter, which took place in lower (*Amtsgericht*) courtrooms, the investigating prosecutor filed this case in the regional court (*Landgericht*).[71] Although regional court panels usually contain three professional judges and two lay judges, the presiding judge assigned the case to a smaller panel and appointed a less experienced colleague to serve as the presiding judge.[72] As will become apparent, the judge's inexperience and personality complicated the truth-finding process as the judge lacked the requisite skill necessary to question the key witness in the case—the victim. In addition, the two defense attorneys adopted a combative trial strategy that was more reflective of adversarial trials.[73]

To begin, by the time that the trial prosecutor received the case file, the case had already been sent to the court and, it was evident to the trial prosecutor that the investigation had been hastily performed. As I learned from trial prosecutor, the prosecutor assigned to the case at the investigation stage had been about to go on maternity leave when the alleged rape occurred. Rather than send the case to a colleague to complete the investigation, the prosecutor elected to file charges without sending the evidence for DNA testing or ordering that a psychologist evaluate the victim's credibility. According to the trial prosecutor, the original prosecutor had expected that the judge would order the DNA testing as well as the psychological evaluation if necessary.

By the time the trial reached its second day, the uncertain nature of the victim's testimony, as well as the escalating conflict between the presiding judge and the defense attorneys had created an uncharacteristically contentious trial. It had become apparent to both the prosecution and the defense by the second day of trial that the evidence presented in court so far had been inadequate to establish the defendants' guilt. Consequently, a key issue put to debate in the trial's second day was whether or not the trial court should order that the state further investigate the case.

---

[69] Participant Observation [13WT], 8 December 2005.

[70] According to §176a StGB, the minimum punishment is a term of imprisonment no less than 1 year the maximum punishment is 10 years of imprisonment. *See* §176a StGB.

[71] Participant Observation [4BI], 24 February 2006.

[72] German procedural law permits a smaller panel of *Landgericht* judges to hear less serious cases. *See* GVG, §76(2) (providing that the chief judge may decide, at the beginning of the main proceedings, whether it will be composed of only two judges unless the participation of a third judge appears necessary due to the scale or complexity of the case).

[73] Although prosecutors and judges acknowledge that defendants have a right to an attorney under German law, many of them look on the so-called "conflict defense attorneys" (*Konfliktverteidiger*) with disdain. Public Prosecutor Interview [13WT], 18 November 2005 (noting that these attorneys are "bad lawyer[s]" whose clients receive a "higher punishment… The defense counsel's job is to secure a confession.").

As the second day of trial began, the defense called into question the victim's credibility by highlighting differences between the victim's original statement to the police and her testimony on the stand. On the night of the alleged rape, the victim had told the police that two young men had climbed into her open bedroom window. While one of the unknown suspects threatened her with a gun, the other suspect raped her. On the stand however, the victim testified that only one young man had entered her room that evening and that she had previously met that young man at a party. Complicating the fact-finding process further was the fact that the initial interview conducted by a police officer was replete with leading questions and answers in which the victim essentially confirmed verbatim the wording of the officer's questions.

The inconsistency in the victim's testimony was not the only reason that the truth-finding process at trial proved to be difficult. During trial, the victim's parents admitted that the victim had been previously hospitalized several times for mental health issues. Had the investigating prosecutor petitioned the court to order a psychological exam of the victim, the court and the prosecutor would have had the benefit of expert witness's evaluation of the victim's credibility. As the trial continued, the factual uncertainty increased. A key witness on the trial's second day was, the victim's close friend, who testified that both she and the victim had conducted a séance after the alleged rape and a ghost had appeared and told the victim that she had not been raped. Unfortunately, the ghost could not be called into court to verify this testimony.

The testimony of the two defendants was also problematic. While one of the defendants testified that he had in fact slept with the victim, he claimed that the sex was consensual.[74] Although the second defendant denied having had sex with the victim, when the police searched his bedroom, they found the gun that the victim had identified as having been used in the rape. The available forensic evidence could not settle the testimonial uncertainty. Although medical personnel had examined the victim immediately following the incident and her medical exam had showed evidence of trauma, by the time of the trial, neither the prosecutor's office nor the court had ordered the forensic lab to test the DNA evidence collected during the exam.

Halfway through the trial's second day, both defense attorneys moved the court to appoint a psychologist to evaluate the victim's credibility. According to a prosecutor who routinely prosecutes sexual crime cases, expert witnesses are routinely used to assist the court in evaluating the victim's credibility:

> [With sexual crimes involving children] it is the task of the expert witness to investigate whether or not the child has been exposed to suggestive influences ... There are many possibilities which must be properly investigated ... I have also seen expert opinions where the expert states that there has [sic] been so many statements that the expert can no longer discern what the truth is.[75]

[74] Public Prosecutor Interview [4BI], 3 February 2006.

[75] Public Prosecutor Interview [5CK], 22 January 2006.

Although the trial prosecutor confided to me that he would have petitioned the court to appoint an expert psychologist had he supervised the case investigation, he took no position in open court on the defense motion.[76] By failing to support the defense motion, the prosecutor's actions did not advance the truth-finding process.

The defense also requested that the court order the forensic laboratory to test the evidence collected at the scene and from the victim. Complying with this request was well within the power of the court. According to the Code of Criminal Procedure, when it becomes apparent during the main proceeding that the investigation conducted by the prosecution is insufficient, a court is free to extend the taking of evidence "in order to establish the truth ... [of] all facts and means of proof relevant to the decision."[77] Moreover, this provision grants the court the authority to summon witnesses and experts not interviewed during the case investigation process. Under German law, both the prosecutor and the defense counsel possess the right to petition the court to hear the testimony of additional witnesses.[78] The prosecutor failed to support this motion as well despite the fact that DNA testing is a common forensic tool in sexual assault cases.

The defense argument regarding the two motions provoked a contentious exchange between defense counsel and the presiding judge. As the prosecutor stood silent, the presiding judge denied both motions and stated that it was obvious that there was no need to take further evidence to render a verdict. The judge then closed the proceeding's evidentiary phase and announced a short break. During the break the judge pulled the prosecutor aside and informed him that he should prepare to make his closing argument. Ironically, the prosecutor did object to the judge at this point as the clock was approaching 7:00 p.m. This objection, however, drew a curt response from the judge to the effect that "he [should] start living in the real world."

Prior to the reading of the court's verdict, I asked the prosecutor whether he believed that the victim's testimony was sufficiently credible to recommend that the court convict both defendants. The prosecutor responded: "I believe [the victim] but only in a small part because there are so many inconsistencies."[79] The prosecutor further explained to me:

> I am only sixty percent convinced that the second defendant is guilty. I have been thinking about my closing argument and I am having difficulty reaching a "certain" decision because the victim's statements are inconsistent. This is only the second time in my fifteen[−]year career that I am not satisfied with the evidence presented during the main proceeding ... The maximum sentence available against both defendants is four years. They are both very young. I think I will recommend a sentence of four years for both defendants. I think that the Federal Criminal Court will overturn the decision in any case ... I have a bad feeling in my gut about this case. Although there is uncertainty, there is not enough uncertainty to

[76] Public Prosecutor Interview [4BI], 3 February 2006.

[77] §244(2) StPO.

[78] §245(2) (obliging the court to extend the taking of evidence to witnesses summoned by the defendant or prosecutor).

[79] Public Prosecutor Interview [4BI], 3 February 2006.

recommend that the court acquit the defendants ... I believe at the center of the case is a truth but around the center are inconsistencies. I wish that we had had an expert report in the case on the subject of the victim's truthfulness.

In this case it appeared that the decisions made during the investigation stage of the proceeding had a binding impact on the trial prosecutor's conduct. In particular, neither the judge nor the prosecutor was inclined to stop the proceedings to allow more evidence to be collected. While the judge was convinced that the evidence presented during the trial was sufficient, the prosecutor was more equivocal; he merely wished that he could rely on an expert witness's report. Moreover, the prosecutor recommended that the court convict both defendants and impose a prison sentence despite the fact that he was not fully convinced of their guilt. While he doubted the reliability of some of the testimony, he was also confident that the higher court would overturn the convictions. That result, however, would have imposed an additional cost on the victim. A new trial would have forced the victim to testify a second time.

In this case the trial prosecutor's decision-making could be categorized as an *acquiescent* strategy. Although the trial highlighted gaps in the investigation, the prosecutor was unwilling to support the defense attorneys' requests to supplement those gaps. While the prosecutor who handled the case at trial had the advantage of viewing the evidence through fresh eyes, the prosecutor's timidity in confronting the court and his unwillingness to side with the opinion voiced by conflict-oriented defense attorneys led him to acquiesce to the opinion of the presiding judge. Rather than challenge the court's opinion, his commitment to objectivity consisted of merely hoping that the appellate court would overturn the decision. In this case, the prosecutor's allegiance to informal collegial controls and his acquiescence to the presiding judge's courtroom decisions suggest that, under certain conditions, some prosecutors may be reluctant to perform a robust fact-finding role in the courtroom.

Although German law envisions that courts will aggressively pursue the truth at trial through a full examination of the evidence, that truth-finding process was certainly short-circuited in this case. The confluence of dynamic relational forces between the investigating and trial prosecutors, between the presiding judge and defense counsel, and between the prosecutor and the presiding judge, handicapped the search for truth. Concomitantly, a series of unique circumstances created a decision-making dynamic that was far different from the process of constructive compromise reflected in the *Schneekopf* case. These circumstances included the fact that the initial prosecutor on the case had filed the charges prematurely because she was leaving on maternity leave. Due to the chief judge's decision not to participate in the case, a less experienced judge, who had difficulty managing the proceeding, directed the proceeding.[80] The two defendants were represented by attorneys who elected to pursue a conflict-oriented strategy. Finally, the prosecutor's last argument to the court assumed the character of a hedged bet. While he

[80] Public Prosecutor Interview [4BI], 3 February 2006.

recommended that the court convict the defendants, he fervently hoped that the higher court would overturn the conviction.[81] The prosecutor's acquiescent strategy did nothing to countermand the direction of a truth-finding process that fell short of a thorough investigation of the facts.

Ultimately this case underscores the fluid and contextual nature of the evidence-weighing process. The interrelationships between the parties involved in the case strongly impacted the case outcome. The prosecutor's decision-making process seemed calculated to preserve the prosecutor's relationship with the presiding judge, rather than to uphold the system's commitment to finding the truth. The prosecutor did not act as a truly independent second judge; rather, the prosecutor chose to speak out in favor of a conviction despite questionable decision-making by the presiding judge. He relied on the appellate court to serve as a check on the decision-making of the inexperienced judge, rather than to fulfill the duties of his own position. The prosecutor's decision to recommend that the court find the defendants guilty was far removed from a detached weighing of the facts and the law and, instead, underscored the interdependence of the prosecutorial and judicial functions. The case raises questions as to whether the prosecutorial and judicial branches can truly function independently as well as the extent to which trial prosecutors are willing to *correct* mistakes made by the investigating prosecutor. In order to act in a manner that evidenced a stronger commitment to supporting a full investigation of the victim's allegation, the prosecutor would have had to adopt a more confrontational tone against the presiding judge. That strategy could have compromised the prosecutor's relationship with his colleague as well as with the presiding judge and violated unwritten norms of collegiality between judges and prosecutors. More problematic was the fact that, by joining in the defense motions, the prosecutor would have had to violate a clear norm against cooperating with conflict-oriented defense attorneys.[82]

---

[81] Public Prosecutor Interview [4BI], 3 February 2006.

[82] When I asked prosecutors what the role of the defense attorney was, many prosecutors criticized defense attorneys who adopted a confrontational courtroom style. As one prosecutor explained to me:

> I think it's good to be aggressive, if you feel that there's a chance for you at the end that the judge thinks that, "Okay, maybe he hasn't committed the crime." That's okay. It is the task of [a] good defense attorney. But in cases where you have a defense attorney that makes mistakes and I think he is not a bad one but you see I think in those cases then we help him. We say let us do it this way, it is better for the client and if he says okay I think you are right. Then I think it's no problem if you have a bad lawyer. But I think as I told you, these cases, if there's a case, for example. Rape is a typical case. In rape, you have to see at the beginning of a trial if you are a good defense attorney, you have to [look at] this case [and ask] what should you do? Then I think it's better for you to say, 'Okay, my client's guilty, but you have to tell the reasons he did what he did.' But sometimes the lawyer is not good then they blame the victim, the victim was guilty and then you are aggressive against them. I think judges, that is not okay. I think you get a higher punishment. Public Prosecutor Interview [13WT], 18 November 2005.

7.7 Conclusion: The Relational Construction of Prosecutorial Objectivity

The face of objectivity in German courtrooms is both constitutive and relational. According to German law, prosecutors possess a duty to conduct an objective investigation while trial courts are bound to ensure that all evidence that is necessary to discover the truth is presented at trial.[83] Ideally, the presiding judge serves as a check on the prosecutor's decisions during the investigation stage, while the prosecutor serves as a check on judicial decision-making at trial. Although German law posits that the prosecutor and the court function as independent organs of justice,[84] a desire to achieve consensus affects the interrelationship between the two institutions at trial. Because the two institutions function in an interdependent manner through their courtroom decision-making, prosecutors are more likely to support or acquiesce to judicial decision making. As a result, trial outcomes are a function of a "relational dance" between the judge and the prosecutor and the other parties involved in the case. Although the institutions of the prosecution and the judiciary are separated on paper, my research demonstrates that they often dance together. In this respect, my research confirms Grande's characterization of Continental procedure as a "rumba" dance "in which many dancers of different capacities dance together in the common enterprise of discovering the truth" (Grande 2008, p. 155).

While prosecutors and judges play interdependent roles, that interdependence does not completely handcuff prosecutorial decision-making at trial. As these three cases illustrate, individual prosecutors interpret the principle of objectivity differently. That difference manifests itself in the courtroom decisions that prosecutors make. Whether a prosecutor chooses to adopt an acquiescent, supportive, or independent strategy towards the presiding judge, those decisions help not only to shape case outcomes in the criminal justice system, but also to determine the extent to which the truth-finding process mirrors the normative ideal of neutrality.

For comparison purposes I have summarized the key characteristics of the three cases below. In the *Rosenberg* case, while the prosecutor played a neutral role and challenged the credibility of several of the witnesses, his view of the evidence in the case ultimately coincided with the presiding judge's vision. Although he appeared to play the role of the "bad cop" towards courtroom witnesses, in the end, the prosecutor and court agreed on the case disposition. Together, the presiding judge and the prosecutor in that case dominated the trial process and guided the trial's outcome.

In contrast, in the *Schneekopf* and *Strehlen* trials, the assessment of the evidence made by the prosecutors and the presiding judges differed. Although the prosecutors in both cases possessed varying levels of doubt about whether a conviction was

[83] §244(2) StPO.

[84] §150 GVG.

warranted, neither prosecutor openly challenged the court's decision-making. The dynamic of both cases differed considerably. In the *Schneekopf* case, the presiding judge reached out to the prosecutor to determine his opinion of the evidence. The prosecutor responded by voicing his doubts. In essence, the collateral prosecutor resolved the disagreement between the prosecutor and the judge by pushing for a "confession agreement." Ironically, it was the actions of an interested party, working on the victim's behalf, and the acquiescence of defense counsel that led to the case's cooperative resolution. Despite his doubts about the case, the prosecutor was not willing to "hand over the store" to reach an agreement. He insisted on a sentence that would cost the defendant his employment and pension. Absent an activist collateral prosecutor, it is likely that the prosecutor would have recommended that the court acquit the defendant.

Finally, in the *Strehlen* case, neither the court nor the prosecutor took the steps necessary to supplement the evidence presented in court when it became apparent that the victim's credibility was open to question. While the prosecutor had doubts about the case, he recommended a conviction hoping that an appellate court would overturn it. Although the defense attorneys in the case petitioned the court to supplement the case investigation, the prosecutor failed to support that motion. Through his acquiescence, the prosecutor did not attempt to navigate an intermediate truth-finding path that might have dampened the impact of the defense attorneys' aggressive, conflict-provoking strategy, or the presiding judge's inexperience.

Table 7.1, detailed below, summarizes the strategies implemented by the various players in these cases.

In each of these cases, the evidence presented in court did not present a clear picture of guilt. The malleability of facts and memory, which occurs regularly in sexual assault cases, shaped the fact-finding process at trial. In all three cases, victim interview evidence, which appeared reliable during the case investigation stage, morphed into inconsistent memories at trial. In two of the cases, the prosecutor responded to that uncertainty by affirmatively questioning the witnesses in an attempt to pin down the truth. In the third case, where the evidentiary uncertainty was perhaps the highest, the prosecutor took no affirmative steps to reduce that uncertainty and in fact, recommended that the court convict the defendants. The level of evidentiary uncertainty that prosecutors are willing to tolerate and still proffer a conviction recommendation obviously varies. The fact that some German prosecutors do indeed wrestle with the truth at trial shows that, in major crime cases, German prosecutors take their commitment to serve as objective fact finders seriously. Further empirical research will be necessary to identify both the degree as well as the extent to which prosecutors evidence a commitment to objectivity at trial. This chapter has merely opened the door to that inquiry.

The degree of that commitment varies substantially. While it would be imprudent to draw broad conclusions based on the excerpts of only three trials, it is clear that the parameters of prosecutors' role in the truth-finding process are drawn not only by the law, but also by the beliefs of individual prosecutors about the scope of their duty. Although I did not personally observe a case in which a prosecutor

Table 7.1 Summary of cases

Case	Judge	Prosecutor	Defendant	Collateral P.
Rosenberg	Leads questioning and conviction	Supports judge	Mild opposition	N/A
Schneekopf	Convinced of guilt	Unconvinced	Wants a deal to preserve job	Pushes for tough plea
Strehlen	Cuts further investigation short	Not happy with judge but will not challenge judge	Conflict defense strategy	Supports victim

recommended that a court acquit a defendant, my interview data indicated that such cases do exist.[85] Several prosecutors related to me that in the course of their careers, they had participated in trials in which their opinion of the evidence shifted dramatically.[86] With few exceptions, every prosecutor that I interviewed could proudly point to a case in which they personally had recommended an acquittal or filed an appeal on the defendant's behalf. Although that anecdotal evidence falls short of conclusive proof, it suggests that prosecutors' duty of objectivity is part of the organizational norms.

The face of objectivity is not merely the product of organizational norms. An individual prosecutor's self-image is a key factor that determines whether a prosecutor is simply content to remain on the sidelines during the truth-finding process. When I asked one senior prosecutor to describe the characteristics of an ideal prosecutor, he responded:

> [Y]ou must reflect about what you do. [You must ask] what will be the effect of your accusation on the accused? What will be the impact on the social situation of the accused? ... Prosecutors have a clear self-understanding ... Naturally, the personality of the prosecutor, whether they are active in the main proceeding, [is important]. There are also those who make no comments and do not talk. On the other hand it is also true that the judge will sometimes also [take] a difficult [position]. One would [prefer prosecutors] who represent [themselves] well in court [by presenting] the state's view of the law and [reflecting on] the personality of the suspect.[87]

These cases demonstrate that, despite the fact that judges structure the presentation of evidence during the main proceeding, prosecutors may influence trial outcomes. There is a wide variation in the approaches that particular prosecutors adopt when assessing the credibility of testimonial evidence. In particular, prosecutors interpret their duty to investigate the facts differently. As a result, while prosecutors possess the ability to actively participate in the truth-finding process by directly questioning witnesses and requesting that the court obtain additional evidence, they

[85] *See, e.g.*, Public Prosecutor Interview [8AR], 23 May 2006 (asserting that, on multiple occasions, she has petitioned the court for an acquittal because she was unconvinced of the defendant's guilt).

[86] *See* Public Prosecutor Interview [6SB], 23 February 2006 (stating that a colleague had twice filed appeals arguing for a lower sentence).

[87] Public Prosecutor Interview [13BR], 18 November 2005.

may also elect to stand in the background and play an inconsequential role. When a prosecutor elects to play an acquiescent role at trial, that passivity cannot be equated with neutrality. In Germany's nonadversarial system, finding the "objective truth" requires that prosecutors make an affirmative commitment to discovering that truth.

When the evidence presented at trial is inconsistent, prosecutors' individual comfort zones with uncertainty vary. Admittedly, the impact of the choices that prosecutors make at trial may be less significant than the influence that they exert during the investigation stage. Nevertheless, the amount of initiative that prosecutors demonstrate during the truth-finding process may affect trial outcomes. Because judges control the trial process, the impact of prosecutorial discretion at trial is severely bounded and is mediated through the actions of the other players who participate in the proceedings. Despite that limitation, prosecutors possess the potential to function in the capacity of a "second judge" at trial. Whether they choose to exercise that potential remains an open question.

Due to the fact that both prosecutors and judges receive the same legal training and are typically members of the same social class, prosecutors may be reluctant to challenge judges with whom they disagree.[88] Moreover, because prosecutors do not function as adversaries and do not see a need to "win" a case, prosecutors may have an incentive to yield to a judge's perspective of a case. A potential for disagreement between a prosecutor's view of a case and the judge's view exists. A prosecutor, who is intimately familiar with the evidence and may have personally directed the course of the investigation, may see the facts of the case differently than a judge whose first impression of the case is the paper file. A judge who has not previously worked as a prosecutor may have an unrealistic view of the investigation resources at a prosecutor's disposal as well as the realities of a prosecutor's caseload.

In addition, there is a potential for tension between the prosecutor assigned to handle a case in court and the prosecutor who investigated the case. Many prosecutors who handle cases at trial that were investigated by another prosecutor will touch base with the investigation prosecutors to get a sense of their ideal outcomes. In order to preserve collegial relations, prosecutors who handle a case in court are typically reluctant to criticize the investigation decisions made by another prosecutor. In the *Strehlen* case, this desire to preserve collegiality placed the trial prosecutor in a difficult position.[89] It was clear that the investigating prosecutor had not conducted a thorough investigation. In fact, the trial prosecutor told me that one of the reasons why there were problems with the case was that the investigating prosecutor filed charges before she completed the investigation.[90] When the defense attorneys raised issues about the case during trial that the chief judge categorically dismissed, the trial prosecutor was reluctant to challenge the judge

[88] Appellate Judge Interview [22FE], 22 July 2004 (stating that close working and social relationships and similar backgrounds make it unlikely that prosecutors and judges will oppose each other in the courtroom).

[89] Public Prosecutor Interview [8AR], 23 May 2006.

[90] Public Prosecutor Interview [8AR], 23 May 2006.

or to critique the quality of the initial investigation. In the end, she elected not to side with the defense because she was confident that the case would be overturned on appeal. In theory, when a new prosecutor takes over a case at trial, it offers the prosecutor's office the opportunity to double-down on their commitment to finding the truth. In reality, the trial prosecutor appears to adopt a path-dependent approach to the outcome of the original investigation.

In the other two cases, *Rosenberg* and *Schneekopf*, the dance between the prosecutor and the judge unfolded quite differently. In *Rosenberg*, the prosecutor's initial confrontation with the victim concerning her drinking appeared to be a move towards an independent assessment of objectivity. As the case progressed, the prosecutor and judge appeared to work in tandem. In particular, the judge attempted to coax the "truth" out of the victim, urging her to remember what happened. The prosecutor did not hang back and accept the lack of corroborating testimony in the case. He threatened the Turkish witness with a criminal charge and worked to undermine the logic of the defendant's testimony.

The interaction between the prosecutor and the chief judge in *Schneekopf* was extremely interesting. The prosecutor did not hesitate to tell the judge that he had concerns about the victim's credibility during a break in the case. The judge seemed genuinely concerned that the prosecutor might ask for an acquittal at the trial's conclusion. But for the collateral prosecutor's efforts to negotiate a plea, it is possible that the prosecutor and judge might have reached a different conclusion about the evidence in the case. Critically, the source of this tension was not a difference of opinion about the law that applied to the case. Instead the difference of opinion emanated from a different perspective of the main witness's credibility. In a legal system that privileges a positivistic vision of the penal law, on a theoretical level there exists the possibility that a judge and a prosecutor could reach a different conclusion about the facts in a case. In that case, if the judge and the prosecutor strictly adhered to criminal procedure, they might have voiced those differences in the courtroom. For example, the prosecutor could move for an acquittal while the judge leans to convict or the prosecutor could ask for a conviction, while the judge elects to acquit. I would suggest however, that the common socialization of judges and prosecutors and their interdependence in the courtroom would exert pressure on the parties to negotiate their conflicting visions of truth. From a sociological perspective, it is worth emphasizing that the public prosecutor and the judge likely studied the same courses, may socialize together, and must continue to work with each other on future cases. As one appellate judge stated:

> Well, the public prosecutor and the judge twenty years ago studied the same classes at the university. They know each other; in the afternoon they play tennis together, why should the judge blame the public prosecutor? They have to work together the next twenty years and if one person started to bother the other, the other would bother the first person, so you don't want to have any wall between these two institutions. That's how it works in practical life. You will not find any institutional changes. If you want institutional changes, you need a radical turnaround of the legal system.[91]

[91] Appellate Judge Interview [22FE], 22 July 2004.

The downside of the more active role that prosecutors in the United States play is that they may become blinded to contradictory evidence and prosecute a case too aggressively. The more passive role played by German prosecutors possesses a downside as well. When prosecutors narrowly interpret or abdicate their duty to participate in the truth-finding process, they forfeit the opportunity to improve the objectivity of the fact-finding process. While German criminal procedure law does not aim to establish a truth-finding process in which the truth is produced from a battle between adversaries, the system requires prosecutors to fulfill an independent fact-finding role. Although the law posits that the judge and prosecutor will function independently while viewing the evidence through an objective lens, this chapter demonstrates that objectivity is the end product of a constitutive process in which the nature of the relationship between the prosecutors and judges as well as the temporal relationship between the trial and investigating prosecutors give birth to the face of objectivity. In sum, where prosecutors are content to play a passive role in the truth-finding process, that passivity may not satisfy the duty of objectivity. Consequently, in some situations Germany's two-judge system does not create a level of redundancy that enhances the accuracy of the decision-making process at trial. In cases in which a prosecutor possesses a more robust self-image, the prosecutor plays a critical role in the courtroom truth-finding process.

Legislation

Code of Criminal Procedure (StPO)

Sections:

24, 25, 28, 29, 30, 74–76,
142(1) 142(2), (3), 152(1), 153, 153(1), 160, 160(2), 199
200, 238(1), 239, 240, 243, 244, 244(2), 249, 250, 252–60, 257c, 258(1), 296, 296 (2),
323, 324, 395, 397

Code of Criminal Law (StGB)

Sections:

164, 176(a), 177, 179
223, 249

Other Laws

Gerichtsveerfassungsgestez [GVG] [Courts Constitution Act], 12 September 1950, Bundesgesetzblatt [BGBL] 1, amended §§24, 25 (Ger.).

Richtlinien Für Das Stafverfahren und Das BußGeldvergahren [RISTBV] [Guidelines for Criminal and Fine Proceedings] §§138, 139.

Stafgesetzbuch [StGB] [Penal Code], 13 November 1998, Bundesgestezblatt, Tiel 1 [(BGBL 1] at 3322, as amended §177 (Ger.)

Bundesgerichtshof [BGH] [Federal Court of Justice] 3 March 2005, 50 Entscheidungen des Bundesgerichtshofs in Strafsachen [BGHST] 40, 48.

Gerichtsveerfassungsgestez [GVG] [Courts Constitution Act], §§21–21j, 24, 74–74f.

Reports/Statistics

Bundesgerichtshof [BGH] [Federal Court of Justice] 28 august 1997, *Neue Juristische Wochenschrift* [NJW] 43 (195), 1997.

Interviews

Appellate Judge Interview [22FE], 22 July 2004.

Appellate Judge Interview [13MU], 10 April 2004.

Appellate Judge Interview [18UE], 24 June 2004.

Ministry of Justice Interview [9CK], 4 May 2006.

Participant Observation [3TW], 9 November 2005.

Participant Observation [13WT], 8 December 2005.

Participant Observation [4AJ], 1 February 2006.

Participant Observation [4BI], 3 February 2006.

Public Prosecutor Interview [4AJ], 1–2 February 2006

Public Prosecutor Interview [4BI], 3 February 2006.

Public Prosecutor Interview [4GG], 30 January 2006.

Public Prosecutor Interview [5CK], 22 January 2006.

Public Prosecutor Interview [5DK], 19 January 2006

Public Prosecutor Interview [6SB], 23 February 2006.

Public Prosecutor Interview [7CX], 7 April 2006.

Public Prosecutor Interview [8AR], 23 May 2006.

Public Prosecutor Interview [8PT], 6 December 2005.

Public Prosecutor Interview [9BU], 4 May 2005.

Public Prosecutor Interview [12CJ], 29 November 2005.

Public Prosecutor Interview [13BC], 12 December 2005.

Public Prosecutor Interview [13BR], 18 November 2005.
Public Prosecutor Interview [13WT], 6 December 2005.
Public Prosecutor Interview [18UE], 24 June 2004.
Public Prosecutor Interview [24AZ], 10 April 2008.
Senior Prosecutor Interview [5BC], 16 January 2006.

References

Books, Articles and Online Publications

Asmus, H.-J. (1988). Der Staatsanwalkt-ein bürokratischer Faktor in der Verbrechenskontrolle. *Zeitschrift für Soziologie, 17*, 117–134 (April).

Blankenburg, E. K., & Steffen, W. (1978). *Die Staatsanwaltschaft* (ProzeßStrafrechlicher Sozialkontrolle). Berlin: Dunker u. Humblot.

Damaška, M. (1981). The realty of prosecutorial discretion: Comments on a German monograph. *American Journal Comparative Law, 29*, 119–138.

Bryden, D. P., & Lengnick, S. (1997). Rape in the criminal justice system. *Journal of Criminal Law and Criminology, 87*, 1194.

Edwards, H. T. (1997). Comments on Mirjan Damaška's "Of Evidentiary Transplants". *American Journal Comparative Law, 45*, 853–860.

Estrich, S. (1988). *Real rape*. Cambridge: Harvard University Press.

Foster, N. (1996). *German legal system & laws*. London: Blackstone Press Ltd.

Gershman, B. L. (2002). Witness coaching by prosecutors. *Cardozo Law Review, 23*, 829–864.

Grande, E. (2008). Dances of criminal justice: Thoughts on systemic difference and the search for the truth. In J. Jackson, M. Langer, & P. Tillers (Eds.) *Crime, procedure and evidence in a comparative and international context: Essays in Honour of Professor Mirjan Damaška*. Oxford: Hart Publishing.

Hannich, R., et al. (Eds.). (2008). *Karlsruher Kommentar Zur Strafprozessordnung* (vol 258, no. 8, 6th ed.). Munich: C.H. Beck.

Herbert, L. (2009). Prosecutorial discretion meeting disaster capitalism. In M. L. Seigel (Ed.), *Race to injustice: Lessons learned from the Duke Lacrosse rape case* (pp. 211–235). Durham: Carolina Academic Press.

Hermann, J. (1976). The German prosecutor. In K. Culp Davis (Ed.) *Discretionary justice in Europe and America*. Urbana: University of Illinois Press.

Jescheck, H.-H. (1970). Principles of German criminal procedure in comparison with American law. *University of Virginia Law Review, 56*, 239–253.

Langbein, J. H. (1977). *Comparative criminal procedure: Germany*. St. Paul, MN: West Group.

Lovett, J. & Kelly, L. (2009). Different systems, similar outcomes? Tracking attrition in reported rape cases throughout Europe [pdf]. London: London Metropolitan University. Available at http://www.aoef.at/Studien/Final%20Research%20Report.pdf. Last Accessed 5 Aug 2013.

Machura, S. (2001). Interaction between lay assessors and professional judges in German mixed courts. *International Review of Penal Law, 72*, 451–479.

Moderne Staatsanwaltschaft: Notwendige Reformen Staatsanwaltschaft und Polizei, 8 (1975).

Pizzi, W. T., & Perron, W. (1996). Crime victims in German courtrooms: A comparative perspective on American problems. *Stanford Journal International Law, 32*, 37–64.

Turner, J. I. (2009). *Plea bargaining across borders*. New York: Aspen Publishers.

Chapter 8
Juvenile Justice

Treatment of children, who are victims of the conditions in which they are living and children who have violated the law, is a reflection of a society's culture and value system (Junger-Tas 2006, p. 505).

8.1 Introduction

Many scholars have relegated the subfield of juvenile crime to the second tier of criminal justice scholarship. Because state policies towards juvenile crime reflect societal attitudes towards criminal culpability and the purpose of punishment, by understanding the factors which shape prosecutorial discretion in juvenile cases, we can gain rich insights into the nature of the crime and justice in a society. In particular, the latitude that prosecutors enjoy in juvenile cases does not develop by accident but rather reflects societal attitudes, the politics surrounding criminal justice policies, as well as the sensitivity of prosecution practices to external forces. As a result, sentencing polices may or may not reflect actual crime rates.

The idea that special juvenile courts should be granted jurisdiction over juvenile misconduct is a relatively recent one. Specialized juvenile courts began to appear in the western world at the turn of the century with the city of Chicago leading the way in 1899. Thereafter, Canada followed suit in 1908, followed by Belgium, France, and Switzerland in 1912. Although these courts differed in their institutional form, they shared a judicial philosophy that invested large discretionary powers in not only the judge, but other institutional actors as well. Focused on addressing the needs of the individual child, their primary aim was to act in the "best interests of the child" rather than to punish the offense that had been committed (Junger-Tas 2006). While the import of this system of juvenile rights appears innocuous at first glance, paternalistic and patronizing judges often possessed absolute authority over the lives of juvenile offenders and failed to accord juvenile offenders the level of

S.M. Boyne, *The German Prosecution Service*, DOI 10.1007/978-3-642-40928-8_8,

procedural protections available to adult suspects (Junger-Tas 2006). This trend began to change in the United States with the Supreme Court's 1967 decision in *In re Gault* that granted juveniles due process rights.[1]

That shift towards protecting juvenile rights was short-lived. In the United States, the institution of rights into the juvenile justice framework, coupled with declining confidence in the efficacy of non-punitive sanctions, opened the door to more punitive judicial philosophies. Riding a renewed wave of public interest in individual responsibility and accountability, in the 1990s state legislatures sharply stiffened penal sanctions in juvenile cases. Politicians discovered that it was easier to garner votes by "selling" punishment rather than rehabilitation.

During the past 15 years, the juvenile justice policies of many American states have swung in a more punitive direction. Consistent with this shift in sentencing philosophy, between 1992 and 1997, 47 states changed their sanctioning policies by expanding the sentencing options available to judges, increasing the severity of juvenile sanctions, and loosening procedural rules to permit prosecutors to try juveniles in adult court (McCord et al. 2001; Junger-Tas 2006). Ironically these changes occurred at a time when the rate of violent juvenile crime in the United States had dropped 36 % between 1994 and 1999. Due to changing political winds, juvenile incarceration rates rose dramatically during that same period (Klein 2001). In the 3 year period between 1992 and 1995, 41 states enacted legislation to make it easier for prosecutors to try juveniles in adult court (Sickmund et al. 1997). Even the Supreme Court joined in, if not embracing, at least condoning the use of harsh sentencing practices holding in Stanford v. Kentucky (1989), that the Constitution's Eighth Amendment did not courts from imposing the death penalty for crimes committed by 16 and 17-year old adolescents.[2] That decision stood until 2005, when a one vote majority on the court held that the practice was now unconstitutional.[3]

Despite the fact that support for the death penalty in the United States has fallen, state court judges throughout the country have continued to sentence juveniles to lengthy terms of incarceration, including life sentences. The most pervasive change in state sentencing practices occurred in the 1990s as many state legislatures introduced blended dispositional and sentencing options (Sickmund et al. 1997). By the end of 2004, 26 states had adopted blended-sentencing statutes which enabled courts to impose juvenile or adult sanctions (or a combination) on youthful offenders. According to research conducted by the National Center for State Courts (Cheesman 2011, p. 112) at least 60 % of the nation's juvenile population between 10 and 17-years of age resides in those 26 states. While blended-sentencing offers

[1] 387 U.S. 1 (1967).

[2] 492 U.S. 361 (1989).

[3] Roper v. Simmons, 543 U.S. 551 (2005).

courts the option to sanction juvenile crime with an a broad package of graduated responses, strong evidence suggests that race influences courts' sentencing practices. Cheseman (2011, p. 116) concluded:

> Our research, however, suggests that in states employing juvenile-inclusive blended sentencing, minorities will be disproportionately overrepresented among transfers, the most punitive of the processing tracks, and underrepresented among blended sentences, the latter providing the last chance for treatment in the juvenile justice system...
>
> Juvenile judges are currently making informal determinations as to offender needs and risk, but formal risk-and-needs-assessment procedures can improve the validity and fairness of such determinations (Silver and Chow-Martin 2002). Consequently, our principal recommendation is that objective risk-and-needs assessments be used to identify the most suitable candidates for blended sentences and adult transfer. Use of objective risk-and-needs assessments to make these determinations will not completely eliminate risks to public safety, but should reduce them by better informing what have heretofore been predominately subjective decisions.

The comparative leniency of juvenile sanctioning practices in Germany contrasts starkly with American practice. Predominately oriented towards promoting child development and education, German policy continues to experiment with new programs consistent with those goals. The fact that Germany's juvenile justice policy promotes the twin aims of promoting welfare-oriented objectives while achieving justice has produced a broad spectrum of sanctioning practices. These practices offer broad opportunities for prosecutorial discretion. In this chapter, I show how locally developed responses to community crime problems have emerged and helped to shape the arc of prosecutorial decision-making. In fact, in the implementation of juvenile law, it has been local practice, rather than the federal law, that has made the most visible imprint on case handling procedures. Ironically, in the area of German juvenile law, changes in the federal law have merely confirmed changes in local practice. Although the federal juvenile code seeks to loosely enforce uniform sentencing policies, the inherent flexibility in juvenile sanctions has allowed local stakeholders to design and tailor policies which attempt to address particular and locally-defined juvenile crime problems. As a result, stark local and regional differences in practice have developed.

There are downsides to this wide ambit of flexibility. The development of widespread regional disparities has undermined not only the law's uniformity, but also the principle of equal treatment under the law. Moreover, the publicity generated by a small number of sensational crimes has made prosecutors and judges more sensitive to local political pressures in a handful of communities. In some cases, the media coverage has forced some prosecution offices to stiffen sentencing practices.

This chapter presents a snapshot of the specialized nature of juvenile prosecution practice as well as the role of prosecutorial discretion in juvenile practice. I trace the emergence of diverse models of practice and show how those models reflect local and regional attitudes towards the character of juvenile crime. The evolution of distinct local practices poses an intriguing challenge to the premise that prosecutorial decision-making is truly objective, impartial, and grounded in neutral legal standards which are impervious to political influence. To set the stage for this inquiry, I begin by laying out the basic framework of German juvenile law and the ambit of discretion which it permits. I then explore the actual patterns of juvenile criminality and punishment using published statistical reports. In the chapter's core, I delve into prosecutors' perceptions of the purposes of juvenile crime and actual sanctioning practices. This includes a discussion of decision making norms. Finally, the chapter details the aims and practices of newly developed fast-track programs and innovative "repeat offender" units established in some German cities. In the framework of that discussion, I show how the law's inherent latitude, as well as the structure of management controls and workload pressures, empower prosecution offices with the power to tailor prosecution policies to respond to community needs and political pressures.

8.2 The Scope of Discretion in the Juvenile Justice System

8.2.1 Defining the Scope of Juvenile Crime

In the area of juvenile crime, three factors have defined prosecutorial discretion. As a starting point, in 1923, the German legislature suspended the applicability of the principle of mandatory prosecution to the prosecution of juvenile crime. As a result, it was initially in the area of juvenile crime, rather than in low level crimes, where prosecutors enjoyed the widest latitude in their case disposition practices (Dünkel 2006a). Second, the sanctioning strategy present in the juvenile law reflects a preference for "minimum intervention" in the life and upbringing of the child (Dünkel 2006a, pp. 116–118). This policy, which is defined as a preference for education-oriented measures, reflects a strong belief that children lack the cognitive capacity to possess criminal guilt. Consistent with this policy, the primary purpose of juvenile officials is to function as agents of support, rather than as agents of intervention. At the core of modern German juvenile justice policy are two convictions. First, juveniles under the age of 14 lack the capacity to commit crimes. Second, there is a consensus that crimes, such as shoplifting and vandalism, are manifestations of normal adolescent behavior that children will eventually outgrow.

Although the crimes set forth in the Code of Criminal Law (StGB) form the basis for defining the elements of juvenile delinquent acts, the investigation, prosecution, and punishment of juvenile delinquency is governed by a separate federal code of criminal procedure known as the *Jugendsgerichtsgesetz* (JGG) or the Act on Juvenile Courts.[4] This special code of procedure specifies the basis for holding young persons accountable under the law in accord with a graduated system of punishment that is primarily based on the child's age and development level. The Act on Juvenile Courts establishes a two-tiered system of sanctions which aims

[4] In addition, the police laws in each state and the Police Service Regulation (*Polizeidienstverordnung*) (PDV 382) detail the police procedures for handling juveniles. The legal provisions which regulate the provision of Child and Youth Services are contained in the *Kinder-und -Jugendhilfgesetz* (Child and Youth Services Act, KJGH).

first-to respond to delinquency through educative and disciplinary measures. Second, the code permits courts to impose more serious sanctions such as probation and imprisonment. One can construe this two-tiered system as a compromise between "justice" and "welfare" responses to juvenile crime (Crofts 2004). These competing objectives open the door to widespread differences in local practices. In part, the differences in prosecutorial practice are the product of different relationships that prosecution offices enjoy with the local police and a particular community's Department of Youth Service (*Jugendgerichtshilfe*). The mandate of this agency, which was established in the *Kinder-und Jugendhilfegesetz* (Children and Youth Services Act, KJHG) enacted in 1990, is to support and protect children and young people, provide them with socio-educational help, and to positively influence their living conditions (Holthusen and Schäfer 2004).

Under German law, there are three legal categories relevant to juvenile crime. First, the law treats children under the age of 14 as lacking criminal responsibility for their actions.[5] Second, juvenile offenders aged 14–17 may be adjudicated in juvenile courts if, at the time they committed a punishable act, they possessed sufficient moral and intellectual maturity to appreciate the injustice of their actions and to comprehend their behavior. Finally, the law places young adults aged 18–20 in a separate category which allows courts to treat young adults as juvenile offenders if their offense was of a juvenile nature[6] or their development lags behind their peers (Jehle 2005, p. 35). According to Section 105 (1) JGG, prosecutors may apply the juvenile law if "the offender's personality and his social environment indicates that at the time of the commission of the crime the young adult was like a juvenile in his moral and psychological development" (Jehle 2005, p. 35). Where the court determines that an individual's personal development lags behind the child's peers, the court may even adjudicate the young adult under the provisions of the juvenile legal code.[7] From a practical standpoint, because neither the criminal law nor the field of adolescent psychiatry can identify uniform eligibility criteria to support this categorization scheme, courts possess substantial discretion in making these assessments (Weber and Ruth 1997). In an attempt to rectify this problem, Germany's highest federal civil and criminal court, the Federal Court of Justice or (*Bundesgerichtshof*), has attempted to clarify the statutory standard that makes young adult offenders eligible for adjudication in juvenile court. According to the Court, a young adult possesses the maturity of a juvenile if evidence demonstrates that "a considerable development of personality is still to be seen."[8]

---

[5] *See* §19 StGB, which states that: "[w]hoever upon commission of the act is under fourteen years of age lacks capacity to be judged guilty."

[6] § 105(1) 2, JGG.

[7] § 105 JGG.

[8] Federal Court of Justice (Criminal Panel) BGHSt 12:116; 36:38.

Because the juvenile justice system attempts to tailor sanctioning practices to the disparate development levels of young people, the law has widened the discretionary power of judges and prosecutors. The inherent ambiguity present in the assessment of a crime's juvenile character as well as in a child's level of development has opened the door to widespread differences in practice (Dünkel 2006b). The fact that there are extensive differences in practice between how different prosecutors and judges interpret Section 105 JGG raises the question as to whether or not the statute's application satisfies constitutional requirements (Bareinske 2004).

The malleability of these subjective standards has led to some interesting distortions of the law's intent. First, prosecutors are most likely to steer cases involving young adult offenders away from juvenile courts, not when the offense at issue involves a violent crime, but rather when it involves a traffic offense (Dünkel 2003). According to German statistics, 59 % of young adult offenders who violate traffic offenses are prosecuted according to the standard "adult" rules of criminal procedure. The reason for this result is simple efficiency. As I discussed in the prior chapter, the Code of Criminal Procedure provides prosecutors with the opportunity to dismiss cases using the penal order procedure available under Section 153 StPO. In these cases, prosecutors may impose a fine without an oral hearing (Dünkel 2003). Thus, when prosecutors want to simply impose a fine in a youthful offender case, the most expeditious way to achieve that objective is to treat the youth as an adult.

Conversely, when a young offender commits a serious offense such as murder, rape, or robbery, over 95 % of the time, courts will elect to invoke the juvenile procedural code (Dünkel 2003). Courts prefer using this option in serious cases because it increases their discretion in the sentencing process. The juvenile code grants prosecutors and courts the flexibility to impose more lenient penalties than those mandated in adult court. For example, in the case of murder, under the juvenile code, judges are not bound to impose a mandatory life sentence required for murder. In a case involving armed robbery, by using the adult code, judges would have to impose a minimum sentence of 5 years imprisonment. Thus, the fact that the juvenile justice system grants prosecutors and judges greater sentencing discretion than the adult code with regard to serious offenses increases the likelihood that courts will elect to prosecute young adults pursuant to the juvenile procedural code in cases where they are suspected of committing a serious offense. In some cases however, young adult offenders adjudicated under the juvenile rules may suffer a disadvantage as the minimum period of incarceration permitted under the juvenile code is 6 months. The adult code allows a 1 month term of imprisonment in certain circumstances.

Finally, although the Act on Juvenile Courts is a federal law applicable to all of the German states, local attitudes towards juvenile crime has shaped how prosecutors interpret and apply the law. Indeed, since it was the lower courts that pioneered unique ways of dealing with juveniles rather than the federal legislature, local juvenile practices have enjoyed influential track record with respect to the evolution juvenile crime policy. Indeed, the first specialized juvenile courts were created in the cities of Berlin, Frankfurt, and Cologne in the early 1900s. This tradition of reform through practice has continued in modern times as the law has permitted disparate local practices to develop at the community level. For example, during the 1970s social workers, prosecutors, and judges assigned to local juvenile courts revolutionized juvenile sanctioning practices by introducing community-based sanctions designed to reduce the use of more repressive sanctions (Dünkel 2003). The legislature in effect endorsed the direction of these local reform efforts when it when reformed the JGG in 1990. The reforms made in the code at that time stressed the importance of educational and disciplinary responses.[9] In addition, the changes emphasized the role that prosecutors as well as judges play in determining the appropriateness of diversionary measures and in identifying appropriate dispositional alternatives (Junger-Tas 2006). Moreover, according to new provisions in the law, in cases where juvenile offenders have participated in mediation or paid restitution, courts may find that those efforts warrant finding a reduced level of culpability. Consequently, when juveniles meet this reduced standard of culpability a court may dismiss a case under Section 45 (1) JGG. Moreover, in enacting these changes, the legislature has underscored the principle that courts should impose more stringent detention-oriented sanctions only as a matter of a last resort. Most importantly, the reform of the JGG further expanded prosecutorial discretion by allowing prosecutors to defer prosecution where the offense is petty in nature or because educational and social measures are being employed. Unlike the law applicable to adult cases, in some cases, juveniles may avoid punishment even if the alleged crime qualifies as a *Verbrechen* (major crime). As a result, juvenile prosecutors possess a wide range of options. They may either dismiss a case outright or condition a case's dismissal on a number of options which include: issuing a warning to a child, requiring the child to participate in educational, training or mediation programs, paying a fine, or performing community service. The fact that social workers from the social welfare department participate in juvenile proceedings helps the court to find an appropriate alternative sanction.[10] In those cases where the child must perform an affirmative duty, German law permits a prosecutor to dismiss a case with the judge's consent after the child completes their obligation.[11] Under certain circumstances, the public prosecution office may dismiss the charges without the court's approval.[12] The range of more severe sanctions applied to juveniles include: a fine and detention on weekends, probation, detention up to 4 weeks in a juvenile detention center (*Juggendarrest*) and youth prison sentences. Juveniles aged 14–17 may, as a last resort, receive a sentence ranging between 6 months and 5 years. Where juveniles up to 20 years of age commit serious crimes, the maximum length of imprisonment available to courts is a 10 year sentence.[13] In order to impose a sentence of that length, the

[9] *See* §§ 45 (1) and (2) JGG.

[10] § 38 (2) JGG.

[11] § 45 (3) JGG.

[12] §§ 45 (1) and (2) JGG.

[13] §§ 18 and 109 JGG.

court must find that a child's "dangerous tendencies" preclude the imposition of community sanctions or that the juvenile's degree of culpability is severe-for example, the crime involved is extremely serious.[14]

8.2.2 *Juvenile Crime Rates and Trends*

There has been little change in Germany's overall juvenile crime rate during the past two decades (Police Crime Statistics 2003, p. 47). However, the combination of heightened media attention on a handful of brutal crimes and an increase in crimes of violence has stoked cries for sentencing reform and the toughening of sanctioning practices. While public and political attention given to a handful of extremely violent crimes may overestimate the problem of juvenile crime in Germany today, a number of developing trends indicate that Germany faces a juvenile crime problem which has been largely fueled by a small proportion of repeat offenders. Although the reported rate of simple assaults committed by juveniles increased by 2.7 % and the rate committed by adolescents rose 4.6 % in 2006 (Spiegel 2007a), criminologists, politicians, and practitioners continue to debate whether or not the rate of violence has actually increased (Spiegel 2005). Indeed, in a 2007 Spiegel article, Berlin's Police Chief argued that, although violence among adolescents had risen, the rate of overall juvenile crime had actually decreased. In fact, according to statistics released from Germany's Federal Statistical Office (Lorenz 2008, p. 2), between 1990 and 2006, courts convicted three times as many individuals under the age of 21 for violent offenses (Lorenz 2008, p. 2). During that same time period, the rate of violent crime convictions for adults doubled. More recent statistics from 2010 (*Deutsche Welle* 2011) however, show a 6.9 % drop in juvenile crime from the prior year. Violent youth crime among 14–18 year olds dropped even more significantly, falling by 9.9 % (*Deutsche Welle* 2011).

Cities like Berlin face a juvenile crime problem which, for a time, appeared to be skyrocketing. In Berlin between 1989 and 1997 for example, the crime rate among German children (8–14) rose 43.1 %, while the rate among non-German children rose 48.7 % (Möhring 2002). Still, Germany's juvenile crime rate is far lower than that of the United States. What is new for Germany is the phenomena that, when news of a vicious crime hits the media, politicians try to exploit the public's fear. This is particularly true of parties on the far-right who use the incidents to peddle anti-immigrant propaganda (Warner 2011).

A particularly contentious issue is the rate of violent crime committed by immigrant children who face hurdles integrating into German society and enjoy fewer economic opportunities (Pfeiffer and Wetzels 1999). While Germany adopted a more restrictive immigration policy in 1993, Germany's criminal justice system still faces challenges from young immigrants and ethnic minorities (Dünkel

---

[14] § 17(2) JGG.

2006b). In urban environments in particular, the rates of violent crime committed by immigrant youths far outpace the rate reported among the total population. For example, in 2006, the German news source, *Deutsche Welle* (Kouparanis 2006) reported that young male immigrants in Berlin were three times more likely to commit violent crimes as their German peers. The problem is particularly acute in large cities such as Berlin, Hamburg, Munich, Cologne, and Frankfurt. In 2006, 80 % of the violent crimes committed by juvenile offenders in Berlin were committed by youths belonging to immigrant families (Spiegel 2007c). One figure which has particularly alarmed politicians in the nation's capital, is the number of juvenile crimes committed with weapons. This figure Berlin grew by over 30 % in Berlin during the first three quarters of 2006 (Spiegel 2007c). This trend is not unique to Germany however. It mirrors a similar trend reported within ten member states of the European Union (Pfeiffer 1998). In particular, rates of violent juvenile crime, committed by young people with lower levels of education and fewer integration prospects, have been rising. Several scholars (James 1995; Pfeiffer et al. 1996; Pfeiffer 1998) have argued that differences in social class variables such as educational levels, income, and dependency on social welfare lay at the root of juvenile violence. However, the co-director of the Max Planck Institute for Foreign and International Criminal Law, Hans-Jörg Albrecht, disagrees:

> As a rule, criminal or violent careers usually begin at an age when jobs and the job market do not yet play a role, which is between 14 and 17 ... Access to criminal groups is a key factor. If a person grows up in an area where there are lots of criminal gangs ready to welcome him into the fold, then the risk that he gravitates towards crime is significantly greater than in would be in other areas. In this respect, ethnic considerations play no role at all (Kouparanis 2006).

The increase in the rate of violent crime among juveniles has attracted the attention of the public as well as politicians. The heightened media attention given to juvenile crime is a relatively new phenomenon in Germany as, in general, politicians have left the design of criminal justice policy to practitioners and experts. The increasing politicization of juvenile crime is reflected in a statement issued by traditionally conservative Christian Democratic Party (CDU) in 2005 after a 16-year-old boy beat his neighbor as well as a child to death in 2005:

> The soft touch era is finally over. The justice system should react more swiftly to the first cases and signs of a criminal career, and be quicker to sentence violent young criminals to imprisonment (Walker 2005).

Sentences for even violent crimes committed by juveniles are mild by U.S. standards. As one example, a court sentenced an 18-year-old youth, who beat his victim over the head with a soda bottle on the Berlin subway platform and then stomped his head repeatedly as he lay on the ground, to a term of incarceration of only 2 years and 10 months in 2011 (Spiegel 2011). The victim suffered head injuries, a broken nose, contusions, and ongoing psychological trauma and might have been hurt worse had a bystander not come to his rescue. Because the suspect was 18 at the time of the attack, the court could have sentenced him to 15 years in prison had the court elected to apply adult sanctions. Between the ages of 18 and 21, youthful offenders fall into a legal grey area in which the court may impose adult sanctions. At the time of sentencing however, even the prosecution only recommended a sentence of 4 years in juvenile detention (Spiegel 2011). The court's decision to sentence the youth under the juvenile code is not surprising as, it is estimated that, judges elect to adjudicate some 60 % of cases involving offenders in this age group in juvenile court even when the crimes involved are violent ones (Sinico 2007).

The media attention devoted to violent crime, as well as to crimes committed by non-German citizens, has helped to fuel the debate concerning the efficacy of the juvenile justice system's traditional education-oriented focus. Compounding the perceptions created by the media's fascination with immigrant crime, Albrecht (1997) reports that German criminological research on immigrant populations has also been preoccupied with the topic of crime. The recent heightened attention on this problem is not wholly disconnected to the reality of crime trends. Although Germany experienced high waves of immigration since after the Second World War, in the initial decades after the war, the correlation between immigrant status and crime rates was a negative one (Chapin 1997a). This relationship reversed in the 1970s and, by 1993, the percentage of foreigners arrested for criminal activity was more than three times the rate for the general population (Chapin 1997b). Data suggests that this disparity is more pronounced in the area of juvenile and young adult crimes. For example, in Frankfurt in 1993, almost 75 % of 18–21 year old suspects were members of minorities (Albrecht 1997).

In many cases, integration problems lie at the root of higher crime rates among young immigrants. According to the Organization for Economic Co-operation and Development (OECD), young immigrants in some city neighborhoods often attend schools with a high percentage of foreign students, making integration more difficult (Möhring 2002). This "closed educational and cultural circuit" helps to perpetuate assimilation problems (Möhring 2002, p. 6). Lacking sufficient language skills, young immigrants have a difficult time completing training programs and gaining meaningful employment (Möhring 2002).

In evaluating the statistics related to crime committed by "foreigners," it is important to remember that, because German citizenship is not automatically awarded to the children of immigrants born in Germany, many members of ethnic minorities who have been born in Germany do not possess German citizenship.[15]

[15] Until 1993, first generation foreigners had to reside in Germany for a period of 15 years before applying for citizenship. In addition, an individual had to forfeit their original nationality, have a clean criminal record, not depend on social welfare, and identify with the German culture to receive citizenship. After 1993, the requirements were slightly relaxed. In contrast, immigrants who claim Germany ancestry (*Aussiedler*) are automatically awarded citizenship upon entry.

Thus, the simple fact that an individual is classified as a "foreigner" does not necessarily mean that they arrived only recently on German soil.[16] Moreover, the possession of a German passport does not by itself guarantee that an individual is well-integrated into German society. The end of the Cold War brought a wave of immigrants into Germany of the so-called ethnic German "resettlers" from the former Soviet Union and its' satellite states. Lured to Germany with the promise of generous benefits packages, this group of immigrants has been a particular challenge to the justice system. The rates of crime among the younger generation of resettlers have been particularly problematic. Attracted by the promise of a better life, Russian-German juveniles emigrated to Germany became quickly frustrated with the German language and their limited job prospects (Ewald and Feltes 2003). Police agencies, as well as prosecutors, complain that a large percentage of Russian-German juveniles are active in gangs involved in organized crime and drug-trafficking.

8.3 A Changing Landscape: The Politicization of Juvenile Delinquency

The rapid increase in rates of juvenile crime in large cities has led some of the politicians who lead Ministries of Justice on the state level to implement special polices which target repeat offenders. Current statistics indicate that, while repeat offenders comprise only 10 % of the juvenile offender population, they are responsible for over 30 % of juvenile criminality. The media has played a pivotal role in fueling the creation of these special units. In Berlin, for example, the police department reorganized their juvenile crime units to focus on repeat offenders back in 1994. Prior to that time, police investigators often had to start from scratch to familiarize themselves about the background of a particular juvenile because police units were organized on the precinct level hampering the exchange of background information. This system prevented police officers from compiling a comprehensive picture of juvenile's background and personality (Steffan 2003). Despite the fact that the police department reorganized its juvenile units to focus on repeat offenders, Berlin's justice officials resisted creating a special repeat offender unit at that time because it would divert personnel away from the general crimes units (Reusch 2007). This impasse continued until early 2003 when the Berlin press began publicizing reports that highlighted the lax and ineffective punishment that

[16] To qualify for German citizenship, children born after December 31, 1999 to foreign parents in Germany must be born to at least one parent who has been a legal resident in Germany for at least 8 years at the time of their birth . In addition, at least one parent of the child must possess a unlimited residence permit *(unbefristete Aufenthalsterlaubris)* or a residence entitlement *(Aufenthaltsberechitgung)* at the time of their birth (German Consultates of the United States 2007).

repeat juvenile offenders received (Reusch 2007). In response, Berlin's Senator for Justice instructed the prosecution office to create a special prosecution unit to target repeat offenders (Reusch 2007). Since that time, the concept has been adopted by several other major cities in Germany.

However, the acceptance of these programs has not been uniform. Juvenile advocacy experts have criticized the programs on the grounds that they ignore the competence and input of experts in juvenile development (Spiegel(a) 2007). A major organization that advocates on the behalf of juvenile rights, the German Association for Juvenile Court and Juvenile Offenders (DVJJ), has staunchly criticized any movement to simply stiffen juvenile sanctions (Abramsolhn 2006). While the majority of German judges and prosecutors remain committed to the system's preference for non-punitive measures, there are signs that that support is equivocating. The members of the German Jurist's Assembly, sharply debated the efficacy of the system's preference for educational measures at their 2002 meeting (Kilchling 2005). In 2004, the German Association for Juvenile Court and Juvenile Offenders (DVJJ) presented a series of proposals which, if adopted, would broaden and stiffen the range of sentencing alternatives. The chief proposals included: (1) increasing the maximum term of imprisonment from 10 to 15 years, (2) introducing summary written procedures for minor traffic and property offenses, and (3) abolishing the possibility that courts could imprison juveniles simply on the basis of their alleged "dangerous tendencies" (Sonnen 2004). In their recommendations, the organization also moved beyond proposing specific, minor changes in the juvenile law and sharply criticized the ambiguous nature of juvenile law itself. In particular the organization asserted that the law's lack of clarity as to what constitutes an "educational measure" has lead to juvenile judgments which often to promote inconsistent and unclear objectives (Sonnen 2004, p. 3).

The existence of this ongoing debate has impacted the implementation of juvenile justice policy on the state and local levels. Critically, during the past 30 years, although the content of the juvenile law itself has not changed radically, the interpretation and implementation of the law has shifted to reflect the political realities of both the particular period as well as the particular community. As a senior prosecutor in a large German city explained:

> So we have developed a very modern, very liberal law to deal with young criminals... It was believed that in many cases [juvenile crime] is just a short phase of normal development It comes and goes... In the years after, the cultural revolution of 1968, this was the official point of view ... The jurisdiction was harsher before [that period]. For example, until the 1970s, it was absolutely normal that people between the ages of 18 and 21 were under the jurisdiction of adult law. So our law allows the court to decide whether to treat them under adult rules or juvenile rules. Up until the 1970s, it was normal to use adult law ... You have criminologists who influenced the public opinion, not the public opinion [of] the people on the street, but the public opinion in lawyer's circles[to believe] that imprisonment causes the severest harms.
>
> At the same time, we had increasing numbers of these crimes committed by young people and so public opinion, this time, of the real public. They pressured the politicians. Newspapers were full of examples of young guys who committed dozens of severe crimes. It was written [in the newspaper] that nothing happen[ed]-[that there were] no [legal

consequences.] This is not true, but okay. And this caused the Minister of Justice to order that our office ... do something about it. So this special department was founded.[17]

Throughout the remainder of this chapter, I will lay out in broad terms the assumptions and nature of traditional juvenile crimes practice as well as introduce the reader to the newer practices which are continuing to evolve.[18] This chapter will demonstrate how changes in practice, motivated by local conditions, have reshaped the nature of prosecutorial discretion.

8.4 The Specialized Nature of Juvenile Crime Units

While general crimes departments are dominated by prosecutors at the early stages of their careers, the prosecutors who staff juvenile crime departments possess a range of experience levels. Although German law stipulates that juvenile crimes prosecutors should possess specialized training and have experience in socio-educational affairs related to juvenile development,[19] in practice many departments substitute a prosecutor's own experience as a parent as a proxy for the attainment of this specialized knowledge.[20] Because the law requires that prosecutors possess special competencies in juvenile development, typically a prosecutor will not begin his or her career in a juvenile crimes department. However, one senior prosecutor complained to me that there has been a recent trend towards assigning younger prosecutors to juvenile crimes departments. Because many young prosecutors possess little life experience, they may have difficulty seeing a crime in proper perspective.[21] Frequently, offices will pair responsibility for juvenile crime cases with crimes committed against juveniles since it can be too stressful for a prosecutor to concentrate only on cases involving the physical or sexual abuse of children.[22] Even when the department is comprised in this split manner, the majority of the individuals whom I interviewed in the juvenile crimes departments were women. The pattern of frequent consultation among colleagues that I observed in the general crimes departments was also present in the juvenile departments. As one prosecutor commented:

---

[17] Senior Prosecutor [9LJ], 12 June 2006.

[18] I use the term "traditional practice" as a moniker for the diversion and education-oriented focused juvenile crime departments which are organized according to the offender's last name. In these units, a prosecutor will only receive a new, open case when a juvenile commits a crime. In contrast, in "repeat offender" departments, a prosecutor monitors a smaller ongoing caseload of juveniles who have already violated the juvenile law several times.

[19] § 37 JGG.

[20] Senior Prosecutor Interview [5CK], 22 January 2006.

[21] Senior Prosecutor Interview [13EU], 6 December 2005.

[22] This would include violations according to §§ 174, 177 (rape), 180, and 182 (sexual abuse of a child ages 14–16).

> One must work diligently so that one has a good reputation. You can be creative and determine for yourself how you will handle your work and develop your own methods. One must be sociable and not appear across as elitist or be a deadbeat. There is nothing as bad when a person projects themselves as a know-it-all when in reality they do not have all the answers.[23]

8.4.1 Prosecutorial Discretion and Informal Dispositions

The wide range of informal sanctions in the juvenile system, coupled with the system's strong emphasis on education and rehabilitation, accords both judges and prosecutors substantial leeway in determining whether and how juvenile offenders should be sanctioned. At the federal, Land, and sometimes local levels, guidelines are in place that attempt to structure prosecutorial discretion under the Juvenile Justice Act. However, while the uniform guidelines under the Juvenile Justice Act (1994) (*Richtlinien zum Jugendgerichtsgesetz*) stress the importance of measures designed to education and socialize juveniles, they do not define in detail the types of cases where that disposition may be appropriate (Kilchling 2005, p. 237). According to Kilchling (2005, p. 237), even the guidelines on the Land level leave some discretion to local prosecutors.

When we examine actual sentencing statistics, a strong pattern emerges. While juvenile crime rates remained flat during the 1980s and increased during the 1990s, during the past 20 years judges and prosecutors have increasingly relied on diversionary measures to dispose of juvenile cases.

Although the United States began to experiment with the use of diversionary programs in the 1960s, the German use of the term is not quite identical to the American term. It is perhaps easiest to understand these differences if we keep in mind that, although the effect of diversion is that it often reduces the burden on the judicial system, from a criminological perspective, the purpose of diversion is to: (1) Reduce the stigmatization of the juvenile, (2) Implement a swifter response to the delinquent act, and to (3) Increase the options available for prosecutors and judges to address whatever problems the juvenile may be facing (Bareinske 2004). The principle diversion measures are prescribed by law under Section 45 JGG and Section 47 JGG summarized below in Table 8.1.

When we examine the use of diversion practices over time, one notes that, in 1981 (Heinz 2006, Fig. 25), the percentage of cases that resulted in a dismissal either with or without the offender satisfying certain conditions accounted for 44 % of the total number of sentenced offenders. By 2003 however, that figure had risen to 69 % (Heinz 2006). Moreover, the statistics show that prosecutors and judges have, to an increasing extent, simply decided to dismiss cases without any sanctions at all. According to Heinz (2006), the percentage of dismissals rose from roughly 12 % in 1981 to over 50 % in 2003. That increase has been driven primarily by an

[23] Senior Prosecutor Interview [13EU], 6 December 2005.

Table 8.1 Juvenile law provisions relevant to diversion

Section	Conditions (in summary form)
45 (1)	A prosecutor may, without judicial agreement, terminate a proceeding if the preconditions stated in Sect. 153 are satisfied.
45 (2)	A prosecutor may discontinue a proceeding if: 1) The prosecutor believes that an educational or instructional program is sufficient and 2) The child is participating in this program. A judge's participation pursuant to paragraph 3 is not necessary and a juvenile proceeding pursuant to Section 76 JGG is also not necessary under this paragraph.
45 (3)	A proceeding may be terminated by a judge if a child has completed their participation in an education or instructional program.
47	After charges have been filed in a juvenile case, a judge may dismiss the charges if: 1) The preconditions stated in Sect. 153 are satisfied; 2) The developmental measures included within Sect. 45 (2) have been satisfied or implemented and it is not necessary for the court to reach a decision based on the evidence; 3) The court has reached a judgment against the child and has ordered that the child complete an educational or instructional program consistent with 45 (3); or 4) The child cannot be held criminally liable because of a lack of maturity. In the case of paragraphs (2) and (3) a judge may, with the agreement of the prosecutor, temporarily suspend the proceedings and give the juvenile a deadline of, at the most of 6 months, to comply with the court's instructions, orders or educational/instructional measures. If the juvenile complies with the court's conditions, the court may dispose of the case through Sections 11 (3) and 15 (3)2. In the event of new criminal acts or evidence, new charges may be filed.

increase in cases dismissed by prosecutors rather than the courts (Heinz 2006). The rate at which the public prosecution office is determining case outcomes absent judicial involvement is increasing (Jehle 2005, p. 38). It is thus fair to conclude that the expansion in prosecutors' discretion with respect to the handling juvenile crimes has gradually shifted the locus of decision-making from the court to the prosecution office.

The existence of opportunities to dismiss or divert cases has profoundly impacted the scope of prosecutorial discretion in juvenile proceedings. The vast majority of juvenile "crime" includes traffic offenses and other easy-to-prove minor offenses. In 2001, for example, prosecutors chose to dispose of cases with diversionary measures rather than file formal charges in 45 % of their cases (Kilchling 2005). Moreover, the fact that a prosecutor elected to file charges in a case did not preclude the court from sending the case to diversion. In 29 % of the cases in which charges were filed, the cases were disposed of through diversionary measures (Kilchling 2005). A portion of these diverted cases contain cases in which the prosecutor has filed an application with the court requesting that the court impose diversionary measures using expedited procedures. In these cases, the court will issue instructions which carry the status of a judgment.

As Kilchling (2002) notes, courts prosecute and sanction only one-third of juvenile offenders. In almost 1/3 of the juvenile cases, prosecutors or judges dismiss without imposing a sanction.[24] Pursuant to Sect. 45 (3) and 47 JGG, prosecutors and judges, respectfully, may dismiss cases dismissed under these provisions on the condition that the offender satisfy a condition such as attending a training course, performing community service, or receiving traffic instruction. The category of educational measures, which only totaled 5 % of the sanctions imposed in 2003, includes court orders that direct the juvenile to notify the court of their whereabouts, perform community service, participate in victim-offender mediation, or attend social training courses.[25]

Even when an offender falls between the ages of 18 and 21 years of age, prosecutors elect to proceed under the juvenile, rather than the criminal, code in the 64 % cases (Lorenz 2008, p. 3). In those cases involving a minor offenses committed by youthful offenders, courts often impose a penal order adults (Lorenz 2008, p. 3). In contrast, in 2006, courts sentenced only 16 % of youthful offenders to juvenile detention. However, in the bulk of those cases, 60 %, the court suspended the period of detention in lieu of vocational training or work opportunities (Lorenz 2008, p. 3).

In assessing both the severity of the sanctioning scheme as well as the degree of discretion which it injects into the juvenile justice system, it is important to recognize that, according to the German principle of "subsidiarity," courts may only impose the more formal sanctions of disciplinary measures or youth imprisonment after educational sanctions prove to be insufficient.[26] While the disciplinary measures include the more severe sanction of detaining juveniles in a youth detention center,[27] the measures also include merely cautioning a youth,[28] or imposing conditions which, in part, mimic the directives included under the range of educational measures.[29] The pattern of this sanctioning is duplicated under the code sections that authorize youth imprisonment as courts possess a series of step-down options short of imprisonment such as suspending a sentence of imprisonment or imposing probation.[30] According to Holthusen (2004), sentencing statistics at the beginning of the decade indicate that courts elected to suspend custodial sentences between 6 and 12 months over 60 % of the time and more severe custodial sentences ranging from 12 to 24 months approximately 50 % of the time. At the end of the scale are custodial sentences, which under the Youth Court Act, range between 6 months and 10 years.[31] Despite the importance of diversionary measures, youth prison rates have been increasing since the 1990s.

---

[24] Statistics are limited to the cases processed in the states of the former West Germany and Berlin.

[25] §§51 and 9 JGG.

[26] § Nr. 2 JGG.

[27] § 16 JGG.

[28] § 16 JGG.

[29] Under § 15 JGG the condition which qualify as disciplinary measures include making reparations, issuing an apology, performing community service, and paying a fine.

[30] §§ 5(2) JGG & Sect. 17 JGG.

[31] §18 JGG.

The driving force behind this trend has been an increase in the number of juveniles convicted of assault and street robbery (Junger-Tas 2006).

8.4.2 *The Mindset of Traditional Juvenile Practice*

How does the juvenile law's emphasis on education-oriented measures play out in practice? To begin with, because the purpose of the juvenile code stresses diversion and education-oriented measures, diversion-related sanctioning processes predominate. As noted previously, courts impose sanctions which include youth imprisonment only as a last resort when informal and formal community sanctions or probation fail (Dünkel 2005, p. 22). The nature of prosecution practice, defined in terms of the flow and nature of decision-making, reflects this philosophy. A juvenile crimes prosecutor will typically handle 120–150 new cases per month. Although this number far exceeds the typical incoming caseload of even the general crimes departments, juvenile department prosecutors typically process cases more quickly than a comparable adult case. Moreover, there is a special provision in the juvenile law which permits prosecutors to combine several pending cases against a particular juvenile together to facilitate a speedier resolution.[32] Despite the fact that juvenile cases are often easier to resolve than adult cases, the reality of juvenile practice is that prosecutors must learn to quickly process an extraordinary number of files. In one office I visited, an experienced prosecutor told me that, he had decided to retire early because the juvenile case load had become so heavy that, he no longer had enough time to adequately read through the case files.[33] High case loads place a premium on efficient decision-making routines:

> The normal prosecutor in this department must handle approximately 120 new cases ... That means that, since there are 22 working days in a month, one must dispense with 5 to 6 cases per day. [On average] every day you will receive 5 to 6 new cases and you must close those cases by filing charges or dismissing the case. Some of the cases can be dispensed with easily. For example, if the police conduct an investigation on a child under the age of fourteen. Children under fourteen can not be criminally punished, so we have a special form [that the prosecutor can fill out] to dismiss the case. That is one reason for the high case loads. We also handle simple cases like shoplifting, traffic cases, and so on. But [we also have] a certain number of complicated cases that we must devote a substantial amount of time to... .When I began my career in 1977, each prosecutor handled half the caseload that we handle now. This is a [significant] problem and the cases have also become more complicated ... The stress of the job has vastly increased.... My shoulders must carry a heavier load. To keep up with the workload I often work weekends as do many of my colleagues... [As a result] we can no longer devote as much time to complicated cases.[34]

[32] §31 JGG.

[33] Prosecutor Interview [5LY], 19 January 2006.

[34] Senior Prosecutor Interview [5CK], 22 January 2006.

In order to deal with heavy case loads, prosecutors must develop systems which prioritize cases according to the case's time deadline, sorting out the cases which involve non-routine decision-making. The dozens of case files which cross a prosecutor's desk each day require prosecutors to make a variety of routine decisions. For example, one experienced prosecutor related to me that,[35] when a new stack of files appears in her office, she will immediately tackle the cases that deal with detention decisions and questions relating to specific proceedings that possess an impending time deadline.[36] After she clears those files from her desk, she will review the *new case files* which have just arrived from the police to determine whether or not the case will require further investigation. If further investigation is required, most often she will send the file back to the police with a written instruction. However, rather surprisingly, this particular prosecutor told me that she will often complete the investigation herself. The next order of business is the *quick decision files* which are files that require a simple signature or the inscription of a new follow-up date in the file. For example, a file which fits in this category might be a case where she has proposed that the case be disposed of with a fine, and she has sent the file to the juvenile authorities to solicit their approval, but the file has not yet returned. She will handle the file at this juncture simply by writing a new follow-up date in the file. Finally, as she is going through her stack of files, she will place all of the files which require a longer and deliberate review on the bookcase behind her. On the particular day I interviewed this prosecutor; the file stacked on top of her back bookcase was actually a case that was assigned to another prosecutor. Because that prosecutor was out sick, the department leader had assigned the case to her for follow-up.

The case processing nature of juvenile practice may lead prosecutors to focus on simply getting their work done. Despite this pressure to focus on case completions, closing cases is seldom cited by prosecutors as a source of job satisfaction. Over 85 % of the eight juvenile crimes prosecutors whom I interviewed stated that their primary source of job satisfaction was not related to merely processing cases or imposing punishment. The diverse nature of the sources of job satisfaction as well as the work in this department itself is reflected in the range of interview responses detailed below. These prosecutors paint a picture of practice that is both unpredictable and that offers opportunities for prosecutors to approach their jobs creatively.

> [*Question*: *What part of your job do you enjoy the most*?]
>
> I like it when I can work through the small cases quickly and then spend time on the larger cases where there will be a main proceeding. However, sometimes the satisfaction comes from finishing small cases. Besides earning money, what I derive satisfaction from on the job is when the court imposes an appropriate sentence. . .Also, in juvenile cases, once

---

[35] Prosecutor Interview [6SB], 23 January 2006.

[36] The department's secretarial staff will place the files requiring immediate attention in a yellow jacket and/or make a notation on the outside file cover which indicates that the file requires immediate attention.

> in awhile a juvenile will approach me and tell me that they had no chance of changing the circumstances of their life until the sentence was imposed on them.[37]

> That is a difficult question. There are many dimensions of my work that I enjoy. In a special crimes department, one is not bored. The work load is very diverse. In a juvenile proceeding one must often deliberate about what has happened. Sometimes one must go to the library and research a legal question-what has the Federal Criminal Court said about this issue? Not only must [I] clarify the facts with the police by telephone but also one must think about the circumstances that have influenced the child-the circumstances surrounding the case. It can also happen that the testimony during the trial differs from the facts which appear clearly in the file. This makes the proceedings interesting.[38]

> The spectrum of cases that we deal with is very large and, in comparison with other departments that also work with social relationships between husbands and women, between children and parents and with these types of histories, I must genuinely say, that the juvenile crimes department is the most important and difficult area. Because the focus of our juvenile law is not punishment in the first instance but personal development, we work closely with the juvenile social workers, parents, schools, social insurance agencies, sports authorities and the like. As a result, as an individual, one can have a large impact. You have the opportunity to take the initiative.[39]

> Here in the juvenile crime department, every prosecutor handles about 120 new cases per month. That is 1,440 cases in a year. Personally, I enjoy participating in court proceedings because the proceedings are simply more interesting [than working on files]. Many days of the week I must work at my desk and read files.

> . . . The desk work is very routine. I personally enjoy my work when it is a little more difficult. That is usually the case when I go to court. I think most of my colleagues feel the same way.[40]

8.4.3 The Mindset of Practice in Repeat Offender Units

In contrast to normal juvenile case loads, which are often assigned based on the suspect's last name, in the repeat offender unit which I visited, prosecutors are assigned a caseload of 50–60 specific juveniles. All of these individuals have a record of multiple offenses, which has earned them the distinction of being labeled an "*Intensivtäter*" or juvenile habitual offenders, as well as their own personal prosecutor. Under this system, a "new case" will come across a prosecutor's desk only when a juvenile who is assigned to them is suspected of committing a new infraction. The goal of these units is not to target the most serious individual crimes per se, but rather to deter the criminal lifestyle of habitual offenders. With this group of offenders, the mindset of practice is no longer driven by the assumption that

---

[37] Prosecutor Interview [6SB], 23 January 2006.

[38] Prosecutor Interview [12CJ], 29 November 2005.

[39] Senior Prosecutor Interview [5CK], 22 January 2006.

[40] Prosecutor Interview [5DK], 19 January 2006.

low-level juvenile delinquency is part of the experience of growing up. In essence, the children who have been identified as serial repeat offenders no longer comport with the archetype of a typical juvenile. While prosecutors in typical juvenile crimes units view of typical juvenile delinquency as part of the normal process of growing up, repeat juvenile offender units view their charges has having stepped beyond the bounds of normal juvenile behavior. While prosecutors in typical juvenile units regard low-level juvenile delinquency as posing little threat to the societal fabric, prosecutors in these repeat offender units consider the lifestyle of serial repeat offenders as a threat to the social fabric of specific neighborhood communities.

> In order to handle juveniles, we have created a habitual offender unit. The main purpose of the unit is to ensure that all of the information dealing with a particular person is centralized so that the judges and prosecutors know a juvenile's full history before sentencing them. There have been many reports in the press advocating for higher sentences for juveniles. [However] the main purpose of the unit is not necessarily to increase the punishments.[41]

> [W]ith these people, we have many, many problems ... They control much of the illegal drug market. They are in every criminal branch you can imagine ... [I]t developed as a crime among very young people, absolutely youngsters. It began with jackets, with shoes, fashion labels, etc. And nowadays, mobiles, money, necklaces, whatever is electronic, MP3 players, what the kids are carrying. So this is our main problem. In certain areas of *Frankenstein* where the concentration of these people is high up to a majority, it's a daily risk for school children to become [a] victim of such a crime. And it's not only robbery. They're beating people. Rap[e] is a problem-at least sexual attacks. If they get a girl or young woman, they take what they want. That's their point of view. 'I am the king. I can do whatever I want to do.'[42]

As a result of this case assignment system, prosecutors become well-acquainted with the social backgrounds and juvenile records of the offenders who fall within their area of responsibility. A consequence of this familiarity is that a prosecutor's sense of job satisfaction may become tied, not simply to disposing of cases, but rather to affecting a change in a juvenile's development.

> As a general rule, I know these people very well. [When I see a case], it usually is not the first time [that I have met the offender]. I know their life history. I know where they live. I know what is going on with their parents. I am familiar with their record. With what happened before. Most of the cases involve young adults between 18 and 21 and a lower number of juveniles above the age of 14. In a typical [juvenile crimes] case, the case will be dismissed or the juvenile will be sent to a special school. Those decisions are completely random. Here it is different because we are orientated to handle particular offenders and I really know them.
>
> In this department, I feel satisfied when an offender stops committing delinquent acts. For example I had a case where I had the impression that the young person should be incarcerated in a detention center or youth facility. The sentence was severe. After he had served a 3.5 year sentence and was 19 years old, he came to see me. He told me that I had been right. I felt good about that. He said that he was now free and that he had completed his vocational training and would visit me again![43]

[41] Justice Ministry Official [9RR], 30 June 2006.

[42] Senior Prosecutor Interview [9AI], 14 June 2006.

[43] Prosecutor Interview [9QL], 14 June 2006.

This can be a tall order given the recidivism rates of the target offender populations of the repeat offender units. According to statistics released by the Worker's Welfare Organization (*Arbeiterwohlfahrt-ABO*) between 80 and 90 % of juveniles reoffend after being released from confinement (Sommer-Guist 2005). In an effort to make a strong impression on repeat offenders, the Berlin repeat offender unit frequently recommends that the court detain a repeat offender in investigative detention (*Untersuchungshaft*) prior to trial. The group targeted for this treatment includes youthful offenders who, because of the nature of their offense, will be eligible for sentencing to a juvenile or an adult facility if they are convicted. The use of pre-trial detention with this small number of hard-core offenders appears to have a slightly positive effect (Reusch 2007). While the reoffense rate among repeat offenders sentenced to probation is approximately 53 %, the reoffense rate for the group of more serious offenders who have been held in some form of pre-trial detention is 56 % (Reusch 2007). The department leader in charge of the repeat offender unit, views this slight gap as success given the fact that the individuals held in pre-trial detention are typically extremely difficult offenders (Reusch 2007). In interpreting the results obtained by the Berlin unit, one must also consider the costs of "expedited justice." A key practice employed by the unit is to petition the court to incarcerate young offenders prior to trial as a form of deterrence. Although the prior offense records of repeat offenders are extensive, pre-trial detention not only serves to ensure that the suspect will be present for trial, but it is also conceived as a form of punishment itself. Viewed from this perspective, repeat offenders are, in essence, convicted and preliminarily punished on the basis of their past records. The harsh practices of the unit have been criticized in the press (Anker 2007a) by defense attorneys who claim that the unit's harsh tactics result in disproportionate punishments. According to Nicholas Becker, speaking in the *Berliner Morgenpost* (Anker 2007a), "for young repeat offenders it is important that they are handled justly. Justice means that the justice system should react quickly, but with a proportionate response."

According to a press release issued by the Ministry of Interior in the state of Nordrhein-Westfalen, the creation of a repeat offender unit in *Mönchengladbach*, a suburb of Düsseldorf, has had a positive effect in terms of reduced crime rates. Notably, the crime rate among repeat offenders dropped almost 50 % between 2003 and 2004 (Behrens 2005). While the Mönchengladbacher model aims to reduce the time between the initial offense and the date of adjudication by 50 %, the core of the program is that as a result of close cooperation between the police, prosecution office, and youth workers, an offender is placed under intensive supervision before their adjudication date (Behrens 2005). However, it is still too early to gauge whether the intensive interagency cooperation necessary to produce results can be sustained and whether any significant improvement in delinquency rates can be made in Berlin's tougher neighborhoods absent a change in the underlying socio-economic conditions. Absent those factors, these programs may only produce short-term, symbolic results.

8.5 Fear, Fairness, and Citizenship

A key question in the juvenile crime system is the issue of whether or not juvenile justice system treats immigrants differently than native Germans. On their face, incarceration statistics raise troubling issues. If we examine those statistics, it is evident that young foreigners are overrepresented in youth prisons by a factor of close to 2.3 times (Holthusen 2004). Young ethnic German immigrants are over-represented by almost double (Holthusen 2004). At least part of the explanation for differences in youth incarceration rates is that foreigners report violent conflicts to the police more often than native Germans and the conflicts that they do report are more likely to involve a foreign suspect (Dünkel 2003). Despite stark differences in incarceration rates, a few research studies show that, prosecutors do not treat young foreigners more harshly than ethnic Germans (Dünkel 2003, p. 14). In fact, while there is scattered evidence showing that police agencies engage in discriminatory enforcement practices, other studies suggest that prosecutors dismiss cases against foreigners at a higher rate than cases involving German suspects (Dünkel 2003; Geißler and Marissen 1990; Mansel and Raithel 2003). According to Dünkel (2003, p. 15), the net result is that:

> [T]he prevalence rates of foreign compared to German offenders are still higher but not as much as the police data would suggest... This means that prosecutors somehow "de-dramatise" (petty)offenses of foreigners to a more "realistic" level.

While Albrecht (1997, p. 71) supports Dünkel's position and claims that prosecutors act as a "counterweight against a trend toward over-reporting of minority offenders by police," this phenomenon may be based more on the evidentiary weaknesses inherent in cases involving foreign suspects rather than prosecutor's desire to preserve the system's overall fairness. Indeed, Bareinske's 2004 study of case dispositions in the state of Baden-Württemberg cast doubt on Dünkel's thesis. In a study of over 25,000 juvenile cases, Bareinske (2004, p. 75) found that juveniles who possessed German citizenship received an informal sanction 72 % of the time; while non-German juveniles received the benefit of an informal disposition only 68 % of the time. Although this variance is a small one, it is evident that further research on the potential existence of discriminatory practices in the justice system should be conducted to determine the source of the substantial differences in youth incarceration rates.

Even where the criminal law is facially neutral with regard to the treatment of foreigners, the use of so-called neutral decision-making criteria may foreign residents differently. Albrecht (1997, p. 37) points to a two-prong reason for this disparity:

> System processing in the case of members of minorities is heavily influenced by two characteristics: legal particulars and certain types of crime involvement. Foreign offenders are likely to be handled differently compared with German offenders are legal grounds, as decision-making in the criminal justice systems in several respects takes account of bonds to conventional society such as place of residence. Participation of some ethnic minorities in black markets, especially drug markets, is likely to lead to disproportionate use of pretrial

detention and prison sentences. This reflects concern not for ethnic minorities but for illicit drugs, which continue to provoke massive criminal justice reactions.

The fact that many immigrant children possess few social bonds, lack a stable residential pattern, and belong to families that are socio-economically disadvantaged increases the likelihood that young foreigners, who are suspected of committing a moderate to serious offense, will be held in pre-trial detention. Thus, the use of justifiable routine decision-making criteria, such as an individual's ties to the community and their ability to flee out of the country, may inadvertently produce unequal outcomes such as higher pre-trial detention rates. Michael Tonry (1997, p. 16) succinctly summarizes the problem:

> The difficulty is that the rational and humane policy of restricting pre-trial confinement to those least likely to appear for trial means that those who live the least settled lives-those without permanent residences, or stable family lives, or jobs-will be held. Those traits more commonly characterize disadvantaged people, and many minority groups are disadvantaged.

This outcome Germany is apparent in as statistics regarding juvenile pre-trial detention rates show that young foreigners are overrepresented in the ranks of pre-trial detainees throughout the country (Albrecht 1997).[44]

Thus, however impartial the law may be on its face, the fact that both judges and prosecutors possess substantial latitude in their decision-making processes, opens the door to accusations that the law is being implemented in a discriminatory manner. Consider the case of Nidal R., a young man from Lebanon whose repeated criminal exploits help trigger the creation of Berlin's repeat offender unit (Anker 2007b). He first attracted the attention of the police at age ten (Anker 2007b). For 4 years his notoriety an a string of repeated offenses attracted the attention of the press who singled his case out as an example of the juvenile justice system's ineffectiveness. Against a backdrop of rising rates of violent juvenile crime, the publicity surrounding the case prompted members of both the conservative Christian Democratic Union (CDU) and the Social Democratic Party (SDP) to take notice. The case's trajectory is a disturbing one. One the one hand, the fact that the youth, who is now over 30 years old, committed over 80 criminal acts within a 10 year period indicates that his decision-making was impervious to punishment. Arguments can be made however; both that the judicial system intervened too late and that, when it did intervene, that the harsh judgments that it imposed were driven by the case's extensive publicity. The case of Nigal R. is one of a handful of cases throughout Germany whose every development seemed to provoke media frenzy. Illustrative of the coverage which Nigal R.'s case received, the Berlin media labeled him as Berlin's "Number one Problem Child" and at one point, the headline of a popular Berlin newspaper described him as "20 years old, 80 crimes, 100 percent violent" (Werwigk-Hertneck 2004).

[44] Albrecht reports that in 1994 foreign youth made up 57 % of the youth imprisoned in Hessen. In Niedersachen and Berlin, foreign pretrial detainees approached the 2/3 mark in 1993.

According to a Berlin defense attorney, as a result of the publicity surrounding Nigal's case, prosecutors sought and courts inflicted unusually harsh sanctions on the youth including a lengthy period of imprisonment. As the attorney explained:

> No reasonable appe[llate] judge dared for a long time to do anything for Nidal. When they finally had to release him he was so hungry for life and poor that it was very easy . . . to get a new arrest warrant for him for stealing cigarettes and [for] pushing away a policeman who just wanted to arrest him. The details of all these procedures are very interesting because they show that the concept beyond this new prosecut[ion] department is deterrence by super harsh treatment and provisional arrest . . .as a kind of fast punishment before a juvenile delinquent [can be found] guilty.[45]

Nor is the case of Nigal R. unique. The continued attention devoted by the Berlin media to the case histories of a group of serial offenders continues to call into question the efficacy of the system's response. Given the fact that over 80 % of Berlin's serial offenders lack German citizenship, media discussion of this crime problem has drawn attention to the fact the bulk of these offenders are non-German citizens. The link between immigration status, criminal justice system's impotency, and demands for an even stiffer response can be seen in this excerpt from a February 2007 article drawn from the *Berliner Morgenpost* (Oldenburger 2007). The article focuses on the case of Levent U. who committed over 200 crimes between the ages of 12 and 25 and was on the run as a murder suspect at the time of the article's publication.

> Politicians and representatives of the police are angry and upset. Law-abiding citizens have become desperate about the judicial system. The domestic politics spokesman for the Christian Democratic Party in the Berlin Senate, Frank Henkel, said yesterday: 'Why is this criminal still at large? The citizens and the police no longer agree with judicial leniency and softness.' The leader of a police organization (*Gewerkschaft der Polizei*), Klaus Eisenreich stated that: 'These people present a danger to the public. They must be imprisoned.' We must ask the question, why are these people still in Germany? (Oldenburger 2007).

While a connection exists between juvenile criminality and the cultural backgrounds of many juvenile offenders, it is impossible within the confines of this chapter to adequately explore any causal connection which may exist between a juvenile offender's citizenship status and prosecutorial decision-making. It is evident however, that the German media has played a key role in drawing attention to the problem of juvenile crime in Germany's larger cities and that that attention has provoked a policy response that has affected prosecutorial decision-making. A significant question which remains unaddressed and lies beyond the scope of this book, is the degree to which the criminal justice system can, by itself, efficaciously address a state's underlying societal problems.

---

[45] E-mail from Berlin defense attorney (9DEP) (June 13, 2007) (on file with author) (In accordance with my policy of preserving anonymity, I have elected not to cite the attorney's name).

8.6 Decision-Making Norms

For the past several decades, the prevailing norm in juvenile departments has been to give juveniles multiple opportunities to turn their lives around.[46] This case handling philosophy is dominated by a preference for using a wide range of mild pedagogical measures with juvenile suspects and harsher sanctions with young adults.[47] In concrete terms, this policy translates into case-handling practices dominated by case dismissals and a slow progression towards stiffer sanctions with each new offense. Given that juvenile cases are often less complicated from an evidentiary standpoint than many adult crimes, one might expect that the model of delegating case investigation practices to the police that German prosecutors use in handling low-level general crimes would be duplicated in juvenile crime departments.

Indeed the softer sanctions imposed in juvenile cases, combined with higher caseloads, provide few incentives and little time for prosecutors to work closely with the police during the investigation stage.[48] Where cases require further investigation a prosecutor might send the file back to the police with instructions regarding further areas for investigation or even attempt to perform the investigation themselves.[49] In a typical juvenile crime crimes department, prosecutors will interface with police units who do not specialize in juvenile crime. There may be a few officers who specialize in handling sexual crimes or violence in the schools for example, but the bulk of the officers may not possess any specialized training or competency.[50]

Where cooperation between police agencies and prosecution offices is only loosely coupled, the action taken in an individual case fluctuates greatly depending on a particular prosecutor's level of initiative and interest. This argument is supported by Asmus's (1998) research on the German prosecution service in which the German sociologist posits that German prosecutorial practice is constituted by bureaucratic decision practices. According to Asmus (1998), particular practices emerge out of the tension between legal norms and practical constraints. Of particular interest here is an interview that Asmus (1998, p. 122) conducted with a juvenile crimes prosecutor regarding the prosecutor's decision to arrest a juvenile suspect. In the case being discussed, the prosecutor first related the sequence of background events that influenced his decision to arrest the suspect. At the time of the arrest, the juvenile had a documented history of minor offenses. During the suspect's most recent crime spree, the prosecutor had been in almost daily telephone contact with the police. In the passage below the prosecutor described the case's recent history:

[46] Prosecutor Interview [6SB], 23 January 2006.

[47] Senior Prosecutor Interview [5CK], 26 January 2006.

[48] Prosecutor Interview [6SB], 23 January 2006.

[49] Prosecutor Interview [6SB], 23 January 2006.

[50] Senior Prosecutor Interview [5CK], 26 January 2006.

Prosecutor: I now have a case: The police called me, last week, and explained to me: The [suspect] had also stolen three mopeds and had committed a burglary in a supermarket. We searched by him and found ... an entire storeroom. [The police asked] Should we summon him? I said, well, does he have a job? Yes he works somewhere. Does he live with his parents? Yes. Also not [a sufficient condition by itself to warrant an arrest]. The day before yesterday the police called and said: The "wretch" has stolen a moped again. What should we do now? He simply will not stop. And then I said. Well okay. Then [the police] said: 'But we don't have him [in custody].' [I]n the meantime he has absconded. Then I said, 'Good, bring us the file, we will file a motion for an arrest warrant and then if you catch him, then we can hold him in custody.'

Now yesterday I was not here. The police went to my [the prosecutor who was standing in for me] and my replacement said, Hmm merely a moped-well the theft of a pair of mopeds, no we will not detain him. Today the police called me again and said. Now he has again broken into a store and stood behind a case of mineral water, and then loaded the case onto another stolen moped (laughing). I said, it is too much, now he will be arrested, now is the end.

[My substitute] is lazy. Yes that is true! That I must honestly say, because the reason for the arrest, everyone [finds] for themselves ... There is the danger of harm, which is not present from this dimwit. He is too dumb. Then there is the danger of flight-that is probably also not present. He stays ... and steals again. Then there is the risk of repeat offense but for that he must have already been appropriately punished [for a similar crime](sic). That has not happened.

And I must say, that a ground for an arrest was found. One says... it exists in the danger of flight, probably he could go. This is the case of an investigative detention which the law is not designed for, which is called the "educative" detention, in narrow circumstances and which I find very sensible (Asmus 1998, p. 122).

The prosecutor's rendition of events as well as his comments about the inaction of his stand-in supports the thesis that, in a typical juvenile crimes department, the character of the actions taken are strongly influenced by the prosecutor's own level of initiative. Although the law seeks to define a series of legally binding prerequisites for taking action, ultimately the prosecutor's own judgment, shaped with the input of the investigating officers, and his or her preference for action will shape the arrest decision.

While individual prosecutors' preferences for action shape case outcomes, by far the strongest impact on sanctions is exerted by regional norms of practice. As I have already pointed out, prosecutors throughout Germany are bound to enforce the same juvenile code. While the law is defined at the federal level, standards of interpretation develop at the regional and local levels. This development is reflected in the widespread variations between the diversion, pre-trial detention, and incarceration rates at the state level. When we examine the diversion rates for 2003, the three states with the lowest diversion rates include: Saarland (51 %), Bavaria (60 %), and Niedersachsen at 66 % (Dünkel 2006b). In contrast, the states with the highest diversion rates are the city-states of Bremen (86 %), Hamburg (82 %), and West Berlin with a diversion rate of 81 % (Dünkel 2006b). One might expect higher diversion rates in prosecution offices located in large cities because larger cities must typically deal with higher crime rates than those found in rural areas. In fact, the rates of juvenile crime in these three cities are among the highest in Germany. When we examine juvenile crime rates per 100,000 residents; Hamburg

(11,007), Bremen (10,268), and Saxony (9,771) Berlin (9,649) top the list of German states (Dünkel 2006b).[51] At the other end of the scale are Baden-Würtemberg (5,151), Hessen (5,506) and Bavaria (5,736), the states with the lowest juvenile crime rates (Dünkel 2006b).

8.7 New Models of Practice

The search for new responses to address juvenile crime began in the early 1990s when projects such as victim-offender mediation were introduced. These programs targeted offenders who had committed minor offenses who would typically be destined for diversion with the imposition of certain conditions. Although an amendment to the Juvenile Code enacted in 1990 opened the door to mediation programs,[52] in some areas these programs eventually closed down because prosecutors refused to support them (Kilchling 2002). In many cases the diversion-related programs that have survived have been sustained by closer working relationships between police, social workers, and prosecutors.

The increase in juvenile crime rates in some German cities has opened the door to, if not mandated, closer working relationships between local branches of government responsible for responding to juvenile crime. As working relationships have become more closely knit, there has been an increased sharing of information between the police officers, prosecutors, social workers, and judges during the investigation and adjudication stages of the proceedings. As a result, within the past 10 years in particular, local juvenile justice agencies have been experimenting with a variety of programs which aim to increase the system's responsiveness to such problems as juvenile delinquency and violence. While these projects take various physical forms-from housing police officers, juvenile welfare officers, and prosecutors under one roof to the simply scheduling regular information sharing meetings, the goal of many of these projects is to improve the coordination between agencies (Bässman 2006). For example, the program initiated in the city of Mönchengladbach, Germany aims to reduce crime committed by repeat offenders by improving the exchange of information between agencies, accelerating the adjudication process, and instituting home visits to the residences of repeat offenders by police and youth welfare officials. This program, which has shown promising results in reducing delinquency rates, has cut the time between the investigation and adjudication stages in half (Bässman 2006, p. 17).[53] Similarly, the Stuttgart's "House of Youth Law" (*Haus des Jugendrechts*) decreased the

---

[51] Citing 2003 data.

[52] First Amendment Act to the Juvenile Acts [*Erstes Gesetz zur Änderung des Jugendgresichts-gesetzes-1 JGGÄndG*] (August 30, 1990) BGBI. Ip. 1853.

[53] According to this report, the rate of repeat offenders among 14–18 years old declined from 45.88 % between 2003 and 2004.

average case processing time from 230 days to 86 days during the project's implementation period (Werwigk-Hertneck 2004). Similar programs, which have been introduced on the local level, have restructured interagency relationships as well as case decision-making processes. In particular there has been a blurring of traditional decision-making competencies that mandated that the police collect the "facts" surrounding a criminal incident while the prosecutors made legal decisions based on those facts. The joint nature of the decision-making process is reflected in the description of the working relationships between police and prosecutors detailed by these prosecutors.

> [*Q*: *How would you describe your working relationship with the police?*]
> We get to know each other and [as a result] can work better with each other. We get together with each other in training sessions, meetings, and conferences... The decisions take shape through an impression we [form] ... when we make a decision whether or not to seek an arrest [and must determine] whether the preconditions for an arrest are present. The police come to us in the larger cases and we talk about what the case looks like and how we should proceed. We coordinate our actions so that there is no superfluous investigation... We work with each other. As a result, we also learn what we have to offer each other. For example when we need a search warrant we must go before the judge with all of the facts. We must prepare the motion. That means that the police must come to us with the file and prepare the motion. The police will often come to us in person.[54]

> With the repeat offender program, I work very closely with the police ... We telephone each other daily and make many decisions together. A police officer will call and say "the witness said this and that, should I send you the updates?' Should I talk to the accused again? Should we do this?" The relationship is very tight.[55]

> When I have a case where the juvenile has committed several crimes and there is a possibility of punishment, the police will contact me early in the investigation. This [is especially true] when they would like to make an arrest. Then we stay in contact with each other throughout the investigation. When a suspect has been arrested we will work very closely together to bring the case to court.[56]

A key assumption which underlies many information-exchange programs is that too often cases processed according to the traditional investigation and prosecution model take too long to adjudicate (Gabriele 2004). When a period of several months to a year elapses between the commission of the delinquent act and the system's response, the connection that the offender will draw between the commission of the act and the subsequent punishment is too attenuated to provoke a behavioral change. This premise was borne out in a number of the cases that I observed as cases were often continued and rescheduled for a variety of reasons for example, if the child had another pending case in another court, or if the court decided that it needed a psychological evaluation of the child. While, these delays were warranted in some cases, in other cases prosecutors complained to me that judges delayed

[54] Senior Prosecutor Interview [13EU], 6 December 2005.

[55] Prosecutor Interview [9QL], 14 June 2006.

[56] Prosecutor Interview [12CJ], 29 November 2005.

adjudication because they were reluctant to impose the stiff sentence that appeared warranted under the circumstances.[57]

As I noted previously, in the past, the traditional form of inter-agency communication used in prosecution practice relied heavily on time-consuming written communications between the prosecution office, investigative agencies, and the courts. To achieve change, local communities have sought to restructure the relationships between organizations by mandating more timely and frequent inter-agency communication and formulating joint strategies. While implementing these operational changes did not require local communities to seek any changes in the existing juvenile laws or regulations, the changes could not occur without changing the organizational structure and decision-making processes in the cooperating local organizations. This decision-making freedom on the local level has positive and negative aspects. On the positive side, local communities are free to implement modest change without petitioning the federal legislature. On the negative side, local communities were free to introduce new programs that impacted the delivery of criminal justice services without a national debate.

Not surprisingly, some of the most effective local projects have involved eliminating the physical distance between the agencies, either through the Stuttgart model of housing the police, prosecutors, and youth welfare workers in a single building or, as the state of Sachsen has done, by housing representatives from the Youth Services Agency (*Jugendgerichtshilfe*) (JGH) within police agencies. Regardless of the physical proximity of the cooperating agencies, the essence of the fast-track approach is that the representatives from the police, prosecutor's office, and the JGH cooperate with each other and coordinate their responses as soon as possible after a suspect has been identified.

A question that has been largely unaddressed to date is the impact that fast-tracking a case may have on the offender-not only on their development but on their legal rights as well. As (Gabriele 2004, p. 103) states:

> Without detailing all the possible constellations, it can be established that arguments in favor of fast-tracking should be qualified in a number of ways. For one thing, although procedures extending over a long period of time do indeed run the risk of losing context with the context, dynamics and background of an offense those who work in the area are familiar with many constellations in which permitting time to elapse is the appropriate and necessary response because it enables the suspects and their families to >cool down< and acquire a more detached view, irrespective of possible official intervention. Indeed, it should not be forgotten that the fast-tracking discussed here is invariably official action, taken in name of the States, and that, rather than solving a problem it can make matters worse.

Since many innovative programs aim to reform the procedures used and decisions made during a juvenile proceeding's investigation stage, the decision-making processes of prosecutors and the range of their discretion inevitably stand at the focal point of questions which challenge the efficacy of reform. A key question is whether or not improved case communication and the fast-tracking of cases has led

[57] Prosecutor Interview [7SE], 5 April 2006.

to prematurely introduce sanctions for minor offenses (Gabriele 2004). If this proposition were true, we would see an increase in the number of cases disposed of under Section 45 (2) JGG, which requires the offender to comply with certain socio-educational measures, and a relative decrease in the number of cases which are summarily dismissed without consequences pursuant to Section 45 (1) JGG. As I noted above, the percentage of cases disposed of under both sections steadily increased between 1981 and 2004. Although, no comprehensive study of fast-track programs has been completed to date, initial data from the Stuttgart program has been published. This data indicates that, while the cases disposed of pursuant to Section 45 (1) JGG during the tenure of the model program increased 30 % (from 6.8 to 8.8 % of total dispositions), dispositions imposed pursuant to Section 45 (2) JGG registered an over 80 % increase (5.8–10.6 %) (Feuerhiem 2003, p. 74).

The sanctioning processes used by some fast-track programs also raise distribution of powers concerns. With many fast-track programs, it is not the courts that determine what programs should be "recommended" to offenders eligible for diversion programs, but rather police officers who work in consultation with prosecutors. Ideally, the decision-making of front-line personnel is guided by recommendations formulated by community workgroups. For example, in 2004, a working group drawn from the police, prosecution office, and related municipal departments in the city-state of Berlin devised guidelines that specify the eligibility standards for the different types of diversion permitted under the law (Gabriele 2004). The highlights of these guidelines are detailed below in Table 8.2.

Diversion guidelines assist the agencies who participate in inter-agency task forces to navigate the conflicts that emerge between the competing mandates imposed on their own organization's mandates and help to facilitate interagency cooperation. For example, social workers may be reluctant to report crimes because it may undercut their effectiveness and credibility with their clients. At the same time, police officers are bound by the principle of legality to register and investigate every potential offense that comes to their attention. On the other hand, the realities of tight fiscal constraints have forced prosecutors to loosen their faithfulness to the principle of mandatory prosecution. While programs which attempt to fast-track juvenile cases offer the promise of breaking the pattern of sanctioning practice which has imposed too few consequences, too late in the game, those programs require an additional investment of both time and personnel. Without a net gain in overall agency resource levels, the increased time and effort devoted to fast-tracking cases may be achieved at the expense of attention paid to other cases. Critically, if the Ministries of Justice at the state level assign prosecutors and judges to offices and courts strictly on the basis of average case load levels, the introduction of new programs may improve prosecutorial effectiveness in one area while creating shortages in other areas. In sum, in an era in which prosecution offices have faced tight budget constraints, implementing new programs which require prosecutors work more closely with other agencies and to do more than routinely process files, may lead to higher case dismissal rates in other departments which experience stiffer resource constraints.

Table 8.2 Berlin diversion guidelines

Relevant provision under juvenile code	§45(1) JGG	§45(2)	§45(3)
Offender-based characteristics	First offender[a] A second-time offender where significant time has elapsed since the first offense or, in hindsight the object of legal protection is insignificant or unimportant. A guilty plea is not required.	First time offender of a more serious offense which can no longer qualify for dismissal under § 45 (1) JGG. Repeat offender of an offense typically dismissed under §45 (1) JGG. A guilty plea is not required.	First time offender of a more serious offense. Repeat offender of a less serious to mid-level offense. A guilty plea is required.
Nature of the offense	The offense is a *Vergehen* (lowlevel crime). It is a typical juvenile offense with a low level of culpability and few repercussions. It is not likely that the youth will reoffend even if they do not participate in educational measures.	Qualifies as a more serious *Vergehen* (low-level crime) and in some cases as a *Verbrechen* (major crime) (i.e. a robbery committed through extortion). Participation in an educational measure has been effective as the youth realizes the consequences of his or her actions and is unlikely to reoffend.	Offense may be a *Vergehen* (lowlevel) or a lesser *Vebrechen* (serious offense). The prosecutor believes that an informal judicial disposition will be successful because the offender is likely to respond to judicial authority and the prosecutor was unable to convince the juvenile to voluntarily participate in educational measures.
Principal decision-maker	Prosecutor	The prosecutor or the police in consultation with the prosecutor initiate the youth's participation in a suitable educational measure.	The prosecutor monitors the conditions. The child must reappear before the court after fulfilling the conditions.
Sample disposition options	Case dismissed without sanctions	An apology to the victim. Restitution. Mediation. First-offender course.	Similar to § 45 (2) JGG.

[a]The guidelines define a first offender as an individual who has not previously participated in a criminal proceeding, has been previously adjudicated as not guilty, or an individual who has had an investigatory proceeding deferred pursuant to §170 (2) StPO

Source: Berlin Senateverwaltungen für Justiz (2004)

8.8 Court Hearings and Sentencing Practices

Although a key goal of juvenile proceedings is to ascertain the state of the juvenile's mind and the status of their development, the proceedings must first establish the suspect's guilt before formal sanctions may be imposed. Nevertheless, the procedural rules which govern juvenile proceedings contain several provisions which attempt to balance the judicial system's quest for truth and transparency with the system's aim to encourage child development. For example, to protect children from publicity, juvenile proceedings are closed to the public.[58] In addition, the juvenile code instructs prosecutors to exclude information from the charging document which could harm a child's development.[59] In the small number of children's court proceedings that I observed,[60] both prosecutors and judges did not simply accept the allegations as filed but weighed through witness testimony and dismissed charges that could not be substantiated. In addition, rather than project a distant, authoritative air, several judges and prosecutors attempted to establish a friendly, but stern, parental tone. Thus, through the tone and communication style of the proceedings, judges and prosecutors attempt to cajole and persuade young offenders to return to the fold of good citizenship. In this sense, the proceedings themselves possess a certain performance value that goes beyond the mandate of the law to "find the truth." The fact that a young suspect has participated in the process and appears to amenable to reform possess a value in and of itself. As a result, the judicial process enjoys its own independent educative value. That fact, plus the fact that the system is oriented towards child development, rather than the imposition of punitive sanctions increases the likelihood that cases will be dismissed and that no sanctions will be imposed.[61] The predominant assumption underlying the treatment of juvenile crime is the thesis that society should tolerate a certain level of juvenile delinquency because it is a normal part of the development process. As one prosecutor explained:

> If you asked a number of university students how many of them had broken the law growing up, most of them would say "yes." Because of that the sanctions that we use to respond to this behavior should be minimal. That is the reason that we work with the office of youth services and the juvenile court workers to ascertain what is happening in the child's life. These social workers also participate in the court proceedings as they are familiar with the child's history. The interviews that they conduct do not focus exclusively on the actions at issue but also the nature of the child's family relationships... So when the case is not

[58] §48 JGG. Where the proceedings also include charges filed against young adults (aged 18–21) or adults the proceedings are open to the public unless the court elects to hold closed hearings.

[59] §46 JGG.

[60] Due to the fact that I only observed a small number of juvenile proceedings, the findings in this subsection must be interpreted as preliminary in nature. In the future, I anticipate conducting more extensive participant observation studies focusing on juvenile court proceedings. Of particular interest would be to compare proceedings initiated by the repeat offender units with the typical juvenile proceedings.

[61] Prosecutor Interview [6SB], 23 February 2006.

serious, the court will require the child to participate in a so-called 'growing up talk,' mediation with the victim, or community service.[62]

The familiarity that develops between judges, prosecutors, and social workers assigned to assist in juvenile proceedings breeds a feeling of community and a sense of familiarity. In most cases the prosecutors and judges who work on juvenile cases specialize in handling juvenile cases, so they know each other well. In the proceedings that I observed, the prosecutor was able to "guess" with uncanny accuracy what the outcome would be before the proceeding started. This prescience is the product of the prosecutor's prior experiences before the court. Judges and prosecutors in particular communities possess a similar knowledge base of shared experience. While this premise holds true to a certain extent in all communities, the fact that juvenile courts form their own communities within a community heightens the level of familiarity of the participants.

At the same time, the predictable nature of case outcomes did not necessarily signal that prosecutors agreed with a particular judge's sentencing philosophy or that prosecutor's relinquish their role during the fact-finding and sanctioning proceedings. As the interview excerpts below indicate, prosecutors are not only aware of differences in judicial sentencing philosophies, but in some circumstances, they will engage in or support efforts to steer cases to judges whose sentencing philosophies they support. While this is a common practice in the American system, it is almost unthinkable in a civil law system founded on the premise that law can and should be uniformly implemented.[63]

> I know the juvenile judge in *Falkenberg* very well and I know most of the time what the outcome is likely to be. . .However the juvenile judge in is too lenient. In one serious case that I was handling he dismissed the case with only the requirement that the juvenile had to complete forty hours of work. When possible I will avoid that judge by filing more serious cases before the *Jugendschöffengericht*.[64] This goes against the spirit of the regulations.[65]

> [W]e are very happy that we could come to a change of [sentencing philosophy with the repeat offender unit] which goes hand in hand with a change in thinking in general. So the generation of 68'ers goes to pension . . . Thank heavens.[66] And we have [new] judges for young people. It is now the generation of forty- somethings. . .They see things absolutely different than the [judges who are] twenty years older or so. And that leads to the effect that the prisons for young persons are overcrowded and [our unit] is one of the reasons that they

[62] Senior Prosecutor Interview [5CK], 22 January 2006.

[63] While a prosecutor or a defense attorney may file a challenge against a judge, according to §24 StPO, challenges may only be filed if there is a fear of bias or a reason to doubt the judge's impartiality.

[64] The *Jugendschöffengericht* is a juvenile court comprised of one professional judge and 2 lay judges.

[65] Prosecutor Interview [6SB], 23 February 2006.

[66] The "generation of 68'ers refers to the individuals who received a university during the turbulent societal upheaval of the late 1960's and early 1970's in Germany-many of whom possessed liberal attitudes towards sentencing and societal problems."

are over-crowded... .A mugger [that comes to our unit] normally is sentenced to imprisonment. Sometimes [a] suspended sentence with imprisonment.[67]

Finally, while there is a high percentage of routine decision-making in juvenile crime cases, the decision-making process in more complex cases can be a more deliberate one that requires skills and knowledge beyond those that a prosecutor acquires during their university training.

[*Q*: *What type of skills does a prosecutor need to function in this department*?]

A: First, one must be able to weigh the evidence clearly and to apply the law... .You must be able to sift through the testimony of the witnesses. One must understand the psychological testimony and weigh it accurately. I must say that that requires having a knowledge of society and psychology. For this one needs experience and ongoing education...What is most important is that one must possess a desire to achieve justice ... This means finding the sanction that fits the crime ... We must protect society.[68]

8.9 Management Controls & Hierarchical Review

As noted in the previous chapter, a key function performed by department leaders is to review the new cases which come into the department and to assign the cases to particular prosecutors. To facilitate this task, department leaders use the case processing reports mentioned previously that detail the number of cases which each prosecutor has opened as well as the average investigation and case closing rates. Because there is an incoming stream of new cases, a central role of department leaders is to ensure that prosecutors in their department stay motivated and keep up with the incoming files. Because disparities in workloads can create dissension in the ranks, department leaders strive to ensure that the workload is evenly distributed and that no one prosecutor is taking too long to move cases through the system. While there can be a production-line type feel to this task, a department leader must also ensure that certain normative standards are met. A key normative standard of juvenile crimes, as well as adult crime practice, is that similarly situated cases should be treated uniformly. How department leaders interpret their roles varies:

[*Question*: *What are your chief duties as a department leader*?]

I am responsible for motivating [the prosecutors in this department] and ensuring that they do not have too much work. It is [also] my responsibility to ensure that all of the cases are dealt with in a uniform manner. [To this end] I decide whether or not we will file an appeal in a particular case-that means all of the *Handakte* [smaller court reference files] will come across my desk with the prosecutor's notes from the court proceeding. I receive all of the *Beschwerde* [complaints] relating to cases where the prosecutor dismissed the charges ...I determine for myself how a particular case should have been handled and forward my

[67] Senior Prosecutor Interview [9AI], 14 June 2006.

[68] Senior Prosecutor Interview [5CK], 22 January 2006.

opinion of the case back to the prosecutor and then to the General Public Prosecutor [himself]. In addition, I write personnel evaluations of my staff.[69]

Currently I am responsible for [supervising] ten prosecutors and two paralegals. I also handle some cases personally. This is an asset because it enables me to appear before all of the judges. If one of my prosecutors has a problem with a particular judge, I am in a better position to handle it. I try to hold a meeting with the department twice per month where everyone can bring up issues. I will also point out recent changes in the law as the prosecutors do not have time to learn about these changes on their own. We will also discuss difficult cases. For example, we recently had a court decision in which the court stated that the prosecutor had misinterpreted the law. That should not happen. . . . It is my job to ensure that the prosecutors follow the law and to make reports to the Ministry of Justice on cases that are important politically. When a victim files a complaint, I will review the file myself and make sure that the prosecutor has explained the case adequately to the victim. If I agree with the prosecutor's decision, I will forward the complaint to the General Prosecutor's Office. Often, in cases where I disagree with the dismissal; the prosecutor will have overlooked something in the file.[70]

When I see my colleagues in the hallway or on the street I will ask them how a particular case is progressing. It is my job in serious cases to follow what is happening. Because I have the most experience in this department, I will talk about the cases with my younger colleagues. I do not give orders. I might share with my colleague how I would handle a similar case. In this office, we respect each prosecutor's independence. We take it for granted that there are decision-making boundaries. . . But since we have the same education and training as judges we try to honor prosecutor's independence. This is true for our chief office prosecutor as well as for our General Public Prosecutor.[71]

8.9.1 Staffing and Workload Pressures

Like their colleagues in "general crimes" departments, juvenile crimes prosecutors face varying degrees of time and workload pressures depending on office staffing levels. There is some evidence which suggests that the introduction of new statistically-driven staffing guidelines have subjected juvenile crimes prosecutors to acute time pressures in some offices. A key reason for this is that Ministry of Justice officials in many states use various case valuation systems to determine office and court staffing requirements. While it is true that all organizations must find efficient and rational methods to allocate personnel, both prosecutors and judges have attacked the PEBB§Y system used by ministry officials. Because the system was developed according the model of practice used in a small number of field sites, prosecutors who work in large offices have complained that the system underestimates the time it takes prosecutors to negotiate the bureaucratic hurdles

[69] Senior Prosecutor Interview [13EU], 6 December 2005.

[70] Senior Prosecutor Interview [6PB], 22 February 2006. This department leader supervises a unit that handles both adult and juvenile crime cases.

[71] Senior Prosecutor Interview [5CK], 22 January 2006.

present in larger offices.[72] A particular office's workload level was determined based on the average amount of time that prosecutors in the test sites devoted to particular types of cases. The system presumed that the work practices used in all prosecution offices were substantially similar. Although the system continues to undergo refinement, a Ministry of Justice official admitted to me that juvenile prosecutors continue to complain that the system does not take into account the work environment of their particular office.[73] In addition, juvenile crimes prosecutors have complained that the system ignores the fact that case proceedings in juvenile cases may be particularly lengthy as the participants search for an appropriate sanction.[74] The PEBB§Y system's valuation guidelines indeed appear to presume that juvenile cases are less time-consuming than adult cases and ignore local and regional differences in case handling procedures.

This assessment of the system is shared by the German Association for Juvenile Courts and Juvenile Offenders (DVJJ). According to the DVJJ, the guidelines ignore the fact that prosecutors and courts must invest additional time in a juvenile case trying to understand the juvenile's character and to ascertain an appropriate sanction (Sonnen and Scholz 2005). In a position paper released in 2005, the organization attacked the system's valuation guidelines and argued that juvenile prosecutors and courts faced severe workload pressures. It is the organization's position that, at minimum, cases involving drugs, repeat offenders, and violence must be accorded a higher valuation or their will be negative consequences for society (Sonnen and Scholz 2005). Moreover, cases in which prosecutors fashion an alternative sentence involving diversion pursuant to Sect. 45 (2) require a higher valuation to give prosecutors adequate time to devote to finding an appropriate solution (Sonnen and Scholz 2005). A consequence of the introduction of the PEBB§Y and other similar systems is that prosecutors and judges are expected to handle almost a 50 % higher case load than prosecutors who handle adult cases (Sonnen and Scholz 2005). Several experienced prosecutors criticized the nature of workload pressures:

> Early in my career I had fewer cases. After the computers came, caseloads rose. Now we have statistics which show how many cases we open and how many we close. I no longer have enough time to read the case files . . . The case load has become too heavy.[75]

> One must be able to make decisions . . .Communication skills are important as well as being able to keep things in perspective so that you do not go crazy when one must work quickly. That is important. You need to pace [yourself]. There is pressure from the defense attorneys. There is always more pressure. It depends on the defense attorneys and the parents. [When the child is being held in investigative detention] the parents will call every day and ask when their child is coming home. . . However, when one has a good relationship with [the parents] one must try to speak with them. The pressure is a bit stressful and I have not experienced this type of pressure in other departments.[76]

[72] Ministry of Justice Interview [9RR], 30 June 2006.

[73] Ministry of Justice Interview [9RR], 30 June 2006.

[74] Ministry of Justice Interview [9RR], 30 June 2006.

[75] Prosecutor Interview [5LY], 19 January 2006.

[76] Prosecutor Interview [9QL], 14 June 2006.

> It can be difficult. We have no possibility here to recognize how hard a prosecutor works. No way to commend what type of impact a prosecutor may have on a juvenile's life . . . The workload has increased greatly. It is often necessary to send files back to the police because more investigation is required because a witness or suspect must be questioned further. [As prosecutors] we question the investigation results. Because of the rising workload pressures, this has become more difficult. I think there have been more acquittals in the past few years as a result of the workload pressures. We can forestall an acquittal in some cases if we have the time to review the investigation and conduct a more thorough investigation.[77]

> One [must handle] a certain number of cases. Many prosecutors have too many cases. I have too many cases to handle. The head of the office cannot really change the situation. The authorities try to plan and calculate case loads but there is not enough [money]. Many of my colleagues are working longer hours. It is difficult when you have a family.[78]

In one prosecution office that I visited (*Cosel*), because of personnel shortages, prosecutors in the a specialized crime departments had to pitch in and handle an overflow of general and juvenile crimes cases. The two juvenile court proceedings which I observed in this city were actually handled by a prosecutor from another specialized unit. Despite this fact, the prosecutor seemed to have no problem changing "hats" quickly reorienting herself to the educative function of a juvenile crimes prosecutor. The nature of this form of case-assignment process however precludes the development of closer cooperative relationships between the prosecution and police agencies which develop in fast-track and repeat offender units.

[*Question*: *How would you evaluate the work of the social workers and police officers who handle juvenile cases*?]

Prosecutor: I like the work of the juvenile court workers, however the politicians do not know what is going on and how the system works.[79]

The DVJJ's criticism of the PEBB§Y system highlights the fact that, the juvenile law cannot achieve its primary goal of promoting the development of juvenile offenders unless prosecutors possess sufficient time to work the case. For the purposes of understanding the factors which influence prosecutorial discretion, the DVJJ's critique brings to the fore two further points. First, however the prosecution of juvenile crimes is organized-either through special programs such as repeat offender units and the fast-tracking of juvenile cases or "traditional" juvenile crimes units, these units cannot fulfill their mandates unless they are adequately staffed. Inadequate staffing reduces the likelihood that prosecutors will have time to share and exchange information with police and social workers to discover case-appropriate sanctions. It also reduces the possibility that prosecutors will possess enough evidence to proceed with the prosecution of a case. Moreover, the pressure to simply close cases in a timely manner may facilitate a

[77] Senior Prosecutor Interview [13EU], 6 December 2005.

[78] Prosecutor Interview [12CJ], 29 November 2005.

[79] Senior Prosecutor Interview [10BJ], 26 June 2006.

rapid case closing mentality in which cases are inadequately investigated and merely closed. Under this scenario, juvenile offenders could commit an endless stream of offenses before receiving a sanction from the court. In the case of offenses involving alcohol or drug use, one could imagine that, a delayed intervention would increase the risk of multiple negative consequences. Second, the fact that the DVJJ acknowledges that regional differences in case handling practices exist and advocates that those differences should be preserved indirectly undercuts the premise that the law operates in a formulaic manner (Sonnen and Scholz 2005).

8.10 Conclusion

Despite the fact that German cities have seen an increase in the number of violent crimes committed by youthful offenders, the modern thrust of German juvenile law remains tilted in favor of rehabilitation. The law's dualistic nature, however, which also sanctions the imposition of punitive measures as a last resort, has created a large space for prosecutorial discretion. This widespread potential for discretion has helped to spawn a variety of community-level initiatives including efforts to fast-track juvenile cases, repeat offender departments, and coordinated diversion programs. While many of these programs have been created with the input of experts in the field of juvenile crime and development, political concerns, stoked by portrayals of violence in local media outlets, have also influenced program design. The imprint of political considerations and popular fears of violent crime is particularly strong in cities that possess large immigrant populations. While there is a danger that the pressure created by populist forces may constrain prosecutorial discretion to the point that decision-making no longer takes the characteristics of the individual offender into sufficient consideration, it is also apparent that in some cases, the combination of wide prosecutorial freedom and inadequate resources spawned a pattern of decision-making that inadequately sanctioned repeat juvenile offenders.

The traditional mode of juvenile crimes practice, which is dominated by case dismissals rather than punitive sanctions, often provides juvenile delinquents with multiple opportunities to reoffend. In some cases, this pattern of practice has proved to be impotent in combating more severe forms of delinquency. However, stiffer sanctioning programs run the risk of failing to attack the roots causes of juvenile delinquency and achieving only symbolic, politically-responsive gains. In the exercise of their discretionary authority, juvenile crimes prosecutors stand at the focal point of these sentencing dilemmas. Absent an adequate flow of information about a juvenile offender's history, sufficient cooperation between community agencies, time, and sufficient resources, prosecutorial discretion may reflect narrow policy preferences which fail to advance the goals of the juvenile justice system. An additional significant concern is whether courts and prosecutors are judiciously exercising their power to determine whether youthful offenders are tried in juvenile or adult courts. The combined impact of regional preferences, judicial desires to preserve discretion in the sentencing extremely violent offenders, and prosecutors' preferences for utilizing Section 153 StPO has led to incongruous, and perhaps unconstitutional, differences in practice.

Court Cases

U.S. CASE LAW

In re Gault, 387 US 1 (1967)
Stanford v. Kentucky, 492 US 361 (1989)
Roper v. Simmons, 543 US 551 (2005)

Legislation

Code of Criminal Procedure (StPO)

Sections:

24
170(2)

Code of Criminal Law (StGB)

Sections:

19,
174, 177, 180, 182

Other Laws

Federal Court of Justice [Criminal Panel] BGHSt 12:116; 36:3.
German Act on Juvenile Courts (JGG)
First Amendment At to the Juvenile Acts [*Erstes Gesetz zur Änderung des Jugendgresichtsgesetzes-1 JGGÄndG*], 30 August 1990 BGBI, 1p. 1853.
Sections:

5 Nr. 2, 9, 11 Nr. 3, 14, 15, 15 Nr. 3 (2), 16, 17, 17 Nr. 2, 18
31, 37, 38(2), 38 Nr. 2, 45, 45 Nr. 1, 45 Nr. 2, 45 Nr. 3, 45 Nr. 7, 46, 47, 48, 51, 76, 105, 105(1), 2, 105 Nr. 1, 109.

Interviews

Berlin Defense Attorney [9DEP], 13 June 2007.
Justice Ministry Official [9RR], 30 June 2006.
Ministry of Justice Interview [9RR], 30 June 2006.
Prosecutor Interview [5LY], 19 January 2006.
Prosecutor Interview [6SB], 23 January 2006.
Prosecutor Interview [12CJ], 29 November 2005.
Prosecutor Interview [5DK], 19 January 2006.
Prosecutor Interview [9QL], 14 June 2006.
Prosecutor Interview [7SE], 5 April 2006.
Senior Prosecutor Interview [9LJ], 12 June 2006.
Senior Prosecutor Interview [5CK], 22 January 2006 and 26 January 2006.
Senior Prosecutor Interview [13EU], 6 December 2005.
Senior Prosecutor Interview [9AI], 14 June 2006.
Senior Prosecutor Interview [6PB], 22 February 2006.
Senior Prosecutor Interview [10BJ], 26 June 2006.

References

Books, Articles and Online Publications

Abramsolhn, J. (2006). Torture Death in Juvenile Jail Sparks Round of Soul Searching. *Deutsche Welle*, [online] 24 November. Available at http://www.dw-world.de/dw/article/0,2144,2246874,00.html. Accessed 29 July 2013.

Albrecht, H. (1997). Ethnic minorities, crime and criminal justice in Germany. In M. Tonry (Ed.), *Crime and justice, ethnicity, crime and immigration: Comparative and cross-national perspectives* (Crime and justice: A review of research, Vol. 21, pp. 31–99). Chicago: University of Chicago Press.

Anker, V. J. (2007a). Intensivtäter zeigt Rechtsstaat die Grenze. *Berliner Morgenpost.De*, [online] 1 March. Available at http://www.morgenpost.de/printarchiv/berlin/article188519/Intensivtaeter-zeigt-Rechtsstaat-die-Grenze.html. Accessed 29 July 2013.

Anker, V. J. (2007b). In der Hauptstadt jer Jugendgewalkt. *Welt Online*, [online] 22 February. Available at http://www.Welt.de/politik/article730948/In_der_Hauptstadt_der_Jungendgealt.html. Accessed 29 July 2013.

Asmus, H. (1988). Der Staatsanwalt-ein bürokratischer Faktor in der Verbrechenskontrolle? *Zeitschrift Für Soziologie, 17*, 117–131.

Bareinske, C. (2004). *Sanktion und Legalbewährung im Jugendstrafverfahren in Baden-Württemberg. Kriminologische Forschungberichte.* Freiburg: Max Planck Institute for Foreign and International Criminal Law.

Bundeskriminalamt Kriminalistiches Insstitute (2006). In: J. Bässman (Ed.), *Crime prevention in Germany: selected examples of projects in the "Infopool Prevention" database*. Bundeskriminalamt. http://www.bka.de/vorbeugung/pub/crim_prev_eng_2006.pdf

Chapin, L. (1997a). Out of control – The uses and abuses of parental liability laws to control juvenile delinquency in the United States. *Santa Clara Law Review, 37*(3), 621–672.

Chapin, W. (1997b). Ausländer Raus? The empirical relationship between immigration and crime in Germany. *Social Science Quarterly, 78*(2), 543–558.

Cheesman, F. (2011). A decade of NCSC research on blended sentencing of juvenile offenders: What have we learned about 'Who Gets a Second Chance?' pp. 112–117. Available at http://www.ncsc.org/sitecore/content/microsites/future-trends-2011/home/Special-Programs/~/media/Microsites/Files/Future%20Trends/Author%20PDFs/Cheesman.ashx. Accessed 5 Aug 2013.

Crime Rate drops to Record Low. (2011) *Deutsche Welle* [online] 20 May. Available at http://www.dw.de/crime-rate-drops-to-record-low/a-15093336. Accessed 5 Aug 2013.

Crofts, T. (2004). The rise of the principle of education in the juvenile justice system. *The International Journal of Children's Rights, 12*, 401–417.

Dünkel, F. (2003). Youth violence and juvenile justice in Germany. In F. Dünkel, & K. Drenkhahn (Eds.), *Youth violence: New patterns and local responses—Experiences in east and west* (pp. 96–142). Mönchengladbach: ForumVerlag Godesberg.

Dünkel, F. (2005). Migration and ethnic minorities in Germany: Impacts on youth crime, juvenile, justice and youth imprisonment [online]. Available at http://www.rsf.uni-greifswald.de/fileadmin/mediapool/lehrstuehle/duenkel/Germany_youngMig.pdf. Accessed 29 July 2013.

Dünkel, F. (2006a). Juvenile justice in Germany: Historical aspects of juvenile justice in Germany: The compromise between welfare and justice. In E. Jensen & J. Jepsen (Eds.), *Juvenile law violators, human rights, and the development of new juvenile justice systems* (pp. 115–154). Oxford: Hart Publishing.

Dünkel, F. (2006b). Juvenile justice in Germany: Between welfare and justice. In J. Junger-Tas & S. H. Decker (Eds.), *International handbook of juvenile justice* (pp. 225–262). New York: Springer.

Ewald, U., & Feltes, T. (2003). Multicultural context, crime and policing and Germany: Challenges after unification. *Police & Society, 7*, 165–196.

Feuerhiem, W. (2003). Das Haus des jugendrechts in Stuttgart Bad Cannstatt: Konzeption und empirische Befunde (INFO 2003), pp. 56–87 (*Institut für Sozialpädagogische Forschung Mainz* 2004). Available at http://www.uni-heidelberg.de/institute/fak2/krimi/DVJJ/Aufsaetze/Feuerhelm2003.pdf. Accessed 5 Aug 2013.

Gabriele, G. (2004) Fast-tracking and co-operation between police, justice and social services – Crime as a cause for looking if support is required. In Centre for the Prevention of Youth Crime (Ed.), *Prevention of youth crime in Germany: Educational strategies*. Trends, Experiences and Approaches. Deutsches Jugendinstitut: Munchen

Geißler, R., & Marissen, N. (1990). Kriminalität imd Kriminalisierung Junger Ausländer: Die TickendeSsoziale Zeitbombe-Ein Artefackt der Kriminalstatistik. *Köhler Zeitschrift für Soziologie und Sozialpsychologie, 42*(4), 663–687.

Gemeinsame Allgemeine Verfügung über die vermehrte Anwendung des §45 JGG im Verfahren gegen Jugendliche und Heranwaschsende (Diversionsrichtslinie), 2004. SENATSVERWALTUNGEN FÜR JUSTIZ, FÜR INNERES UND FÜR BILDUNG, JUGEND UND SPORT (Oct. 5, 2004).

German Consulates of the United States, 2007. *General Information on German Citizenship* Available online http://www.germany.info/relaunch/info/consular_services/citizenship/generalinformation.html#q2. Accessed 23 July 2007.

Heinz, W. (2006). Penal sanctions and sanctioning practice in the Federal Republic of Germany, the Konstanz repository on crime and sanctioning, 1882–2004. Konstanz: Konstanzer Inventar Sanktionsforschung (KIS).

Holthusen, B. (2004). Ultima ratio? Deprivation of liberty measures for children and young people. Findings and need for research. In: Centre for the Prevention of Youth Crime (Ed.),

Prevention of youth crime in Germany: Educational strategies: Trends, experiences and approaches (pp. 133–156). München: Deutsches Jugendinstitut. Available at www.hm.ee/index.php?popup=download&id=11006. Accessed 29 July 2013.

Holthusen, B. & Schäfer, H. (2004). Strategies and organization of youth crime prevention in Germany. The importance of the educational approach. In: Centre for the Prevention of Youth Crime (Ed.), *Prevention of youth crime in Germany: Educational strategies: Trends, experiences and approaches* (pp. 11–23). München: Deutsches Jugendinstitut. Available at www.hm.ee/index.php?popup=download&id=11006. Accessed 29 July 2013.

Judging Subway Violence: U-Bahn Attacker Sentenced in Berlin, 2011. *Spiegel Online* [online] 19 September. Available at http://www.spiegel.de/international/germany/judging-subway-violence-u-bahn-attacker-sentenced-in-berlin-a-787135.html. Accessed 4 Aug 2013.

James, O. (1995). *Juvenile violence in a winner-loser-culture: Socio-economic and familial origins of the rise of violence against the person*. London: Free Association Books.

Jehle, J.-M. (2005). *Criminal justice in Germany: Facts and figures*. (Fifth ed.) Godesberg: Federal Ministry of Justice (ed.) Mönchengladbach:Forum-Verlag. Available online at www.bmj.bund.de/files/-/1556/criminal%20justice%20for%20all.pdf. Accessed 5 August 2013.

Junge gewalttätige Migranten machen uns am meisten Sorgen. (2007). *Spiegel Online* (b) [online], 5 February. Available at http://www.spiegel.de/politik/deutschland/0,1518,druck-463236,00.html. Accessed 4 Aug 2013.

Junger-Tas, J. (2006). Trends in international juvenile justice: What conclusions can be drawn? In J. Junger-Tas & S. H. Decker (Eds.), *International handbook of juvenile justice* (pp. 503–532). New York: Springer.

Kilchling, M. (2002). Victim-offender mediation with juvenile offenders in Germany. *European Commission Grotius II Criminal Programme* (September). Available at http://www.irsig.cnr.it/reports/testi_reports/dpf_reports/report_germanyfinal_01sept02=3.pdf.

Kilchling, M. (2005). Victim-offender mediation with juvenile offenders in Germany. In A. Mestitz & S. Ghetti (Eds.), *Victim-offender mediation with youth offenders in Europe: An overview and comparison of 15 countries* (pp. 229–256). Amsterdam: Springer.

Klein, M. (2001). Thoughts in juvenile justice system and research. *European Journal on Criminal Policy & Research, 9*, 273–281.

Kouparanis, P. (2006). Identifying the roots of immigrant crime: Inner city life leaves kids alienated and angry. *Deutsche Welle* [online] 8 April. Available at http://www.dw-world.de/dw/article/0,2144,1953916,00.html. Accessed 29 July 2013.

Lorenz, A. (2008). *Juvenile delinquency in Germany*. Wiesbaden: Statistisches Bundesamt. Available at https://www.destatis.de/EN/Publications/STATmagazin/Justice/2008_1/PDF2008_1.pdf?__blob=publicationFile. Accessed 5 Aug 2013.

Mansel, J., & Raithel, J. (2003). Verzerrungsfaktorem im Hell-und Dunkelfeld und die Gewaltentwicklung. In J. Raithel & H. Mansel (Eds.), *Kriminalität und Gewalt im Jugendalter Hell-und Dunkelfeldbefunde im Vergleich* (pp. 7–24). Weinheim: Juventa.

McCord, J., Widom, C., & Crowell, N. (2001). *Juvenile crime, juvenile justice. Panel on juvenile crime: Prevention, treatment, and control*. Washington, DC: The National Academies Press.

Mehr Gewalt, Weniger Haftbefehle, 2007. *Spiegel Online* (c) [online] 22 February. Available at http://www.spiegel.de/politik/deutschland/jugendkriminalitaet-in-berlin-mehr-gewalt-weniger-haftbefehle-a-467955.html. Accessed 4 Aug 2013.

Möhring, J. (2002). Creating opportunities for young people in Berlin: Support for self-employment. In: Joint OECD-Investitions bank Berlin Seminar, *OECD Urban Renaissance Studies: Berlin – Towards an Integrated Strategy for Social Cohesion and Economic Development*. Berlin. 12 December 2002. Available at http://www.oecd.org/regional/leed/2485266.pdf. Accessed 31 July 2013.

Oldenburger, P. (2007). Kriminell-und doch auf freiem Fuss: Polizei und Politiker Krüitisieren "richterliche Milde" bei Intensivtätern. *Berlinder Morgenpost.De* [online] 21 February. Available at http://www.morgenpost.de/printarchiv/berlin/article187074/Kriminell_und_doch_auf_freiem_Fuss.html. Accessed 30 July 2013.

Pfeiffer, C. (1998). Juvenile crime and violence in Europe. *Crime and Justice, 23*, 255–328.

Pfeiffer, C., Brettfeld, K., & Delzer, I. (1996). *Kriminalität in Niedersachsen – eine Analyse auf der Basis der Polizeilichen Kriminalstatistik 1988–1995*. Hannover: Kriminologisches Forschungsinstitut Niedersachsen e. V. – *Forschungsberichte*, Nr. 56. Available at http://www.kfn.de/versions/kfn/assets/fb56.pdf. Accessed 30 July 2013.

Pfeiffer, C. & Wetzels, P. (1999). *The structure and development of juvenile violence in Germany*. Hannover: Kriminologisches Forschungsinstitut Niedersachsen e. V. – *Forschungsberichte*, Nr. 76. Available at http://www.kfn.de/versions/kfn/assets/fb76.pdf. Accessed 30 July 2013.

Police Crime Statistics 2003: Federal Republic of Germany. (Abridged Version). BUNDESKRIMINALAMT. Available at www.bka.de/pks/pks203ev/pcs_2003.pdf.

Polizeistatistik: *Kriminalität sinkt, Gewalt nimmt zu*, 2007. *Spiegel Online* (a) [online] 8 May. Available at http://www.spiegel.de/panorama/justiz/polizeistatistik-kriminalitaet-sinkt-gewalt-nimmt-zu-a-481693.html. Accessed 5 Aug 2013.

Press Release- Innenministerium Nordrhein-Westfalen, 2005. Innenminister Behrens Lobt Vorbildliche Ordungspartnerschaft: Straftaten von 'Jugendlichen Intensivtätern' Gehen um Fast 50% Zurück. 3 March. Available at http://www.im.nrw.de/pe/pm2001/pm2001/news_1361.htm.

Reusch, R. (2007). Intensivtäter in Berlin: Rechstaatsächlice und Kriminologische Aspekte. *Zeitshrift Für Judgendkriminalrecht und Jugendhilfe* 2, 295–291. Available at http://www.glueckliche-familie-ev.de/wp-content/uploads/2011/05/Artikel-Intensivt%C3%A4ter-Reusch-2007-Internet.pdf. Accessed 5 Aug 2013.

Sickmund, M., Snyder, H., & Poe-Yamagata, E. (1997). *Juvenile offenders and victims: 1997 update on violence*. Washington, DC: Office of Juvenile Justice and Delinquency Prevention.

Silver, E., & Chow-Martin, L. (2002). A multiple models approach to assessing recidivism risk: Implications for judicial decision making. *Criminal Justice and Behavior, 29*(5), 538–568.

Sinico, S. (2007). In Germany, focus on preventing not punishing youth crime. *Deutsche Welle* [online] November. Available at http://www.dw.de/in-germany-focus-on-preventing-not-punishing-youth-crime/a-2810444. Accessed 4 Aug 2013.

Sommer-Guist, C. (2005). Giving young convicts a break. *Goethe Institute*, November 2005. Available at http://www.goethe.de/ges/soz/thm/hjs/en955599.htm.

Sonnen, B. (2004). *Stellungnahme zum "entwurf eines Gesetzes zur Stärkung des Jugendstrafrechts und zur Verbessurung und Beschleunigung des Jegendstrafverfahren."* DVJJ-Deutsche Vereinigung For Jugendgerichte und Jugendgerichtshilfen e. V., 19 April 2004. Available at http://www.dvjj.de/veroeffentlichungen/stellungnahmen/stellungnahme-zum-entwurf-eines-gesetzes-zur-staerkung-des. Accessed 30 July 2013.

Sonnen, B., & Scholz, C. (2005). *Stellungnahme PEBBY§Y: Bewertung von Jugendsachen bei Staatsanwaltschaft und Gericht*. DVJJ-Deutsche Vereinigung Für Judgendgerichte und Jugendgerichtschilfen e. V., 30 Aug. 2005. Available at http://www.dvjj.de/nachrichten-aktuell/stellungnahme-pebb§y-bewertung-von-jugendsachen-bei-staatsanwaltschaft-und. Accessed 30 July 2013.

STATISTISCHES BUNDESAMT: DEUTSCHLAND. *Rechtspflege: Staatsanwaltschaften 2004*. Fachserie 10, Reihe 2.6. Available at https://wwwec.destatis.de/csp/shop/sfg/bpm.html.cms.cBroker.cls?cmspath=struktur,vollanzeige.csp&ID=1018469. Accessed 22 May 2006.

Steffan, W. (2003). Junge Intensivtäter – Kriminologische Befunde. Landesgruppte Baden-Würtemberg-Jugendkriminalität und Reform des Jugendstrafrechts, ed. Deutsche Vereinigung für Jugendgericht und Jugendgerichtshilfen e.V. Heidelberg: DEUTSCHEVEREINIGUNG FOR JUGENDGERICHT UND GUGENDGERICHTSHILFEN e.V

Todt, J. (2005). Interview zur Jugendkriminalität: Kein Grund zur hysterie. *Spiegel Online* [online] 6 September. Available at http://www.spiegel.de/panorama/justiz/interview-zur-jugendkriminalitaet-kein-grund-zur-hysterie-a-373166.html. Accessed 5 August 2013.

Tonry, M. (1997). Ethnicity, crime and immigration: Comparative and cross-national perspectives. *Crime and Justice, 21*, 1–29.

Walker, T. (2005). The lot of young German offenders: How far can youths go before they wind up behind bars? *Deutsche Welle* [online] 12 September. Available at http://www.dw.de/the-lot-of-young-german-offenders/a-1705805. Accessed 30 July 2013.

Warner, M. B. (2011). Vicious attack in Berlin: Subway beating becomes campaign issue, *Spiegel Online* [online]. 9 September. Available at http://www.spiegel.de/international/germany/vicious-attack-in-berlin-subway-beating-becomes-campaign-issue-a-784959.html. Accessed 4 Aug 2013.

Weber, M. M., & Ruth, U. (1997). Forensic psychiatric evaluations of young persons in accordance with § 105 JGG – between punishment and therapeutic help. *Fortschritte der Neurologie, Psychiatrie, 65*(6), 247–255.

Werwigk-Hertneck, C. (2004). Bekämpfung der Jugendkriminalität aus strafrechtlicher Sicht. In: H. J. Kerner, & E. Mark (Eds.). *Internetdokumentation deustcher Präventionstag*. Hannover: Internetdokumentation Deutscher Präventionstag.

Chapter 9
Conclusion: Achieving the Promise of German Criminal Law

> Truth is more than just a first principle in law and procedure, in science, in politics, in social life. Truth is an essential, and for many the essential, moral value of humanity (Jung 2004, p. 147)

In adversarial systems of justice like the United States, prosecutors possess a tremendous range of discretion. They may leverage that power to bring criminals to justice, as well as to ruin the lives of the innocent. In contrast, since the enactment of the first codes of criminal law and procedure in the late nineteenth century, the German criminal justice system has attempted to constrain, if not banish, prosecutorial discretion. In this book, I have demonstrated that, while the German attempt to banish discretion has failed, German prosecutors today struggle to balance their duty to find the truth with rising caseloads. In the final analysis, the organizational culture of the prosecution, rather than the law decisively shapes how prosecutors exercise discretion. Whether driven by the public's appetite for vengeance, a prosecutor's career aspirations, or a misguided sense of justice, some prosecutors continue to abuse that power to manipulate the truth by harassing the innocent and overcharging the guilty. At present, no serious efforts to hamstring that power or to stiffen sanctions for prosecutorial misconduct exist. While the vast majority of prosecutors act within the bounds of the law, the nation's harsh sentencing practices accentuate the harm caused by prosecutors who put their conviction record ahead of securing equitable outcomes.

In contrast, since the enactment of the first codes of criminal law and procedure in the late nineteenth century, the German criminal justice system has attempted to constrain, if not banish, prosecutorial discretion. Rather than foster a "conviction mentality," the German Code of Criminal Procedure charges prosecutors with the mandate to investigate the facts "for" and "against" the defendant. The principle of mandatory prosecution likewise seeks to ensure that prosecutors do not turn their eyes away from any criminal behavior. While these statutory provisions are

---

Some of the material in this chapter originally appeared in an article printed in the Journal of Crime, Law and Social Change. It reappears here with permission.

S.M. Boyne, *The German Prosecution Service*, DOI 10.1007/978-3-642-40928-8_9,

admirable, their efficacy is limited. Prosecutors may comply with ritualized norms that attempt to mandate objectivity and conduct a minimum investigation of criminal complaint. Indeed, the law has turned out not to be quite the science that German legal theorists predicted it would be. Despite the fact that many learned scholars attempted to write objectivity into the Code of Criminal Procedure, the law cannot adequately guide every step of prosecutorial decision-making. The law's indeterminancy inevitably opens the door to discretion.

In the last 30 years, German prosecutors and judges, burdened by the strain of increasing case loads, have found numerous ways to short-circuit the truth-finding process envisioned by Code of Criminal Procedure. Gradually, step by step, the German legislature, with its eye on balancing the federal budget, has amended the code to bring these changes in practice in to the statute books from the shadows of the law. As each revision widened prosecutors' decision making options, the criminal justice system appeared to drift ever more further away from its normative foundations. For many commentators, the judicial approval of confession bargaining practices in 2009 signaled the death knell for the criminal justice system's truth-finding aspirations. However, there has been judicial pushback against the use of confession bargaining practices. In March 2013, Germany's Constitutional Court (FCC) struck down three plea deals because the deals did not conform to the law's strict legal framework and short-circuited the truth finding process. In one of the specific cases, the FCC held that a Court could not use an unverified confession as the basis to support a judgment of guilt.[1] In the press release (17/2013) announcing the decisions, the Court called on the prosecution service to play an integral role of monitoring the legality of confession agreements:

> Of particular importance is the monitoring by the prosecution. The prosecution is not only obliged to refuse to agree to an illegal plea bargain, but also has to lodge appeals against judgments that are based on such an agreement. The fact that the prosecution is a hierarchical system and has reporting obligations makes it possible that this monitoring capacity can be exercised according to consistent standards.

The Court's decision lends support to the prime thesis of this book, namely that the law, standing alone, is not adequate to constrain prosecutorial decision-making. While everyone may not agree upon what "objectivity" means in a particular case, the most effective way to ensure that prosecutors view a case through a neutral lens is to design organizational incentives and reporting requirements that support that vision. Provisions in the Code of Criminal Procedure may establish the system's normative aims, but they cannot ensure that prosecutors function as the guardians of the law and of neutrality.

During in my 3 years of travels through German prosecution offices, I found cause, not for dismay, but for cautious optimism. While it is true that many prosecutors are struggling with caseloads that are simply too heavy, prosecutors' commitment to objectivity ultimately rests not on the law, but in the degree to which it may be embedded in the organizational culture. While the top bureaucrats

[1] 2 BvR 2155/11.

attempt to curb discretion through the use of guidelines, the most meaningful guidelines are communicated during informal coffee "meetings" where prosecutors collectively gather and share "stories" and advice on case decisions. This collaborative decision-making is not the technocratic decision-making envisioned by nineteenth century legal scholars. But it is a truth-determining exercise. When prosecutors discuss their decision options in a collegial setting, they strive to define a common approach shared among peers. By sharing oral stories and formulating common approaches, prosecutors engage in the social construction of knowledge. While we may debate whether a particular prosecutor views the evidence in a case with a sufficiently "objective" lens, when that prosecutor seeks to align their decision-making with group norms, those norms constrain the free exercise of discretion. The strongest piece of evidence that prosecutors strive to be objective, is that they continue to use the term in their everyday conversations about justice-be it in their offices, in meetings with law enforcement, or in the courtroom hallways.

While German law classifies the prosecution service as a judicial authority, the service's function is not wholly part of the executive or judicial branches. The prosecution service's uncertain institutional position helps to create the daily decision-making gap that exists between prosecutors, practice routines and the system's normative goals. Although the law charges prosecutors with the mandate to function objectively, their ability to achieve that mandate is constrained. Prosecutors do not act independently; rather they are ensconced within a hierarchical organization and constrained by political, fiscal, and bureaucratically driven pressures.

In seeking to fulfill their mandate to function as objective decision-makers, German prosecutors face a number of barriers. Chief among those is the size of the stack of files sitting in their in-box, the court's docket, and whether their "efficiency" statistics lag behind those of their colleagues in their department. In more serious cases that have attracted media interest, a prosecutor's investigation decisions may be influenced by the monitoring practices of their superiors. Although the law mandates that prosecutors find the "truth" by serving as neutral fact finders, a variety of factors influence how that truth is defined. Those factors include not only local conceptions of justice, but also the nature of the relationships between the prosecutor's office and law enforcement as well as the judiciary. Where department managers and chief office prosecutors have little tolerance for bureaucratic red tape, prosecutors may be given free rein to focus on conducting investigations. In many parts of Germany, joint investigation teams devoted to prosecuting specialized crimes, are leading the way in breaking down the archaic art of issuing written instructions.

At the same time, unless the Land-level legislatures decide to appropriate more funding to the criminal justice system, it is inevitable that prosecutors will feel pressured to compromise the search for truth. A prosecutor's ability to function in an objective manner is driven, not only by organizational norms, practices, and inter-institutional relationships, but also by resource levels. The continued underfunding of prosecutor's offices in general and the judicial system as a whole, combined with the use of the PEBB§Y system, threatens to further erode prosecutors' ability to investigate criminal activity. This is especially true in the case of complicated economic crime and corruption cases. At present, prosecutors lack the resources to adequately prosecute these cases. In an ideal world, the German legislature would reclassify, or at least define with more specificity, many of white collar crimes that currently fall into the "minor crimes" category to minimize the use of diversionary proceedings. Absent an infusion of funding however, prosecutors will continue to settle many of those cases because they lack sufficient resources to adequately track complex financial transactions. The low political standing of the Ministries of Justice at the Land level and the concomitant adoption of efficiency-driven metrics at the top level of the judicial administration poses a substantial threat to the system's normative goals. While "finding the truth" is a difficult enterprise under any circumstances, it is impossible to find the truth when the guiding decision-making metric is to close an investigation as soon as it starts. The severity of resource constraints facing the German criminal justice system threatens to produce uniform injustice.

In any large bureaucracy with life time tenure, there are undoubtedly individual prosecutors who fall below the standards set by the law and by informal norms. Ironically, while their decision-making practices may be "efficient," they may have long ago lost their commitment to the full search for the "truth." As Chap. 7 demonstrated, prosecutors may "enact" their duty to function objectively in an aggressive or passive manner. Prosecutorial passivity in the courtroom does not always serve the cause of justice. As the law is currently written, the Land level Ministries have insufficient power to terminate these employees. That is one price of life-time tenure. It may be a price worth paying however, as prosecutors must be able to make decisions without fear of losing their jobs. To this end, Germany should take action to depoliticize the career decisions in those *Länder* where attorneys rotate every 3 years between prosecution offices, judicial positions, and the Ministry of Justice. The *Länder* should cede control of individuals' career rotation schedules to an independent judicial organization. Until that occurs, Ministry officials will continue to call or "informally chat" with prosecutors and jangle offers of plum assignments in front of them in an attempt to sway decision-making. By continuing to grant officials in the Ministry of Justice leverage over an individual's career path, these Länder compromise the integrity of the criminal justice system.

Though recent literature has pointed to the increasing use confession agreements as evidence that the German criminal justice system has strayed from its normative foundations, the variance between the law on the books and the law in practice in German criminal law is not a new development. In fact, four decades ago, Marcus and Goldstein argued that prosecutorial discretion in Germany was not effectively constrained by judicial control and strict statutory language. As I have shown here, prosecutorial decision-making is constrained. However, the decisive constraint is no longer the law, but rather organizational factors. While the law sets the broad parameters and normative goals of prosecutorial decision-making, the principal factors that influence daily decision-making preferences are organization-based. Moreover, training programs and collegial standards continue to inculcate prosecutors with the importance of objectivity. As a side point, while one cannot completely discount the impact that historical attitudes towards crime and punishment has on criminal justice outcomes, the imprint cast by organization-based factors is a consequential one.

It is tempting to point to the existence of regional and local variations in practice as evidence that prosecutorial discretion is not strictly controlled. The research presented here however demonstrates that the variance does not show that discretion is uncontrolled, but rather that it reflects differences in organizational controls and practices. While prosecutors possess a duty to follow the law's normative goals, their ability to achieve those goals is strongly affected by whether the organization supports or undermines the system's commitment to objectivity and to a full-fledged search for the truth.

To those legal scholars who would prefer not to eschew the German system's normative demise, my research offers a basis for hope. Throughout Germany at the department, office, and even Ministry level in some cases, individuals in management positions have begun to implement new practices that aim to turn the tide against entrenchment of efficient case processing practices as the system's lodestar. In some cases, the commitment of an individual prosecutor to justice has made a difference, albeit within a narrow sphere of influence. In prosecution offices throughout the country, there are individual departments and in some cases, entire offices, that can serve as models for teamwork and best practices.

Although the restraints posed by factors such as fiscal restrictions may be immutable, changes in incentives, work routines, and organizational culture are within reach. A first step in the direction of organizational change is to identify the institutional level where change is possible. The key to the reforming the criminal justice system lies, not in devoting more time and resources towards perfecting our understanding of the law as a science, but in devoting significant attention to the organization of prosecution system. In particular, reformers must understand the impact that the organization of work has on the achievement of the system's normative goals. The key to reform lies first in identifying the organizational level at which reforms could be made and second in identifying the constraints blocking reform.

It is evident that change requires prosecutors and upper levels of management to adopt a proactive, rather than a reactive, strategy towards improving case investigation practices. Even at the level of a single, individual prosecutor, change is possible. A proactive approach may be as simple as a single prosecutor electing to interview a witness in their office rather than writing an instruction and waiting for the file to return to their office with the transcribed interview. A prosecutor handling the main proceeding may decide that objectivity requires more than their passive presence in the courtroom.

At the department level, the department manager may streamline case handling practices and encourage prosecutors to work in investigation teams with law enforcement in more complex cases. In some offices, managers who have introduced open door policies and worked with prosecutors on an equal playing field have set the stage for improved decision-making. To the extent that a department manager has input on the department staffing, managers should choose prosecutors who possess strong social skills and are not afraid to pick up the phone to cajole law enforcement and other agencies to conduct a thorough investigation.

The most important potential agents of change in the career prosecution service are the individuals who sit in the position of leading office prosecutor. Because the chief office prosecutor determines the extent of hierarchical decision-making controls within an office and sets the tone for the office climate, provided that they can secure department managers' cooperation, they possess the power to introduce innovative case processing practices. In an era of tight resource constraints, the fate of the prosecution service's ability to achieve its key normative goal of objective fact-finding rests with the adoption of innovative case disposition practices. Efforts to shunt off the "processing" of the majority of simple, low-level cases to specific days of the month, a certain percentage of a prosecutor's case load, or into expedited procedural practices offer a glimmer of hope that prosecutors will have the time and dedication to investigate major cases in a fair and thorough manner. The top manager may encourage department managers to innovate rather than to be content with the use of antiquated case processing practices.

In terms of their leadership style, top managers may either cultivate an environment of independence and trust or one of oppressive control. In the vast majority of cases, prosecutors enjoy remarkable decision-making freedom. However, individuals in the prosecution hierarchy and even the top office prosecutor may attempt to influence decision-making in a particular case. Prosecutors' self-identity oftentimes chafes against such interference. Where the chief office prosecutor can shield prosecutors from pernicious interference or scapegoating by officials in the General Public Prosecutor's or the Ministry of Justice, those actions may positively influence office morale. As one prosecutor stated to me, "office morale is high because our chief protects our backs."

At the level of the General Public Prosecutor's Office, one of the important ways in which the General Public Prosecutor may effect change is to set strategic objectives that facilitate the achievement of the system's normative goals. For example, the General Public Prosecutor has the power to identify a particular type of case as a prosecution priority and to establish specialized regional prosecution units staffed with experienced prosecutors. A prime example of this impact can be seen in the statistics presented in Chap. 6. The failure to create specialized units or to adequately staff such units once they have been created leads to the predictable result that prosecutors cannot adequately investigate cases. As a result, sanctions are pled down, charges are not filed, and, in some cases, investigations are not even initiated although the requisite suspicion levels exist. Because prosecutors possess insufficient resources to investigate cases involving corruption and white-collar crime, it leads to investigation delays and milder punishments. The problem is so severe that Germany's Federal Court of Justice in a 2005 opinion criticized the state for devoting insufficient resources to the prosecution of economic crimes cases. In the case at issue, the Court held that the defendant's punishment had to be lowered because the case investigation had taken too much time. The Court went on to state that, it felt compelled to remark that, too often in complex economic crimes and corruption cases, courts cannot satisfactorily punish the defendant because the state lacked sufficient resources to conduct an adequate investigation.

Situated above the General Public Prosecutors is the Land Ministry of Justice. At the level of the Land Ministries of Justice, the Ministry determines budget and staffing levels and sets policy priorities at the Land level. The Minister is a political appointment made by the Land President who is elected. Thus, the overall direction of the justice policies at the Land level reflects the majority party's political direction. According to the law, ministers may not issue instructions in individual cases. They can however, set the overall priorities for the judicial system as a whole. In some cases, ministers will attempt to implement Land-wide reforms or to introduce special programs such as victim-offender mediation programs. For example, one Minister encouraged prosecutors to use an expedited case handling procedure that is permitted under the law in cases where a suspect confesses to the crime during the case investigation process. Under this procedure, the prosecutor may file a motion to expedite the case with the defendant's consent. Once the motion is filed, the court will hold a hearing within 2 weeks and adjudicate the case.

A key problem that Ministers face lies in trying to defend the size of their budgets. In recent times, the budgets of the Ministries of Justice within German states have been treated as distant step cousins. Ironically, because law enforcement budgets are part of the more politically prominent Interior Ministries, law enforcement budgets in many states have grown. As a result, the problem of workload pressures and resources has not been distributed equally across all prosecution offices. As I detailed in a Chap. 5, in some cases, financial constraints have privileged the pursuit of efficiency above the fulfillment of prosecutors' commitment to function objectively. While efficiency is a laudable goal for many front-line bureaucratic agencies, in the field of justice, efficiency is not always compatible with finding the truth. Ultimately, the fate of the German criminal justice system rests in the hands of the legislators who must find adequate ways to support the prosecution of serious crime, and the hands of the Ministries of Justice, who must stop privileging efficiency over truth-finding in the handling of major crime cases.

Court Cases

Judgment of 19 March 2013, 2 BvR 2628/10
Judgment of 19 March 2013, 2 BvR 2883/10
Judgment of 19 March 2013, 2 BvR 2155/11

References

Books, Articles and Online Publications

Jung, H. (2004). Nothing but the truth? Some facts, impressions and confessions about truth in criminal procedure. In A. Duff et al. (Eds.), *Trial on trial* (pp. 147–156). Portland: Hart Publishing.

Press Release, Federal Constitutional Court. 19 March 2013. No. 17/2013. Legal Regulation of Plea Bargaining is Constitutional-Informal Agreements are Impermissible. Available at: http://www.bundesverfassungsgericht.de/pressemitteilungen/bvg13-017en.

Appendix: Methods & Research Design

Overall Research Design: Research Narrative

At its core, this book examines the decision making practices of German prosecutors. Because decision-making is not a formulaic process, I used research methods drawn from ethnographic studies. Those methods allowed me to investigate how German prosecutors both viewed and applied the law in their everyday decision-making.

Lawyers, in general, and prosecutors, in particular, can be a particular difficult group to "understand" because their facility with language and the language of law can provide one with a version of the "truth," but not necessary the "truth" in its full richness. For these reasons, the primary source material used in this study consists of ethnographic data—principally semi-structured interviews of German prosecutors, participant observation notes of their daily work routines, and "file reviews."

I elected to use qualitative research methods in this project because the bulk of scholarship published on German prosecutors in English focuses on the legal structure within which prosecutors operate rather than how prosecutors interpret and apply the law. The principle shortcoming of existing research is that it focuses on the law and generalizations about practice and understates the impact that organizational and cultural factors play in shaping the implementation of the law. The key advantage which qualitative research methods offered this project is that they enabled me to understand how the process of prosecutorial decision-making is situated in and influenced by the organizational context. Even though I was familiar with the German Criminal Code and Code of Criminal Procedure before beginning my field research, I was did not appreciate the degree to which organizational factors affected the implementation of the law. By using open-ended questions, I was able to probe how prosecutors interpreted the law in particular situations. On many days, I would sit with a prosecutor as he or she opened the case files which had been sitting in their in-box and discuss with the prosecutor the actual decisions facing that prosecutor at that moment in time. By observing prosecutors in their daily routines, I began to understand the degree of discretion they enjoy. I also read

S.M. Boyne, *The German Prosecution Service*, DOI 10.1007/978-3-642-40928-8, through stacks of closed files and their heavily detailed notes of the prosecutor's actions. The utility of that practice was undercut by the fact that, typically the closed cases that I reviewed were hand chosen by a senior individual in the office.

By far, the richest source of information came from the dozens of coffee meetings that I was privileged to observe. In these small informal gatherings, prosecutors, not only discussed the latest gossip in the office, but also their "hidden knowledge" regarding how they interacted with particular judges as well as their investigation tactics. In order to protect my interview subjects, I promised every individual that I would not disclose the source of the interviews in any publication. On rare occasions, individuals asked me not to write about a particular matter, I honored those requests.

Potential Disadvantages of Ethnographic Methods

From my perspective, the major disadvantage of using qualitative methods was the time and energy consuming nature of the field work. In addition I greatly underestimated the time and energy required to transcribe tapes and type up observation notes. Although methods books attempt to answer the question of how many interviews is sufficient, the process itself was not merely a method of data collection, but an education process as well. The more interviews I conducted, the more incisive my questions became, and the more useful the data I collected. During my first year of fieldwork, I thought that I would hit the ground running because I had spent a semester in a German law school and had already interviewed a number of prosecutors. In reality, I hit the ground limping and learned to walk only after a few months of interviewing. Many of my initial interview questions reflected my own experience working in an adversarial system and were ill-suited to the probing the factors that motivate German prosecutors' decision-making. At the same time, I learned useful information even where my questions "missed" the mark. While most German prosecutors do not view case dispositions in terms of winning and losing, the degree of agency that they attach to the case outcomes varied depending on the type of crime being prosecuted.

In my data collection procedures, I sought to address the issue of internal validity by using multiple sources of data collection at each research site. My data collection methods included semi-structured interviews, participant observation studies, file reviews, and file research. The core of my data includes 117 semi-structured interviews conducted with prosecutors, judges, and Ministry of Justice officials. I conducted another 20 or so interviews with defense attorneys, law enforcement officers, and collateral prosecutors. At least half of the interviews were recorded and transcribed. I recorded the remaining interviews in note form.

In total, I visited prosecution offices in 18 different cities. These visits ranged from a 2-day visit spent primarily with a single prosecutor in a small city to several 2-week visits in which I interviewed multiple prosecutors and viewed multiple proceedings per day. The "interviews" ranged in length from one hour to several hours over multiple days. The number of interviews listed above does not include any incidental or unplanned conversations which occurred during my field research. Those conversations were included in my field notes and not counted as interviews. In addition, I interviewed police officers, defense attorneys, law professors, members of the ministry of finance, and members of related nonprofit associations in an effort to triangulate the information that I collected from members of the judicial service. I also interviewed officials who worked in the Ministry of Justice at both the Land and federal levels.

For better or worse, conducting qualitative interviews is a skill honed more in the field than in the classroom. In addition, despite my "research plan" sometimes I stumbled onto rich sources of information serendipitously, most often when I was lost and knocked on the wrong door or appeared at the wrong office. On the flip side, it takes a streak of stubbornness to conduct qualitative research at multiple sites in a foreign country. I experienced inevitable moments of doubt—most often on Mondays when I visited a new site research site. In addition, one must not be afraid to appear "dumb" either by design or unwittingly. Informants will often take extra time to explain a process or a technical point in richer detail when you tell them that you do not understand their initial explanation. One must also project a thick skin in those inevitable moments when you encounter a speaker with a dialect or attitude for which you were not prepared. While methods textbooks do not contain chapters that dispense advice on traits such as perseverance, at times I had to push myself not to be tempted to terminate an interview or cancel a site visit altogether when it was not proceeding smoothly.

The best methods training that I have received occurred not in the classroom, but through my training as a prosecutor and as a defense attorney. The process of interviewing witnesses, listening to their accounts, and sorting through the inconsistencies in the evidence honed my listening and inductive reasoning skills. It also taught me to listen to my intuition and common sense in developing follow-up questions and in pushing witnesses to question their own memories. It is the open-ended questioning style that I used in witness preparation, rather than the leading questions of courtroom questioning, which I emulated in my research process. In this respect, I emulated those researchers who maintain that one should trust their own personal biographies as a significant source of knowledge. My instincts as both a lawyer as well as a social scientist enriched the research process.

Since the broad object of my research was the decision-making processes of German prosecutors, I set out to interview a regionally diverse cross-section of German prosecutors. Consistent with research tradition initiated by Lipsky (1980), my primary focus was the decision-making which occurs on the front lines of a public service organization—in Lipsky's words—"the street-level bureaucrats." To this I conducted the majority of my interviews with public prosecutors (*Staatsanwälte*) and department managers (*Oberstaatsanwälte*) rather than with higher level supervisors, office directors, and ministry officials.

In addition to formal question and answer sessions I conducted "file reviews" with several prosecutors. During these file reviews I would ask a prosecutor if we could go through the cases currently stacked in their in box as they would process them and discuss the current decision facing the prosecutor in the case and their decision process. These file reviews helped me to understand the types of decisions prosecutors in different departments make daily. Moreover, the information which I gathered through the file review process had an advantage over interview answers. Namely, with the file reviews, the prosecutor did not pre-select the cases which they wished to talk about. We talked about the cases brought to his or her office that day. Thus, in essence, the cases were selected randomly, because they were the cases sitting in the prosecutor's in-box that day. Towards the middle of my fieldwork, one prosecutor surprised me by handing me a stack of case files to read and we shared our opinion on how we would handle the cases. This process forced me to reflexively think through the decision-making process. I later repeated that process at another research site. This was an interesting exercise which helped me to understand my own preferences for action as well as to talk through the process by which particular prosecutors approached and taught case decision-making skills.

During the participant observation portion of my field work, the activities which I observed blanketed the wide spectrum of activities in which German prosecutors are engaged. These included appearances in court for detention hearings and main proceedings, plea discussions, meetings with law enforcement, as well as meetings of investigation teams. During court proceedings, I typically sat in the audience. On some occasions, the prosecutor or judge invited me to sit at the prosecution or expert witness's table. Because juvenile proceedings are closed to the public, in order to observe those proceedings I obtained the permission of all of the parties involved in the case. To protect the privacy of the individuals involved in those cases, I have elected not to describe specifics related to those particular proceedings.

Despite the amount of time and effort which I invested in conducting interviews, absent the periods of participant observation, the usefulness of those interviews would have been limited. It was the mix of periods of participant observation with interviews which, in combination, generated rich insights that led me to continue refine my interview questions as well as to trust the answers I was receiving. For example, there were frequent moments when I was in the midst of conducting an interview and another prosecutor would enter seeking advice on how to handle a case. These moments convinced me more than an answer to an interview question that the prosecutors in a particular department did in fact frequently consult each other on case decision-making and showed me in practice what types of decisions prosecutors ruminated over. Moreover, inevitably, unplanned events would occur such as a phone call from a superior, a visit from a representative of the Ministry of Justice, or a call from the press which gave me the opportunity to verify my perception of the event with the prosecutor I was visiting. Obviously a researcher's ability to "sense" what is happening in a research environment improves with months spent in the field. It was in these unplanned moments where I gained the most useful insights into the flow of decision-making and the prosecutor's perceptions of the nature of their work environment. In one of my first site visits to a prosecution office in a large city, I had difficulty finding the office of the prosecutor with whom I was to meet. As I was walking through a hallway filled with offices with closed doors, I mentally compared the office atmosphere with often raucous, open-door atmosphere of a prosecution office where I had worked in the United States. Immediately I began to doubt, not only that I would find the right office but also that I would be able to report any interesting information at all. Finally I knocked on the door of an adjoining office and found the prosecutor I was scheduled to interview sitting at a small table sharing coffee with a group of other prosecutors from the department. Alas, the higher authorities had scheduled my interview right in the middle of the department's informal daily coffee break. The group of prosecutors, who were laughing and sharing stories, invited me to sit down. As the conversation continued, my fears vanished. Despite the quiet hallways in many prosecution offices, I discovered that I could learn a great deal from the stories exchanged over a cup of coffee.

In some of the adult cases which were scheduled for trial I observed closed door discussions of potential "confession agreements." Sometimes these occurred at the start of the proceeding or midway through a proceeding. In terms of the daily office routines I observed informal coffee meetings in which cases and gossip were discussed, informal consultations between prosecutors to discuss cases, routine office work, department meetings, and office trainings. With respect to the investigation stage of proceedings I observed meetings between police and prosecutors as well as meetings of case investigation teams. I visited prison facilities with representatives of prosecution offices and in the guise of a "consultant" working with a defense attorney. I also toured the facilities and meet with individuals of other auxiliary investigation facilities including a forensic lab and the offices of the *Finanzamt* (fiscal and tax authorities) and a forensics lab. To get a sense of the working relationships between prosecutors and judges as well as those which exist between prosecutors and defense attorneys, I participated in social events when invited to do so including one interesting meeting of local attorneys which was held in a restored butcher's guild.

Reliability

Since my book examines the decision-making processes of German prosecutors, I elected at the project's start to visit a large number of research sites including sites in the former East Germany. The research sites were diverse from both a regional perspective as well as from the perspective of the size of the office itself. To gain access to interview sites, I relied on a network of contacts that I had built up during two prior visits to Germany. In the summer of 2003, I visited Germany for 2 weeks courtesy of a Scott-Kloeck-Jensen Pre-dissertation Fellowship to research Germany's responses to terrorism. During the course of this visit, I made contacts with several law professors and federal government officials upon which I later relied.

In the spring of 2004, I was a visiting student at the Justus-Liebig-Universität in Gießen, Germany. The bulk of my contacts in prosecution offices resulted from contacts which I made through law professors in Gießen and researchers at the Max-Planck-Institute in Frieburg. I supplemented these contacts with contacts established through my position as a Visiting Fellow in the Berlin Program for Advanced German and European Studies at the Freie Universität in Berlin. I also initiated direct contact with several prosecution offices with whom I had no "way" in. In the end, no office which I approached denied me access.

I conducted site visits in 11 of the 16 German *Länder*. I discovered in the course of my interviews that, in several of the interview sites which I had visited, the Land-level Ministry of Justice had approved my research visit. It is doubtful that I would have enjoyed the same level of access without the network of contacts I had established during my prior visits to Germany. The 18 research sites that I visited ranged in size from an office with 24 prosecutors to an office with over 300 prosecutors. In terms of regional variation, my site visits were distributed throughout 11 of Germany's 16 *Länder* and represented geographically diverse locations. The prosecutors whom I interviewed prosecuted the full gamut of crimes. Although each the departmental configurations of prosecution offices in Germany varies, the prosecutors I interviewed were drawn from the following departments: general crimes, economic crimes, capital crimes, state security, juvenile crimes, environmental crimes, sex crimes, organized crime, and corruption.

Other Data Sources

In addition to the data described above, I also collected a sample of training materials, office organization plans, internal memos, and statistical reports. In a number of cases in which prosecutors discussed the handling of high profile cases, I researched media accounts of those cases to verify case details. While field researchers who use organizations as research sites often confront individuals who attempt to paint the organization in its best light, I feel confident that I conducted sufficient "soaking and poking" over a long enough period of time to penetrate the idealized portraits of German prosecution taught in many German universities. At the same time, in the writing process, I steered clear of the impulse to jump on interesting but anomalous examples of prosecution practice.

Notes on Reflexivity

My own experience as a prosecutor in the United States served as both an asset as well as a potential bias during my field work. By introducing myself as a former prosecutor both in my initial contacts with research sites and at the start of each interview, I helped establish my own credibility beyond that of a social science researcher. Although social scientists are held in high regard in Germany in general, the fact that I had also served as a prosecutor raised the confidence level of my informants that I myself was familiar with the realities and challenges of prosecutorial practice. Without question, my own background as a prosecutor facilitated my access to research sites. Moreover, it also established a common framework of trust during many of my interviews. During several interviews prosecutors told me that I must have faced similar problems as a prosecutor in America. Despite the differences in the two systems, with many informants I sensed that we shared a common membership in a similar professional fraternity.

In addition, my own frame of reference for prosecution practice served to starkly highlight the differences in the two systems. For example, when I first observed main proceedings where the prosecutor asked few questions of witnesses, it initially troubled me. But it then led me to ask prosecutors how they observed their role in court and ultimately helped me to sort out the differences in prosecutorial performance which could be attributed to the structure of the German system and those attributable to the prosecutor's lack of effort and disinterest. With other informants however, the combination of the portrayal of American practice in films and the perception of the America's lack of respect for international law, the informant either outright stated or strongly implied that the American criminal justice system was inferior to the German system. In one respect this attitude enhanced my research as it increased the amount of time that informants were willing to spend with me as some these individuals were eager to teach an American about the German legal system. One informant even stated explicitly: "I think more highly of America because you are here" In another sense, however, when interviewees gave no quarter about potential weaknesses of the German system, it gave me cause for caution in trusting the reliability of their responses in general. In many of my interviews, my informants asked me if they could ask me questions about the American system or my own experiences as a prosecutor. Grateful for the level of cooperation I received in Germany for my research project, I was happy to answer questions when I felt sufficiently qualified to do so. Often this give and take provided me with the opportunity to ask interviewees how their experiences compared with my own experience and gave me an entry point to more probe areas of inquiry more deeply.

Although I devoted much time and effort to developing a list of appropriate questions for my semi-structured interviews, the questions that I used evolved throughout my field research. The ongoing evolution of the questions that I used reflected not only my increasing knowledge of the subject but also the size of the hurdle which a foreign researcher faces in trying to understand another culture as well as another legal system. I worked with two different native speakers in formulating my interview questions. Often we would hit roadblocks formulating what I thought were straightforward questions. The process of translation was not a simple exercise in converting language. With the help of a German law student, I had to find ways to formulate questions which were intelligible not only in German, but also in the abstract paradigm of German law. This was a time consuming process which continued to evolve as my own knowledge grew as conducted more and more interviews. For example, in attempting to craft interview questions such as "What are your department's goals for the next year?", it became apparent that I was viewing German prosecutors through a lens colored by my own perspective as American lawyer but also through my knowledge of management practices which I assumed to be universal. The existence of these gaps in understanding validated the selection of qualitative research methods for this project.

Protection of Confidentiality and Privacy

Prior to beginning my field research, I obtained an exemption from the University of Wisconsin's Institutional Review Board for my field research. As I continued the project while I worked as a professor at Indiana University's Robert H. McKinney School of Law, I obtained a second institutional review board exemption. Because the bulk of my interview subjects were both legally trained and occupied positions of power, they were in a stronger position to protect their rights than typical informants. In fact, in some offices, the tables were turned when the office research liaison or manager asked me to sign a document in which I certified that I would not publish or otherwise communicate information related to ongoing case investigations. Despite that fact, several of my interview subjects did share information with me which, if disclosed, might conceivably alter the trajectory of their careers. In those cases, I have used that information only as background material to deepen my own understandings, and elected not to use it in my book.

In order to protect the confidentiality of my interview subjects, at the start of each interview, I promised each informant that I would not use their name, nor would I use the location of their particular prosecution office in my written work. I addition, where the disclosure of the details of an event or conversation might identify the informant, I have altered details to protect the informant's identity while preserving the import of the significance of the event. In some instances I observed meetings and phone conversations which my informants explicitly asked me not to report in my research. I have honored their request. Several of my informants requested that I send them a copy of my book. I intend to honor that request. For citation purposes, I assigned each interview subject a unique identifier based on their office location and identity. The office locations are indicated by a numerical identifier while the subject's identity has been given a two letter designation. This system allows the reader to get a sense of the number of interviews cited in the text as well as their distribution across different cities.

For ease in reading, I have assigned a fictitious name to the location of particular prosecution offices, drawn from the German names of counties or other locations in former areas of Germany which existed before the Second World War. I chose those names to gently remind readers that we referring to Germany and not cities in the United States. The reader should not draw any conclusion from the particular names used. The particularly detail driven reader may note that, according to my coding schema, the number of cities which I reference exceeds the number of prosecution offices that I visited. The explanation for this is that, in a few cases, I interviewed an individual such as a defense attorney or judge who was based in a city in which I did not conduct a site visit.

Reference

Lipsky, M. (1980). *Street-level bureaucracy: Dilemmas of the individual in public services*. New York: Russell Sage Foundation.

The manufacturer's authorised representative in the EU is Springer
Nature Customer Service Centre GmbH, Europaplatz 3, 69115 Heidelberg,
Germany. If you have any concerns regarding our products, please
contact ProductSafety@springernature.com

Printed and bound by CPI Group (UK) Ltd, Croydon, CR0 4YY
08/10/2026
02229823-0001